The Inner Side of History

A professional historian and professor of history at Empire State College in New York, Charles DeMotte combines his knowledge of history with a long-time study of the evolution of human consciousness to provide a groundbreaking approach to the expanded study of history.

First printing: December 1997

Published by:
Source Publications
P.O. Box 1160
Mariposa, California 95338
source@yosemite.net

Cover by:
Todd Eckhoff - Teck Design
Visalia, California

Printed and bound in the United States of America

Library of Congress Cataloging-in-Publication Data

DeMotte, Charles 1943-
    The inner side of history / by Charles DeMotte.
        p.   cm.
    Includes bibliographical references and index.
    ISBN 0-9635766-1-5 (alk. paper)
    1. History--Miscellanea.   I. Title.
  BF1999.D355   1997
  130--dc21   96-47298
                CIP

The Inner Side of History

Charles DeMotte

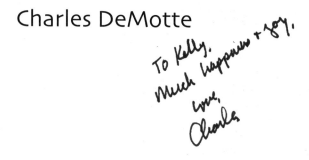

To Kelly.
Much happiness + joy.
love,
Charles

Source Publications
Mariposa, California

Dedicated To

Mabel Beggs and Jane Edwards

Two remarkable women

Contents

Preface

It has been said that, "Those ignorant of history are doomed to repeat it." Perhaps a question might therefore be posed in relation to this wise statement which inquires: "What do we really mean by 'history,' and what do we really *know* of the truth anent the record of history as we are given it?" If we consult a dictionary definition, we are given to understand that this word is derived from the Latin, *historia*, which is from the Greek, *histor, istor,* meaning *inquiry, knowing, learned,* and which is akin to the Greek, *eidenai,* meaning *to know.* One of the first definitions given is that it recounts a "tale, or story," and furthermore that it is "a chronological record of significant events often including an explanation of their causes," "a branch of knowledge that records and explains past events."

That the more recent account of history narrates a chronological record of events may indeed be relatively true, as far as it goes, but are we really given an explanation of causes? The answer to this question would depend upon one's definition of "causes." Furthermore, the conventional chronological view appears to break down with any fresh attempt to penetrate further back in time, as witnessed by the recent controversial debate over the age of the Sphinx, to give just one example. Likewise, are we satisfied that past events are really explained? If so, in what light and from what angle are they explained, and who is doing the explaining? It could be argued that conventional explanations have been, and are, sometimes based upon perceptions filtered through conceptual limitations conditioned by national, political, religious, scientific, and academic bias.

When we introduce nouns such as conceptions, perceptions, and explanations, and conjoin them with the etymological root of the noun, "history," a "branch of knowledge" derived from *inquiry, knowledge* and *learnedness,* as the subject of the verb, *eidenai, to know,* we must ask ourselves how much conclusive justice we can serve upon the subject when we admit our relatively limited knowledge concerning the instrument generating the inquiry, the repository of knowledge—the mind itself. What do we really mean by *know* and what is it that *knows?* The history of man and the development of science should more correctly be studied from the evolutionary angle of the nature of the mind and consciousness itself. Perhaps in this manner, effects or appearances of phenomena as they are conventionally studied, the manner in which they are imputed to exist, and the power by which they are established to exist, can more directly be traced back to causes.

Epistemologically speaking, we could posit that the dualities of ignorance and knowledge are dependent arisings of one another. From a condition of ignorance arises (to the consciousness) the perception that knowledge exists; from knowledge, assimilated and cognized, arises (in the consciousness) the revelation that a condition of ignorance exists. Ignorance and knowledge are therefore mutually dependent upon one another, for where one exists the other exists, and where one does not exist the other does not exist—to the perceiving consciousness. The concept of *knowledge* implies that there is something to be known, but the basis of this "knowing" must be acknowledged to be relative to the perceiving consciousness studying the subject about which one attempts to know something about.

We might add, from the angle of logic (an attribute of the mind), that whatever exists (to the consciousness) may be known, and whatever does not exist (to the consciousness) may not be *known*— which is to say that whatever is established by the power of reasoning may be found concordant with valid cognition and verified in the consciousness, but whatever is not established in the consciousness by the power of reasoning remains non-verified and non-proven. This does not mean that *whatever* one may think is correct, just because one thinks it, but that valid reasoning will establish only what is correct and concordant with valid cognition and valid proof to a verifying consciousness thus engaged in the subject-predicate relationship.

It could be proposed that knowledge may essentially be divided into three types: concrete knowledge, abstract knowledge, and self-knowledge. Concrete knowledge is the most familiar to us, for it concerns our relative knowledge of the way in which phenomena, persons, and events "appear" to exist (or have existed) and have their being to our perceiving consciousness as it is conditioned by conceptual limitations governed by time and space. This is the conventional view of the world, the one that we are habitually conditioned by and the everyday manner by which events, phenomena and persons are "explained." This sphere of knowledge, from certain angles, could be said to be primarily one of an observation of effects, though the conventional view posits of such knowledges a concrete reality of substantially inherent self-existence.

Abstract knowledge is less familiar, for it concerns spheres of awareness and existence(s) abstracted (in their essential nature) from the phenomenal conditions of time and space, transcending conventional conceptual limitations and synthesizing all that is known (about a subject) into the realization of a "single moment." To those who have investigated it, this realm of knowledge reveals a dynamic world of ceaseless interacting, interrelating, and impacting energies and forces, operating under their own laws, and subject to their own definitions, which transcend normal conventionally held views, but which convey more meaningful definitions concerning the nature of causes. This is a more unconventional view of "the world." No thought of "personal self" or separative inherent self-existence can enter this realm, nor any dualistic personalized thought. It is a realm into which some of the farthest reaches of science penetrate, the awareness which those who practice the more strenuous aspects of meditation and other self-applied disciplines develop (or seek to develop), and the type of consciousness-knowledge which advanced yogis and initiates of the greater mysteries of being *have* developed.

Self-knowledge concerns that sphere of knowledge which fundamentally bridges these two aspects of knowledge. "Man, know thyself," says the ancient injunction. It is a psychologically established basis that the way in which we view and understand ourselves conditions the manner in which we view that which we conventionally perceive and interpret as lying outside ourselves in the environment, circumstances, other persons, and events. Those who investigate this branch of self-knowledge—from the first tentative steps of mundane psychology to that more expanded and transcendent or transpersonal psychology which posits the existence of an immortal spark of *psyche*, or the *soul*, resident within each and every one of us—gradually develop the understanding that it is the limiting nature of our perceiving consciousness itself which separates our view of ourselves as being isolated from the greater whole in which we live and move and have our being.

It follows that those who develop a more expanded awareness of themselves and their consciousness potential simultaneously and gradually expand their awareness to become more inclusive in their consciousness of other sentient life forms, as an extended factor of their own developing self-consciousness principle. The concept of "self" begins to take on a more inclusive and expansive meaning. Such persons begin to note causes, promptings, or impulses in the form of motives arising in their own consciousness which produce effects in their environment, circumstances, and themselves, and thereby develop the realization that in fact we are not merely spectators of a vast life drama into which we insert ourselves, but that we are intrinsically active participants in that greater evolving life process (involving many levels or degrees of consciousness) which we individually and collectively help shape and mold by virtue of the uniquely human self-consciousness principle expressing itself through the power of thought.

The investigation naturally turns towards an examination of the motives prompting thought, which reveals that certain laws are conspicuously operative which appear to govern the nature of the effects. Simply put, selfish motives produce undesirable results, pain and suffering; altruistic motives, prompted by love and unselfish dedication to the welfare of others, produce desirable results, freedom from limitation, and relief of suffering. Thus, is gradually revealed to the consciousness, through trial and error, a redefinition of the concept of "self," as a more transpersonal, impersonal, and inclusive Identity makes its presence felt within the sphere of one's cognitive awareness. Eventually, this selfless Self, along with all its myriad attributes and powers, begins to dominate one's consciousness as the source of one's true identity, and all former identifications begin to lose their imprisoning, illusory grip upon the consciousness.

The record of history could be rewritten from the angle of motive. From the record of the effects produced by certain persons, groups of persons, and events, motive would not be difficult to ascertain. Contrary to superficial opinion, humanity is not traveling upon an uncharted course. Even a cursory view of history reveals a gradual evolution of human consciousness from a primitive intelligence concerned with self-preservation to that of a highly developed logic and creative ingenuity, and from which have arisen expressions, experiments, and evolutions in the sciences, technologies, arts, institutions, and ideologies of the varied civilizations which have appeared and disappeared.

History, from the point of view of humanity, could be rewritten as a narrative upon the long, slow process of the liberation of the spirit aspect from the limitation and bondage of the matter or form aspect, via the evolution of the mind nature or aspect. Those with no vision scoff at the idea of a greater Plan generating the evolutionary process. They are ignorant of history. Yet it does not take so much of a stretch of the imagination to inquire that if it is possible for a human being to plan his or her affairs and arrange them into a neatly organized mental package to determine the course of his or her life, then could it not also be possible that greater Intelligences transcending human intelligence could also formulate a more extended version to include entire kingdoms of nature, including the human. Those who think not merely rest back upon the conceit that it is only humanity who is endowed with intelligence, and that greater Intelligences cannot exist.

We are reminded that whatever does not exist to the consciousness *may* not be known, but that whatever exists to the consciousness may be known—through investigation—and established by the power of reasoning, leading to valid cognition, direct perception, and a verifying consciousness. "Seek and ye shall find; knock and it shall be opened," said one of the greatest Minds of the ages when speaking of kingdoms of greater Intelligence, which, He added (along with His Brother, the Buddha), lies within.

The Buddha and the Christ came before mankind and established stupendous Ideas within the body of humanity. This They accomplished through the power of Their living example, Their embodied teaching, the fearless expression of Their love, wisdom and compassion, the highest spiritual and moral rectitude, and the stupendous power of Their Minds, interrelating all three types of knowledge earlier mentioned, and demonstrating their perfected expression. They swayed hemispheres to such an extent that the power of Their lives continues to this very day, having inspired millions of persons for over two thousand years, as a forceful argument for a universally recognized correct mode of being.

This recognition is not based upon a mere wish-life of escape, but is registered as concordant with an internal valid cognition that such a condition of selflessness and universal goodness, exemplified by these two dynamic Lives, is also the major potential of our own livingness, present within each and every one of us. That distortions (and sometimes gross distortions) and reductions of Their essential teachings have colored the institutions which have been built up in Their name is also true, but we are here only considering the actual living example of Their Being. If we could but see it, They demonstrated and summed up in Themselves the goal of human evolution. Both of Them told us that we could become as They are, and gave us rules and disciplines to follow—if we dare. Countless mystics, saints, and holy persons in all departments of life expression heeded the call, and the chain of history is decorated with accounts of their jeweled lives. They thus advanced towards the stage of a verifying consciousness. Many such persons appeared before these two great Personages, and many will continue to appear. Such initiates are the *cause* of civilizations and cultures, not the result, as holds the normal conventional view.

The conventional superficial view that considers such a mode of spiritual being to lie exclusively within the religious department, having nothing to do with political, educational, scientific, and artistic concerns, is a basic misconception of the separative mind. No atheist ever created anything of lasting value. "Where there is no vision, the people perish . . . ," and for that vision to have a lasting value and usefulness to others, it can only be gained from limitless sources. To study "the world" from the historical angle of the views presented through concrete knowledge is not to be considered "wrong," nor "incorrect," but merely limited. It is true that empirical modes of investigation protect mankind from superstition and the wonder-world of illusion, as likewise a healthy skepticism, but it is also true that those areas of awareness normally considered "mystical" and "esoteric" will admit empirical investigation, prompted by right motive.

It could be argued from certain angles that the fundamental ignorance to be defeated is the belief in the substantially, inherent, self-existence of phenomena, of persons, of events, and of the nature of existence itself. That is to say, the conventional view or belief that phenomena and persons exist in and of and by themselves, that they exist from their own side alone, without taking into account their dependent causes, their interdependent relationships, and the way in which relative consciousness perceives or imputes their existence. Such a misconception inevitably leads to an erroneous and partial interpretation of events and persons as isolated phenomena, devoid of a larger context of interdependent causes, and seemingly without purposeful direction in time and space.

That persons, events and phenomena exist, or have existed, is not to be disputed, for it is self-evident; but the *way* in which they exist or have existed, and the *power* by which they exist and have existed is still open to investigation and debate if they are to be more satisfactorily "explained." If we can apply this epistemological investigation to a study of history, perhaps we can then uncover deeper meanings and causes behind past events and, with a more holistic and hylozoistic sense of proportion, cast our sense of vision towards a more glorious future in which we all have a part to play.

A point first to be addressed in this enterprise is a question of a conceptual framework from which to proceed. In this book, *The Inner Side of History*, Charles DeMotte has drawn upon and compiled from many sources much of what has been written about this subject from the angle of what comes under the generic term, the Ageless Wisdom. Combining his academic knowledge of history together with that which has been proposed through the Ageless Wisdom teachings, he seeks to develop for us a greater and more inclusive conceptual framework within which to work. Many areas are touched upon and indeed many of the propositions are open to dispute, mainly because we lack, at present, the scientific means of proof. But the fact that so much has been written about this subject from this angle—much of which, though from varied and different sources, *agrees* in fundamentals—must give pause for consideration, and must present questions to the open-minded, intelligent, and inquiring investigator, and cannot be dismissed lightly.

In *The Inner Side of History*, Charles DeMotte presents a more unconventional view of history from the angle of cause and effect. In this, he has not confined his attention to the obvious, but drawn upon what we have been told about the vast system of interrelating, interacting, and impacting energies and forces, (cosmic, solar, and planetary), in which and of which we are intrinsically a part. This ceaseless dynamic array of forces and energies are qualified by attributes which produce and have produced conditioning psychological impacts upon the mind of humanity, as humanity—in turn, and relative to its degree of conscious unfoldment—has responded . . . for good or ill.

In *The Inner Side of History*, Charles DeMotte presents a view of history from the angle of a "Plan," again, an unconventional approach. This "Plan" is essentially one which concerns the evolution of consciousness itself; the results, as they work out through phenomena and events, being considered more proportionately as *effects*. This architectural blueprint, or pattern, sets the design for the evolution of consciousness on a greater or vaster scale than the individual is normally capable of comprehending but, nevertheless, the individual is thus shaped and molded in his consciousness as he responds to this greater design in group or mass response. Whether the individual likes to think it or not, he is a part of the greater whole of humanity itself and cannot avoid this mass response. This is obviously a crushing blow to the egocentric attitude which prizes individuality above all else, but it is not difficult to come to terms with if we consider that such attitudes of "individuality" are basically illusions when considering the mass conditioning impacts the media and convention have upon attitudes and consciousness. However, we may gain some sense of the prevailing argument for this greater plan if we consider the correspondence in the individual ability to formulate (mental) plans, patterns, or designs for his own individual welfare and personal affairs, and then extend the idea.

Not only are we made aware of a greater plan directing the evolution of consciousness behind the scenes or drama of the outer appearing circumstances or events, but we are also made aware of a group of custodians or formulators of this plan, a vast group of superior Intelligences (to that of the human) responsible for its direction. Another crushing blow to human conceit. However, the annals of history (both recent and ancient) are decorated with persons who have appeared and demonstrated wondrous, super-normal powers. They are usually negated because they defy conventional explanation. Yet, from time to time, certain of these superior Intelligences in Their many grades continue to appear before mankind to help guide it—in consciousness— forward in time and space.

Thus is defrayed any notion or fear that this "Plan" infringes upon the "free-will" of humanity at large. Humanity determines its own destiny, as demonstrated by the insanity of the wars and suffering it has inflicted upon itself and which are narrated throughout the annals of history, as likewise by its more altruistic achievements such as its endeavors and abilities—through right response to that which is for the greater good—to solve its own problems . . . but within certain limits. Behind the scenes stand the Guides of the race, Beings of wondrous power, Who work ceaselessly through infinite love, wisdom, and compassion on our behalf. Quite often, when One is sent among us to help us forward, our gratitude has been expressed through crucifying, killing, or attempting to destroy him or her, merely out of superstitious fear of the threat such a One poses to convention.

So too, does this book present a challenge to convention. No doubt it will meet with scoffing. But the author does not claim infallibility. He only requests that we reconsider our views, and has taken the trouble to compile a significant amount of material to help us reconsider those views. It is not an end in itself, but merely a beginning. Topical studies can also be compiled along similar lines which would also help substantiate certain of the views presented in this more generalized overview. The question may arise, why should we reconsider our views, when history is already "explained" by the experts? The answer may be given that the more we understand about the possible truth anent the past, the more are we better equipped to deal with the present and safeguard the future. The more we understand about a greater plan, the more directly we can begin to cooperate with it, set in motion those causes which will produce desirable effects, and learn to subordinate our intensely personal considerations to the greater good.

Much has been given in the teaching of the Ageless Wisdom that demands to be taken as hints and suggestions to be followed up and investigated. If it is not studied and not taken into account—in all its ramifications and not just merely its concrete form as it appears to the materializing mind—then who can really say whether or not it is true? If it is true that cycles of conditioning energies impact our consciousness, thus presenting fresh opportunities for furthering the greater good, then surely it is the part of wisdom to take heed of what we have been told and learn to cooperate with these inflowing energies, rather than work against them through ignorance and defiance.

The history of ignorance and defiance is well documented. Now is the time for universal cooperation!

Keith Bailey
August, 1997
Encinitas

Introduction

Several years ago, a student of mine wrote in a paper about going to Germany, the land of her ancestors. Although she was part Irish, she never had a desire to visit Ireland, but was ecstatic when presented with the opportunity to travel to Germany. Arriving there, she felt that she had come home, so familiar was the experience. "That type of feeling, " she said, "can certainly cause one to ponder the possibility of reincarnation."

Windows into the unseen world, such as the one experienced by my student, are not uncommon. Such experiences have helped to fuel a growing interest in psychic phenomenon, mysticism, and the occult. Books on so-called "new age" topics are among the fastest growing body of literature to be found in bookstores. Periodicals and even films devoted to esoteric themes are far more plentiful than they have ever been. So to is the curious, yet often insincere interest taken by the mass media on occult subjects. While many people who are attracted to mysticism and the occult have mixed motives, there is a substantial core of the honest seekers who are often uncomfortable or dissatisfied with conventional explanations of reality and are gallantly looking for greater meaning in life, or a deeper truth, or both.

Such a person was myself who, as a graduate student in history in the mid-1970s, began to read the books of Alice Bailey on that which comes under the general heading of the ancient or Ageless Wisdom, first with casual interest and then with relish. Naturally, my mind soon turned to the question of how the great cosmic overview, as presented in the Bailey material, could be reconciled with the events and developments in my chosen field of study. Initially, few connections were evident. It was not long before I became a student with the School for Esoteric Studies, which set me on a formal path of occult study.

For many years the application of the Ageless Wisdom to the study of history seemed vague and unrelated. However, over time, through the persistence of study, meditation, and inner work in reordering my perceptions and service, the relevance of the teachings to the material world of everyday existence became more apparent. The writing of this book is an attempt to develop some gestating ideas that have been evolving for some time into an esoteric perspective on history.

All serious books have a specific readership in mind and this one is no exception. Although students of esotericism will undoubtedly find it useful, it is my intention to reach out to a broader audience of those who have an interest in history, philosophy, or related subjects, and others who are open to newer ideas. I must first offer a disclaimer. What is presented in this book is not a claim to truth but a perspective on how history might be considered. Since there is no hard evidence to substantiate many of the assertions that are made, the material given must be viewed as a set of hypotheses to be contemplated and tested according to the law of analogy. If the paradigm and the arguments presented in this book are found to be interesting, thought-provoking, useful, or even inspiring, then it will have served its purpose. Certainly, the reader is not asked to accept what is written at face value.

In the same vein, it should be noted that the ideas expressed in this book are far from complete. Like the proverbial "Murphy stew," a vast array of thoughts and ideas have been thrown into the pot, yet the reader may find that many of them are raw or only partially cooked. My purpose in writing this book has never been to present a tour de force of esoteric history, rather to offer some intriguing and useful associations that may provide insights and an impetus for further reflection and research into more specific areas. Some time ago, a physicist, in presenting testimony before a subcommittee of Congress, observed that the essence of science is the dynamic interconnection between facts, and that the more distant the connection, the more highly it is valued. The goal of this book is to make certain connections, many of them speculative, between the inner world of substance and the outer world of form.

Increasingly we are coming to realize that the realm of objective knowledge is, comparatively, a very limited space and most of what we know, or claim to know, emerges from perceptions derived from our experiences and understanding of the wider environment. An historian, like Arnold Toynbee, who views history at the level of a civilization, will have a different picture of the social world than someone who is writing a biography or is studying a particular event, such as a the British General Strike of 1926 or the Kennedy assassination.

Similarly, a person who sets out to chart the relationships and correspondences of the inner realm of energies and forces and connect them to events in the tangible world will see things differently from someone who assumes that the totality of existence and physical plane reality are one and the same.

In discussing matters esoteric, one must start with definitions. The word esoteric itself relates to the realm of energies and forces. According to one source, the term esoteric is used to signify all that does not concern form life or consciousness in the three worlds of everyday living.[1] By this it is meant that which is beyond the scope of physical, emotional, and mental awareness. The fundamental principle of esotericism is that all is energy. Many physicists who have studied the nature of matter are arriving at the same conclusion. In the words of physicist Fritjof Capra, "relativity theory showed that mass has nothing to do with substance, but is a form of energy."[2] Forces are defined as those energies which are limited or imprisoned within a form. Put another way, energies are subtle and potent and are thus spiritual in nature, while forces denote the ways that energy is used and expressed.[3] If the term esoteric is taken to mean those energies and forces that are subjective and are generally hidden from the world of appearances, the term exoteric relates to the externalization of energies and forces in physical manifestation.

Words such as mysticism and occultism are also casually used but often little understood. Mysticism, in the esoteric sense of the term, refers to a desire for union with the divine. It is based upon the experience of this unity and hence is more of a sentient realization than a mental process.[4] Occultism, on the other hand, is simply the intelligent study of that which is hidden.[5] By this I mean that it is a loosely defined scientific effort to make manifest the laws, principles, life, and consciousness aspects of the unseen world. Hence, an esoteric history is, in essence, a form of practical occultism.

When one sets out to write about things from a spiritual or esoteric perspective, the problem is complicated by not only a lack of familiar territory but also an array of knowledge that seemingly runs counter to conventional wisdom and evidence. A fundamental postulate of esotericism is that all levels of existence are governed by law. One of the masters of the wisdom, the Tibetan Djwhal Khul, who is responsible for the material in most of the Alice Bailey books, which is the major source of ideas for this book, defines a law as the imposition (upon both the lesser and more important) of a greater will or purpose. He goes on to say that all laws in nature have their higher, spiritual counterparts.[6] This points to another basic principle of esotericism, namely that predicates can be based upon correspondence and analogy, which is the primary means of supporting seemingly unprovable statements with evidence. "As above so below" is an esoteric maxim, which is also a key to the essentially scientific nature of spiritual or occult study.

Esoteric history, of which comparatively little has been written, seeks to do just that. This relatively uncharted course of history accepts as its starting point the reality of the esoteric or unseen world and tries to make correlations with observable events, movements, and cycles of time. Divinity, as understood esoterically, is composed of a triad of energies. The lowest manifestation of this triad is active intelligence. There is an increasing realization that all forms in nature possess symptoms of a rudimentary form of intelligence. Physicist David Bohm has stated that "spirit has always been thought of as something very subtle, something that at times we call intelligence."[7] Hence all forms contain spirit and spirit is composed of intelligence. Alice Bailey writes that insofar as an atom demonstrates a quality of discrimination, and possesses the ability to attract or repel, it embodies intelligence.[8]

The second aspect of divinity is love-wisdom. According to the Tibetan Master Djwhal Khul (D.K.), love involves a realization of the laws of attraction and repulsion, the magnetic interplay between all forms, and the attractive power of one unit upon another, whether it is (according to the law of correspondence) an atom, a human, or a solar system.[9] Whereas intelligence tends to diffuse as spirit encounters denser fields of matter, love is the energy of attractive power that keeps the units of a system together. Therefore, gravity could be considered a phenomenon of this love force within the solar system, and the urge to group formation is a demonstration of this law of attraction (which we call love) working itself out in human affairs. At the atomic level, love is what keeps electrons in their orbit.

Thirdly, divinity is an expression of the will aspect. Will embodies intention and purpose and is expressed through the law of evolution. The term evolution suggests a process of unfoldment towards something greater and may be defined as "the unfolding of a continually increasing power to respond."[10] It is important to stress that evolution relates not only to the form aspect, as Darwin and others have theorized, but also to consciousness and life itself. Karl Popper, in his influential book, *The Poverty of Historicism*, makes a distinction between what he calls the evolutionary hypothesis, as applied to biological and paleontological observations, and evolution, as it would relate to human history. He writes:

"Now I do not intend to deny...that history may sometimes repeat itself in certain respects, nor that the parallel between certain types of historical events...can be significant for the student of sociology or political power. But it is clear that all these instances of repetition involve circumstances which are vastly dissimilar, and which may exert an important influence upon further developments."[11]

Popper makes the error of accepting that, while evolution may operate consistently in one sphere of nature, it fails to do so in another sphere, which violates the law of correspondence. Such a view also takes little note of the immense complexity of the law of cycles, which govern all aspects of the macrocosm and microcosm in constant rhythmic order. As philosopher and astrologer Dane Rudhyar has written, "The structures of cycles are, in the occult sense of the term, archetypes. Archetypal knowledge does not deal with events per se but with their structural sequence."[12]

Taken together, the intelligence, love, and will aspects of divinity comprise what is called the "divine plan." From an esoteric standpoint, what we call history is but a map of the Plan as it unfolds in time and space. Popper's arguments against historicism are rooted in a denial of the presumption of the rhythms, laws, and patterns that form the basis for historical prediction.[13] Here again, the question is one of perspective. Insofar as esoteric history assumes that human history unfolds within larger cycles of time and space, the vast interplay of rhythms, patterns, and laws appear as self-evident. Teilhard de Chardin, who was both a priest and a biologist, saw within the diverse process of evolution a purpose leading to unification, or what he termed humanization. His reasoning was contained in two propositions: the first equating evolution with the rise of consciousness, and the second linking the rise of consciousness with the effect of union. He writes:

"The general gathering together in which, by correlated actions of the without and the within of the earth, the totality of thinking units and thinking forces are engaged—the aggregation in a single block of a mankind whose fragments weld together and interpenetrate before our eyes (indeed in proportion to) their efforts to separate—all this becomes intelligible from top to bottom as soon as we perceive the natural culmination of a cosmic process of organisation which has never varied since those remote ages when our planet was young."[14]

Esoteric history forces us to re-examine certain fundamental assumptions about man's place in the universe, his impact on world affairs, and his future. The lineage of the Ageless Wisdom teaches that humanity is not the end of evolution, but a stage of development within the unfolding sphere of apparently limitless consciousness. Nature is organized in terms of kingdoms. Within the physical sphere of the earth plane we can identify the mineral, vegetable, animal, and human kingdoms. These kingdoms are not isolated from one another but are interdependent. But where does one go from here? According to the law of correspondences, humanity would appear to be a link in a continuous chain of kingdoms, or hierarchies, that extend, perhaps even beyond our comprehension. This corresponds to the model of the "great chain of being," which was the dominant cosmology of western people up to the eighteenth century. The analogy holds if we shift our focus from material form to consciousness.

Consciousness is the sentient response of an entity to its environment and is critical to understanding man's position within the historical process. The term consciousness is derived from the Latin words *con*, meaning with, and *scio*, to know, and literally means that which we know. We might understand consciousness in different ways as awareness, the condition of perceiving, an ability to respond to stimuli, the faculty of recognizing contacts or relationships, or the power to synchronize. Consciousness can also be comprehended in an absolute sense as the totality of that which can be possibly conceived of as having occurred, is occurring, or is going to occur. Likewise, we can understand consciousness in a universal context as defined by time and space and having a specific location. Herein consciousness is relative. In terms of space we may talk about individual, group, or planetary consciousness or, with reference to time, there is medieval consciousness, revolutionary consciousness, modern consciousness, and so on. Each kingdom in nature has its own sphere of consciousness as well. Minerals, although inert, have an atomic structure and are therefore able to respond to stimuli. Plants are said to possess sensation, which is a rudimentary form of feeling. Further up the chain of evolution, animals have the power to instigate action, and thereby possess a low grade form of intelligence that we call instinct. The faculty of self-consciousness, of course, does not appear until evolution reaches the human kingdom.[15]

Esoteric history is more about causes than effects. This may come as a surprise to some since many conventional histories would make a similar claim. Here again, we need to be careful about the use of terms. According to the Ageless Wisdom, all created manifestation is part of a vast hierarchy of graded energies; that which produces causes always descends from a higher (or deeper) plane of reality to that which is more dense and, consequently, from some angles, more illusory. The glib statement that all forms are but illusions is true if seen from a greater sphere of consciousness. The Tibetan, in discussing the idea of meaning, cause, and being, observed that meaning is the light of life, cause is the breath of experience, and being is the initiator of all that is.[16] A whole treatise could be written on these three concepts alone. Reflecting solely on the principle of cause, the above reference to the "breath of experience" can esoterically be understood as the whole creative process underlying the unfoldment of the divine plan, or purpose of God. This is what one might define as absolute cause. Causes can also be relative to time and space. An event may be seen to have a noticeable cause, which is but a reflection of a more general cause that may not be so evident, and this may be the consequence of some greater cause, or causes, and so forth. Cause and effect are considered from the perspective of the Ageless Wisdom to be central to the law of karma, which in itself is a subject of unfathomable dimensions.

"The testimony of the ages points to a spiritual force or life in the world; the inference to be garnered from the life experience of millions is that spirit exists; the deduction to be gathered from the consideration of the world or of the great maya is that a Cause, self-persisting and self-existing, must be back of that maya."[17]

From Hinduism and Buddhism we learn that cause and effect are central to the understanding of karma and reincarnation, which function as laws governing all forms in the universe. Suffice it to say that karma is based on causes which are inherent in the constitution of matter itself and are generated through the interaction of atomic units at all levels of existence. It is important to understand that an atomic unit, in the occult sense, is a systemic term and may apply to an atom, a human being, or a solar system. Causes produce consequences, which in turn produce further causes and effects in an endless chain of events. Over many lifetimes, links in the chain of karma are forged (for good and for evil) and these links create opportunity and impose limitations at all levels of life. This is a very complex subject, and one which D. K. maintains is "too involved for average comprehension but a factor of real importance…in connection with the evolution of the world."[18]

Finally, it is important to make a distinction between the history of esotericism and esoteric history. The former, of which a significant amount has been written, is basically the history of esoteric movements, secret societies, and occult practices as they appear in the annals of history. Frances A. Yates's *The Occult Philosophy*, Joscelyn Godwin's *The Theosophical Enlightenment*, and Stephen A. McKnight's *The Modern Age and the Recovery of Ancient Wisdom*, are a few examples. These works, many of which are pieces of academic scholarship, offer interesting and often useful insights into an esoteric subject as it exists within the ebb and flow of recorded history. They do not, as a rule, approach the subject from an esoteric perspective. Conversely, the latter seeks to place history within a matrix of energies and forces by which change is measured not so much by the interplay of forms as by the evolution of consciousness.

This book is divided into three sections and eight chapters. The first chapter relates to the question, "what is esoteric history?" In one sense, esoteric history involves looking at the same data and information only with different eyes. In another sense, it is the recognition that such a history is part of a lineage of the Ageless Wisdom, the essence of which can be found in the deeper mysteries of the world's religions and the great conundrums of philosophy. The implication here is that the exterior events and processes of history are sustained by a composite stream of thought from deeper or higher levels of consciousness.

Chapters two and three focus on the nature of man within the macrocosmic universe. The question of what constitutes a human being is raised. The answer given involves a brief analysis of the sevenfold levels of consciousness, some of which are known to us and others that are presently beyond our comprehension, which according to the

Ageless Wisdom is known as the Constitution of Man. Whereas man within the more visible realms of form, corresponding to the physical, emotional, and concrete mental planes, is recognizable and familiar, by analogy he also exists in archetypal form within a vast scheme of evolution, ordered on what is called the cosmic physical plane by chains, globes, manvantaras, and rounds. Within these grand cycles are micro-cycles consisting of root races, subraces, and branch races. These racial groups, or distinct evolutions of consciousness, overlay the progress of cultures and civilizations in history. In attempting to appreciate these vast schemes and cycles, we are hampered by the poverty of nomenclature that limits our ability to explain that which lies beyond our normal comprehension.

Chapters four, five, and six discuss history in relation to the forces of will, love, and active intelligence. In esoteric parlance, these energies flow from three planetary centers referred to as Shamballa, Hierarchy, and Humanity. The reader must be constantly on guard against the tendency to reduce and materialize concepts which, from our vantage point may be intangible or formless, by use of the concrete mind. Difficulties arise through the lack of a conceptual framework that allows us to put such concepts into context. For this, the cultivation of abstract thought, or the use of the intuition, is required. This is necessary when one seeks to comprehend terms such as Shamballa and Hierarchy.

There are many legends surrounding Shamballa, known as the "City of the Gods," which is thought by some to exist in etheric substance (technically, a network of interlacing substance that surrounds and interpenetrates denser matter and corresponds to it). Some legends hold that Shamballa can be pinpointed to an exact location within the region of the Gobi Desert. Wherever and at what level Shamballa is to be found is secondary to the nature of this will energy, which is understood by esoteric students to be a force of great destructiveness and also great synthesis within human and planetary affairs. The effects of Shamballa are reported to be found in the great cataclysms of global upheaval, the forces that initiate new cycles and bring old cycles to a closure, and that which engenders a synthesis of ideas, events, and movements.

The lineage of the Ageless Wisdom refers to a planetary Hierarchy which consists of those groups of spiritually advanced human beings, known as disciples, initiates, and adepts, as well as those who have transcended human form (for the most part), known as the Trans-Himalayan brotherhood, yet work to help guide the affairs of humanity. Known in different religious traditions by other names, the ashrams (spiritual communities) of these evolved beings are said to provide a model for the spiritual government of the planet. Whereas vague references to the impact of these great beings on human affairs can be implied, in no way is the Hierarchy said to intrude on human free will. Therefore, within certain parameters, the events and trends of history are largely an expression of human activity.

Finally, the history of humanity is seen not as the affairs and activity of men and women within the context of nations and civilizations, but rather as the evolution of human consciousness. Insofar as the Ageless Wisdom measures human evolution in millions of years (not thousands of years), human development can be understood in terms of latent patterns of consciousness, conditioned by past and present root races, which influence the ways that men and women respond to their environment. This phenomenon explains, to a large extent, the reason why certain civilizations or cultures flower at particular times while others are fallow and appear to be in a more primitive stage of development. History cannot be fully comprehended without reference to the process of reincarnation and the law of karma, which underscore and explain the human predicament in both an individual and a collective sense.

The last two chapters, seven and eight, further reinforce the point that history, understood esoterically, is a maze of cycles of varying duration. The Alice Bailey books, which contain the teachings of the Tibetan Master, Djwhal Khul, highlight an analysis of the seven rays, which are the seven qualities of energy to be found in the universe. It is this teaching of the seven rays that is the primary contribution of D.K. and separates the Alice Bailey books from the earlier Theosophical writings. As with all things esoteric, the seven rays are part of a hierarchy of graded energy so that corresponding to the primal ray of a solar system, for example, one finds a whole system of rays and subrays and more minute subrays. The seven rays, as they flow in and out of season, can be interpreted as providing an important conditioning element in history. For example, it is said that the influence of the sixth ray of devotion and idealism is presently passing out of manifestation and is being replaced by the seventh ray of ceremonial order. The influence of certain other rays is also present, which adds complexity to the fabric of human history. Our planet is also affected by ray energy that is colored and modified by the planets and constellations. These energies are thought to govern planetary cycles and form the basis for the study of esoteric astrology. Chapter seven deals directly with ray cycles, whereas chapter eight discusses some aspects of astrology as they condition historical events. In both cases, the analysis of these cycles barely scratches the surface of what is a most profound and fathomless subject.

Since history is like a tapeworm that can be cut in any number of ways and still survive, my cut of the worm is to put greater emphasis on Western Civilization, and more specifically, modern European history. Indeed, the history of Asia and the Americas is almost entirely ignored. This is not a political statement but rather a recognition of the fact that European history is the area in which I possess a little knowledge and so feel free to address some comments. Also, Europe has been the center stage of historical development over the past millennium, and therefore has had a greater impact and influence on planetary affairs as a whole than have the nations and peoples of Africa, Asia, South America, or even North America. Within the framework of esoteric history, the present fifth root race, known as the Aryan root race, has culminated in the flowering of European civilization. This offers additional justification for giving the western world a higher profile in this study

I would like to especially thank Keith Bailey and Daniel Krummenacher for their helpful comments on the draft of this book. I would also like to acknowledge Kevin Townley, Matthew Alagich, and Daisy Kirkpatrick who also provided me with feedback. I am indebted to Carole Beckham, who encouraged me to publish this book and provided me with the vehicle for doing so, and to my wife, Jane Edwards, for her continued love and support and for her questions.

Section One—
An Historical and Cosmic Overview

...Modern academic history constitutes only one page in a vast historical record and that the initiating events of which we are in search and which are working out as effects in the planetary life at this time belong to an age so distant that no modern historian recognizes its episodes. Information anent this ancient period must be sought in the many world scriptures, in ancient monuments, in the science of symbols, in the racial myths, and in inherited and transmitted legends.

—Alice A. Bailey, *The Externalisation of the Hierarchy*

Throughout the entire history of the world, waves of attention to the inner forces of man have been perceived. These waves are linked with the periods of evolution. In any case, a growing attention to the essential nature of man will always be indicative of an especially significant period. If, at present, there are observed particular strivings for cognition of the essence of man's forces, such aspiration corresponds to cosmic conditions.

—Agni Yoga Society, *Brotherhood*

Chapter 1—
What is Esoteric History?

The historian Herbert Butterfield shrewdly remarked in his book, *The Origins of Modern Science*, that great changes in science (or history) come about, not by new observations or additional evidence, but through transpositions that take place within the minds of people themselves.[1] This reference suggests that what in recent times is often tediously referred to as a paradigm shift is not the assimilation of new information into new models, but the ability to place knowledge and information within a new set of relationships, so as to generate a different framework of perception.

This point can be clearly illustrated in relation to the juxtaposition of two unrelated frameworks, such as those which define our current perceptions about health. Not so long ago an important series of programs were aired on PBS television called "Healing and the Mind," narrated by Bill Moyers. Two questions posed by Moyers shaped the series: the first question addressed the way thoughts and feelings influence health, and the second question was concerned with the relationship of the mind to the healing process. In his first set of interviews, Moyers went to China where he toured the various healing facilities and talked to David Eisenberg, an American doctor who had trained and practiced in China for many years. Eisenberg was very upbeat about Chinese medicine. He observed that Chinese culture is based on the notion that there is a correct way to live, and that how you live ultimately affects your health. He further added that the Chinese medical system, founded on the Taoist tradition, stressed not only diet and nutrition as the basis of good health, but also psychological and spiritual well being.[2]

When Moyers turned his attention to the impact that the mind had on health in American medicine, the responses were more reticent. David Felton, a Professor of Neurobiology at the University of Rochester, when asked about the role of science in discovering the mechanisms by which causes produce effects, admitted that science had as yet not caught up with medical speculation. In terms of how some drugs affect depression, for example, he noted that "in some cases we don't have a clue. ...We haven't worked it out even though we still use the drugs."[3]

Why Chinese medicine should confidently make the connection between spirit/mind/body and health whereas western medicine is still mystified by the role that mind plays in healing is an interesting question and one which has far wider implications. The answer must surely be that, while Chinese medicine retains a connection with its spiritual source, western medicine has been cut adrift from its metaphysical roots; hence it can deal with the effects of a problem but not its causes. In other words, the framework that defines western medicine has become too rigid to allow for a deeper understanding of a problem.

The point of departure is not hard to find. Somewhere between the late seventeenth and early eighteenth centuries, artificial pharmaceuticals began to replace natural and alchemical medicines, which were linked through an intricate code of astrological signatures to the cosmos. Earth, air, water, and fire (the four archetypal elements) were seen as vital entities with values, properties, and intelligences. By losing its connection with nature (and hence the universe) scientific medicine, through an elaborate system of classification, codification, and reductionism, has deciphered all aspects of matter but remains ignorant of its essence, interrelatedness, and metaphysical roots.

Ironically, the new form of mental activity to which Butterfield referred was material science. He writes that the modern law of inertia, the modern theory of motion, was the vehicle by which seventeenth-century scientists used to drive the spirits out of the world, opening the way to a universe that ran like clockwork.[4] Keith Thomas, in his book *Religion and the Decline of Magic*, makes the point that modern science replaced occult explanations of the world due to the emergence of a renewed faith in the potentialities of human initiative. He believes that the decline of interest in the "magical arts" and metaphysical explanations can be explained by the growth of more superior methods of prediction.[5]

Be that as it may, the new thinking that underscored changes in perception, which brought about new approaches to science in the seventeenth century, have now been called into question. Physicist

Fritjof Capra has written that physics has undergone several conceptual revolutions in the twentieth century that show the limitations of the mechanistic world view. In its place, he argues, there is emerging a more organic and ecological view of the world which resembles the observations and experiences of mystics of all ages and traditions.[6] Marilyn Ferguson talks about "a leaderless but powerful network" that is working to bring about radical change by cutting loose from certain key elements of western thought and even with historical continuity.[7] Writer Morris Berman states:

"For more than 99 percent of human history, the world was enchanted and man saw himself as an integral part of it. The complete reversal of this perception in a mere four hundred years or so has destroyed the continuity of the human experience and the integrity of the human psyche. It has very nearly wrecked the planet as well. The only hope, or so it seems to me, lies in a retrenchment of the world."[8]

The creation of a new, or more accurately put, a different system of mental relationships is neither abrupt or clear-cut. Patterns of thought at any point in time are complex and often contradictory. Aristotelian theories, which dominated the intellectual life of the Middle Ages and had been integrated into Christian thought, stood apart from the ground-water streams of esotericism. Yet both were predicated on a world view where unseen forces, energies, and entities intermingled with the affairs of people. It is also true that many of the intellectual giants of the early modern period, including Johann Kepler, Francis Bacon, and Isaac Newton, had strong esoteric interests while promoting new methodologies and modern scientific theories.

Paradoxically, even though Christianity has been in a profound sense otherworldly, it has been largely accommodating to a materialistic view of the universe. In this respect, it has become more the apologist for modern science than its antagonist, with some exceptions of course. Conversely, the lineage of the Ageless Wisdom has held that the world of material forms is but a delusion, perpetuated by our senses, and cloaking that which is true. Thus, to an esotericist, life on the physical plane is a shadow world that is animated by an inner light. To understand history, esoterically, requires us to metaphorically stand on our heads. This perception will require, in the words of Butterfield, light from heaven so as to break the old framework and allow a new understanding to take hold.

Western Religious Cosmology

In relating the evolution of the western religious tradition to the emergence of a scientific-materialistic world view, three important points can be made. The first has to do with the orientation of western religious thought. Religious historian, Houston Smith, believes that the great world religions can be divided into three groups: the religions of southern Asia, namely Hinduism and Buddhism, speak to the psychological dimension in humanity; the east Asian religions of Confucianism and Taoism address the question of human relationships and social conduct; while the western religious tradition confronts the problem of nature, or humanity's relation to the physical universe.[9]

According to Smith, the West has developed three distinctive ideas, which have transformed Western Civilization and have percolated throughout the world. These ideas include the scientific method, the notion of progress, and the concept of individual rights. If we ask "what is nature?" we would find that it is composed of matter, time, and space. Smith sees a strong correlation between religion and the material world. Since the religions of the West, what Smith calls the Abrahamic religions, picture God as the ruler of the physical universe, the material world, which is all but denied in the eastern religions, is elevated to a central position.[10]

The second aspect of nature, time, corresponds to the concept of progress. Judaism, Christianity, and Islam are unique insofar as they represent the views of the oppressed and dispossessed. If you are at the bottom of the heap the only way out is up, so each of these religions is future-oriented towards a time when suffering will end and the good will reign. The Jews saw this as the advent of the Messiah, for the Christians it was the second coming of the Christ, for the eighteenth-century rationalist it was the belief in material progress, and for Karl Marx, a century later, it was the inevitable classless society. Such has been the power of the idea of progress that it has moved beyond its purely religious form.[11]

Space, the third aspect of nature, relates clearly to individualism. Smith rightly points out that individualism has no real connection with the Occidental religions, but developed organically as western people moved out of the Near East, through the Mediterranean world, into Europe and, eventually, across the ocean to the New World. Restless people on the move lose the context of their identity and are more apt to fall back on their own resources. The idea of individualism carries with it the sense of individual rights. Over time, there developed a polarity between the well being of the individual and the power of the collective, as expressed through the authority of institutions, such as church and state.[12] It was this tension, in part, which underscored the Protestant Reformation and later, the American and French revolutions.

Time and space have esoteric correspondences which are based on consciousness and the flow of energy. Time relates to the length of a thought. A thought may be a fleeting idea that is briefly modified in some way or it can be the length of a solar system, when generated through the mind of a great deity, such as the Solar Logos. Space, on the other hand, in an idealistic sense, relates to the substance of a thought. The word "substance," meaning that which lies behind or stands underneath something else, refers to the aggregate of atomic builders out of which all forms are built.[13] Essentially, the transformation of energy from cause to effect involves the cyclic ebb and flow of energy streams, known as the seven rays, about which much will be discussed throughout this book.

The second point that Professor Smith makes about the evolution of the western religious tradition is that it led to the perception of a cleavage between spirit and matter. Judaism, Christianity, and Islam all characterize God as an external power, which acts upon nature and often, capriciously, interferes in human affairs. On one hand, the separation between spirit and matter prompted much aspiration and devotion, which united the faithful into a community of believers. While the Christian Church conceived of itself as the body of Christ on earth, the focus of the believing Christian was always directed towards heaven and the hope of salvation in the afterlife. Humanity existed as a link in the "great chain of being," which connected God through the angels and other celestial entities with the animal kingdom and other lower forms of life. This static, hierarchical image of the cosmos must have given some reassurance to western people, who at least knew their place in the scheme of things.

The downside of this cleavage has been the removal of people from their divine source. At the sixth council held at Constantinople in 681 CE, a doctrine was proclaimed which ascribed to Christ two wills flowing from two natural energies, one divine and one human.[14] The implications of this resolution are clear: if Christ had two natures, then people were represented by their lower nature and, hence, were not divine. It therefore follows that divinity remains something beyond humanity's grasp and can only be experienced through some form of mediation, which is the role given to the Church, the saints, and ultimately to the Christ. In a very real sense, the Church replaced the idea of the soul with itself. As the medieval world view gradually eroded, a competing cosmology emerged in the seventeenth century, claiming that the universe was merely a collection of bodies acted upon by natural forces. Thus the external reality of divinity appeared to inquiring minds to be increasingly abstract and remote.

Certainly by the late seventeenth century, the Platonic world view, which the Catholic Church embraced, with its hierarchy of perfected spheres presided over by angelic entities, no longer made sense as a physical reality. As a subjective map of the human constitution, there were many correlations relating to the Ptolemaic cosmos. However, few would have realized these connections at the time. Christianity could accommodate the scientific revolution by relinquishing its metaphysical explanations for the material world, while at the same time claiming exclusive jurisdiction over the non-material realms of divinity. Hence men and women in the West have adapted themselves comfortably or uncomfortably to two apparently irreconcilable explanations of humanity, nature, and the cosmos.

The third and final point that can be made about the western religious tradition is that it is overtly historical. Houston Smith has written that Judaism, and later Christianity, found great meaning in history simply because human society represented the sphere of God's purposeful activity.[15] In other words, God manifested himself in human affairs over time, so to understand the will of God one had to have a model of history. The notion that God was the engineer of history was the standard interpretation up through the seventeenth century. When Sir Walter Raleigh wrote his *History of the World* in 1614, he began this study with the creation of the world and recounted the high points of Old Testament history to the destruction of Jerusalem. The rest of Raleigh's history covers the rise of Greek civilization from the time of the Persian Wars (490 to 449 BCE) to the Second Macedonian War (200 to 197 BCE). For Raleigh, history was seen merely as a repetition of events and trends in the ancient world and the great events of Western Civilization, up to his time, did not merit any mention.

The most noted apologist for the Christian view of history was Augustine. In his famous book, *The City of God*, Augustine structures history around two distinct realms; the City of God, which is eternal, and the City of Man, which is corrupt and transitory. History begins at the moment of creation and continues in a progressive and linear fashion up to the Day of Judgment. What really mattered to Augustine was salvation or damnation in the world to come, and salvation could only be guaranteed through absolute faith. This line of thinking denied that history was cyclical in nature, which was the prevailing paradigm of classical thinkers in the ancient world, and the linear and literal unfoldment of human history governed by a celestial destiny remained the official view of the Church up to the eighteenth century. Bishop Bossuet, a French cleric and counselor to king Louis XIV, writing in the late seventeenth century, became one of the last apologists for a full-blown Christian perspective of history. According to Bossuet, the whole course of human history is guided by providence, which could be seen in all spheres of life.

The Isolation of History

The removal of God as the controlling force of history did not cause an abrupt change in perspective; rather it led to a shift in focus towards a history guided by the laws of nature. Whereas medieval church history had sought to put faith and salvation at the center of the historical narrative, the philosophers and historians of the eighteenth century concentrated more on morality, civic virtue, and human nature. Philosopher David Hume remarked in his *Essays* that the chief use of history was to uncover the constant and universal principles of human nature.[16] Denis Diderot's *Encyclopedia* was even more specific. In the words of Voltaire, the probable collaborator of the section on history, it states:

"We demand today of historians more minute details, facts more completely authenticated, exact dates, precise authorities, more attention to customs, laws, manners, commerce, finance, agriculture, and population: it is the same with history as it is with mathematics and natural philosophy."[17]

The next step in the evolution of history was in the direction of objectivism. The German historian, Leopold von Ranke, known as the father of objective history, believed that it was not the role of the historian to sit in judgment on the past but to show what really happened.[18] One thinker who did sit in judgment was Karl Marx who, though impressed with many subjective insights, produced a model that sought to explain history and society in materialistic terms. History was based on what Marx called dialectical materialism, which involved conflict between the dominant social classes and those classes who were exploited. Class conflict eventually led to revolution and a new historical synthesis. The ultimate goal of history, according to Marx, was the creation of a classless society through communism.

Auguste Comte, the recognized founder of sociology, argued that history evolved through three stages, which he called the theological stage, when the thoughts of people were guided by religion; the metaphysical stage, when people gradually came to understand society as a natural, rather than a supernatural phenomenon; and, finally, the scientific stage, where human affairs would be studied objectively and scientifically. Under the influence of positivism, a term coined by Comte, there developed a methodology of history based upon the evaluation of empirical evidence, the objective analysis of source material, and the scrupulous employment of research techniques. Whereas the scope of history has expanded in recent times, which has led to new questions, methods of research, and theoretical models, the methodology and concerns of the historian have not changed that much in over a century.

Readers of professional historical journals will have no difficulty in deducing that history, as a field of study, is in a state of crisis. The lack of interest in the study of history in schools and colleges, coupled with an ignorance of general historical knowledge among many young people, points to an extreme and unprecedented provincialism by which an awareness of the past has been cut adrift by a preoccupation with the present. Within the historical profession itself, there appears to be a lack of direction and vision. Academic history has become increasingly specialized and theoretical. Ironically, in spite of their claims to re-create objective reality, historians often perpetuate myths. Indeed, the interpretation of historical events quickly dissolves into mythology and, given the pressures from many sources to have the past reflect their interests, much history today has become ideologically driven.

The problems confronting history have also spread across the entire educational system. College faculty have become more absorbed in technology, the accessing of information, and administrative matters than with ideas and the interchange of thought. The information explosion, brought about by the revolution in computer and information technology, has helped to expand and break down the barriers within and between different disciplines. However, easy access to information has led to an overload whereby we have more data than can be actually processed.

By the same token, the accumulation of information is at the bottom rung of the ladder. It is through the synthesis of information that one gains knowledge and it is through the synthesis of knowledge, in the light of one's soul or higher mental and intuitive faculties, that one achieves wisdom. Whereas conventional history, along with many other disciplines, tends to generate knowledge through information, esoteric or occult approaches seek to create knowledge that is inspired by wisdom. This is an important distinction.

History and the Ageless Wisdom

Behind the official view of history, whether Christian, scientific, or secular, there is an undercurrent of thought which has been largely invisible. Modern physicists, dating from the work of Werner Heisenberg in 1927, have raised serious questions about the nature of matter and objectivity. Quantum physicists tell us that the subatomic world appears as particles and waves of energy.[19] If we use particles and waves as metaphors for viewing civilization, then it is clear that history has both an exoteric and an esoteric nature. Exoteric history relies on concrete sources to re-create the past along the line of identifiable images, while esoteric history represents the shifting sands of consciousness, rhythmic patterns, and energy relationships.

In its outward material form, history consists of visible institutional development. We see the evolution of political forms—monarchies, nation-states, constitutions, bureaucracies: of economic forms—money, trade, industry, guilds, trade unions, banking: of religious forms—churches, sects, cults, religious activities, rituals: of educational establishments—schools, colleges, universities: and of private life—family patterns, manners, customs, and moral life. What social institutions share in common is longevity. They link us to the past and define, in many ways, our social reality. Institutions are to be found in all cultures and civilizations and give rise to a variety of customs and practices which sociologists term cultural universals. Relating back to our metaphor, therefore, institutional development can be seen as particles of matter on the broad canvass of history.

On the other hand, there is a realm of history which operates as a wave pattern. Throughout the ages there has been an invisible matrix of energies which, arguably, underscores and gives direction and life to visible forms. Nowhere can this be seen more clearly than with respect to religion. The life of any religion is closely associated with its mystical or occult roots. At the height of its power in the fourteenth century, the Church confirmed at the three councils in Constantinople (1341, 1347, and 1351) the teachings of St. Gregory Palamas that, whereas the energies of God are unknowable, these energies "come down to us, and the saints participate in them by grace through a union of love."[20]

In the centuries following the Counter Reformation, the Catholic Church began to lose touch with the esoteric world of active energies and forces. By the seventeenth century, according to McManners, a new spirituality had arisen, a common spirituality for ordinary people.[21] One might ask, where are today the great visionaries, mystics, and seers, such as Meister Eckhart, John Ruusbroec, Julian of Norwich, Brigitta of Sweden, Catherine of Siena, Teresa of Avila, and St. Francis of Assisi? They certainly have been absent from Christian religious life in recent centuries. Though still a potent force today, the Church has become less a vitalized mystical community and more a crystallized shell surrounded and impacted by the forces of materialism. Needless to say, the number of true occultists at any point in time is relatively few. Helena Petrovna Blavatsky has written that there are not in the West a half-dozen people among the hundreds who call themselves occultists who have any idea as to the true nature of occult science.[22]

What can be termed the history of the Ageless Wisdom should in no way be confused with popular culture. From the time of the Middle Ages, there developed a two-tiered society which unfolded in parallel fashion until the nineteenth century. The ruling classes who dominated the basic institutions of Europe also dominate the pages of history books and are well known to us. On the other hand, within peasant society, which comprised the vast majority of people in Europe up to recent times, there could be found a whole range of subcultures which rested upon an oral tradition of legends, ballads, superstitions, and fantasies. Witchcraft, sorcery, and the other cunning arts were common fixtures within the peasant frame of experience. Conversely, the learned astrologer, alchemist, magician, cabalist, and occult philosopher occupied a different social and intellectual universe, although there are points of common identity. The occultist and the sorcerer were the defined enemies of the Christian Church, both Protestant and Catholic. The Renaissance of the fifteenth and sixteenth centuries gave rise to a flowering of occult thought and practice. However, the spiritual unity of humanity in the West and the unification of philosophy and religion, which cabalists like Pico della Mirandola dreamed about, were quickly squelched by the hardening of church attitudes in the sixteenth century.[23] To understand the history of esotericism, or the Ageless Wisdom, one must look for patterns of synchronicity, moments of sudden change, and dramatic departures from the past.

Kenneth Clark, in his talks on "Civilisation," observes that in the whole of recorded history there have been three or four moments when "the earth seems suddenly to have grown warmer and more radio-active." He goes on to say that it is during these times that "man has made a leap forward that would have been unthinkable under ordinary evolutionary conditions."[24] The dates that Clark gives for these "bursts of radio-activity" are 3000 BCE, during the high point of the Taurian age, when the centralized civilizations of Sumeria and Egypt, complete with new myths and gods, replaced the more decentralized goddess-centered cultures of the Neolithic world during the Age of Cancer; the late sixth century BCE, with the flowering of Greek philosophy, art, and science along with the great religions/philosophies of Buddhism and Confucianism in the East; and the twelfth century CE, when centers of learning emerged, cathedrals sprouted up all over Europe and, in the words of Clark, "there was an extraordinary outpouring of energy" in every phase of life.[25]

Whether we agree with Clark's periodicity, the important point to be grasped is that during times of great creative manifestation there is always some deep esoteric cause. The Tibetan Master D.K. also refers to cycles of radiation, leading to a realized expansion of consciousness. He states that one such period occurred during the prehistoric Atlantean civilization, thousands of years ago. Another period of radioactivity coincided with the time of the Buddha and, again, to a lesser degree, about the time of the Christ. More recently, there is a cycle of radiation that has been gaining momentum since the fourteenth century, and the human kingdom, in an esoteric sense, is becoming increasingly more radioactive. We are told that it promises to become even more intense in the future.[26]

An explanation for why certain periods of history are more prone to explosions of consciousness, or radioactivity, than others may relate to the influence of those people of genius (from Clark's perspective) or advanced initiates, masters, disciples (if one adopts the esoteric paradigm of the Tibetan) who exist at such times. To contend that certain heroes in history are, in fact, initiates who are privy to the inner mysteries of the Ageless Wisdom is, in one sense, merely a point of speculation. This leaves us with the question, however, as to why certain individuals, based on their wisdom, compassion, or genius, emerge individually or as a group to cast their light across history for hundreds, or even thousands of years. Whatever epithets we might give such persons, it is difficult to deny that they stand "head and shoulders" above the lot of ordinary men and women and are, in a very real sense, the teachers of humanity. The ability to distinguish true greatness and quality in the lives of historical personages is essential for any spiritual comprehension of history, since it is primarily thorough the lives of "great beings" that wisdom can be distilled and vision becomes realized. As it says in the Bible, by their fruits they shall be known (Matthew 7:16).

Following this line of argument, the Ageless Wisdom teaches that the god-kings of Sumeria and Egypt in the ancient world were, in fact, masters of the wisdom who had been sent to rule over the affairs of men. The emergence of the great religions of the East, including Buddhism, Confucianism, Taoism, and Zoroastrianism in the sixth century, and the Greek mystery schools growing out of the teaching of Pythagoras and Plato, were also the work of great initiates and spiritually charged beings representing the ashrams of the planetary Hierarchy. The twelfth century witnessed less exalted personages but could still point to great men, no doubt advanced disciples and initiates of the inner mysteries, such as St. Anselm of Canterbury, John of Salisbury, Peter Abelard and, of course, St. Francis of Assisi. In each case the external events, which fill the pages of history texts, arose from the thought or invisible activities of some spiritual being or mystery school. Generally, a mystery school is a group of spiritual disciples who participate in occult study and ritual and who guard the secrets of the Ageless Wisdom.

If we quickly scan our eyes across antiquity, we will catch a glimpse of dozens of occult groups and spiritual movements. We see the emergence of Neoplatonism through the works of Plotinus in the third century CE and the rise of Gnosticism two centuries earlier. Then there was Mithraism, which spread among the Roman legions and has been called the Freemasonry of the ancient world.[27] Add to this the mystery schools of Egypt and Greece, the Dionysian cult, the teachings of the occult architect Marcus Vitruvius Pollio, along with the writings of great initiates, of which Plato, Aristophanes, Apollonius of Tyana, Plutarch of Chaeronea, Virgil, and Marcus Aurelius Antoninus are some examples. Together, they comprised a few focal points in a vast network of esoteric thought and practice which had a potent impact upon the ancient world.[28]

With the rise of Christianity, dating from 313 CE when the Roman Emperor Constantine turned this cult into the official religion of the Empire, various mystery schools were forced underground. Each century found a number of secret or quasi-secret, or not-so-secret societies which perpetuated esoteric wisdom. Some of those groups are listed as follows:

- **Third Century**: Manes, Gnostics, Marcionite Churches, Magian Brotherhood
- **Fourth Century to the Tenth Century**: Neoplatonists, Manichaeans, Nestorians, Euchites, Ophites, Paulicans, and Bogomiles
- **Eleventh and Twelfth Centuries**: Albigensians, Knights Templar, Cathari, Caputiati, and Hermeticists
- **Thirteenth Century**: Brethern of the Free Spirit, Apostolikers, Brotherhood of Winkelers, Lollards, and Albigensians
- **Fourteenth Century**: Heschasts, Adam-cult, Fraticelli, Lollards, and Friends of God
- **Fifteenth Century**: Taborites, Waldensians, Fratres Lucis, Rosicrucians, Alchemical Society, and Hussites
- **Sixteenth Century**: Waldensians, Rosicrucians, Order of Christ, Neoplatonists, Christian Cabalists, Hermeticists, Militia Crucifera Evangelica, and followers of Paracelsus, Cornelius Agrippa, and Francesco Giorgi
- **Seventeenth Century**: Rosicrucians, Quietists, Pietists, Diggers, Order of the Quest, and Templars
- **Eighteenth Century**: Knights of Light, Rosicrucians, Martinists, Freemasons, Illuminati, Knights of the Holy Grail, Lodge of Perfection, Universal Society, and the first Theosophists

- **Nineteenth Century**: Brotherhood of Light, Swedenborgians, Rosicrucians, Mesmerists, Hermetic Order of the Golden Dawn, Freemasons and other Masonic groups, and Theosophists
- **Twentieth Century**: Masonic Order, Ancient Universal Mysteries, Theosophists, Anthroposophists, Arcane School, School for Esoteric Studies, Philosophical Research Society, Society of the Inner Light, Findhorn Foundation, Agni Yoga Society, and Meditation Mount. There are many others.

Several of these esoteric groups merit further elaboration. One occult movement that may have contributed to the "great thaw" of the twelfth century, referred to by Clark, were the Knights Templar. Formed in 1118, the poor knights of the Temple of Solomon, as they were called, emerged as a religious order dedicated to protecting pilgrims in the Holy Land and restoring the principles of knighthood. A less obvious agenda was the reconstruction of Solomon's Temple, the synthesis of the Ageless Wisdom with Christian faith, and the creation of a United Europe, however it is unclear what form this would take. So successful were the Templars that by the thirteenth century they had become the international bankers of Europe and were chosen to be the treasurers of the Vatican and the French royal family.[29] More esoterically, the Templars lived like an order of monks and adopted many of the rituals and practices of the Masonic tradition, which had gone underground during this time.

The downfall of the order came when the French king, Philip IV, who was bankrupt at the time and coveted Templar funds, formed an alliance with Pope Clement V, who had become fearful of Templar power. Together they formulated a plan to capture and execute the Grand Master of the Order, Jacques de Molay. The Templars were formally disbanded in 1312, but they continued for centuries as a clandestine organization working to promote occultism and new political ideas. Eliphas Levi, in his book, *The History of Magic*, saw the Templars as a movement which had become corrupted not only through their material success but through a degeneration of their spiritual disciplines, even to the point of dabbling in black magic.[30]

Another movement, more ancient in origin, has been Masonry. Some sources consider Masonry to be a modern phenomenon. Michael Baigent and Richard Leigh, in their book, *The Temple and the Lodge*, state that Freemasonry generally looks to its origins in the seventeenth century,[31] however, this is only the tip of the iceberg. Theosophy and other esoteric traditions imply that Masonry, in its earliest form, is as old as humanity and dates back to a time when, so it is argued, the planetary Hierarchy of spiritual beings was installed on earth during the ancient Lemurian civilization, millions of years ago. It existed in Egypt, so we are told, where Masonry became a custodian of the mysteries, which were communicated by the priesthood to initiates in a secret language. The Egyptians related the teachings of the Ageless Wisdom in their rituals and dogmas for many centuries, until this knowledge became diluted and the keys to these mysteries were gradually lost. The Semites inherited the mystery teaching from the Egyptians and Chaldeans. Two of the seven keys to the ancient mysteries were adopted by the Jews while in captivity, and brought to their homeland. The Jews set up certain mystery schools and adopted into Masonry their own symbols, words of power, and allegorical stories—for example, the story of King Solomon's Temple, which existed in myth if not in fact. In Roman times, Masonry developed as a kind of ascetic practice among the legionnaires, who introduced into their ceremonies weaponry in the defense of the downtrodden.

From the fourth century, with the fall of Rome and the rise of a fanatical Christianity, Masonry went underground and was kept alive in the guilds of builders called "masons," which met in secret and passed along the esoteric mysteries and rituals from one generation to the next without committing anything to paper. It was during this period that Masonry developed a more hierarchical structure with Operative Masons being the custodians of the inner mysteries. This was at about the same time that the Roman Collegia, which had been the guardian of the Masonic mysteries, disappeared, and the rituals and teachings continued to survive among the lodges of guild masons in various regions. Included here would be the Comancini in Italy, the Stonemasons of Germany, and the Compagnonnage in France. Many of the great cathedrals, such as the cathedral at Chartres, which emerged during the twelfth and thirteenth centuries, were built by guild masons who incorporated esoteric symbolism into their work. Because the Masonic guilds were outlawed and persecuted during this time, the symbolic aspects of the mysteries were preserved in what was termed Blue Masonry, and the more esoteric aspects of the wisdom temporarily disappeared. Thus these speculative secrets became concealed behind the operative forms of Masonry for much of the duration of the Middle Ages.

With the coming of the Reformation, Masonry began to emerge from obscurity and reassert itself. Freemasonry appeared in Scotland during the sixteenth and seventeenth centuries, but it was not fully revived until the opening of the Grand Lodges in England during the early eighteenth century. Many Protestant Christians flocked to Masonry (it was still outlawed by the Catholic Church) and many lodges emerged in Europe. Masonry thrived in the American colonies and it should be noted that many who fought in the American Revolution were Masons. Twenty-five signers of those who authored the Declaration of Independence were known to be active Masons. In France, Masonry was dominated by progressive thinking aristocrats and those persons who possessed influence and power. One source claims that on the eve of the French Revolution in 1789 there were between six- and seven-hundred lodges in France, with an approximate total of 30,000 members.[32] The contention that Masonic ideas of liberty and brotherhood directly contributed to the Revolution must, therefore, be taken seriously.

The rise of materialism, with its narrow focus on objective reality, adversely affected the appeal and quality of Masonry in the nineteenth century. Co-Masonry, which was open to women, was instituted in France in 1893 through the efforts of Mme. Marie Deraismes, who was the first woman since ancient times to be admitted to a Masonic order. Soon lodges spread to other countries and, in England, Masonry received the support of the Theosophical Society. On the whole, however, Masonry in its various forms has continued to decline as its esoteric meaning and practices have withered away.

A recent development in Masonry has been the formation of Ancient Universal Mysteries (A.U.M.), which has attempted to bring about a spiritual reformation and thus inject new life into the old forms. A.U.M. lodges have started in several cities across the United States, in Australia, and in New Zealand. To date, this revival of Masonry represents one of the most promising developments in an effort to restore the ancient mysteries.[33]

The Renaissance and Reformation period not only led to the externalization of Masonry, but gave rise to a whole range of occult and esoteric practices. Astrology, of course, is of ancient origin and can trace its roots back to Egyptian, Babylonian, Greek, and Arabic traditions. Some would suggest that astrology was originally given to humanity by great beings of superior intelligence who came to earth to guide us.[34] Astrology is based on the law of analogy, meaning that planetary movements and rhythms have a correspondence on the earth plane. "As above, so below," states the Hermetic axiom. Astrology was widely accepted and practiced through all levels of society until the eighteenth century, when the desire to probe the nature of matter itself replaced the law of correspondences as the guiding principle of science.

Another early and influential esoteric tradition was Cabalism which, according to Manly Palmer Hall, rose, flourished, and declined in Europe between the tenth and seventeenth centuries.[35] Cabalism emerged during the Middle Ages on the Iberian peninsula—the home of the three great western religious traditions: Christian, Moslem, and Jewish. Although based upon the Jewish tradition, Cabalism, like all esoteric knowledge and practices, has universal significance. Cabala is a kind of esoteric mathematics, derived from the Pythagoreans, which can be translated into the letters of the Hebrew alphabet—Hebrew, itself, is a sacred language. The structure for Cabala numerology is what came to be called "the tree of life," which symbolizes the inner or esoteric structure of the cosmos. The Cabala was not only a useful tool for occultists seeking to unravel the inner mysteries; it also gave support to treatises in alchemy, astrology, Hermeticism, and Neoplatonism, all of which staged a revival during the sixteenth century.

The Rosicrucian movement is an important beneficiary of Cabalism. As with Masonry, the origins of Rosicrucianism are somewhat obscure. Sources tend to link the movement to the writings of a fourteenth-century mystic, known by the pseudonym of Christian Rosenkreuz who, it was said, left monastic life to travel to the Middle East where he studied the Cabala and Arabian occultism. Upon his return to Europe, he became involved with alchemy, Hermeticism, and the "secret arts," which led to a number of manifestos that were later published in the early seventeenth century. With the publication of these tracts and their dissemination, the Rosicrucian movement formally began in the early seventeenth century. There is some debate over the popularity and coherence of this movement, which overlapped with other occult groups. Those wishing to establish clear boundaries between the different streams of occultism will be frustrated because of the universal nature of the Ageless Wisdom, which seeped into the various movements and secret societies.

At the heart of the Rosicrucian teachings is the Secret Doctrine, a body of esoteric wisdom, ancient in origin, given to humanity, so it is said, through initiates and disciples in their schools, temples, and lodges. It is certain that the Secret Doctrine did not come from a single source, namely Rosenkreuz (if he existed at all), but through delegates of the Hierarchy, such as John Dee, Edmund Spenser, and Francis Bacon. Rosicrucian doctrine can be seen as an attempt to synthesize religion (as expressed through the Ageless Wisdom) and science. Had this movement exercised greater influence on the cosmological debates, which emerged in the seventeenth century and centered on the implications of new scientific theories in relation to the Ptolemaic-Christian world view, the course of history would have been altered significantly. Rosicrucianism, however, like other esoteric movements, was still out of favor and could not, as yet, be discussed openly.

The Secret Doctrine consists of seven aphorisms of creation which, in veiled language, present an occult analysis of creation, the symbolism and function of the world soul, the origin of generation, how unity becomes diversity, the mysteries surrounding the flame of life, the seven planes of consciousness, and the sevenfold soul of humanity. According to Rosicrucian teachings, the universe is divided into seven different worlds, which include the world of God on the highest plane, followed by the world of virgin spirits, the world of divine spirit, the world of life spirit, the world of thought, the desire world, and the physical world. Beyond the sevenfold planes of consciousness, which define earthly existence, there is an interpenetration of other worlds, planetary systems, and cosmic realms, all guided by a supreme being or intelligence.[36]

Theosophy and Its Offspring

A more recent dispensation of the Ageless Wisdom has been Theosophy. As a movement, Theosophy dates from the late nineteenth century. In 1875, the Theosophical Society was formed but, like all esoteric groups, its shadow extends far back into antiquity. In the short term, Theosophy, as stated by Joscelyn Godwin, owed much to the skeptical thinking of the eighteenth century[37] which helped to create a suitable environment in which Theosophy could thrive. One of the things that made the Theosophical movement different was that it was the outgrowth of a small group of people dominated by a single outstanding initiate, Helena Petrovna Blavatsky (H.P.B.). Books could be written, and many of them have been written, on this remarkable and bizarre person. However, suffice it to say, chief among Blavatsky's abilities were intuitive powers, which were reported to reach into planes of consciousness beyond the grasp of most other living souls. Stories as to Madame Blavatsky's extraordinary mediumistic and intuitive abilities have been detailed by her biographers, most notably Sylvia Cranston, Charles J. Ryan, and A.P. Sinnett.[38]

These abilities allowed her not only to communicate with the Masters of the Wisdom (especially the Master Morya) but, it is said, enabled her to draw ideas from the akashic records. There are frequent references to these records in the esoteric literature. They have been described as an immense photographic film, registering the desires and earthly experiences of our planet. These include the life experiences of every human being throughout history, the reactions to experience of the entire animal kingdom, the aggregate of thoughtforms based on desire, and the planetary "dweller on the threshold," meaning all the aggregated forms that exist in the environment.[39]

A clearer understanding of the akashic records can be gained through an appreciation of the nature of thought itself. Esoteric students generally hold the view that thoughts have a life on their own plane and are essentially ideas in transit. Strictly speaking, thoughts, or one should say ideas, are not created by individual minds; instead, minds attract certain kinds of thoughts or ideas which are then modified and directed outward into the ethers, as it were, or towards some object. It could be said, therefore, that the mind will become receptive to thoughts or ideas on the plane where it is focused. The platitude that small minds think small thoughts whereas big minds think big thoughts has some truth. The Tibetan refers to "reservoirs of thought" onto which the focused mind alights and then translates thoughts derived from this "reservoir" into words and phrases.[40] The akashic records, in a corresponding sense, are reservoirs of thought on a higher plane of consciousness.

The Master Morya, in a letter to A.P. Sinnett, relays the following: "I have a habit of often quoting…from the maze of what I get in the countless folios of our akashic libraries, so to say—with eyes shut. Sometimes I may give out thoughts that will see light in years later; at other times what an orator, a Cicero may have pronounced ages earlier, and at others, what was only pronounced by modern lips."[41] Reading the akashic records involves focused mental polarization. The power of thought is essentially the power of directing energy and the source of thought is esoterically believed to derive from electrical vitalized substance, which is the template for the whole of history, human and cosmic.

The core of Theosophy is contained in H.P.B.'s last great work, *The Secret Doctrine*. H.P.B.'s volumes cover the same territory as Rosicrucianism and go much further. The books are essentially treatises on seven stanzas translated from what H.P.B. calls the *Book of Dzyan* and deal with both cosmic and human evolution. In an age that had reached the nadir of materialism, *The Secret Doctrine* presented a complex world of infinite proportions that is governed by sacred numbers and geometry. H.P.B. devoted much of her treatise to decoding myths, sacred writings, ancient texts, and esoteric symbols to show how they support a cosmology that has been for ages at the root of the Ageless Wisdom.

At a time when scholars and clergymen were hotly debating whether the Biblical story of creation or Darwin's biological theory of evolution was the true explanation of human origins, H.P.B. presented a far more radical and mind-boggling view of human development. She held that humanity had emerged through a complex evolution of schemes, rounds, chains, and root races and had individuated into distinctly human form during the Lemurian age, twenty-one million years ago. Contrary to conventional evolutionary thinking, human existence was seen to be a link in a vast evolutionary chain stretching from the world of atomic substances through the infinite world of great cosmic entities. Beyond the human kingdom stood the planetary Hierarchy, the elder brothers of humanity, who sought to guide human affairs in accordance with the divine plan.

In addition to revealing in great detail the teachings of the Ageless Wisdom, H.P.B. contributed two more important perspectives. The first, hitherto mentioned, was to challenge the materialistic world view of the late nineteenth century and to offer an alternative vision. To this end she carried on a voluminous correspondence with writers, scholars, scientists, skeptics, spiritualists, and others, as well as contributing articles to journals and newspapers, which amounted to an uncompromising war of words in defense of occultism. Her reward was stinging abuse from all quarters, which reached hysterical levels, even by the standards of the time, and even still continues.

H.P.B.'s second contribution was to bring into western intellectual life the teachings of the Orient so as to provide a synthesis of religious thought. Of course, the ideas of Buddhism and Hinduism were not unknown to the western world but it was H.P.B. and other prominent Theosophists, such as Colonel Olcott and A.P. Sinnett, who integrated these traditions, along with Christianity, into a universal philosophy. What the East gave to the West, apart from profound psychological insights on life, was an understanding of the complex, yet subtle, interplay of cycles, of which karma and reincarnation are the most obvious examples.

As with Masonry, Rosicrucianism, Hermeticism, and other esoteric schools, Theosophy had a profound impact upon the intellectual climate of its time, and one can see that in each case the leaders and thinkers of the age were privy to and/or actively involved in occultism. Prominent persons influenced by Theosophy, for example, included writers—W.B. Yeats, James Joyce, Jack London, E.M. Forster, D.H. Lawrence, T. S. Eliot, Ralph Waldo Emerson, Thornton Wilder, H.G. Wells, and the Irish poet G.W. Russell (A.E.); scientists—Albert Einstein, Thomas Edison, and Alfred Russell Wallace; musicians—Richard Wagner, Gustav Mahler, Jean Sibelius, Alexander Scriabin, Arnold Schoenberg, and Cyril Scott; psychologists—Carl Jung and Roberto Assagioli; and artists— Wassily Kandinsky, Piet Mondrian, Paul Klee, and Nicholas Roerich. And, of course, there are many more. Abner Doubleday, whose name has mistakenly been linked to the origins of baseball, was a charter member of the Theosophical Society. Whereas some of these great leaders and thinkers, like Yeats, have been active participants in esoteric circles, a much larger number have been sensitive to the patterns of the divine plan and have expressed them in their art or work. This reiterates the point that esotericism acts like an invisible guiding hand in human affairs which, like the metaphor of the wave as opposed to the particle, is seldom seen but is continually present.

While there have been a number of important offshoots of Theosophy, particularly Rudolf Steiner's development of Anthroposophy and Helena Roerich's transmitted Agni Yoga books, the most direct line has been through the writings of Alice A. Bailey (A.A.B.).

Alice A. Bailey was born into an aristocratic English family in 1880, grew up in comfortable but strict and formal circumstances and, as a young adult, went to India as a Christian missionary. She was approached by one of the Masters of the Wisdom at several points in her life and she finally agreed to undertake the task of acting as the amanuensis for the telepathically transmitted teachings of the Master D.K. These teachings comprised many volumes, which stand today as the most comprehensive and up-to-date revelation of the Ageless Wisdom.[42] These writings recapitulate and extend the material presented by H.P.B., although in a different voice. However, they are most important for their revelatory teachings on the seven rays.

What are the seven rays? More about this vast subject will be discussed in a later chapter. As a way of putting a discussion of the rays in context, let us begin by recognizing that what we know of the universe is based upon ideas, sensations, and impressions that are filtered through three planes of our consciousness. We know there is a physical world because we can directly experience it. By the same token, we are aware of the planes of emotion and thought (mostly in a concrete sense), again through our experiences. These three realms condition our understanding of reality, which is the world of form. Try as we will, it is virtually impossible to imagine anything, no matter how ethereal or subtle, that is truly formless.

But what would happen if the veil of form suddenly disappeared and we could view the ordered flow of intelligent energy that transmits the qualities of life as they actually exist? From the esoteric perspective, the answer would point to the complex web of ray lives. Helen S. Burmeister, in her book, *The Seven Rays Made Visual*, writes: "As we strive toward this cosmic consciousness and oneness with all, veil after veil falls off that hides our innate essential divinity, our Christ-consciousness, our true Self, which is ever trying to reveal itself under the influences of the seven great Rays that function on cosmic, solar and planetary levels."[43]

Generally speaking, the rays are considered to be seven streams of force, or seven great lights of the Logos (God), each of them embodying a great cosmic entity. The seven rays then divide into three major and four minor rays.[44] The seven rays, as intelligent entities through which the divine plan manifests, function ultimately as sound and color. Each ray note vibrates at a certain frequency and has its own shade and quality of intelligent life. Consequently, as the rays radiate through the seven planes of manifestation, they saturate the life forms on each plane in descending order. History is shaped by the interplay of ray notes and light qualities on the three lower planes: the mental, the astral, and the etheric/physical. As these rays are governed by the law of cycles, they play upon the consciousness of humanity according to rhythmic patterns. Thus, the whole of human history can be understood as a melody of ray and subray interactions.

Table 1. The Seven Rays and Some of Their Qualities

- Ray 1 - Will and Power: courage, strength, fearlessness, pride, synthesis
- Ray 2 - Love and Wisdom: faithfulness, magnetic love, sensitivity, fusing power
- Ray 3 - Active Intelligence: abstract thought, strategizing, action, manipulation of energy
- Ray 4 - Harmony from Conflict: love of beauty, mediation, mathematical exactitude, creative aspiration
- Ray 5 - Concrete Knowledge: technical expertise, scientific thought, logic, power to define, accuracy and precision, idea of cause and results
- Ray 6 - Devotion and Idealism: single-mindedness, humility, self-sacrifice, emotionalism, fanaticism, idealism
- Ray 7 - Ceremonial Order: planning and organization, power to build, management of detail, sense of rhythm and timing, ritualism

In terms of esoteric history, the end of every great age is significant insofar as it represents a period of transition and the culmination of forces that have been building up over long periods of time. The fact that we are presently living through such a transition period is no secret. This period, whether seen as long or short, can be considered no less remarkable. Historian Eric Hobsbawm states that there can be no serious doubt that, in the late 1980s and early 1990s, an era in world history ended and another one began.[45] Periods of transition can be seen as somewhat arbitrary. While there is no overwhelming evidence in favor of selecting one date over another as a benchmark for beginning a transition, a good case can be made for 1875 CE, the date that *The Secret Doctrine* was published. The emergence of Theosophy has, therefore, been timely.

In one of her books, *The Rays and the Initiations*, Alice Bailey observes that the teaching planned by the Hierarchy to guide humanity into the coming age was to be presented in installments. The first, marking the preparatory stage, was written down by H.P.B. between the years 1875 and 1890; the second or intermediate stage was presented by A.A.B. from 1919 through 1949; a third or revelatory stage was scheduled to be transmitted after 1975 through the media; and "in the next century and early in the century, an initiate will appear and will carry on this teaching."[46] It would appear that this revelatory aspect is not far away.

The Methodology of Esotericism

Technically speaking, of the twenty-three books written by A.A.B., all but four owe their authorship to the Tibetan Master Djwhal Khul, who used her as his amanuensis through transmitting thoughts to her telepathically. The question as to how a master communicates with his disciple is a fascinating subject, but we shall confine ourselves to the important question of how can one measure the validity of the ideas presented? After all, much information is being given out today based on claims that it is channeled from some master, avatar, or even the Christ. According to one source, researchers have estimated that about 85% of all guidance and channeling comes from a person's subconscious or from his or her astral or emotional plane of consciousness. Of the remaining 15%, less than 2% represents transmitted ideas from an actual spiritual master, while approximately 8% are insights gleaned from the individual's soul, and the remaining 5% are the telepathic transmissions of an advanced disciple.[47]

Based on a pamphlet authored by Corinne McLaughlin, the difference between the vast amount of astral plane channeling and spiritual transmissions of a higher order represents the difference between lower and higher psychism. Of the former, one finds information that is self-serving; flattering to the personality ego; motivated by fear or some strong desire; vague and platitudinous in nature; often long, flowery, confusing, and contradictory; passed through a trance or mediumistic state; proclaiming of itself sole authority; and of the conviction that spiritual growth requires no particular effort.[48]

Higher psychism, on the other hand, is always good for the whole group or society; focuses on service or helping others; never demands the surrender of one's free will nor denies personal responsibility or decision-making; always recognizes a higher power than the authority itself; presents a profound and thoughtful synthesis of new information or a new synthesis of spiritual teachings that does not contradict those of the major world religions; comes across as short, to the point, and intelligent; generates love, inspiration, and empowerment; and emphasizes personal effort as a prerequisite for spiritual growth.[49]

There is another problem that deals specifically with the use of evidence in writing esoteric history. The question is one of authority. Conventional history and scholarship, based upon recorded facts, is skeptical about relying on the words or insights of any particular observer. If the Tibetan Master D.K. writes "the history of mankind is, in reality, the history of man's demand for light and for contact with God,…"[50] what are we to make of this? The Tibetan offers a sound guideline for how to use the material contained in the Bailey books through a disclaimer, as mentioned earlier, which is printed at the beginning of each of the works for which he is responsible. In essence what he says is that the truth or value of these teachings can be measured only in terms of its ability to correspond with truth already found in the world's great teachings; its capacity to raise the point of focus from the emotions to the mind, to bring forth flashes of intuition; and to prove true under the test of the law of correspondences. Otherwise, the reader should not accept what is said. Keeping this in mind, it is clear that the proper approach to using inspired thoughts in writing esoteric history is to approach everything as an hypothesis to be proven. By the same token, speculations are permissible insofar as they are an inducement to further thought, analysis, and research.

Rudolf Steiner, in a series of lectures which he called *Methods of Spiritual Research*, makes the useful point that when we penetrate human experience from the vantage point of the soul, we attain a real state of self-observation.[51] The concept of the soul has been obscured in Christian theology and stripped of its essential nature. From an esoteric perspective, the soul is the bridging point between spirit and matter, the true ego or self, and the unified point of consciousness. However, it is much more. The Tibetan writes that the first step towards substantiating the fact of the soul is to establish the fact of survival. If there is a part of us that survives earthly existence, and this can be proven by the near-death testimony of thousands of people, then the question is, what survives?[52] The esoteric answer is the soul, which is, relatively speaking, that element of a living form which is immortal. The soul, like all things, is a corresponding value and may pertain to an atom, a person, a planetary unit, or to a solar system.

Conventional scientific thinking generally denies the soul and presupposes that it is through reason that we become impartial observers whereas, by basing our thoughts on emotion or feelings, we become subjective. Thus it is axiomatic to orthodox science that impartiality through reason is to be cultivated while all else—feeling, mystical experience, or intuitive insight—cannot be substantiated through empirical insight and hence must be dismissed as irrational. From a spiritual perspective, however, true objectivity can only be experienced from the point of soul consciousness (which is unattached from the myriads of thoughts and feelings flowing through the lower vehicles), whereas the personality, driven by thoughts conditioned by modified desires, drifts into patterns of separative thinking.

Experiencing the world through the vehicle of the separated mind induces habits of linear thought. Historians usually imbue their histories with a notion of continuity that tends to put events and ideas into categories and classes, which are then arranged in sequential order. Common to many histories is the concept of progress which sees the past as way stations in the march towards a bigger and more improved present. Regardless of the ideological bent of the historian, there is an assumption that history consists of a corpus of ascertained facts which can be manipulated in a variety of ways so as to achieve a desired conclusion.[53]

However, what is lost from this perspective is the understanding that historical events almost immediately become translated into symbols which live on as myths. Whereas myths are commonly thought of as fictional stories or half truths, in a deeper sense they represent ancient facts or figures long forgotten, preserved through archetypes that are repeated over and over again, which give them a timeless quality. History abounds with myths. President Reagan's star wars initiative was launched within the framework of the cosmic battle between good and evil; ethnic cleansing, as has occurred in Bosnia and Rwandi, is merely the latest in a long series of attempts at genocide, which is rooted in the myth of a vengeful god; Nazism was a reversion back to Nordic paganism and the return to the age of Ragnarok with the death of the gods, the regression of the world into chaos, and the distorted myth of the Aryans; the conquest of the Aztec Indians by the Spanish conquistadors was a visitation of the myth of the fall from innocence; and the explorations of the sixteenth-century navigators, looking for gold and trade, flows in the footsteps of the Grail myth of the hero in search for truth and immortality. Myth, therefore, characterizes the vision of the soul, which views history as the perpetual reenactment of divinely inspired ideas.

It should be stressed that a spiritual approach to historical and social research is not a retreat from reason, but an application of reason using often different assumptions. The importance of defining terms cannot be overstated. Within Tibetan Buddhism the basis of philosophy is the employment of definitions. Definitions lead to an understanding of syllogisms, which is an elementary form of logic within each sentence. To prove the occult statement "energy follows thought," one would start with a definition of energy, which esoterically is substance, and a definition of thought, which is the expression of that substance on the mental plane. Hence, logically, one proves the other.

Words in themselves have not only literal meanings but also symbolic and metaphorical meanings. The word "revolution" in a political and historical context refers to radical change, but it also means the completion of a cycle or the orbital spin around an axis. This expanded understanding of the term gives one a clearer insight into the true nature of a revolution as a compressed cycle of events that interferes with and creates impacts on those cycles of a longer duration. As in all other respects, a spiritual approach strives to comprehend the essence of a thing, not the meaning that may be the most obvious.

Towards an Esoteric View of History

Throughout the Alice Bailey books, the Tibetan makes numerous references to history. We find in *The Reappearance of the Christ*, for example, the observation that "history will some day be based and written upon the record of the initiatory growth of humanity; prior to that we must have a history which is constructed around the development of humanity under the influences of great and fundamental ideas."[54] In *Destiny of the Nations*, he states that "all history is the record of the effects of energies or radiations as they play upon humanity in its varying stages of evolutionary development."[55] In other references, the Tibetan discusses history in terms of the growth of human consciousness;[56] as the growth of man's perceptive faculties under differing national and racial conditions;[57] as the power to recognize ideas and push forward towards their fulfillment;[58] and as man's cyclic reaction to some inflowing divine energy, to some avatar or some inspired leader.[59]

These statements about esoteric history can be summed up in three words: ideas, cycles, and consciousness. Before we can fully understand history as the impact of "great and fundamental ideas," it is first necessary to comprehend what is meant by an idea. Esoteric students generally hold the view that an idea is a point of energy. Plutarch wrote that "an idea is a being incorporeal, which has no substance in itself, but gives figure and form unto shapeless matter and becomes the cause of manifestation."[60] Ideas, therefore, do not originate in the minds of people but are impressed upon them from other and deeper sources. One truly experiences ideas through the means of soul awareness which, according to the Tibetan, is the bridge between humanity and "the ideas which lie back of our world evolution..."[61]

Human history revolves around the ontological point that all creative manifestation is the result of ideas. In one sense history is measured by time, which is the life cycle of an idea, and space, which is the substance accumulated around an idea. What we call cultures and civilizations are, from an esoteric perspective, the result of ideas that have originated in the mind of the Logos, have been stepped down by the planetary Hierarchy, and have then been impressed upon the minds of humanity. Western Civilization is a synthesis of ideas that have reached their highest expression in previous civilizations with the addition of a new ingredient or component, in this case Christianity. Thus, so the argument goes, history is most fruitfully understood within the context of large time units, which embody a particular set of ideas. On the other hand, since history is holographic in nature, every event is encoded with the patterns and ideas of that culture and civilization. Ideas are, therefore, the fingerprints of history and all its components.

If ideas are the originators of history, consciousness is the means by which ideas can be manifested. The Ageless Wisdom teaches that all forms possess consciousness, which obliterates the belief held by some scientists (and most people) that matter is both animate and inanimate. Hence, consciousness is what underscores evolution. The archetypal pattern governing the history of all life is the involutionary descent into matter and the evolutionary return to divinity. The fall and redemption of man is the constant underlying theme of the Bible. Religions of the Orient stress the awakening of consciousness and the struggle to overcome desire. Cultural historian, William Irwin Thompson, tells us that the myths of the world indicate that consciousness is universal and precedes the formation of our solar system.[62] Ken Wilber expresses a companion view held by others (most notably J.G. Bennett and Teilhard de Chardin) that history is expressed through the evolution of consciousness and involves a slow and tortuous path to transcendence.[63]

What is significant about any period of history is the level of consciousness that one finds. In the teachings of the Ageless Wisdom, humanity, during the course of its long evolutionary history, has had the overriding task of developing consciousness, first by responding to various stimuli on the physical plane, then through the development of simple cognition and the full expression of the emotional life, and most recently through becoming receptive to ideas and learning to generate thought on the mental plane. Correspondences can be found in all phases of evolution, as exemplified by the maturing of consciousness historically and the natural course of child development. The Swiss psychologist, Jean Piaget, in tracing the unfolding of human cognition, noted that an infant experiences the world through sensory contact, next through language and other symbols, followed by the use of simple logic and a rudimentary knowledge of cause and effect, resulting in the final stage of development that is characterized by abstract thought and the ability to imagine different realities.

The Tibetan has noted throughout his books, and this can be confirmed by empirical observation, that humanity today is largely emotional in consciousness and is now making significant strides towards achieving mental polarization. The most striking evidence in support of this statement is the level of consciousness at which the mass media operates. While the bulk of the media, with its use of symbols to arouse the emotions, is concentrated primarily in the West, its impact is mostly global. By the same token, at no time in history has humanity been so awash with information and avenues to knowledge. The fact that the collective consciousness of humanity changes very little over the course of centuries is a sobering thought, given the ultimate goal of human evolution, which is to become fully conscious on many other planes.

The underlying laws of evolution are understood through a study of the ebb and flow of cycles. The oft-stated phrase that "history repeats itself" is true in one sense, but it is far from being a mechanical repetition of events that leads nowhere. The law of evolution, in accordance with the divine plan, drives onward towards an increasingly complex, interrelated, and larger reality so that history in its geometric form resembles an ever-spiraling cycle.

The length, duration, and intensity of cycles are determined by number, what Bertrand Russell eloquently termed "the Pythagorean power by which number holds sway above the flux."[64] Within Hindu cosmology there is an elaborate numbering system for measuring cycles of time ranging from a split second (Nimesa) to a hundred years of Brahma, which is over 311 trillion years, an occult century. What the Hindus referred to as a Kali Yuga, or "Black Age" was 432,000 years. Joseph Campbell points out that a great cycle to the peoples of Iceland during the Middle Ages, known as a "Day of the Wolf" was 432,000 years; whereas the estimated time in the mythology of Babylonia between the rise of the first city, Kish, and the coming of the legendary flood was also 432,000 years.[65] As a sacred number, 432, it seems, was widely used as a fundamental unit of calculation for peoples throughout the ancient Near East.

We know, for example, that scholars during the Middle Ages were obsessed with the meaning of numbers, particularly Biblical numerology. What, they wondered, was meant by the four beasts with ten horns in Daniel's vision, or the significance of the lamb breaking the seven seals in the Book of Revelation? Far from idle speculation, the significance of numbers to medieval humanity reflected a desire to substantiate the truth that the cosmos was orderly as well as divine. In the world we have lost, everything had its place, and meaning within a hierarchical universe was governed by the mind of God. When a world view becomes too static, forces are generated to break it apart, which leads in the other direction towards constant change, relativism, meaninglessness and, ultimately, confusion. This is where we are today. The role of esoteric history, which will be explored in greater detail in the following chapters, seeks to revision the past so as to provide a broader understanding of where we have been and, perhaps, where we will be going.

Chapter 2—
Man and Cosmos: A
Constitutional Analysis

In the last chapter, an analogy was made comparing observable (or exoteric) historical development with the esoteric stream of the Ageless Wisdom in terms of particles and waves. This correspondence also provides a convenient metaphor for the change in consciousness which, arguably, we are now experiencing and have been experiencing for the duration of this century, involving a change in perception from objective reality to subjective interrelationship. The evidence for this shift in consciousness is not hard to find. Discoveries in physics by Einstein, Heisenberg, and others coalesced into two concepts which have caused major fissures in the landscape of objectivity. Einstein taught us that in the universe everything is relative according to our perceptions, and Heisenberg went further in noting that nothing for certain can be said to exist. Recently, some superstring theorists have begun to doubt whether matter really exists at all. Together these concepts have opened the door to a vast terrain of uncharted territory that invites a deeper sense of awareness.

Not only has theoretical science changed our perceptions of reality: so have the arts. The genre of cubism controverted principles of painting that had prevailed for centuries by substituting a radically new fusion of mass and void. In so doing, cubism provided an unstable structure of dismembered planes in indeterminate spatial positions.[1]

With reference to the equally revolutionary developments in music, Keith Bailey writes: "Two very important composers to the early twentieth century were Igor Stravinsky and Arnold Schoenberg, both of them releasing a destructive type of energy that would assist with the destruction of certain ancient and crystalised thought-forms. While both of them were careful to acknowledge tradition, both composers reorganized their music, away from the established order and accepted forms."[2]

Further evidence of a shift from the world view of concrete objectivity to the relative realms of subjectivity is provided by Thomas Harrison, who in a recent book, *1910: The Emancipation of Dissonance,* notes the resurgence during the first decade of the twentieth century "of the traditional European ideal to liberate human spirit from the pressures of material reality." Here he is referring to the rise of occultism, as propagated by the Theosophical Society, the teachings of Rudolf Steiner, and related movements.[3]

To conclude that reality is based on subjective perceptions, not objective appearances, has staggering implications. In one of the books by Carlos Castaneda, documenting the wisdom of Don Juan, a Yaqui Indian shaman and medicine man, Don Juan makes the distinction between what he calls the tonal and the nagual. The tonal, he says, consists of everything that we are. It has a beginning and an end, it can be visualized, measured, and categorized. In other words, it is the realm of appearances. Beyond the island of the tonal is the nagual which is, according to Don Juan, "that part of us for which there is no description—no words, no names, no feelings, no knowledge."[4]

It is the nagual that underscores the Ageless Wisdom. To understand history in this light requires a different set of maps so as to charter this unfamiliar terrain. Classical Theosophy, the books of Alice Bailey based on the thoughts of the Tibetan Master D.K., the writings of Rudolf Steiner, and other currents within the stream of the Ageless Wisdom provide the coordinates for the creation of such maps. It needs to be stressed, yet again, that these are not the only guideposts nor, according to some perspectives, even the best ones. They do, in a very basic way, provide us with a point of departure.

The coordinates contained in the Ageless Wisdom for mapping the topology of the unseen world is predicated on the constitution of man. The first question that might be asked is, "what is a man?" Here, many answers are possible. In her book, *The Consciousness of the Atom,* Alice Bailey defines a man as "that central energy, life, or intelligence, who works through a material manifestation or form, this form being built up of myriads of lesser lives."[5] The Tibetan characterizes man as a psychic entity, a life who has built a form through radiatory influence and has colored it with some psychic quality[6] or, more esoterically, as "the Flame Divine and the fire of Mind brought into contact through the medium of substance or form."[7] H.P.B. has simply said that man is an animal plus a living God residing in a physical shell.

What is common to each of these definitions is that man is a life occupying a form. In this respect, what appears to us as a human being is merely an outer form masking subtle dimensions of consciousness and life. It should be noted that within the framework of esoteric science, appearances count for little. The relationship between spirit, consciousness, and matter, in their various manifestations, is a complex subject from concrete angles, but from conceptual angles it is simplified through the law of correspondences. The Tibetan refers to a man, an atom, and a solar system in the same breath since they are analogous in essential composites, even though their forms vary considerably as to size and composition. Hence, what is called the "constitution of man" has reference to the entire seven planes of our solar system, which is the cosmic physical plane of an even greater entity, the Cosmic Logos.

The Constitution of Man

The chart of the seven planes, as seen below in Table 2, may seem bewildering to most people, yet it conveys a beautiful pattern of orderly correspondence. It is essentially a diagram outlining three periodical vehicles, man's seven principles and corresponding vehicles, which are located along seven planes of consciousness. The three vehicles can be characterized in the following manner:

aspect		form	quality
Spirit	Father (Siva)	Monad	Will
Soul	Son (Vishnu)	Ego	Love
Body	Holy Spirit (Brahma)	Personality	Active Intelligence

These three aspects of divinity are present in every form and can be viewed in a variety of ways. The lower form is always the vehicle for a higher form so that a body is the form for the soul, just as the soul is the form for spirit. A similar correspondence exists between the personality, the ego, and the monad. From another perspective, what we consider to be a personality is essentially the integration of the concrete mind, the desire or emotional body, and the physical form into a functioning unit, representing, in humans, the lowest expression of spiritual consciousness, which is active intelligent life.

At the next turn of the spiral, or stage of evolution, one develops the quality of love and recognizes a true identity with the ego, or self. The soul, within its form, the causal body, is the same triplicate of energies, which are vibrating and revolving at a greater speed and frequency. In gaining soul awareness, one loses any sense of separation and embodies the perspective of inclusiveness, which is the expression of love. From Table 2, following, we see that the ego or soul is located on the mental plane. This points to the often misunderstood fact that love is essentially a quality of mind. We see also that there is a gap between the threefold nature of the personality and the threefold spiritual triad. Esoteric students generally hold the view that it is the goal of the spiritual disciple, in esoteric terms, to make the link in consciousness, by means of the soul, between what might be called the lower and higher states of consciousness. This process is referred to as building the rainbow bridge, or antahkarana which, technically speaking, involves the projection of light energy between the mental unit and the mental permanent atom on the mental plane. Building the antahkarana is a group effort and, at the same time, is a prerequisite for passing into higher spheres of evolution.

The spiritual triad (atma, buddhi, and manas) is the higher correspondence of the personality. Whereas the personality is expressed through the concrete mind, its spiritual correspondence is the abstract mind; whereas the personality seeks to express love through emotional desire, at the level of the spiritual triad there is conscious realization through the intuition (buddhi), which is pure love; whereas the physical/etheric vehicle embodies the most rudimentary element of will or purpose, it has its correspondence in the spiritual will, which is the revealer of the divine plan. The synthesis of the higher triad is the monadic triad, which it could accurately be said is the evolutionary goal for humanity in this solar system. At each level the law of analogy holds true.

Table 2. The Seven Planes of the Solar System/The Constitution of Man

The Seven Planes of Our Solar System

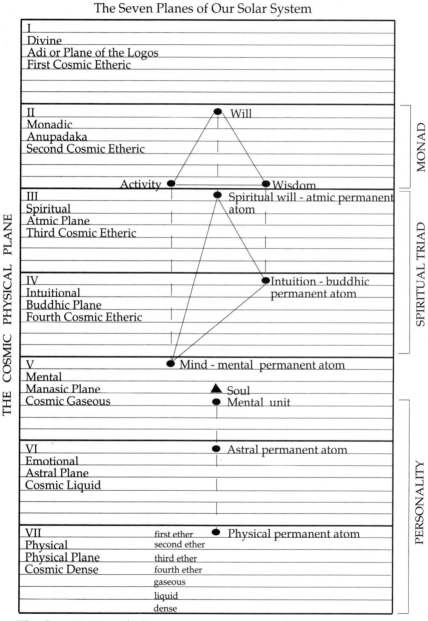

The Constitution of Man

The seven principles pertain to the qualities of energy that are generated on each on each of the seven planes, which can be characterized accordingly:

Plane	Qualities
1. Spiritual	all knowledge, perfection
2. Monadic	will, love-wisdom, intelligence
3. Atmic	pure will, realization
4. Buddhi	pure reason, love, intuition
5. Higher manas	abstract or pure mind
5. Manas	lower concrete mind
6. Kama-manas	desire mind
6. Astral	pure desire, emotion, feeling
8. Etheric	the sensory apparatus

It will be quickly observed that the physical vehicle is not included in this list of principles. Esotericism teaches that the physical body is not a principle, but is simply an automatic agent for manifesting a hierarchy of energies. Those principles of a purely spiritual nature, as mentioned above, flow through the monad and the spiritual triad (atma, buddhi, higher manas) and, for the most part, are beyond the reach of ordinary people. The principles of one's lower nature, relatively speaking, involve mind and desire (the latter being will shrouded with emotion). Mind is an all-encompassing sphere of intelligent life through which thoughts (compressed points of energy that are linked together) pass. A thought is rarely experienced in its pure form and quickly becomes modified by desire. It has been reported that the Master Morya would ask his disciples, "who among you can even think a thought?" with the assurance that the answer would probably be none of them. As is most often the case, one thinks or expresses not the thought itself, but a feeling or perspective about the thought. This is the phenomena known as kama-manas, or desire mind. Below the threshold of mind is the realm of emotions. It was no less a person than Oscar Wilde who wisely observed that the emotions of man are stirred more quickly than man's intelligence.[8] Without being condescending, the Master D.K. observes that the majority of the human race function from the level of the emotions and is only vaguely aware of, if at all, the impact of thought.

The relationship between principles and qualities is mapped out on the seven planes. A plane can be defined as the range or extent of consciousness, or the perceptive power of a particular range of senses, or the action of any particular force. Each of the seven planes is divided into seven subplanes, making forty-nine in total. We can see from Table 2 that dense matter is merely the lowest subplane of the physical plane, with liquid and gaseous matter occupying the next two subplanes, respectively. From that point there is a departure from the physical world, as it is generally understood, into the etheric, super-etheric, subatomic, and atomic realms of matter. The etheric levels of the physical plane are a replica of its denser counterpart, composed of force currents and fine channels of radiatory substance called nadis, which provide the vehicle for prana, or life energy. The etheric planes are also the focal point for the physical senses.

There is a similar correspondence on each of the other six planes. The lower subplanes of the astral plane provide the field of emotional activity, including the emotions of fear, envy, anger, possessiveness, likes, and dislikes, which most people experience on a daily basis. On the higher subplanes of the astral plane, one finds emotional idealism (the experience of many mystics), imagination, and clairvoyance. Likewise, on the lower rungs of the mental plane, one becomes receptive to undeveloped fragments of thought. At this level, one latches on to clichés and platitudes that are unsustained or undeveloped. On the level of the concrete mind, one also becomes receptive to the thought patterns of other people in the environment. Eventually, this fragmented receptivity becomes synthesized into discrimination, which is found on the fourth subplane of the mental plane. With this comes critical thinking and the generation of logical thought patterns. Beyond this point, one lives the life of the soul and gains access to spiritual discernment, subjective responses to group vibratory thought, and spiritual telepathy. The subconscious manifestation of telepathy is often observed when a team of scientists working on a problem in one part of the world comes up with a solution at the same time as another group of scientists working elsewhere. The law of analogy holds for the higher spiritual planes, but these realms of abstraction cannot, from our vantage point, be appreciated or even comprehended.

Two final points need to be made in considering the constitution of man. The first is that while we can diagram these planes, vehicles, and principles on a logical and orderly map, the subjective experience of living (causes emanating from a divine source or some plane other than the physical plane) within these fields of forces and energies has no such relationship. Energies and forces, at whatever level, intermingle and flow together in constant vibratory and cyclic motion. Students of the esoteric teachings generally believe that nothing is, in reality, separate and reducible and that the only way we can discern changes in essence or quality is through registering subtle changes in quality and vibration. It is for this reason that conscious spiritual living can only take place at the point of soul awareness.

Secondly, insofar as the law of analogy always holds true, the constitution of man functions at all levels simultaneously. Whereas we may see some relevance of this schematic for human evolution, it may seem less comprehensible in relation to the evolution of our planetary system itself, which the Tibetan refers to as one of the Heavenly Men. The same applies to solar and cosmic evolutionary schemes. Consequently, two fundamental principles can be deduced. The first is that all of creation, from atomic to cosmic levels, is an orderly rhythmic pattern of evolutionary progress. Likewise, the greater scheme is primarily a template of energies for a lesser scheme. This is what is meant in the Bible when God said, "Let us make man in our own image, in the likeness of ourselves…"[9] Thus the constitution of man can be read at many different levels, and at each level it provides a blueprint, albeit a limited one, for the working out of cosmic law.

The Universe as an Interplay of Number

Throughout the teachings of Theosophy and the Ageless Wisdom, there is a constant uniformity of numbers. At the core of every system, one finds unity represented by the Logos. The term Logos comes from Greek meaning speech, word, or reason. H.P.B. uses such terms as the absolute, the first manifestation, spirit of the universe, and cosmic ideation to characterize the Logos.[10] The Tibetan gives a more arcane definition of a Logos. "We are dealing with solar fire per se, with the essence of thought, with the coherent life of all forms, with the consciousness of its evolving aspect, or with Agni, the sum total of the

Gods."[11] A Logos is a systemic entity, which exists on different levels. The Solar Logos is understood to mean that great entity who thinks the solar system into perpetual existence and who steps down and transforms the potent energies from the cosmic schemes for the use of lesser solar entities. On the planetary level, there is the Planetary Logos, who in the esoteric literature is called Sanat Kumara, the Lord of the World, or the Ancient of Days in the Bible. This great being sustains and watches over the entire process of planetary evolution and is in one sense the One who is referred to as God. (The notion of God is relative since all things are governed by the law of correspondence and therefore are analogous to that which is similar but greater or lesser.)

The unity of logoic energy is the sum total of the three fundamental and pervasive energies of will, love, and active intelligence. The Christian notion of God the trinity is a theological expression of this esoteric reality. In the same way, the Hindus view the divine as a trinity consisting of Brahma, the creator of the universe, Vishnu, the preserver, and Siva, the destroyer. The correspondences here are obvious. Joseph Campbell tells us that the numbers three and nine (3*3) figure predominately in both Greek and Indonesian mythology.[12] We are also told that the ancient Mesopotamians divided the cosmos between three gods. In the Hermetic literature, there are three organizing principles of the universe, and Plato, in his *Republic*, refers to three fates who spin the planetary spheres.[13] Clearly, the trinity is a cultural universal.

There is a law in the universe that translates triplicities into sevens. One can find numerous proofs of this law in the mundane world. In terms of binary language, the sequential steps from 000 to 111 is a sevenfold progression. If one were to shine three colored lights onto a pure white background, four more lights would appear, making seven in total. Acoustic symbolism in the Hindu *Atharvaveda* teaches that the three primary sounds produce four minor sounds which, of course, equal seven.[14] Likewise, according to Theosophical cosmology, out of the threefold aspect of God (the Logos) comes the seven planes of the solar system on which the seven rays (three major and four minor rays) give substance to form. The arithmetic interplay of three, four, and seven provides the mathematical structuring for the spiritualization of the material world.

Therefore, the cosmic order is nothing more than a symphonic interplay of septenary systems: solar or planetary. Scientist Arthur

Young provides strong evidence for the organization of the universe based on the number seven. He argues that there are seven kingdoms in nature that have emerged during the course of evolution. They are: 1) light, which represents potential; 2) nuclear energy, which is the binding force of attraction and repulsion; 3) atomic force, representing identity because it acquires its own center; 4) molecular force, generating the combination of various properties; 5) vegetable life, which characterizes growth through cellular organization and entropy; 6) animal life, reflecting mobility, whereby force becomes volitional; and finally, 7) the human kingdom, which, through consciousness, gains dominion over the other kingdoms.

Young then maintains that within each of these kingdoms there are seven stages which go through an analogous sub-process of potential, binding, identity, combination, growth, mobility, and dominion. Light, for example, evolves from cosmic waves, in the stage of potential, to low frequency waves in the dominion stage. Atoms evolve through seven stages from hydrogen to radon; molecules from elementary metallic bonds to DNA; vegetables from unicellular bacteria to flowering plants, and so forth. The evolution of human consciousness, in parallel fashion to the constitution of man, follows a sevenfold progression.[15]

Involution and Evolution

All scientists would agree that matter in the universe is in a constant state of flux, which can be detected on every level. Esoteric students generally hold the view that this motion is far from random and moves in orderly and cyclic patterns. One such pattern, which is characteristic of all life, is the breath cycle. Breathing involves the act of forcefully drawing air into the body and the release of the breathed air into the atmosphere. Shirley Nicholson, who has written a book on the adaptation of the Ageless Wisdom to modern science, characterizes this cycle as the movement from superphysical fields into the physical and then the movement back into superphysical realms.[16] Alice Bailey describes this process of involution and evolution in terms of the law of attraction and repulsion. The involutionary arc is when an entity takes to itself its vehicle of expression, and the evolutionary arc is when the imprisoned entity is gradually released into liberation.[17]

Table 3. Solar Cycle of Manifestation or Logos of a Solar System

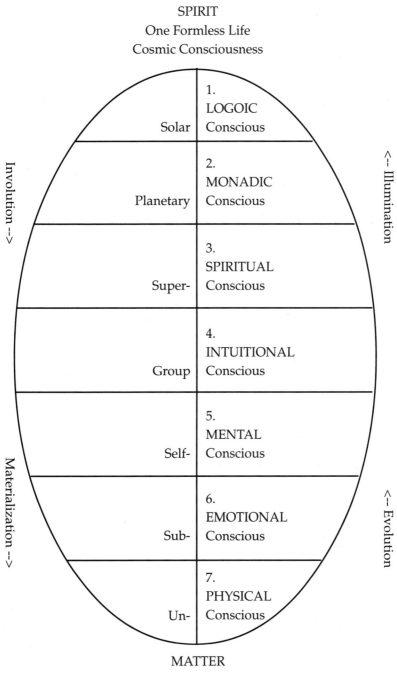

SPIRIT
One Formless Life
Cosmic Consciousness

Involution -->

Materialization -->

<-- Illumination

<-- Evolution

Solar	1. LOGOIC Conscious
Planetary	2. MONADIC Conscious
Super-	3. SPIRITUAL Conscious
Group	4. INTUITIONAL Conscious
Self-	5. MENTAL Conscious
Sub-	6. EMOTIONAL Conscious
Un-	7. PHYSICAL Conscious

MATTER
Atomic Consciousness

If we impose the cycle of involution and evolution onto the constitution of man, then we see the relationship of the Logos, in its relative states, to the various grades of matter. This can be seen in Table 3. If we employ, again, the analogy of the breath cycle, it appears that some great entity breathes life into matter until it reaches its point of maximum density, at which point it turns in upon itself and completes the cycle back to the point of origination.

An analysis of the involutionary and evolutionary cycle shows a four-stage development. The projection of force from unity into form involves a process of differentiation whereby the negative atoms of matter predominate over the positive atoms of spiritual substance. At the nadir point, there is a change in polarity in which the positive atoms become more attractive and begin to transmute the negative atoms. This leads to a movement towards synthesis and homogeneity, whereby the negative atoms become stimulated and either dissipate back into a central electrical reservoir, or merge in their opposite pole.[18] The atoms increase their vibratory velocity and the vortices approximate their positive pole. At the point of synthesis, obscuration occurs and the recycled energy is liberated.

Evidence of involution and evolution comes from both religion and science. In Christian theology, this is an archetypal pattern that is played out in human history, beginning with the fall of man and culminating with his resurrection into eternal life. Cosmologists view the history of a solar system as starting with the "big bang," when matter and energy exploded into the universe, and culminating with entropy, when the system loses energy and begins to turn back on itself. As Jeremy Rifkin has demonstrated, the law of entropy cuts across all phases of human existence.[19]

Arthur Young, in describing the seven-stage evolution from light substance to man, also defines this process in terms of an involutionary and evolutionary cycle.

third-degree freedom	Light	Man
second-degree freedom	Particles	Animals
first-degree freedom	Atoms	Plants
zero-degree freedom	Molecules	

The above chart shows that at the level-one stage, light has a high degree of freedom because it lacks symmetry and is therefore almost completely free of form. Particles of light, or photons, also exhibit a high degree of freedom but, as invisible units of matter, they are somewhat more restricted. Atoms possess a greater degree of symmetry than particles insofar as they have a central nucleus with orbiting electrons and can be identified. Molecules are the most dense, given that they have three directions of symmetry (rows, columns, layers) and can occur in crystalline form. On the upward sweep of evolution, plants exhibit one degree of freedom through vertical growth. This is known as radial or cylindrical symmetry, or two axes of symmetry. Animals differ as to front and rear but also as to top and bottom so they are said to have one axis of symmetry. Since animals can move about two-dimensionally on the earth's surface, they are classified as having two degrees of freedom. Finally, man has control over three dimensions of space and through being divided into three parts—head, trunk, limbs—tends towards being asymmetrical.[20] This biological model corresponds to that of the esoteric teachings since both indicate a process of movement from freedom into restriction and then back to liberation. The difference between the esoteric model, which views physical man as matter at its lowest manifestation, and Young's typology, which sees man in the same form as the final stage of freedom, is purely relative, based on varying perceptions.

Evidence of involution and evolution can furthermore be seen in the life cycle of a human being. People live to different ages, of course, but imposed on each life is a pattern of rhythmic transitions, based on seven-year cycles. Early childhood, childhood, adolescence, and early adulthood follow an orderly sequence marked by the ages in which children start school, reach puberty, become an adult in the legal sense, and usually undergo a major conflict or crisis. This period of crisis is often referred to by astrologers as a Saturn-return cycle because it takes Saturn, the great tester—known esoterically as the Lord of Karma— twenty-eight years to complete a single revolution around the sun. The transition from early adulthood to middle adulthood and the culmination of the Saturn-return cycle correlate with the nadir point of the involutionary path. The turning point from the involutionary to the evolutionary path in a human life, according to astrologer, Dane Rudhyar, "constitutes a probable critical state; the impulse may scatter itself and lead to disintegration or failure, or it may find in the integrated materials gathered into the field the organized concrete vehicle for complete actualization and fulfillment."[21]

The evolutionary path in the cycle of life is marked by stages of adulthood when a person assumes a unique identity and enters into his or her life's work. Whereas the first thirty years are often characterized by the desire to experience many different aspects of a life, leading to the dissipation of energy, the second half of life usually involves a greater consolidation of energy and a more sustained purpose. During the various transitions of adulthood, a person (depending upon the point in evolution) may seek to detach oneself from the desires of the outward life of appearances and become more subjectively responsive to the inner light of the soul. On or around age fifty-six, one is confronted with a second Saturn-return cycle. It is thought by some that if a person has not discovered one's purpose or "life mission" by this time, it will have to wait for another cycle of manifestation. With the increase in life-expectancy, particularly in the westernized nations, there is a good indication that people are entering into additional cycles of learning experience, which may diverge sharply from the life patterns of their earlier years.

The Esoteric Cosmos: Systems, Chains, Globes, and Rounds

The Ageless Wisdom teaches us that human existence is technically a finite point within a vast scheme of cycles within greater cycles. Although the process carries on theoretically to infinity, the largest unit of practical consideration is a solar system. It is generally believed by esotericists that we are presently passing through the second of three solar systems, which is an expression of the love-wisdom aspect (the previous solar system emphasized the active intelligence aspect and the next solar system will highlight the will-power aspect). A solar system is thought to comprise ten planetary schemes, which number among them the schemes of Vulcan (a hidden planet), Mercury, Venus, Earth, Mars, Jupiter, Saturn, Uranus, and Neptune.

Within each planetary scheme, there is a whole hierarchy of cycles based on the number seven. They are as follows:

A Planetary Scheme

Major Manifestations:

one scheme of an evolution	=	
seven chain periods	=	seven rounds of seven chains
one chain period	=	seven rounds of one chain
seven globe periods	=	one round of one chain
one globe period	=	one round of the life wave (manvantara)

Minor Manifestations:

one manvantara	=	seven root races
one root race	=	seven subraces
one subrace	=	seven branch races

An investigation of the figure, following, reveals a pattern of involution and evolution on a grid that roughly corresponds to the constitution of man. The earth scheme, being one of the ten planetary schemes, or Heavenly Men, comprises seven chains of planetary evolution. So complex is this schemata that, for the sake of convenience and relevance, we will focus on one of these chains, the earth chain.

We can see from the following diagram that the earth chain, from the standpoint of materialization, is the most dense within the entire scheme. The highest level of manifestation for this chain begins on the lower mental plane and descends through the astral and etheric planes to the realm of dense matter. It then evolves back to the lower mental plane. The fact that earth is the only known planet in the solar system to have physical expressions of life within the plant, animal, and human kingdoms is indicative of the fact that it is the only planet that is currently in a fully flowered stage that exists in tangible material form. Some planets have not as yet reached this stage of flowering; others, such as Venus, have gone beyond it.

According to Theosophical sources, it has been during the fourth round of the earth chain (the fourth chain) that the template for human forms has been developed. In the previous chain, animal forms emerged. Prior to that, plant forms were created in the second round, whereas the same thing took place with respect to mineral forms in the first round. These earlier chains have since passed out of manifestation. Likewise, earlier globes of the earth chain would not have been visible to the physical eye and have since disappeared. A similar point can be made regarding future involutionary and evolutionary round of globes through this chain.[22]

The Seven Chains of the Earth Scheme

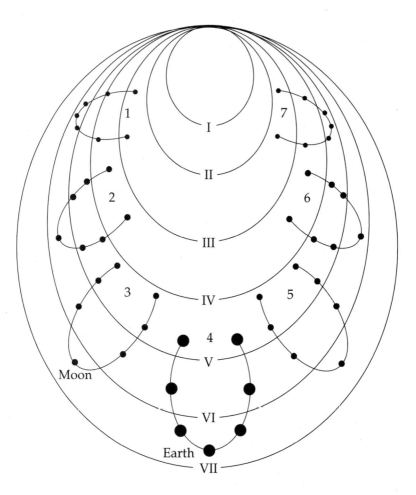

The directed force behind these greater or lesser cycles is symbolized by some great logoic entity who breathes life through the entire cycle of manifestation. As this breath, or life force, moves through one scheme, chain, or round to the next, it coalesces momentarily into sequential septenary globes, planets, or racial groups before passing on. Round and round this life force travels in its involutionary and evolutionary arcs, sweeping all before it towards greater and greater levels of self-awareness and perfection. These cycles cover tremendous periods of time. A round of seven chains is a year of Brahma (3,110,400,000,000 mortal years). A period of seven rounds lasts for one week of Brahma (60,480,000,000 mortal years). The period of a single solar system, in all of its levels of manifestation, is one hundred years of Brahma (311,040,000,000,000 mortal years). Some sources believe that these vast periods of time are largely symbolic as they tend to defy even our imagination.

Not only do cycles, large or small, pass through involutionary and evolutionary rounds, they also have day and night phases. A day phase in esoteric terminology—when a planetary scheme, chain of globes, or rounds is in objective manifestation—is called a manvantara. Relating to the cycles of a Planetary Logos, a manvantara at the schematic level consists of seven chains and forty-nine globes; at the level of a planetary chain, it comprises seven globes and seven rounds; and at the level of a planetary round, it is made up of seven root races, forty-nine subraces, and 343 branch races.

The night phase is called pralaya. The Tibetan describes the pralaya that takes place at the close of a manvantara in the following manner: "The Logos will withdraw within Himself, abstracting His three major principles [will, love-wisdom, and active intelligence aspects]. His body of manifestation—the Sun and the seven sacred Planets [Vulcan, Mercury, Venus, Jupiter, Saturn, Neptune, and Uranus], all existing in etheric matter—will withdraw from objectivity and become obscured. From the usual physical standpoint, the light of the system will go out. This will be succeeded by a gradual inbreathing until He shall have gathered all unto Himself; the etheric will cease to exist, and the web will be no more."[23]

This arcane language aside, the principle of forces and energies withdrawing out of manifestation into a condition of rest is not hard to grasp. *The Secret Doctrine* refers to many kinds of pralaya, of which there are three fundamental types. The first is called incidental pralaya and is triggered by the period of destruction that follows the end of a round (a day of Brahma or kalpa) that is characterized by cataclysms and destructive changes on a planetary scale. The second form of pralaya is referred to as individual pralaya when persons who have achieved a high degree of spiritual unfoldment, and have undergone in consciousness an advanced level of initiation, have achieved, in Hindu terms, a state of Nirvana. The final type of pralaya (mahapralaya) concerns the death of a cosmos, marking the closure of a hundred years of Brahma, in which an entire solar system passes out of existence.[24]

The length of pralaya appears to be somewhat relative. H.P.B. notes that a mahapralaya lasts the length of a century of Brahma, or 311 trillion years. In other cases, the time period could be shorter or longer. In the case of Nitya pralaya, which relates to the decay and regenerations of form, the process is almost constant.[25] At this micro-level, the cells of one's body are experiencing continuous pralaya.

Pralaya always refers to a relative state of rest (or non-existence) as opposed to an absolute state of rest. Through the law of reincarnation, all things in manifestation are subject to the wheel of continuous birth and death and, at the end of a great cycle of activity (pralaya), a new cycle of activity will eventually take place on a higher turn of the spiral. We see here the symbolism of the Hindu trinity at work. Brahma, the creator, brings the void into form; Vishnu, the preserver, maintains the life of form through its various rounds and cycles; whereas Siva, the destroyer, annihilates the form at the start of pralaya.

A Planetary Round

Broadly speaking, a unit of esoteric geological history is a round. Rudolf Steiner writes that at each stage of human evolution, consciousness must pass through seven subordinate conditions. Seven stages of consciousness equals root races or forty-nine lesser cycles, called subraces. These stages add up to a round, which is a life cycle, or a manvantara. A round, the equivalent of 4,320,000,000 years, is known in the Hindu system as a kalpa. If we break this cycle down into seven smaller branch races, we find, in the words of Steiner, that humanity passes through 343 (7 * 49) conditions of form.[26]

Humanity in its evolution has passed through its mineral, vegetable, and animal phases in earlier rounds and, in this present fourth round of 4,320 million years, we are experiencing the human phase of development. In later rounds, it will be the lot of humanity to expand its consciousness within the planetary Hierarchy and beyond to other rounds and chains. All rounds are governed by three main principles: the septenary system, which divides all units of time into blocks of seven; the law of periodicity, involving the continuous cyclical intake and outflow of energies; and the duality of evolution, which affects both the involution and evolution of consciousness and its vehicles.[27]

Within the present earth round, man continues to work his way, in consciousness, through the solar system. According to Rudolf Steiner's cosmic scheme, life, through the various cycles of manifestation, is at its greatest speed on Saturn, and then rapidly decreases as man works his way through the wheel of existence on the sun and the moon rounds along the line of involution. The cycles of manifestation reach their slowest and most material phase on earth, at which point self-consciousness begins to develop. The process then speeds up again as man proceeds along the path of evolution. At some future point, man will develop his consciousness on other planets; Steiner mentions only Jupiter and Venus.

Through each of these planetary cycles, man has evolved through unconsciousness, somnambulistic, and dream-like states of consciousness on Saturn, the sun, and the moon respectively, before achieving conscious awareness on this planet. In the future phases of this round, he will be able to gain control over his environment and, later, acquire the ability to create forms out of energy. After a period of rest (pralaya) when, according to Steiner, the earth has transmuted itself into the consciousness of Jupiter, the cycle from Saturn to earth (now part of man's distant past) and beyond, will again be repeated. Only after man has experienced a full round will he have achieved planetary consciousness.[28]

There is some scientific evidence that relates the geological history of the planet to the various rounds of the earth globe. Daniel Krummenacher, a geologist, has made a careful comparative study of the esoteric map of chains and rounds with that of geological cycles.[29] Table 4 is based on information that he provided (part of the information, including that on the rounds, is hypothetical):

Krummenacher points out that the physical earth is 4.5 billion years old, which coincides with the emergence of our present manvantara of seven rounds, in conjunction with the solidification of the earth form. The physical earth was formed from matter generated by a supernova five billion years ago. This matter was injected with heavy elements that coalesced into a solid body. Important to our understanding of geological cycles and rounds is the period of destruction which brings such periods to a close. These moments of cataclysm, resulting in the annihilation of many, if not most, life forms pave the way for new species to emerge.

Table 4. Geological Events and Rounds

Esoteric		Exoteric	
PAST SOLAR SYSTEM			
	5 B.Y.		
SOLAR PRALAYA	4.75 B.Y.	Star from which our matter originated goes supernova	
	4.55 B.Y.	Earth as solid body	
	4.2 B.Y.	Oldest mineral	
	3.8 B.Y.	Oldest fragment of continent/oldest fossil (Prokaryotes)	ARCHEAN
ROUND I			
	2.5 B.Y.		
	2.2 B.Y.	Important glaciation	
	1.6 B.Y.	Eukaryotes appear	PROTEROZOIC
ROUND II			
	700 M.Y.	Metazoans appear/global glaciation	
ROUND III	530 M.Y.		
	246 M.Y.	Permian Extinction	PALEOZOIC
ROUND IV			
	65 M.Y.	Dinosaurs Extinct	MESOZOIC
	NOW		TERTIARY

Time based on radioactivity measurements

In the Theosophical writings, man has evolved through a series of seven races and root races. There is often a source of confusion between races and root races. The esoteric literature reveals that there have been races of man throughout the entire round, however, they existed on the inner planes and were essentially invisible. It was during these earlier rounds that the mineral, plant, and animal kingdoms evolved into full manifestation. Each round recapitulates the forms of the earlier rounds, so we find that in the present fourth round, man has repeated the earlier races through the forms of the first three root races. Man, in his most concretized form, appeared in the fourth root race. Now in the fifth root race, humanity is in the upward swing of evolution in this round.

The first race of man living in the first round was essentially protoplastic in structure and astral in consciousness.[30] Krummenacher sees a correlation between the protoplastic structure of these earliest of men and the earliest form of fossil life, prokaryotes, a simple bacteria lacking a nucleus which was able to live without oxygen.

The shift from the Archean age to the Proterozoic age at roughly 2.5 billion years ago, following a period of glaciation, at first revealed no real difference in life forms. With the advent of the second round at about 1.6 billion years ago, there was a similar appearance of eukaryotes, more complex organisms, possessing one or more cells with a definable nucleus that was capable of different functions. These eukaryotes propagated through gemmation, or budding through the production of spores, which was similar to the asexual reproductive patterns of the second race.[31]

With the coming of the third round, approximately 700 million years ago, and the birth of the Paleozoic age, following another period of glaciation, new multi-celled animals with soft shells appeared. This expanse of time, lasting up to the Permian extinctions in which 75% to 95% of all species were eliminated, marked the appearance of vertebrate animals, fish, insects, and egg-laying reptiles. Whereas early third-race man, so we are told, was androgynous in nature, somewhere during the middle of the third round, two sexes existed in every individual. "The psycho-magnetic activities within those 'human' individuals, of this far-distant geologic past, produced a fertile germ which was cast off from the body as an egg, somewhat resembling the process that takes place in birds and certain reptiles today."[32]

It was somewhere during the third root race in the fourth round that, according to esoteric understanding, man received the spark of divine consciousness and developed some recognizable human form. The progress of human development, and hence human history, from this point will be the subject of the next chapter. Already we can see a correspondence between two lines of evolution, that which is human in contrast to the lower kingdoms in nature. "As above, so below" is the guiding principle through all phases of evolution from the outer reaches of the macrocosm to the smallest infinitesimal sphere of the microcosm.

Chapter 3—
Historical Periodicity:
Rounds and Root Races

It is well known to students of the Ageless Wisdom that the material on the origins and evolution of man presented within this lineage stands in marked contrast to the conventional view of human evolution. One is therefore confronted with the problem of evidence. Our knowledge of human origins is derived from material evidence—bones, fossils, and various artifacts—which have been cleverly and skillfully pieced together to reveal a picture of continuity that stretches into the distant past. Yet this picture is, at best, a sketchy one. Comparatively little is known about life on earth during the vast dimensions of time that stretch back millions of years. As noted in the last chapter, the earth has undergone periodic convulsions which have created and destroyed whole continents, along with plant and animal species. Since our knowledge of the past is predicated on inherited remains, the geological record is silent as to the possibility that some forms merely dissolved or otherwise perished without leaving a trace.

The lack of evidence cannot be used to deny an alternative perspective of evolution, yet one would be advised to be skeptical on this point. The picture presented by the Ageless Wisdom of human origins and development recognizes a lineage of divinity as well as a lineage of man's animal predecessors. By the same token, human development, as seen by esotericists, fits within a complex pattern of cycles that define cosmic evolution as well as history. Here the occult maxim "as above so below" in conjunction with the law of correspondences holds true. While the esoteric accounts of human evolution should be treated as a hypothesis, it does fit into a pattern that gives meaning to human evolution within wider spheres of existence.

Esoterically speaking, the earth phase of the present round is one of the seven manvantaras which, in turn, is divided into seven root races. According to the teachings of the Ageless Wisdom, a race is predominantly a focal point of consciousness that has only vague biological connections.[1] The Tibetan has written that man has developed from an isolated animal, prompted by instincts for self-preservation, eating, and mating, through various stages of family life, tribal life, and national life to the point where a broader vision of international unity can be grasped.[2] Throughout their long history, people have experienced the world as separative beings in which differences in appearance, social rank, and conditions of life have appeared as significant. Behind this "sin of separation" is the spiritual reality of unity, which knows only graded differences in consciousness, not form.

The Emergence of the First and Second Root Races

In our present round, the fourth round, the evolution of the seven root races, of which we are now in the fifth, is analogous to racial development in each of the earlier rounds. The life span of a root race varies considerably. Geoffrey Hodson calculates that the first root race appeared just prior to the start of the Eocene age some sixty-three million years ago, at the end of the Mesozoic era when the earth was being convulsed by volcanoes, avalanches, and extremely high winds.[3] There was also a mass extinction of animal life, termed Cretaceous, whereby dinosaurs and much marine life were destroyed. At the start of the Cenozoic period, the earth became colder and the fauna life of the planet dwindled.[4]

Speaking of the first root race to appear on earth, H.P.B. notes that somewhere during the fourth round a moon-colored race of men appeared who were devoid of all understanding, intelligence and will, insofar as the inner being (the higher self or monad) was as yet unconnected with the outer form.[5] According to Hodson, this root race appeared as large, filamentous, sexless, cloud-like beings residing in etheric form on a tropical continent at the North Pole. These beings multiplied by fission and lacked any sense of individuality.[6] They were, so notes the Tibetan, huge and indefinite with a low state of consciousness exercised through one sense, hearing.[7] dePurucker refers to the first root race as huge astral cells, or "pudding-bags."[8] Note the correspondence of these descriptions to the races of the first round, the difference being that the first root race appeared in a more materialized form.

The second root race is said to have emerged during the Oligocene period, thirty-eight to forty million years ago, following the Eocene catastrophe when, again, many species of animal and plant life were killed off. At that time the planet was covered by lush vegetation and featured more evolved forms of mammals.

The second root race, called "the sweat-born and the boneless" by H.P.B., like its predecessor, lacked a solid physical form, but developed in some degree the sense of touch. Whereas the first race was, in the words of the old commentaries, derived from "the shadows from the bodies of the sons of twilight," they could not be injured or destroyed by death. The second race, on the other hand, was composed of denser material and could be destroyed. In appearance they resembled "gigantic semi-human monsters" insofar as this was the first attempt of the builders of human form to construct physical bodies.[9]

Hodson claims that these early humans lived on a continent south of the polar region known as the Hyperborean land, which lent its name to this race.[10] One source observes that this race formed buds or spores and attached themselves on to other beings, which served as the means of propagation. Many of the offspring, no doubt, perished but others were fertilized and developed into the forms of their parents.[11]

The Debate Over Evolution

Since the mid-nineteenth century, an ideological battle has raged between the scientific community, which supports the view of evolution as presented by the naturalist, Charles Darwin, and the Christian religious community, particularly among its fundamentalist adherents, who deny the existence of evolution, while claiming that all forms of life are God-created.

It is interesting to note that in the Biblical book of *Genesis* there are two stories of evolution. The first story places man at the end of evolution, whereas the second story, situated in the Garden of Eden, places man at the beginning of the creative process. It does not take much imagination to find evidence for both evolution and creationism in these stories. For, as H.P.B. observes, the whole Darwinian theory of natural selection is contained in the first six chapters of Genesis.[12] If one understands the veiled language that is used in the Bible, it is easy to see its pervasive esoteric meaning. Annie Besant, in her book, *Esoteric Christianity*, writes of the creation stories in *Genesis*:

"In the Mysteries this work was shown in its detail as the preparation of matter of the universe, the formation of atoms, the drawing of these together into aggregates, and the grouping of these together into elements, and of these again into gaseous, liquid, and solid compounds. This work includes not only the kind of matter called physical, but also all the subtle states of matter in the invisible worlds. He (God or Logos) further as the 'Spirit of Understanding' conceived the forms into which the prepared matter should be shaped, not building the forms, but by the action of the Creative Intelligence producing the ideas of them, the heavenly prototypes, as they are often called."[13]

H.P.B. asserts that Darwin came close to accepting the perspective of the Ageless Wisdom in one important respect. She quotes a passage from one of his writings that appears to confirm that at some time in the remote past, the whole vertebrate kingdom had been androgynous.[14] This would tend to support the notion of a pre-sexual evolutionary development in the earlier rounds. Indeed, Blavatsky contends that amphibia, birds, reptiles, and fishes are throwbacks to the third round, as are fossil forms, which she claims were stored up in the auric envelope of the earth and then projected into physical objectivity. Mammals are related to the prototypes shed by man and are part of the fourth-round evolutionary stream. This points to the complexity of the esoteric cosmic system in which evolutionary processes from different rounds, chains, and globes intermingle and occur simultaneously.[15] H.P.B. further observes that evolution is an external cycle of becoming, and that "man is the end towards which all animal creation has tended from the appearance of the first Paleozoic fishes."[16] Steiner remarks that when the "watery" moon beings began their earthly evolution there was no mineral, plant, or animal kingdom. Earth, he says, was at the beginning of its evolution and was composed only of human forms.[17]

Occultists and modern scholars violently disagree over the age and origins of man. Esotericists view the emergence of man as a long evolutionary development that is marked by cycles rather than dates. Hence, man today is located on the fourth scheme, on the fourth globe, in the fourth chain, in the fourth round, and in the fifth root race. This explains why man is in physical form on a physical planet, but is beginning to tread the path of return. Other dating schemes chart the development of man in a linear fashion through the development of the species. The first human, homo habilis, is thought to have appeared around 2.6 million years ago, whereas modern man, homo sapiens, is estimated to be only 40,000 years old.[18] Based on the research of anthropologists, J. G. Bennett concludes that the remains of earliest man, known as Australopithecus, can be dated back 1,700,000 years.[19]

The Lemurian Root Race

Practically speaking, from an esoteric perspective, human history starts with the emergence of the third root race, or Lemurian race. There is no clear evidence that this root race ever existed, which begs the question of whether it, in fact, did exist. In the millions of years since this root race allegedly made its appearance, the shape of the earth has changed dramatically. The various convulsions which accompanied these changes may have led to the complete destruction of all physical forms of life so, in truth, as was said earlier, we can only speak of the Lemurian root race and the earlier root races in hypothetical terms. It was during the Miocene period, twenty-five million years ago, when new species of animal life appeared, that the third root race is said to have emerged. At this time, the climate of the planet gradually became warmer. For millions of years, man is said to have changed only slightly from his point of development at the end of the second root race.

At some propitious time near the midpoint of the Lemurian root race, esotericism teaches that the solar angels (also referred to as the sons of mind or manasaputras) descended and man was touched with the spark of individuality. This point is alluded to by C.D. Darlington, a professor of Biology, who observed that the ancestors of modern man separated from the apes about 20 million years ago somewhere on the three old-world continents.[20] Human individualization or, technically speaking, the emergence of self-conscious units on the mental plane, is said to have been synchronized with the emergence of the planet into dense form on the physical plane and the material composition of the three lower planes of the Planetary Logos.[21]

Much could be said about the solar angels, who are defined simply as the builders of the ego (or soul), and the producers of individualization or realized consciousness. The key to the mysteries of individuation lies with an understanding of the relationship between the various creative hierarchies (particularly the third and the fifth hierarchies, which together produced the fourth hierarchy). Each creative hierarchy is an aggregate of lives that is evolving towards liberation within the solar system. Hence, at a given point, the collective lives (or atoms) of animal-man (the third hierarchy in nature) responded on the plane of mind to an electrical impulse from the fifth hierarchy of buddhi, which produced a sense of "I"ness or identity. The Tibetan referred to the awakening of mind in man as the dragon-influence or "serpent energy," which suggests that men were permeated with planetary kundalini, or vital energy. An important consequence of the dragon-influence on human consciousness was an opening of the door to karma. D.K. mentions that karma was brought in by the "serpent religion" in the Lemurian period.[22]

It is from this point that myth and history become intertwined. The Bible characterizes this moment as the Fall of Man, meaning the separation of humanity from God-consciousness through the acquisition of knowledge. Theology sees it as an act of rebellion or sin. As H.P.B. points out, however, it was much the reverse since it was really the fall of spirit or "archangels" on to this plane who fought for supremacy of consciousness within the individual against the "spirits of darkness" or animal passions.[23] These spirits of darkness are referred to in the Alice Bailey books as the lunar lords.

Another noteworthy thing about the Lemurian race is that for the first time humans appeared in physical form. Men developed a fleshy bone structure with recognizable bodily organs and an ability to walk upright. Guenther Wachsmuth, in his book, *The Evolution of Mankind*, commented that during the Lemurian period the human constitution received a major differentiation. The etheric body had not as yet connected itself tightly to the physical vehicle so the Lemurians were not grounded in physical form. On the other hand, the preliminary stages of mind formation were starting to take place. Fragments of memory began to appear, first among women. Since they had no language, the Lemurians communicated through the projection of a picture-consciousness. The pineal gland, referred to by some esotericists as the seat of the soul, was then used as an organ for perceiving warmth in the environment.[24]

The Lemurians were the first people to engage in sexual intercourse as a means of producing offspring. Steiner writes that the division into two sexes took place in Lemurian times when the earth entered into a certain stage of densification.[25] Since the focus of these people was primarily on the physical plane, they were driven by overwhelming instinctual urges. The desire on the part of Lemurians to satisfy these drives and urges reached proportions of excess. The Tibetan comments that it was at this time that the syphilitic diseases first appeared. Sexual excess also led to the emergence of homosexuality, which has been an underlying phenomenon throughout history. Embedded as it was in the Lemurian consciousness, homosexuality has been a dominant social fact (to use a term coined by sociologist Emile Durkheim) during certain historical periods when Lemurian thought-patterns reappeared, such as fifth-century Greece and the present era.[26]

The fact that the Lemurians lived through a period of many earth changes and eruptions probably explains why they had no permanent settlements. These people were also huge, as were men in the previous root races. dePurucker writes that the first root race was gigantic in size compared to our present humanity, as was the second race which was smaller than the first. The third root race was still huge compared to our own "pygmy-humanity" of today.[27] H.P.B. talks about a large cyclopic race of men who lived on the now submerged continent of Lemuria. Whereas the giants of old are buried at the bottom of the oceans where time and the movement of water "would reduce to dust and pulverize a brazen, far more human skeleton," oblique references to huge men can be found in the legends, myths, artifacts, and scriptures of ancient times. For instance, H.P.B. refers to the large statues discovered on Easter Island in the South Pacific by Captain Cook, which measured twenty-seven feet in height and could well relate back to this class of giants.[28] Speculation also surrounds the existence of large megaliths, such as those found at Stonehenge and at Carnac (Brittany) which, as H.P.B. says, had there been no giants to move such colossal rocks, these places would never have existed.[29]

The giants survived into the fourth root race, but a portion of the Lemurians became something of a mixed race due, it is said, to mating with certain animal species. Some tribes in Asia and Africa, so we are told, fell into stagnation at some point and did not become part of the main stream of evolution. Those who escaped from the cataclysms marking the downfall of Lemuria proceeded diagonally across to Africa.[30] Hodson claims that the Australian and Tasmanian aborigines and the African Bushmen are remnants of the Lemurian root race.[31]

The Atlantean Root Race

The fourth root race goes back twelve million years to the Pliocene age, during which time the temperature of the planet began to cool and the great Ice Ages appeared. Following the destruction of the continent of Lemuria, which stretched from Madagascar to the Pacific Ocean covering parts of southern Asia and Oceania, there gradually emerged another root race, the Atlantean civilization, following a period of pralaya. H.P.B. defines pralaya in one sense as a period of obscuration when a root race is brought to an end through cataclysmic activity. For a period covering thousands of years, there existed a blended race of Lemuro-Atlanteans who built cities and spread civilization, such as it was, in a region of the continent in the vicinity of the present island of Madagascar. Two social groups emerged: those preferring to live a nomadic and pastoral life and a lower class of builders, who only gradually developed the power over their physical natures. Here we find a significant and gradual shift in consciousness away from the spiritual and towards the material. As H.P.B. has noted, "civilization has ever developed the physical and the intellectual at the cost of the psychic and the spiritual."[32]

We know a bit about Atlantis from Plato, who left us a history. Though short, Plato's history tells us that Atlantis was a sophisticated civilization in which temples were built and the affairs of men were governed by divine beings, such as Zeus and Poseidon, who appear as prominent Gods in Greek mythology.[33]

"The plan of Atlantis, Plato tells us, 'had been cultivated during many ages by many generations of kings.' If, as we believe, agriculture, the domestication of the horse, ox, sheep, goat, and hog, and the discovery or development of wheat, oats, rye, barley originated in this region, then this language of Plato in reference to 'the many ages, and the successive generation of kings,' accords with the great periods of time which were necessary to bring man from a savage to a civilized condition."[34]

The Orphic Key to the Atlantean Fable

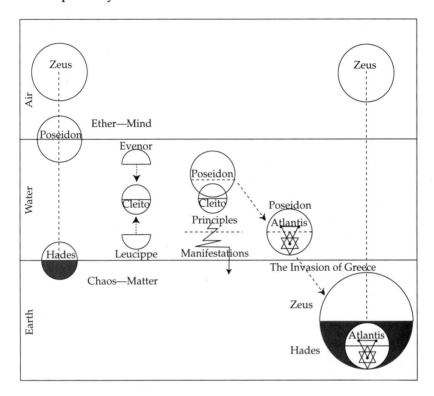

Manly Palmer Hall offers an intriguing chart (above) which presents the fable of Atlantis in terms of Orphic theology. Within this cosmology, the universe is divided into three visible parts: the supreme world which was the bode of pure truth, the superior world in which dwelled the principal gods and manifestations of divinity, and the inferior world, or the plane of corruptible forms. These three worlds corresponded to the three conditions of matter: airy, watery, and earthy. In this scheme, Zeus rules the supreme world, Poseidon rules the watery plane, and Hades rules the underworld. Evenor and Leucippe represent the higher and lower ethers, respectively, and from their union Cleito, or the etheric body of the solar system, is produced. The ten sons of Cleito, based on the Pythagorean numerical system of ten, symbolize the planes of manifestation. Insofar as Atlantis corresponded to the watery or astral realm of consciousness, the sphere of the supreme world represents the point of incarnation of the Atlantean Empire. From there it sinks into form, becomes corrupted, and is eventually lost.[35]

Like the previous root races, Atlantis contained seven subraces. The first subrace, according to one source, was called the Rmoahal, a black-skinned race of people ten or twelve feet tall, who settled on the southern coast of Atlantis and fought endless battles against the Lemurians. Directly descended from the Rmoahals were the Cro-Magnons, who were somewhat shorter than their predecessors and had lighter skins. Next came the Tlavatlis, a red-haired race of people who resided in the region of what is now Mexico. We are told that the Tlavatlis were the first people capable of forming self-government. This effort at establishing political stability provided the basis for hereditary monarchy, which was the achievement of the Toltecs, whose kings ruled for thousands of years, guided by adepts from the unseen world. With the degeneration of the Toltecs came the Turanians, who appeared to be a cruel and ruthless lot and engaged in constant warfare. Through unlicensed sexuality, their numbers increased dramatically. They also were reported to have engaged in sorcery.[36]

Hodson agrees with the ordering of these subraces and concludes that the Rmoahals eventually evolved into the Lapps of the Arctic regions; the Tlavatli became the Patagonians of South America and the Cro-Magnons of Western Europe, the first Europeans; the Toltecs were the root from which sprang the Dravidians and American Indians; the Turanians evolved into the mainland Chinese; the Semites were the forerunners of the Kabyles and Jews; the Akkadians became the Basques, the Etruscans (the predecessors to the Romans), the Phoenicians, and the Carthaginians; and the seventh race, the Mongolians, gave rise to the Magyars, the Japanese, the present-day Mongolians, the Malayans, and the Esquimaux.[37]

According to an ancient writer, Theopompus, who was probably referring to the third and fourth Atlantean subraces, Atlantis was an empire of indefinite size consisting of two countries that were inhabited by two races. One of these races was warlike (Turanians), while the other race was pious and given to subjective exercises (Toltecs). H.P.B. refers to a great continent, inhabited by two distinct races, which perished about 850,000 years ago. Both races were versed in the Ageless Wisdom and the secrets of nature, but were antagonistic towards each other.[38] The origin and history of these two races is little known, but it is possible that the struggle between the forces of light and darkness that helped to bring down Atlantis can be found here. It seems likely that there was a gradual polarization among the Atlanteans, perhaps over several subraces, that accelerated this conflict. The battle of light and darkness also brought in its wake a long period of catastrophe, which eventually brought Atlantis to an end.

The battle between the forces of good and evil, we are told, has occurred at several momentous times in history when the course of human evolution reached a cross road. If certain conditions were allowed to prevail, it could retard human development for centuries to come or it could lead to a significant leap forward. Thus, the conflict between the forces of light and darkness match those who seek to perpetuate the best of a civilization and those who, through extreme selfishness, materialism, and the desire to dominate others, would, if their will prevailed, bring about destruction. Although the details are lacking, this is what appears to have happened on Atlantis. Suffice it to say that catastrophic events of this nature occur not only on the physical plane, but are fought on the inner planes as well.

The demise of Atlantis occurred over a long period of time. There was a major eruption nearly 800,000 years ago, during the Pleistocene age, which caused part of Atlantis to sink below the ocean. Some of the Turanians migrated to Asia where they provided the basis for a more civilized and psychically gifted Mongolian race, the seventh subrace. The fifth and sixth subraces, the Semites and the Akkadians, also emerged after the catastrophe. The former settled in the northern regions of Atlantis and were, as we are told, "a discontented, quarrelsome, energetic folk living under a patriarchal social scheme and constantly raiding their neighbors, especially the law-abiding Akkadians."[39]

Dating from the year 200,000 BCE, there were a series of deluges which completely submerged the Atlantean continent. Esoteric sources maintain that prior to this period, the planetary Hierarchy established the Dynasty of Pharaohs in Egypt, during which time the two huge pyramids at Gizeh were built according to sacred geometry. Seeing the intellectual powers of the Semites to be the best hope for human development, the Brothers on the inner planes, directed by that great spiritual entity, the Manu, guided these chosen peoples to Central Asia where they formed the core of what was to become the new Aryan root race.[40] A branch of the Mongolian root race migrated from Asia to North America, whose progeny formed the basis for the Mayan civilization and the Native American tribes.[41]

H.P.B. observes that the Greeks and Romans, as well as the Egyptians, were remnants of the Atlanto-Aryans who had suddenly disappeared. She notes that Egypt was a civilization that had no infancy but emerged in mature form. They, like the Aryans of India, the Chaldeans, the Chinese, and the Assyrians, grew out of the Atlantean root race and were the result of preceding civilizations lasting many centuries.[42]

The keynote of the Atlantean root race, we are told, had been the development of self-conscious emotion and the sense of taste. The Aryan root race was concerned with recognizing the sense of smell, the power of reason, and the capacity for logical thought. Not surprisingly, one finds this quality of mind more in evidence among the later Atlanteans than among those of the earlier Aryan subraces. Hodson figures that the last remnant of Atlantis disappeared at about 9564 BCE, close to the time when recorded history begins.[43] Legend tells of a great flood which submerged the continent of Atlantis, followed by a series of cataclysms that lasted until about 9564 BCE.[44] Whereas the Atlantean root race came to an end with the last great flood, this did not spell the end for Atlantean consciousness. Esoteric sources generally agree that many people alive today, particularly in the West, are essentially Atlantean in consciousness and astral in nature which, as the Tibetan Master D.K. has often stated, is one of the fundamental problems that the Hierarchy is forced to deal with.

The Aryan Root Race

We are presently living in the fifth root race, dating back to the Pleistocene age, which started over a million years ago. There seems to be common agreement that the end of the Pliocene age, which by Swimme and Berry's calculations ran from five million to 1.8 million years ago, marked the start of the Pleistocene period, when conventional thinking holds that early hominids (homo erectus) first appeared. The Pleistocene era lasted from 1.5 million to 72,000 years ago.[45]

H.P.B. uses the analogy of a tree in describing the relationship of root races, subraces, and branch races. The main stem of the tree would, of course, be the root race; the larger limbs, seven in number, comprise the subraces; and the seven branches from these limbs make up the branch or family races. By her calculations, our present Aryan root race has been in existence for a million years. From this, it can be inferred that each of the subraces lasts approximately 210,000 years, or ten times the length of a planetary ray cycle. By the same token, a branch race is 30,000 years. Thus, the European branch race still has many thousand years to run, although the fortunes of individual nations may rise and fall during this period.[46] The American branch race is barely in its infancy.

It cannot be stated strongly enough that race refers to consciousness and should be seen as matrices of ideas, which are expressed through language, law, customs, and social patterns. It always holds that evil is the flip side of good so whereas both the forces of light and the forces of darkness use a common symbolism, their meanings and purposes are divergently different. The references to Aryan and Nordic super races and the notion of biological racial superiority, which dominated the ideology and propaganda of the Nazis and many of the unthinking masses during the last half of the nineteenth century and the first half of the twentieth century, was a total perversion of the true meaning of race. There are no better or inferior racial groups but only relative degrees of racial consciousness. While one branch race, subrace, or root race may be at its height, others may be in a state of decay. This should not in any way be construed to imply racial superiority at any level.

Subraces as Vessels for Civilizations

The Aryan root race includes seven subraces which, in turn, include seven branch races. A branch race can be interpreted as a synonym for a civilization. Ancient and modern civilizations are covered by the first five subraces of the Aryan root race and, consequently, they are well known to us.

As to the number and type of civilizations, there is wide disagreement. The Russian nineteenth-century historian, Nikolai Danilevsky, noted ten positive or creative civilizations, which he identified as the Egyptian civilization; those of the Assyro-Babylonian-Phoenician-Chaldean or ancient Semitic peoples; the Chinese civilization; the Hindu civilization; the Iranian civilization; the Hebrew civilization; the Greek civilization; the Roman civilization; and the Germano-Romantic or European civilization. His negative or destructive civilizations included the Mongols, the Huns, and the Turks.[47] Oswald Spengler, the author of an influential book at the turn of the century, *The Decline of the West*, thought there had been eight civilizations, whereas Arnold Toynbee, specified twenty-one civilizations.

This raises a fundamental point as to what is a civilization? A dictionary definition of the word civilization, such as that found in the *American Heritage Dictionary*, is an advanced state of social, political, and cultural complexity, which is also associated with a high stage of artistic development. Hence not all societies, even those who have endured for long periods of time and are historically significant, merit being called civilizations. The Tibetan Master D.K. alludes to the fact that a civilization is the repository of racial consciousness and provides a function within the scheme of the divine plan of furthering the evolution of humanity.[48]

A civilization is also tied to the cultural and social development of a particular nation or region. Esoterically speaking, a civilization is the reflection in the mass of people of some particular cyclic influence, leading to an initiation.[49] Put another way, it is the reaction of a cross section of humanity to the purpose of any particular world period.[50] Confusion can easily arise over terminology. Within each racial stream, there are a number of civilizations which rise and fall in order to present a variation of the message enunciated by a world teacher, which is in keeping with the overall theme of the root race, the round, and, ultimately, the mind of the Logos himself. Each civilization has its own nations, states, and empires, which are identified with branch races within the subrace of each root race. From the microcosm to the macrocosm, there is a beautiful interactive and coterminous unity that is hardly seen from the messy and often chaotic perspective of mundane history.

One must carefully distinguish between a racial group and the particular civilization in which it came to fruition. Examples are the Chaldeans and Phoenicians, who rose to prominence during the third subrace of the Aryan root race but essentially were a remnant of the fourth and sixth subraces, respectively, of the fourth Atlantean root race. The Jews date from an earlier root race, but they did not rise to historic visibility until the third Aryan subrace. The great civilization of the Far East, including China and Japan, are descendants of the seventh subrace of the Atlantean root race.

According to Geoffrey Hodson's typology, the five subraces of the Aryan root race included the Indian, the Arabian (Egyptian), the Iranian (Mesopotamian), the Mediterranean (including Greece and Rome), and the Teutonic or Nordic.[51] Within the stream of the fifth root race, Rudolf Steiner notes that there have been five great civilizations to date, including the ancient Indian, the ancient Persian, the Egyptian-Chaldean, the Greco-Roman, and Western Civilization.[52]

The difference appears to be that, whereas Steiner thinks more in terms of civilizations, Hodson emphasizes racial evolution. A racial stream is the subjective nature of a people whereas a nation is the objective factor. By the same token, culture is the soul of a people while a civilization represents the personality. Clearly, Steiner makes no real distinction between a civilization (or what he calls a cultural epoch) and a branch race. Despite differences in terminology, both Steiner and Hodson would see their typologies as representing a similar epoch of consciousness.

The Early Subraces of the Aryan Root Race

Each subrace has its own symbols and social patterns. The ancient Indian civilization, which Hodson dates from 45,000 BCE[53] was, according to the Anthroposophists, founded on a population that was shaped entirely by the forces of the Lemurian root race and had not been touched by Atlantean evolution. Little is known of the history of this earliest subrace, which rose to dominance during the post-Atlantean pralaya. Steiner maintains that in the ancient epoch of India, man was guided by divine imagination. One can thus conclude that these ancient peoples saw dream-like images of the gods while possessing only a rudimentary capacity to think.[54]

Aryan Subrace

The impulses for the Aryan branch race, or civilization, were in evidence from 2500 BCE with the coming of the Harappan Culture, and from 1500 BCE with the migration of the Aryans to India, where they rose to predominance.[55] Wachsmuth maintains that the Aryans emerged from Tibet (Kashmir) and then passed into the Indus Valley at around 2000 BCE.[56] Whereas, in the early stages of the civilization, castes did not exist, they developed initially as a means for delineating spheres of consciousness and then over time evolved into social classifications based on physiognomies.

A perspective on how history develops holds that a subrace and a branch race flows from three key concepts representing the lower aspects of will, love, and active intelligence. Translated into a social framework, they represent the political, the religious, and the intellectual life of any given society. Politics in ancient India initially centered around the Manu who, legend held, was born directly of the god Brahma and was a hermaphrodite.[57] Each new root race was guided by a Manu, with seven adepts, each reflecting Manu-consciousness and overshadowing a particular subrace.

Since, from an esoteric standpoint, myth, legend, and history all converge, it is interesting to note that the Tibetan wrote that the one who is called Vaivasvata Manu is the Manu of the fifth root race, and it is He who has presided over the destinies of the Aryan race since its inception one hundred thousand years ago or longer.[58] It is also said that the Manu ruled with the assistance of seven sages, or adepts, referred to above.[59] Curiously, the ancient Egyptians spoke of a great king, Menes, who united Egypt into a single kingdom before it came under the control of succeeding dynasties. One might easily conclude that King Menes was, in fact, the Manu. Likewise, there may well be a correspondence between the Manu and King Minos, the legendary ruler of the Minoan civilization on Crete, and Mithra, the sun-god of the Persians.

Out of the laws of the Manu, it is claimed that Hinduism arose, the first of the great world religions. At the core of this religion is the Rig-Veda, consisting of 1028 hymns to the gods of the Aryans.[60] It was also from ancient India that Sanskrit emerged, which influenced the development of the Indo-European family of languages. As a sacred language, Sanskrit is structured on divine numbering patterns, providing an esoteric order to the syntax. Sanskrit has provided the basis for the rich intellectual and cultural life of India.

Table 5. Subraces and Religions of the Aryan Race

Date	Name/Place	Teacher	Religion	Keynote	Symbol
60,000 BC	Manoan (Tibet)	Vaivasvata Manu	Hinduism Laws of Manu	Dharma	Swastika
10,000 BC	India	Vyasa Krishna of Gita	Brahmanical		
500 BC-Present	India, Ceylon Burma, etc.	Buddha Krishna (Child)	Buddhism Hinduism	Law Devotion	Wheel Flute
40,000 BC	Arabian Egypt & Arabia	Thoth/Hermes	Egyptian	Light	Winged Disc
570 AD-Present	Arabia/N.Africa	Mohammed	Islam	Sub-mission	Crescent
30,000 BC	Iranian Persia Mesopotamia Chaldea	Zarathustra	Zoroastrian	Purity	Fire
2200 BC	Crete				
500 BC	Persian Empire of Darius				
Present	Parsees				
20,000 BC	Celtic in Mediterranean area				
10,000	Southern Europe	Orpheus	Orphic Mysteries	Harmony & Reality	Lyre & Caduceus
300 BC	Greece	Pythagoras			
300 AD	Rome				
10,000 BC	Teutonic or Nordic				
5000 BC	Europe	Christ	Christianity	Brotherly Love/Self-Sacrifice	Cross
Present	Spread over the World				

Egyptian Subrace

We see an anomaly in dates between the emergence of a subrace and the various branch races which are part of the historical record. The thousands of years separating the two (see Table 5) can be explained in several ways. It seems likely that each new root race somehow recapitulates the earlier root races in the round, although what form this takes is hard to imagine. The most obvious explanation is that there is a great deal of overlapping. For example, Hodson notes that the planetary Hierarchy transferred the White Lodge to Egypt in 400,000 BCE when Atlantis was beginning to break apart. In 210,000, we are told, the first divine dynasty settled in Egypt and the two pyramids at Gizeh were built, well before the dates given by most scholars. Accordingly, Egypt was peopled by remnants of the Toltecs and Akkadians in 150,000 BCE and was repeopled again in 70,000 BCE. The Egyptian subrace was said to have emerged around 35,000 BCE, whereas Egyptian civilization is thought to have come into existence at around 3100 BCE.[61]

As was previously noted, the second subrace, the Egyptian, or Arabian (based upon Hodson's system), dates from 35,000 BCE and emerged while the Third Divine Dynasty was ruling Egypt. In time, these early Egyptians spread westward and extended their hold over all of Arabia, much of Africa, Mesopotamia, and all of Persia. It was during this time that Europe was in the grip of an Ice Age and was peopled by the so-called Raindeer Men and Cro-Magnards.[62]

It was during this period of Egyptian hegemony that civilization became illuminated by Hermes, the first of the great world teachers. The Tibetan notes that Hermes was the first to proclaim himself "the light of the world" and teach the doctrine of immortality.[63] The vision and secret teachings of Hermes gave rise to an important school of occult knowledge, which over the centuries permeated the West. Egypt was ruled by the pharaohs, who were considered to be god-kings and were overshadowed by Amen-Ra, "the heavenly king whose will all men must obey."[64] Insofar as the Egyptian civilization lasted for nearly four thousand years through all kinds of vicissitudes, it would be difficult to ascribe to it a fixed religious and social system. As Professor Toynbee pointed out, while Egyptian society lasted for some four thousand years, it was not so much a living entity but a dead and unburied organism for half that period.[65] Ancient Egypt gave to the world one of the most important myths, that of Isis and Osiris, which has become a prototype for other myths. While ancient India was based on the keynotes of dharma and law, Egypt was guided by the concept of light.[66]

Iranian Subrace

As we have seen, each subrace was initiated by a world teacher. The great teacher of the third root race was Zarathustra, or in Greek, Zoroaster. H.P.B. observes that there were several Zarathustras, the last being the founder of the Fire Temple of Azareksh and the writer of the works on the sacred Magian religion.[67] By some accounts, the first Zoroaster was a prior incarnation of the Buddha. The life of the historical Zoroaster was amazingly similar to that of the Christ, who came after him. He was born, supposedly, of immaculate conception; escaped early death from a Herod-like king; before starting his ministry, he went alone to pray and meditate in the desert; he suffered temptations; moreover, he was later arrested and thrown into prison.[68] The teachings of esoteric Zorastrianism, according to H.P.B., parallel those of *The Secret Doctrine*.[69]

The guiding concept that Zoroaster gave to the third subrace of the fifth root race was the contrast between spirit and matter.[70] As this root race spread across the ancient Near East, from roughly 30,000 BCE, people developed a map of divine intention and cosmology from calculations of planetary and stellar movements, which had emerged during the second subrace. Over time, this subrace gave rise to the branch races or mini-civilizations of Crete, Rhodes, and Cyprus, which later gave rise to the ancient Greek city states of the fourth subrace; also, Aryas, where the Indo-European language was rooted; the Empire of Sumer and Akkad, from which the first written laws appeared; and later to the important Hittite, Babylonian, Chaldean, and Persian civilizations.[71]

From a political standpoint, there developed over the course of this subrace cities, law codes, the domestication of animals, and a written language. Temples were built to the gods and the religion of localized deities emerged. The king was surrounded by a priestly class who advised and carried out the commands of the ruler. The king himself possessed sacerdotal authority to interpret the will of God. It was during the Sumerian branch race of this third subrace that the

Epic of Gilgamesh appeared, which characterized the dyadic relationship between divinity and nature. It dates from approximately 3000 BCE.

Celtic Subrace

The fourth subrace, which Hodson places at 20,000 BCE, originated with the Celtic peoples in the Mediterranean region and was later inspired by the teachings of Orpheus. From Orpheus, the mysteries descended to Pythagoras and then to Plato. According to Orpheus, all existence was derived from a sovereign principle of the good, which was the source of all virtue. From one indivisible unity came a progression of supermundane causes, seven in number, which formed into triads. They are as follows:

1. The One
2. The intelligible order (subjective and causal)
3. The intelligible and intellectual order (subjective and causal)
4. The intellectual order (creator of the mundane world)
5. The supermundane order
6. The liberated order
7. The mundane order[72]

The mundane order, the last and lowest of the creative triads, was the home of the gods, who had their own kingdom and interacted in the affairs of men. Below this realm was the world of human affairs where creative power manifested through the physical elements of nature. Beneath this world was the underworld of fire and death called Hades.[73] Orpheus was a poet and a musician who presented his teachings in the form of musical verse. His music was played on seven strings symbolizing the seven planes of the universe and the sevenfold mysteries of initiation.[74]

The Celtic subrace, in Hodson's view, began in Manoa and then passed through Persia to the Caucasus, where they settled. At about 10,000 BCE, the Celts passed into Southeastern Europe, where they formed the basis of what came to be known as the Pelasgians, or ancient Greeks. After the flood of 9564 BCE, he says, the Celts became the dominant race over most of Europe.[75] It is not known whether the Celts were the peoples classified by conventional history as the Stone Age folk, who were known to be in Europe as early as 2000 BCE. Nor do we know whether the Celts were the pre-existing Minoans, who inhabited the island of Crete and created an advanced civilization at around 1600 BCE. A reference from one source holds that the Slavs, Celts, and Teutons survived in Eastern Europe on cereal crops from about 1700 BCE.[76] Essentially, Hodson speaks to a period of history of which little or nothing is known.

In any event, the span of years covering ancient Greek history, which can be dated from the Homeric period, 850 BCE, to the rise of Macedonia in the third century BCE, and Roman history, from Rome's subjugation of Italy in 270 BCE, to its fall in the fourth century CE, constitutes a major flowering of the fourth subrace of the Aryan root race. Steiner says of this epoch that it was the first time in which man felt that he was entirely on the earth and united with the forces on earth.[77] It was during the Greek and Roman branch races of the fourth subrace that political power began to be shared by an elite oligarchy or aristocracy, who formed a privileged class above and beyond a larger class of freemen and the massive slave populations. Representative democracy had its fledgling origins in the Greek city-state of Athens. States evolved into empires and the material aspects of civilization became more sophisticated, including warfare, manufacturing, and trade. Religion took the form of cults and public ritual. Throughout the classical world, one finds a strong taste of heroism, which was most notably expressed in the poems of Homer and the life of Alexander the Great. Leaders, therefore, were heroes who had distinguished themselves in some manner, usually in combat. Religion revolved around the noble exploits of the gods, whereas intellectual and social life stressed the importance of dying for a cause rather than living the quiet and easy life of a coward.

Among the Jews, however, whose lineage—not its history— preceded the fourth subrace, there developed a tribal religion which emphasized the search for meaning and obedience to a single deity. This historically based religion of the oppressed formed the core of the religion of the fifth root race, Christianity. The cultural flowering of the fourth subrace took place near its end, during the fifth century BCE, with the golden age of Greece. The last great development of the fourth subrace was the emergence of the Roman Empire, which became a global civilization by the standards of the time.

Western Civilization: The Culmination of the Fifth Subrace

It is clear from all accounts that subraces overlap one another. All of the subraces of the Aryan root race continue to exist up to the present day, with the exception of the fourth subrace, which Hodson maintains was terminated with the fall of Rome in the fourth century CE. Actually, it would be more accurate to date the end of Roman civilization with the fall of Constantinople to the Turks in 1453 CE. Europe consists of the Celtic, Latin, Slavic, and Teutonic branch races but only the Teutonic can be included in the fifth subrace.

Configured another way, these four branch races correspond to the four mystery streams found in the writings of Anthroposophy.[78] The correspondences are as follows: the eastern mystery stream, or the post-Atlantean stream, flowed through the sub- and branch races of India, Persia, and Greece, and related to the subjective history of the Slavic peoples; the western mystery stream, flowing through the Druid and early Christian subgroups, was linked to that of the Celtic peoples; the Northern mystery stream, generated through the Nordic peoples, contributed to the Germanic folk; and the Southern mystery stream emerged through the Lemurian, Egyptian, Roman root, sub-, and branch races, and early Rosicrucian mysteries, to the Latin civilizations.[79] A further discussion of these mystery streams will be found in Chapters 6 and 8.

Whereas the civilizations of India and the Near East now exist in the afterglow of their peak periods, the main thrust of the fifth subrace of the fifth root race for the past two thousand years has been, of course, Western Civilization. Hodson believes that Western Civilization emerged primarily from what he called the Teutonic or Nordic racial groups. The Teutonic peoples, so he argues, left Manoa and passed through Persia where they, along with the Celtic race, settled in the Caucasus. They later moved to the area around Cracow, in present day Poland, at around 8000 BCE, and from there spread across Europe, forming themselves into nations, particularly in northern Europe in the lands now occupied by Germany, England, Scandinavia, and Iceland.[80]

This view may be somewhat misleading since, as noted above, Europe can be seen to have been fed by four dominant racial streams, representing the Latin, Slavic, Celtic, as well as the Teutonic peoples. The American branch race was initially an offshoot of the Teutonic subrace, but has been strongly defined, not only by the other three groups, but by subraces and branch races of the third and fourth root race. Each new subrace contains not only a new idea, more accurately three new ideas, but a mixture of various ethnic and racial groups through intermarriage and migration.

Whereas Hodson maintains that the fifth subrace of the Aryan root race began ten thousand years ago in the folk history of the ancient Teutonic peoples, the keynote of this particular epoch was sounded by the Master Jesus, who incarnated in Palestine and became the vehicle for the Christ energy. The story of Jesus's ministry and the early history of Christianity are well known and do not require elaboration. What is important is that the purpose or central theme of a subrace does not appear until that subrace has evolved to a certain point over thousands of years, much in the way that a person is often unaware of his or her destiny until one reaches middle age or later. If we accept Hodson's dates for the commencement of each subrace, then what we call Western Civilization has only covered one-sixth of this entire subracial period. For the early history of the fifth subrace, one must study the origins and development of the Teutonic peoples, who reach back into a more distant past.

Themes in European Civilization

As was stated earlier, each civilization may be perceived as being defined by three currents or streams which weave together its political, religious, and intellectual characteristics. These streams of civilization, incorporating the aspects of will, love-wisdom, and active intelligence, have shaped European civilization from the fall of Rome to the eighteenth century. "Europe," in the words of historian Geoffrey Barraclough, "owes its political existence to the Roman Empire and its spiritual unity to the Catholic Church, and for its intellectual culture, it is indebted to a third factor—the classical tradition."[81] Curiously enough, two of these three dominant currents of consciousness flow from the eastern and southern racial streams of the fourth Aryan subrace and were not derived from the Nordic consciousness of the fifth subrace. Only Christianity, which was conceived in the mainstream of an earlier racial consciousness, was clearly a force of the most recent subrace and it did not manifest through the Nordic stream.

It may seem difficult for us, living in unhistorical times when everything is change and flux, to fully appreciate how backward-looking European civilization has been. The Carolingian emperors, who ruled much of Europe during the eighth and ninth centuries, following the slow collapse of Rome, likened themselves to the descendants of the Roman Empire, and revived many of the trappings of the old imperial regime. With the emergence of centralized European states in the fifteenth and sixteenth centuries, the new monarchs sought legitimacy and power through restoring the cultural and constitutional legacies of Rome. Both church and state adhered to Roman law. The aristocracy throughout Europe formed themselves into a patrician class that was consciously Roman in character, and every educated nobleman knew his Cicero, Pliny, Virgil, Tacitus, and the corpus of Roman letters and thought.

As for spiritual unity, the impact of the Christian Church on Western Civilization hardly needs elaboration. Christopher Dawson defines Europe as a community of peoples who share a common spiritual tradition that has been transmitted from age to age until it has overshadowed the world.[82] In point of fact, it was the Church whose roots sank the deepest into the soil of Western Civilization. Based on his study of a small French village in the Middle Ages, the historian Emmanuel LeRoy Ladurie writes that external repression of the people came not so much from the lay nobility as from the ambitions of a totalitarian church which demanded both material dues and spiritual obedience.[83] Christianity, in its various forms, remained at the center of European political and social life until the mid-nineteenth century, when it gradually succumbed to secular forces.

It would be an understatement to say that education and intellectual life in Europe (the third current of Western Civilization) was characterized by classical thought. The recovery of classical philosophic texts and their incorporation into scholastic thought gave rise to scientific and analytical ideas during the high Middle Ages. These ideas dominated the intellectual life of the universities until they were challenged by the new scientific thinking of the seventeenth century and the intellectual revolution, known as the Enlightenment, in the eighteenth century. Classicism underscored the arts well into the nineteenth century. So powerful have these ideas been that one historian has argued that whenever classical and Christian ideas have come into conflict, as they often have, it is the classical ideas which have won out over the Christian.[84]

New Components of the Plan

Historians of civilizations, such as Nikolai Danilevsky, Oswald Spengler, and Arnold Toynbee, argue that civilizations emerge, grow, decline, and disintegrate over time. Hypothetically, the change from a waxing to a waning phase is accompanied by the advent of new ideas, representing the three divine aspects of will, love, and active intelligence. This marks the maturing point of a civilization, when it withdraws from the domination of those ideas that were carried over from an earlier civilization or subrace and begins to come under the sway of those ideas that will carry it into the next civilization or subrace.

An example of such a transition occurred in the third root race, during what has been termed the Neolithic period, when goddess cults began to decline. Somewhere between 6000 and 4000 BCE, according to William Irwin Thompson, there was a shift towards a more warlike and individualistic set of ideas, which came to dominate the regions of Egypt, the ancient Near East, and Crete[85] and heralded the rise to dominance of the fourth root race. Heroic individualism was carried by various branch races, the Latin in particular, into Western Civilization. In the West, individualism, through the rise to power of Christianity and the emergence of strong nation-states, has been raised to a high level of sophistication. The regularity by which ideas ebb and flow is not accidental but, according to esotericism, is orchestrated from the inner planes by those who interpret and transmit the relevant pieces of the divine plan.

Most recently, dating from the seventeenth century, one can detect the advent of a major shift in ideas that will carry civilization in the direction of the sixth subrace. The impact of these new ideas has affected all levels of society, most particularly through changes in cosmology, the expansion of political life, and secularization. The keynotes for humanity in the next planetary cycle—liberty, equality, fraternity—were the hallmarks of the democratic revolutions of the eighteenth century, particularly the French Revolution. Contained within each of these keynotes is the seed for a new political, religious, and scientific consciousness that could well supersede the more limited thinking of the past.

Liberty might be defined as the restricted evolution towards freedom. This, obviously, means different things to different people. For political theorists of the eighteenth century, the idea of liberty was closely associated with the possession of property.[86] Some associate the concept of liberty with human rights and those basic freedoms found in the American Bill of Rights. Still others maintain that liberty can only be understood within the context of personal responsibility and the rule of law.

The Tibetan has observed that the theme of liberty is of far greater importance than has been previously grasped and involves no less than the establishment of right human relations on a planetary basis.[87] There have been many experiments in right human relations over the past two centuries, ranging from the various mass movements aimed at alleviating political, economic, and social wrongs to the work of establishing an international consciousness along many lines. Such developments would include an economic synthesis among nations, business, and interest groups; the wrecking of old political parties and trade groups; the development of a spirit of internationalism that will overcome isolation, separateness, and egoism; and the ending of class hatreds and racial antagonisms. The impetus for building a brotherhood of nations has been behind the formation of various international groups, organizations, and alliances which have proliferated during the twentieth century.[88] Clearly, this is work that will occupy humanity during the next subrace and, perhaps, extend even into the following root race.

Brotherhood might be seen as the keyword for bringing about a new synthesis in religion. There has been a retreat from the domination of theology and the institutional power of religion in the West since the eighteenth century, and this has been in keeping with the divine plan. D.K. writes that we are now in a period when traditional religious dogma and theology is being brushed aside and new sects, cults, and organizations are emerging to give religious expression new life.[89] As the peoples of the world continue to mix and blend, and thus bring about a cultural synthesis, which is one of the trends leading into the next subrace, then religion will lose its sectarian flavor and recapture the mysteries as have been expounded and perpetuated in the Ageless

Wisdom. This is what D.K. has called the New World Religion. Specifically, the Tibetan predicted that an inner structure of world faith would make its appearance by the end of the twentieth century and that the subjective organization of the World Federation of Nations will emerge, with its outer form taking shape by 2025.[90] Human free will is the final arbiter of its own fate so that all dates, handed down as prophecy, must be considered relative.

Finally, D.K. inferred that intellectual life will foster the principle of equality through the rise of primary and secondary education and the proliferation of knowledge through literature and the mass media. Modern science has its role to play in broadening and educating the masses. Over the latter part of the twentieth century, scientific studies have replaced the humanities as the focal point of academic life, and have contributed to more systematic modes of thinking with the aid of new technologies. Some branches of science are also eliminating the barriers masking the unseen world of phenomena. The new physics, in the words of Fritjof Capra, is "now dealing with a non sensory experience of reality."[91] The Curies' discovery of and experiments with radium at the turn of the twentieth century, Einstein's theory of relativity, Max Planck's quantum theory, Werner Heisenberg's uncertainty principle, David Bohm's implicate order, the recent development of superstring theory, and research into near-death experiences all speak to the renting of the veil between the visible and invisible worlds.

Culture

Culture is a very slippery term that is easily misinterpreted. T.S. Eliot wrote a book on the subject and the closest he could come to a definition was a view of society as a self-conscious spiritual unity, based upon bonds of loyalty, identity, and mutual obligation.[92] Esoterically speaking, culture relates to the cyclical flow of consciousness as it waxes and wanes over time. This differs from the way we have defined civilization as the response of people to a teaching or current of activity—political, religious, or intellectual—that can be found at any point in time.

Consciousness, seen historically, is not time-specific. In other words, whereas the present Aryan root race is a conditioning field for the development of the mental faculty, the state of mass consciousness is still dominated by that of earlier root races. For the past two thousand years, Western Civilization has been predominately Atlantean in consciousness, and that can be seen from the pages of history, which have been filled with the vagaries of human emotion, such as ambition, the lust for power, errant sexual passions, blind devotion to a person or cause, collective contagion of fear, economic acquisitiveness, national self-identification, and heroic individualism. From the standpoint of consciousness, the fifth subrace of the Aryan root race through the branch race of Western Civilization has been an attempt to qualify the excesses of emotion by means of cultivating taste, refinement, and virtue, along with subduing the passions by the use of reason.

Culture and Cycles

History confronts one with a myriad of cycles so numerous they can hardly be delineated. Cycles deal with the ebb and flow of life, consciousness, and thought which, in turn, impact all spheres of activity on the physical plane. The Tibetan has written: "In the understanding of the law of cycles, we gain knowledge of the underlying laws of evolution and come to a realization of the rhythmic work of creation."[93]

More will be said in later chapters about cycles as they relate to the rays and the signs of the zodiac. It is sufficient for now to give a cursory overview as to how events and historical periods are structured by the tidal flow of recurrent cycles. It is first important to say that cyclical activity as it plays upon planetary events is far from arbitrary. In the Hindu system, briefly alluded to in the first chapter, there is a universe of rhythmic evolution, corresponding to the cycle of a Manu, that great entity directing intelligence at the level of a root race, round, globe, or chain period. Thus a round, which constitutes 4,320,000,000 years, the length of a kalpa, can be reduced to 4,320,000 years, the span of a Maha-Yuga or root race and this, in turn, can be divided into a Kali Yuga of 4,320 years. A yuga is 1/1000 of a day and night of Brahma, the length of a round. The planetary and solar cycles comprising globes, chains, and rounds correspond to the greater revolutions of Brahma that extend into billions and trillions of years.

Each yuga has a direct bearing on human history. There is sufficient evidence to show, for instance, that significant historical turning points pass through roughly five-hundred-year cycles. For example, the seed of Western Civilization was planted at the time of Christ; it began to germinate with the collapse of Rome and the barbarian invasions of the fifth century CE; it was nurtured throughout the Dark Ages, lasting until about 1075; it then rose to maturity during the Middle Ages, which underwent a profound change in the fifteenth century; and then was transformed again in the twentieth century, following the World Wars.

H.P.B., in an article written for *The Theosophist*, presents a theory of cycles that was worked out by a Dr. E. Zasse, who published his findings in the *Prussian Journal of Statistics* some time towards the end of the nineteenth century. Drawing upon the Hindu theory of cycles, Dr. Zasse believed that history could be studied by examining cycles in durations of 250, 500, 700, and 1,000 years. He states that if we divide the map of the Old World into six parts—Eastern, Central, Western Asia, Eastern and Western Europe, and Egypt—then it is easy to see that a distinctive wave passes over these regions every 250 years.[94]

The first of these waves began in 2000 BCE China during the golden age of Huangho culture. In 1750 BCE, the Mongolians of Central Asia established a powerful empire. At around 1500 BCE, the Egyptian Empire spread across the eastern Mediterranean and its trade and culture flourished. Around 1250 BCE, the historical wave crossed over into Southeastern Europe with the blooming of Cretan-Mycenaean culture, ending with the destruction of Troy during the Trojan War. The second historical wave appears in Central Asia at about the first millennium before Christ. There we find the migration of the Scythians from the steppes to countries in the South and West. This was followed in 500 BCE with the emergence of the Persian Empire. The wave then moves on to Rome during the time of the First Punic War in 264 through 241 BCE, signaling the rise of that great empire.

The third historical wave starts in the Far East and passes through Central Asia to Eastern Europe, culminating with the Byzantine Empire which, under the Macedonian dynasty, had begun the process of recovering lands lost to the Muslims. The fourth and final wave began in China in 1250 CE; reached Western Asia at about 1500 CE with the rise of the Ottoman Empire; and passed to Russia around 1750 between the reigns of Peter the Great and Catherine the Great.[95]

While the dates given by Dr. Zasse seem arbitrary and many important events are completely neglected, he does emphasize the existence of streams of racial consciousness that flow from one epoch and civilization to another in rhythmic fashion. Rudolf Steiner and the Anthroposophists, as we have seen, refer to four streams of consciousness that grew out of the Lemurian and Atlantean periods and conditioned the development of Europe during the fifth root race.[96]

If civilization, which can be likened to the inflow of triadal energies that influence the political, religious, and intellectual life of a two-thousand-year cycle and addresses the *what* and *how* questions of an historical epoch, culture asks *why*? Culture is therefore concerned with meaning and is characterized by breakthroughs in thought and creativity that lead to an expansion of human consciousness. Unlike cycles of civilization, which are progressive in nature, cultural cycles are regressive, insofar as they start from a point of unity or insight and from there become continually distorted throughout the life span of the cycle. The ancients interpreted a cultural cycle as the diffusion of some divinely inspired impulse through matter. In particular, the Greeks viewed culture as a descent from a high point, referred to as the Age of Gold, through the ages of Silver and Bronze, reaching its nadir in the degenerate Age of Iron.

Vico's Historical Typology

Writing in the eighteenth century, the Italian philosopher Giambattista Vico observed that the cultural evolution of a civilization involved passing through a number of stages which he termed the Age of Gods, the Age of Heroes, and the Age of Men, finally descending into the Age of Chaos. This pattern might well be the case for each root race, subrace, and branch race. For Vico, each age possessed its own set of myths and languages "which tell us the histories of the institutions signified by the words..."[97] The Tibetan writes that as each great ray comes into incarnation and inaugurates a new civilization, the speech of the cycle is transformed, leading to an enriched vocabulary and the presentation of new knowledge to humanity.[98]

Age of Gods

Although Vico makes little mention of dates, the period in the West from roughly the fourth to the twelfth century seemingly corresponds to the Age of Gods. During this time, culture was embodied in hieroglyphs, or myths and divine symbols, which veiled the inner mysteries, what Vico called a mute language.[99] Historian Johan Huizinga, writing about the late Middle Ages, revealed tendencies that were strongly evident centuries earlier. He notes that religious emotion during the Middle Ages tended to be transmuted into images that became graspable to the mind when invested with a perceptible form.[100] Hence the culture of this period involved devotion to and speculation on the nature of sacred symbols and archetypes. Men and women ordered their lives by the ringing of church bells and could be driven to war or intense devotion through the display of the cross or the sanctified bones of some martyr.

Age of Heroes

The Age of Heroes coincided with the emergence of the nation-state and the inception of secularism. This period, generally speaking, might be said to cover the period from the twelfth century to the eighteenth century and was characterized by, in the words of Vico, language which was "equally articulate and mute."[101] It was during this second cultural age that European society underwent a reformation in manners and began to differentiate public and private spheres of activity. More and more national languages emerged to replace Latin. Jacob Burckhardt, an historian of the Renaissance, writes that from the high Middle Ages "the nobility of Western Europe had sought to establish a 'courtly' speech for social intercourse as well as poetry."[102] Whereas the myths of this period tended to be more classical than divine, they did play upon the consciousness of the illiterate masses and expanded the scope of education. The humanist tradition, with its apparent materialism, has had, according to the Tibetan, a deeply spiritual program and purpose.[103]

Age of Men

With the coming of the Age of Men, coinciding with the commercial and early industrial revolutions, language, in the quaint phraseology of Vico, became almost entirely articulate.[104] Less the language of allusion, metaphor, and classical imagery, the new commercial classes used speech that was prosaic, befitting the material environment of the marketplace. The mechanistic world of technical thinking and scientific reductionism did not go unchallenged. Voices in the wilderness—such as Blake who, in his *Book of Urizen*, rails against "a visionless, lifeless, Newtonian world, divided, weighed and measured by the instruments of empirical science;"[105] and Emerson, who, writing *English Traits*—felt that English intellectual life in the mid-nineteenth century was being choked by the consciousness of money, power, and rightness.[106] These men and others presented alternative visions of creative imagination and spiritual insight. It is by no means coincidental that the Hierarchy's efforts to revive the Ageless Wisdom have occurred during a time of profound materialism.

Age of Chaos

The Age of Chaos, inaugurated by the Great War in 1914, has brought in its wake pain, disillusionment, confusion, and death on a massive scale. Historian Eric Hobsbawm, in his history of the twentieth century, *The Age of Extremes*, quotes a number of writers and intellectuals as to their views of this century. Philosopher Isaiah Berlin calls it "the most terrible century in western history," whereas the French scientist, René Dumont, sees the twentieth century only as a time of massacres and wars.[107] No wonder that the Tibetan notes that the Hierarchy has had to work hard to prevent the complete collapse of human civilization "as it exists at this time."[108] Characteristically, language, the unifying factor in a culture, degenerates into slang, cant, and endless babble, reflecting the loss of cultural unity. It is, however, from the debris of a dying culture that a new vision of synthesis is created, which provides the seeds for a new Age of Gods at a higher turn of the spiral.

Summary

What makes this present moment in history so significant is the fact that humanity is entering into a transition from the fifth subrace of the Aryan root race into the sixth subrace that will last for a long period of time. Life will be very different in the years ahead and, although we know little as to the particulars of these changes, certain trends are clearly discernible. The first has to do with globalism and the end to dominant regional civilizations as existed in Europe during the flowering of the fifth subrace and the Mediterranean world throughout the fourth subrace. The second trend is the mixing of populations resulting from migration on an unprecedented scale. This most particularly will occur between the peoples of Asia and the West, and to a lesser extent between white and black populations. Finally, there will be a greater impetus towards the training of the mind, which is the goal of the Aryan root race. Periods of pralaya (times of upheaval that exist between the end and beginning of a world cycle) tend to be unhistorical, but this is only an illusion. As the currents of the next subrace start to flow, our sense of the past will be exceedingly different from what it is today.

Section Two—
The Centers of Planetary History

History, as lies at the root of all science, is also the first distinct product of man's spiritual nature; his earliest expression of what can be called Thought.

—Thomas Carlyle, *Critical and Miscellaneous Essays, I*

The primary distinctive feature of human nature is consciousness, including a human being's consciousness of himself, as well as his consciousness of the Universe outside himself, in which his fellow human beings figure side by side with non-human nature, animate and inanimate.

—Arnold Toynbee, *Change and Habit*

Chapter 4—
The Expression of Power
and Will in History:
Shamballa

Among the Tibetan people there persists the popular belief that the Kingdom of Shamballa exists somewhere in the remote valleys of the Himalayas. Ancient Buddhist texts give directions for reaching Shamballa. According to the *Great Commentary on the Kalachakra*, written by the nineteenth-century Buddhist teacher Mipham, the land of Shamballa exists north of the river Sita and is divided by eight mountain ranges. On top of a circular mountain there is a palace where the imperial rulers of Shamballa reside.[1]

Rene Guénon referred in one of his books to a tri-axial cosmology that has been hidden in various codes and ciphers among the world's sacred texts. The texts that he particularly has in mind include those from Taoism, the Vedanta, the Cabala, and passages from the Pentateuch. According to the tri-axial planetary system, there exists a major axis of energies somewhere in Central Asia, and in the southern hemisphere, in the vicinity of Easter Island, which is distinguishable from the magnetic axis or the spin axis of the planet, and contributes to the dynamic balance of the earth as a whole. Not only that, but this energy field extends far beyond the earth's atmosphere and resonates with the high frequency energies flowing from the various planetary constellations and star systems. The relationship of this energy field to Shamballa is unclear, but it does give a context to some of the legends pertaining to this mysterious force.[2]

Other legends observe that the kingdom of Shamballa disappeared from the planet many centuries ago. The story goes that at a particular point the strides made by men towards enlightenment allowed the rulers of Shamballa to vanish into a more celestial realm where they continue, to this day, to watch over human affairs. More recently, some scholars have suggested that the ancient kingdom of Shamballa may have been a more modern establishment in Central Asia, preferring to believe that the legends of Shamballa and the White Brotherhood are mythical.[3]

Many legends and myths speak of a particular direction or place as being sacred. Concerning the prophesy of Gog and Magog in the Bible, the prophet Ezekiel warns of a storm of the Lord that will rise out of the north to defend Israel against her enemies in which "mountains will fall, cliffs crumble, walls collapse, and...every sort of terror" will befall the enemy.[4] For the Egyptians, the north polar mountain was considered to be the abode of the "dark gods," the fathers of the divine kings. The mysterious Mount Meru was where the gods resided and, like Shamballa for the Buddhists, was the point of the polar axis.[5]

While the legends speak of Shamballa as a particular place involving real people, there is little concrete evidence to support such a physical manifestation. Joscelyn Godwin observes that among the Buddhists the distinction between a real city that could be found on a map and a non-material place is far from being clear-cut. What is real depends upon one's perceptions. A visit to London or New York may seem real enough but, within a particular framework, these places are nothing more than millions of thoughtforms that have coalesced over many years, even hundreds of years in some cases. To the trained seer, who has developed the power of sight on the inner planes, the vision of Shamballa may be every bit as real as a stroll through a large city would appear to us on the physical plane.[6] Likewise, when we are told that Shamballa is the sacred island in the Gobi desert, the question is not so much one of physical geography as esoteric geography. It is at this point that legend often veils an occult truth.

In the esoteric version, as related by the Tibetan, Shamballa became rooted on the planet some eighteen million years ago, when humanity received the touch of individualization. About a million years later, it was decided by the Lord of the World and his assistants, possessing bodies of etheric matter, to send forth adepts and chohans into the physical world to help meet the need of an awakening humanity.[7] This marked the approach of the planetary Hierarchy into human affairs. Initially, the Hierarchy assumed direct control, and many of the so-called divine rulers, or god-kings in the ancient world, were in fact these adepts and chohans.

The first outpost of the Shamballa brotherhood was said to have been the Temple of Ibez in South America. From this temple, a branch emerged at a period, much further removed, which formed the Mayan civilization. A second branch of Shamballa was later established in Asia, and from this center the adepts spread across the Himalayan mountains and throughout southern India. It is said that there is a sacred island in the Gobi Desert where the Lord of the World has his headquarters in etheric matter. The mysteries passed further across central Asia stretching from Chaldea and Babylon through Turkestan to Manchuria. Through the mystery schools of Chaldea, Egypt, and Greece, the secrets of the Ageless Wisdom were taught and disseminated until, eventually, they permeated the whole of the ancient world.[8]

Because of the relatively low state of human consciousness throughout the early eons of human evolution, being focused almost exclusively on the physical plane, the door was open for the influx of planetary evil. The intrusion of evil on this scale, generated by adepts from the Black Lodge and their followers on "the left hand path," forced the White Brotherhood at Ibez and in Asia to withdraw into their temples and to make the mysteries less attainable so as to prevent abuses and distortions.

Given that every positive force has its negative counterpart, it follows that the White Lodge of the planetary Hierarchy would find its polar opposite with the masters of the Black Lodge. Out of this conflict between the White and Black Lodges, a powerful thoughtform was created, comprising the amassed illusions, glamours, and the illusion of outer appearances (maya) at that time. This produced what esotericism refers to as a gigantic "dweller on the threshold," which effectively imposed a barrier to knowledge passing from the subtle realms. The "dweller" we are told still exists and, according to the Tibetan, this ancient thoughtform must be shattered if humanity is to progress further along the path.[9]

The Planetary Centers

In the tradition of the Ageless Wisdom, the planet is seen as a living organism. Because it is a life form, and an extensive one at that, the earth possesses systems that correspond to those found in other forms of life. What many in the Orient have known for centuries (and we in the West are beginning to learn) is that alongside of our physical body there is a subtle body, known in the Ageless Wisdom as the etheric body. By analogy there is an etheric body to the planet as well, which surrounds and intermingles with the physical vehicle. It is also widely accepted in the East that within the etheric body there are a number of centers called chakra points. More about the chakras will be discussed in a later chapter. While it is generally accepted that there are seven major chakra points within the human body, five centers are given for the planet as a whole and three of these centers, corresponding to the head, heart, and throat centers in man, are inlets for divine energy.

The first of these centers is Shamballa, the vehicle for the will aspect and divine purpose, which is known as the conditioner of nations because this energy stimulates the creation and termination of nations, civilizations, root races, rounds, and so forth. Through the second center, known as the planetary heart center, flows the energy of the Hierarchy, which stimulates the ideals of any group or nation, and is therefore thought to reflect the soul of those entities. The last of the three planetary centers is humanity itself, which is understood to embody divine intelligence and, as a result, conditions the mental aspect. These three centers have a correspondence with the first, second, and third rays, respectively. Insofar as human history, seen esoterically, is patterned by these three fundamental energies, our discussion of *The Inner Side of History* must elaborate on their influence.

Of the energies that impact our planet, few are more mysterious than that of Shamballa. The Tibetan writes: "It [Shamballa] is a world of pure energy, of light and of directional force; it can be seen as streams and centres of force, all forming a pattern of consummate beauty, all potently invocative of the world of the soul and of the world of phenomena; it therefore constitutes in a very real sense the world of causes and of initiation."[10]

The phrase "constitutes in a very real sense the world of causes" is a provocative thought. Causes can mean different things to different people but what is of concern here is the role of Shamballa as a moving force that initiates activity. In as much as all forms move through cycles of involution and evolution, Shamballa would appear to cause an explosion of energy so as to drive a body into matter from which it precipitates other causes. At the end of the evolutionary cycle, Shamballa acts as a synthesizing force on an etherealized body before it passes into pralaya. This process would apply to any system, but we might think of it in relation to rounds, root races, civilizations, and nations. This initiatory impulse points to the fact that Shamballa travels along first-ray lines.

Another interesting aspect of Shamballa, contained in the Tibetan's statement, is that it is a world of pure light energy. This speaks to the potency of Shamballa as a great stream of directional force. At numerous places in his writings, the Tibetan refers to the important work of the Hierarchy in deflecting these potent energies so as to safeguard the planet. Whereas the esoteric perspective tells us that it is the destiny of humanity to absorb and be guided by the first-ray energy of Shamballa, such an occurrence remains in the relatively distant future. Conditioned by the fourth scheme, the fourth chain, the fourth globe, the fourth round, and having just moved out of the fourth root race, man and his environment are too material in nature to tolerate such a potent energy on a sustained basis. As humanity and the planet become more etherealized towards the end of this round, their forms will become less resistant to and more receptive to the first-ray Shamballa force.

Whereas Shamballa is often understood in relation to its destructive power, its true purpose is to liberate the life within the form. Thus, in a real sense, Shamballa shrouds the mysteries surrounding death. If we accept that death is the point of transition in the life of an entity, at whatever level, then the function of Shamballa as the great liberator and redeemer of life forms is clear. This was evident during the period of the First and Second World Wars when the death of millions of people (55 million in World War II alone) shattered the collective thoughtforms, glamours, and institutions in the lower three worlds. These happenings, noted the Tibetan, opened the door to a new type of energy which "should facilitate the appearance of the ideas embodying the needed recognitions, ...and their emergence into the realm of human thinking, ...with the formulation of new 'lanes or channels of impression' whereby the minds of men can become sensitive to hierarchical plans and to the purposes of Shamballa."[11]

The Destructive Forces in Nature

The destructive power of Shamballa is somewhat misleading. Essentially, Shamballa is a clarifying and intensifying energy that acts to generate a critical mass which can have destructive consequences. There are primarily two kinds of destructive force. The first type is characterized by a sudden burst of energy in which a force shatters a form, suddenly and decisively, thereby liberating the life or energy from that form.

The Tibetan writes: "The type of destruction here dealt with is never the result of desire; it is an effort of the spiritual will and is essentially an activity of the spiritual triad (linking atma, buddhi, manas on the higher planes of the constitution of man); it involves the carrying out of those measures which will hinder obstruction to God's will; it is the furthering of those conditions which will destroy those who are attempting to prevent divine purpose from materialising as the Plan."[12]

This passage leaves little doubt that human affairs, from an esoteric perspective, are part of a much greater plan that must, by divine law, be fulfilled. The divine plan takes into account not only the fourth round of the earth chain—a fleeting moment in cosmic history—but the relationship of planetary history to schematic, zodiacal, and logoic cycles. Occult law requires that evolution proceed in a timely fashion, subject to the vagaries of human free will. Whereas planetary conditions can temporarily slow the progress of evolution, they can never arrest the purpose or goal of the Plan. It is for this reason that the Shamballa force, modified or unmodified, in its varying potencies fulfills the purpose of the Plan by removing limiting conditions. These hindering conditions can be a culture, a civilization, a root race (or any of the lesser racial cycles), a major ideology or religion, a nation-state, or so on. Shamballa may work through many different agents, such as natural disasters, social revolutions, or an influx in the quanta of energy reaching the planet, forcing accelerated change.

The second form of destruction is inherent in the nature of matter itself. Technically speaking, a seed that begins to germinate, an embryo that has started its journey towards birth, or a planetary system that has begun to coalesce into form is already moving towards its rendezvous with death. It is only a question of time. From an esoteric perspective, death occurs when an entity's purpose or soul withdraws the thread of consciousness and the thread of life, allowing the form to quickly decay. This form of destruction also comes under the direction of Shamballa, but its impact is less obvious and far less potent. The death process involves not only the disappearance of the physical form, but also the astral and mental bodies. By the same token, there is an overlapping between the process of building and destruction. Root races, civilizations, and cultures decline and die while new ones emerge.[13] With respect to the seven rays, some come into manifestation while others pass out, as will be discussed further in a later chapter.

Shamballa and the History of Chaos

As noted above, there is a curious relationship between the impact of Shamballa and the record of natural catastrophes. As the agent of will, the purpose of this directed force has been to force the breakup or dissolution of forms so new life can grow and evolve. We are also told that Shamballa, being the energy of will, causes "certain radical and momentous changes in the consciousness of the race" which can lead to abrupt revolutions in consciousness through the imposition of a crisis.[14] Such crises are sometimes marked by convulsions of the earth resulting in shifts of land masses, ice ages, great floods and tidal waves, earthquakes, and shifts in the polar axis. Insofar as all energy is subject to the law of cycles, Shamballa impacts the planet in a rhythmic manner. However, Shamballa cycles tend to be infrequent. This energy will often be felt in some measure at the end of a major cycle, whether a kalpa (the length of a round) or a planetary ray cycle of two thousand years.

The important and interesting point about Shamballa is the degree of potency by which its influence is directed on to planetary affairs. According to D.K., the full weight of the Shamballa force has only been felt twice in the course of human history: the first crisis occurred at the time of man's individualization in the middle of the Lemurian age, and the other time was during the great struggle between the forces of light and darkness in Atlantis.[15] Thus, our understanding of the Shamballa influence results from a measured awareness of its potency. Given the power of this energy, and its ability to cause havoc on the physical plane, its impact is usually stepped down or deflected by the planetary Hierarchy in accordance with the divine plan.

We should bear in mind that physical plane catastrophes are always the final manifestation of disruptions on the inner realms of the astral and mental plane. As the Tibetan states: "it [the law of economy] works through the great world cataclysms, and we need to remember that it governs, not only the physical plane catastrophes (as we erroneously term them), but the corresponding cataclysms on the astral plane, and the lower levels of the mental plane."[16]

The extent to which natural disasters result from the intensified energies of Shamballa is a useful question, however great cataclysms on a global scale would seemingly have a more definite connection to this force. These events occur towards the end of a geological age, a round, and a root race. We know, for instance, that there were a series of catastrophes during the Paleozoic era. Near the close of the Ordovician age 440 million years ago, when the earth was populated with small vertebrate animals, some kind of disaster occurred. Another catastrophe visited the planet at the end of the Devonian age 370 million years ago, followed by a cataclysm at the end of the Permian age 245 million years ago, when most of all animal species were eliminated.[17]

Catastrophes continued during the following Mesozoic era. The Triassic age, 210 to 235 million years ago, saw the formation of new continents and the creation of what later expanded into the Atlantic Ocean. There was another extinction, about which we know little, at the end of the Cretaceous age 67 million years ago,[18] some say 65 million years ago. Scientists believe that this catastrophe was brought about by an asteroid. The impact of this missile caused dust to be thrown into the stratosphere, leading to a drastic cooling of the planet and bringing to an end the dinosaur population.[19] Whether all of these cataclysms were the result of a comet striking the earth, it is difficult to say. The real question revolves around the force or energy that causes a physical-plane event. The answer may have something to do with the mystery of fire, which is also related to the workings of Shamballa on the inner planes. There is no hard evidence for this assumption, but a curious passage from one of the Stanzas of Dzyan may contain a clue:

"The flames came. The fires with the sparks; The night fires and the day fires. They dried out the turbid dark waters. With their heat they quenched them. The Lhas of the high, and the Lhamayin of below, came. They slew the forms which were two- and four-faced."[20]

The Destruction of Lemuria

There was a further catastrophe during the Eocene age, thirty-seven million years ago, which brought to an end the second root race. This was followed by a massive catastrophe in which animal life almost became extinct.[21] According to one source, the cataclysm eliminated more than half of the original continent of Lemuria and left only a small continent at the center of the Pacific Ocean.[22]

What led to the first great crisis of humanity is difficult to say. The explanation for the breakup of Lemuria favored by students of esotericism was that it resulted from a decision made by the guiding brothers of the race to generate a catastrophe by precipitating a chain of events. No doubt this decision was forced upon them by circumstances which were not of their own choosing. The Tibetan writes of Lemuria:

"As the centuries slipped away and the Lemurian race submitted to the evil impulses of the animal nature, gradually the earliest type of venereal disease made its appearance; eventually the entire race was riddled with it and died out, nature taking its toll and exacting its inexorable price."[23]

The above passage points to one of the fundamental laws of history that whenever a people prevaricate too far, as did the Lemurians in relation to sexual excess, there is always a correcting influence which serves to guarantee future evolution. This is a clear illustration of the law of karma. For every cause there is an effect and this law holds true on all planes of existence. An understanding of karma can serve as a check against some of the more fanciful and nostalgic impressions that people have of the past. Wishar Cerve, in his book on Lemuria, maintains that the moral standard of the Lemurians was extremely high and, so far as anyone could tell, they lived like noble savages.[24] This idyllic image of a people who were one step beyond the animal stage seems unconvincing. More realistic is the view D.K. gives of the Lemurians as primitive people with a physical-plane consciousness. Without the moral and social inhibitions that come with a more sensitized consciousness, the Lemurians became the victims of their own physical urges, which contributed to their virtual extinction.

The Great War on the Astral Plane

The second great human crisis, we are told, happened during the Atlantean root race. There are two significant developments pertaining to this crisis. The first relates to what the Tibetan called "the great war between the forces of light and the forces of evil," which occurred, one supposes, during one of the last root races of the Atlantean period, probably in the period of the Turanians. D.K. writes that the Atlanteans boasted a civilization that was more advanced in many ways than our own. In addition to enjoying material comforts, they engaged in magical work and were able to command enormous powers. Then something went wrong. Power tends to corrupt and it seems as though the elites became drunk with their own power and greed, which led to excesses that provided an opening for the forces of darkness to take hold.[25] This brought on the "great war," which was fought out on the astral plane. The consequences of this epic battle, no doubt, led directly to the floods that submerged this once powerful civilization.

The flood is a universal myth and it is often presented as the story of corruption, destruction, and renewal. There can be little doubt that many of these deluge stories—the Biblical account of the flood in Genesis, for example—hark back to the destruction of Atlantis. We know that Atlantis did not succumb to a single flood but to a series of deluges. H.P.B. contends that the earliest of these floods occurred one million to 850,000 years ago, whereas the last great flood ended 750,000 years later.[26]

Granted, we are dealing with broad epochs, but to place an event within such enormous stretches of time raises questions as to the linkages of these cataclysms. Swimme and Berry note that there was a cosmic happening that resulted in a catastrophe during the Pleistocene age 730,000 years ago.[27] This was the last of the "earth-shaking events" that appear in their chronology, which leads one to suppose that it must have been the great deluge of which myth and legend speak. We can further observe that during this time the planet was in a cycle of ice ages, which would have had some bearing on the flooding.

The point remains, how does Shamballa fit into all of this? The answer is far from clear. We know that the "great war" during the Atlantean period was fought out on the astral plane, which was the plane of consciousness that was being developed at this time.

Furthermore, there appears to be a correlation between the consequences of unbridled astralism and a disruption to weather patterns. The Tibetan writes:

"Heat and cold, as we understand the term, in a most peculiar manner are the result of the interplay of the pairs of opposites, and an interesting line of occult study concerns itself with the effects of racial emotions on climatic conditions. We most truly make our climate in one significant sense. When desire has burnt itself out, planetary life comes to an end, as climatic conditions will negate form—life as we understand it."[28]

This pregnant passage from D.K. says much about our relationship to the environment. It also gives us a clue concerning the role of Shamballa in the "great war" of Atlantean times. We can imagine that the adepts and chohans residing at their secret temples were actively involved in this conflict and utilized the potent first-ray will energy of Shamballa in combating the forces of darkness. The cataclysmic waves of energy generated on the astral plane had a corresponding effect on the physical plane through the "clashing of the tides." As emotion is the symbolic representation of water, it naturally follows that flooding and deluges would follow.

Future Cataclysms

While the cataclysms marking the breakup of Atlantis appear to us to be in the distant past (and in one sense that is true), it would be erroneous to conclude that cycles of disaster on such a grand scale are over. D.K. has predicted that cataclysms of a global nature will occur over the next thousand years, during which continents will be shaken, lands raised and submerged, and material disaster will overtake much of the world. The date he gives for this catastrophe is during the fourth branch race of the sixth subrace, which will usher in the sixth root race.[29] There is a consistency in this prediction with previous events insofar, as we have seen, each root race has ended with a catastrophe of one sort or another. What the Tibetan means by the fourth branch race of the sixth subrace is unclear, but it is likely that the focal point for racial development at this time will be in the Pacific rim region, either in the Far East or the West Coast of the United States.

William Irwin Thompson has stated in his book, *Pacific Shift*, that human society has passed through four different cultural ecologies: Riverine, Mediterranean, Atlantic, and Pacific-Space. He states: "Now a new world-system is emerging around the shores of the Pacific, and as eastern mysticism meets western science, a wholly new Pythagoreanism is being born."[30] While Thompson ascribes many attributes to the coming Pacific cultural ecology, which appear to be projections of new-age clichés, he does have a point with respect to the nature of change. He rightly points out that catastrophe literally means a "turning over" or a composting of history. Whereas an apocalypse often happens within the collective consciousness of a people, who sense that they are at the end of an era and are confused about the future, the transition from one cultural ecology to the next may be subtle, unimaginable, and gradual.[31] Even when the earth is being rocked by cataclysms, the time frame for these upheavals is so long that, to use Thompson's words, "the discontinuity between the rate of change and the rate of adaptation becomes more dramatic."[32]

Seen from the broad perspective of the Hierarchy, a global catastrophe is merely a crisis of human consciousness, which is connected to the cyclical evolution of the Logos. Such is the case with respect to what D.K. calls "the Judgment Day." This little understood and highly misinterpreted event is seen esoterically as a period of strife on the mental plane, much in the same way as the conflict in Atlantean times was a conflict on the emotional plane, and will lead to the ultimate triumph of spirit over matter.[33] At that time, during the next round (the fifth round), three-fifths of humanity, so we are told, will undergo a shift in consciousness to the mental plane, whereas the other two-fifths, who do not make the grade, will pass into temporary pralaya before continuing their evolutionary development on another scheme.[34]

Shamballa and the Completion of Cycles

Out of all these cataclysms, a picture emerges of Shamballa as the cause behind the destruction of forms, which enables evolution to continue. By the same token, Shamballa energy is realized in measured degrees towards the end of one historical cycle and the beginning of the next cycle. Over time, as history in the form of a branch race, subrace, root race, or round spirals from one cycle to the next, the potency of Shamballa becomes stronger and stronger, meaning that humanity is better able to absorb this powerful energy of divine will.

While first-ray energy in its various potencies is an important factor in the termination of a cyclic period, it is not the whole story. The manifestation or obscuration of a scheme, round, root race, or zodiacal cycle, and so forth, is also brought about by the passing away of one ray impulse and the coming into prominence of another ray. This creates a temporary period of confusion and chaos insofar as the conflict between two competing energy cycles "disrupts the waters" of continuity. The Tibetan points out that when a ray passes out of manifestation, it is not completely abrogated. Rather, it simply withdraws beyond the ring-pass-not of its previous sphere of influence and becomes active elsewhere. The previous focal point of its attention then becomes less receptive to the waning ray influence and more magnetically attractive to the incoming ray.[35] A case in point is the present world situation where the sixth ray of devotion is giving way to the seventh ray of ceremonial order and organization.

Shamballa, on the other hand, performs two distinctive functions with respect to cyclical manifestation and obscuration. The first involves the elimination of old forms, including social institutions and even species of plant and animal life. Warfare, invasion, or some other calamity is usually to be seen at such times. The other development is a culmination and synthesis of the essential ideas, which results in the conceptual miniaturization of the past history of the terminating age or cycle. Out of these composted and synthesized ideas, the ground is prepared for the seeding of new ideas and perceptions.

Toynbee concludes that each degenerating civilization possesses common characteristics, such as an emphasis on militarism, division, and discord within the body politic, the increased estrangement between majority and minority groups, and a growing tendency towards standardization.[36] Spengler sees the old-age phase of a culture as a time of synthesis. He writes in relation to the merging of sciences in modern times:

"The separate sciences … are approaching one another with acceleration, converging towards a complete identity of results. The issue will be a fusion of the form-worlds, which will present on one hand a system of numbers, functional in nature and, reduced to a few ground-formulae, and on the other a small group of theories, denominators to those numerators, which in the end will be seen to be myths of the springtime under modern veils, reducible therefore—and at once of necessity reduced—to picturable and physiognomically significant characteristics."[37]

We know from Krummenacher's work that there is a correlation between periods of major disruption, such as was discussed earlier in relation to the great cataclysms, and the ebb and flow of the early rounds of the planetary manvantara. This is also the case with respect to the life cycle of civilizations. Astrologically speaking, the time it takes for the sun to travel through the zodiac is 25,000 years. Broken down into units of twelve, this means that the duration of the sun's passage through a particular sign is close to 2,100 years, which constitutes an astrological age. Over the past two thousand years, since the birth of Christ in 4 BCE, we have been living through the Piscean age. The previous two thousand years marked the Age of Aries, before that the Age of Taurus, and before that the Age of Gemini, and so forth. The fact that each astrological age goes through a cycle of youth, growth, maturity, and decay, as Spengler put it,[38] means that when history is experienced near the cusp of the next age, time speeds up, the old forms are destroyed, and the seeds are sown for the coming cycle.

Although the historical record in the distant past, as recognized by conventional interpretations, is somewhat spotty, there is clear evidence that each astrological age has witnessed a major transition. The first Near Eastern civilizations rose during the Age of Gemini, roughly 6000 to 4000 BCE. (Astrologer Alice O. Howell puts the time period for this age at 6500 to 3750 BCE.)[39] William Irwin Thompson believes that it was during this transition that culture and civilization in the West shifted from matriarchy to patriarchy, characterized by the movement of people from stable agricultural communities to a militaristic and nomadic way of life.[40] From the piecemeal accounts of this period, it appears that there was indeed a migration of people from isolated villages to more centralized communities. Issues of survival aside, this probably had something to do the military threat from warring bands of nomads and the desire for plunder. Militarism and the vast movement of peoples, as we shall see, is an effect of Shamballa energy.

Characteristically, there was an important religious transition away from the worship of the Neolithic Great Goddess, as existed in the Age of Cancer, towards the worship of the masculine sun god-king, as one sees in Sumer. What one finds at the end of each two-thousand-year planetary cycle is a hastening of time, which underscores migration, conquest, and a tendency towards giantism, whether in architecture, economic life, or population growth.

The transition from the Age of Gemini to the Age of Taurus (roughly 4000 to 2000 BCE) was marked by a time of troubles, which brought to an end established civilizations and laid the basis for the creation of new cultural patterns. Professor Toynbee wrote that the Old Kingdom in Egypt underwent three phases of disintegration: "...this apparently moribund society then departed unexpectedly and abruptly, at a moment when it was apparently completing its life course..."[41] From about 3900 BCE to 3500 BCE, historian William McNeill observes that in the lower Tigris and Euphrates valleys "a new style of human life had emerged, characterized by complexity, wealth, and general impressiveness that justify the epithet 'civilized.'"[42] The Sumerians introduced a written language. The growth of cities in Mesopotamia brought on by the migration of people to urban areas was also evident. The estimated population of the world at this time stood somewhere between five to ten million people.

It was during the Taurian age that the historical record caught up with human evolution. The calendar, the use of numbers, the development of wheeled vehicles, and the spread of agriculture all occurred during this period. Professor McNeill observes that a transition, covering a period of several hundred years to 1700 BCE, was characterized by the influx of barbarians from Eurasia, who conquered the peoples of Sumer and Egypt. These conquerors then absorbed the culture of the vanquished and adopted it as their own.[43]

Similarly, Mycenaean culture was spread throughout the Aegean world at this time by the Achaeans, an Indo-European people, who conquered the Pelasgian people of Greece around 2200 BCE. The Achaeans spoke an early form of Greek. They formed cities on the Greek mainland and established the city of Mycenae as the center of their culture. The warlike Mycenaeans remained a dominant civilization in the region until they were destroyed by the Dorians a little after 1200 BCE.

New myths and religious teachings also appeared during the transition from Taurus to Aries. The myth of Isis, Osiris, and Horus emerged in Egypt, along with a belief in the god Ra, who became the chief god in the Egyptian religious firmament during the fifth dynasty at about 2500 BCE. Ra reigned supreme throughout the remainder of the Egyptian dynasties. The goddess Ishtar also became a focal point of veneration at about the same time.

Curiously, the Tibetan specifically makes reference to the intervention of the first-ray energy of Shamballa at a time that appears to have been out of sync with the two-thousand-year planetary cycles. D.K. mentions that a consequence of the Shamballa influence may be a period of ruthlessness and cruelty, if the personality of the individual is not in line with soul impulse. He referred to an era of Jewish history, as recorded in the Old Testament, "when the first ray was passing through one of its rare cycles of activity" and many enemies of the Jews were put to the sword.[44] The period under question could have been anytime from the tenth century BCE, when Israel was ruled by King David and later King Solomon, to 586 BCE, when the Great Temple of Jerusalem was destroyed by the Babylonians. This was certainly a time when ruthlessness and cruelty reigned.

The whole subject of Shamballa cycles poses an enigma since so little is said about them in the Tibetan's writings. Part of the problem is that we can never be sure of the level at which this force is active. We know of two instances in pre-modern history (during Lemurian and Atlantean times) when Shamballa touched the physical plane. At other periods, the Shamballa force may have been felt on the astral or mental planes. A clue may be found in the type of consciousness that characterizes humanity when this potent force is active. Judging from the information given with respect to the Jews of the Old Testament period, Shamballa might well have made its presence felt on the lower mental plane since ruthlessness and cruelty result from a buildup of negative mental energy.

The Transition From the Roman Empire Into the Age of Pisces

Next to our own age, the transition from the Age of Aries to the Age of Pisces is the best documented from an historical standpoint. Here we can more closely see the dynamics of cultural breakup and synthesis that accompany such a transition. The causes of any cultural crisis are a matter of historical debate but, as mentioned before, the actual causes of events in history come ultimately from Shamballa on the inner planes and are modified and directed by the spiritual Hierarchy. Like all periods of cultural transition, the shift from the Age of Aries to the Age of Pisces (illustrated by the decline and fall of the Roman Empire) was a lengthy process.

One can always quibble over dates, but it is arguable that the Roman Republic began to wane as early as the second century BCE.[45] The Empire, dating from the rulership of the emperor Augustus, was certainly on the wane by the third century CE when Rome experienced twenty-two emperors in forty-nine years and a noticeable amount of civic corruption and social decay was evident. Dating also from the third century CE, the barbarian invasions began in earnest and continued through the extinction of the Roman Empire in the West in 476 CE. Over the next five centuries (until the tenth century) much of Europe was in a state of upheaval, as evidenced by the almost continuous warfare and further invasions by the Norsemen.

Many factors can be attributed to the demise of Rome, which have parallels to our own time. Some of these factors involve the residue of an ancient consciousness. The Tibetan writes: "There was a recurrence of pure Atlantean mischief and wickedness in the decadent days of the Roman Empire. Life became tainted by the miasma of unadulterated selfishness and the very springs of life itself became polluted. People only lived and breathed in order to be in possession of the utmost luxury and of a very plethora of things and of material goods. They were smothered by desire and plagued by the dream of never dying but living on and on, acquiring more and more of all that they desired."[46]

One historian writes that "for at least half a millennium the Greeks and the Romans lived convinced that their society was decadent."[47] It is true that as the Roman Empire entered into its final stages of decline, criticisms abounded as to the low standards of public and private life.

There were a number of other factors which contributed to the demise of Rome. Professor A.H.M. Jones writes that the root cause of the troubles was seen in the lack of discipline of the army and the ambitions of Roman politicians.[48] The third century CE was a time when political assassination was common, which mirrors less dramatically the political instability of our present era. There are other linkages too. The barbarian invasions can be compared to the influx of Third World peoples into Europe and America. Similarities to the modern world also include financial chaos resulting in inflation and debt; lack of social discipline leading to rising crime and political corruption; material excess and a growing separation between rich and poor; declining agricultural cultivation and frequent famine; ravaging epidemics, especially among the poor; migration from urban areas to the countryside; weakening loyalties, particularly in relation to civic responsibility and patriotism; and the rise of a new and powerful spirituality within a secular society.[49]

What brought all these conditions to a crisis point was the intensifying energy of Shamballa, filtered through the planetary Hierarchy. As has been said, Shamballa marks the end and beginning of a cycle whereby the crystallized forms are destroyed and the best of the old is synthesized with new ideas and emergent forms. The demise of slavery was an important step in this direction. As a social institution, slavery was pervasive in the ancient world and was considered as natural to "civilized living" as private property is to western people. Whereas, it could be argued that serfdom, which replaced slavery, was only a marginal improvement; from the standpoint of the planetary Hierarchy, it was probably seen as a major step forward for humanity.

Shamballa energy is also directed through the lives of great first-ray leaders, usually in the political field, whose strength of character and dedicated purpose influences events for generations to come. Two such figures are prominent in the Roman Empire during the late third and fourth centuries. One was Constantine, who as emperor legalized Christianity and thus provided a new institutional structure for the coming Piscean age. The other was Diocletian who, although conservative in temperament, took the radical step of separating the Empire into two parts. Whereas the western Empire underwent a transformation and quickly dissolved, the eastern Empire remained intact for centuries, albeit in a crystallized form.

One final consequence of the Shamballa force is the proliferation of religious and ideological thought, which condition the minds of humanity. The spread of Christianity throughout the Mediterranean world and Europe was the single most obvious development in this area. Of equal significance was the proliferation of mystery school cults, particularly Neoplatonism, which kept alive and perpetuated the teachings of the Ageless Wisdom. Interestingly enough, it was at the tension point of crossover from the Age of Aries to the Age of Pisces, marked by the final collapse of Rome in the fifth century AD, that alchemy appeared in the West.

Shamballa and the Currents of Modernization

The Tibetan tells us that a history of the trend towards fusion in the modern world would be a most illuminating study. We are told that this emergence of fusion, through the release of Shamballa energy, was initiated at the centennial conference of the planetary Hierarchy in 1425 CE, and its initial faint impulses were felt around 1575 CE. The first pronounced demonstration of this fusion, seemingly, began to appear in the late eighteenth and early nineteenth centuries, sparked by a tendency towards nation-building and the synthesis of smaller states into larger states.

In modern times, humanity began to experience the "direct line of spiritual, dynamic, electrical energy," characteristic of Shamballa, following the Great Council of Shamballa in 1825.[50] The Tibetan observes that one of the primary causes of the cataclysms of the twentieth century derived from the fact that humanity was considered capable of "receiving a touch from Shamballa" without stepping it down through the Hierarchy, which had hitherto been the case.[51] This energy penetrated into the three lower kingdoms and greatly stimulated the mental, emotional, and physical vehicles of humans, as well as transforming the many levels of the human environment.

The transformative impact of Shamballa in the modern world has been pervasive and, from the standpoint of the contemporary observer, self-evident. The Tibetan writes: "From it [Shamballa] the great political movements and the destiny of races and nations and their progress are determined, just as the religious movements, the cultural unfoldments and spiritual ideas are sent forth from the hierarchical center of Love and Light. Political and social ideologies and world religions, the Will of God and the Love of God, the Purpose of divinity and the plans whereby that purpose is brought into activity all focus through that centre of which we are each consciously a part of Humanity itself."[52]

Shamballa and the Industrial Revolution

Within the framework of esotericism, it could be argued that one of the major manifestations of the Shamballa touch was the Industrial Revolution. Colored by the fifth and seventh rays, the Industrial Revolution represented a tremendous unleashing of power. Voicing his outrage at the effects of factories and industry, Wordsworth wrote in 1814 about "...the force of those gigantic powers that, by the thinking mind, have been compelled to serve the will of feeble-bodied man."[53] What formed the basis for the Industrial Revolution was man's ability to tap new sources of energy. Historian David Landes writes: "The point is obvious: no such industrial world could come into being. It is precisely the availability of inanimate sources of power that has enabled man to transcend the limitations of biology and increase his productivity a hundred times over."[54] In essence, Landes says, the proliferation of factories and industries involved an interrelated succession of technological changes, including the substitution of mechanical devices for human skills, the uses of inanimate sources of power, and the extraction and use of raw materials.[55] Taken together, these changes marked a whole new relationship between humans and the mineral kingdom, which would have important exoteric as well as esoteric consequences.

These material advances in technology provoked and promoted complex economic, social, political, and cultural changes, known as industrialization, which has had a sustained ripple effect, first in parts of Western Europe and North America, then throughout the entire world.[56] Population growth and migration, urbanization, the restructuring of economic life, the demand for political reform, social movements, public health measures, and the rise of representative government are some of the by-products of the energies released by industrialization. Britain, the first nation to industrialize, also became the world's first urbanized society during the early nineteenth century. Between 1841 and 1901, the population of England and Wales more than doubled, growing from 15,914,148 to 32,527,843.[57] Other nations in Europe, and later the United States, followed a similar pattern of development.

Moreover, industrialization contributed to a more complex process, often designated as modernization, which can best be described as the total socialization of a society to the social patterns, norms, myths, symbols, values, images, and artifacts of technology. Whereas the great cathedrals of the twelfth century symbolized the "age of faith," the nineteenth and twentieth centuries have produced more functional symbols, such as skyscrapers and malls, which speak to the values of materialism. The new culture of modernization rests on a world view that was uncompromisingly materialistic, so much so that the Hierarchy was compelled to send into the world groups of creative artists to counteract the dehumanizing impact of industrialization and the new ideology of positivism. These musicians and artists formed what came to be called the "Romantic movement," however, the intent of many artists was less to stir the emotions and more to elevate and etherealize society.

The driving force behind the onslaught of technology was the voracious desire on the part of people to bring about changes in the environment. Shamballa aroused mass desire in people which served to push humanity forward; to eliminate all obstructions; and to bring to the surface conflicts, hatreds, and the desire for liberation. As a consequence, the past two centuries have witnessed an acceleration in the rate of change, which has transformed whole societies in a matter of decades. In terms of consciousness, rapid change leads to "isolation in the present" whereby a society loses its ability to digest and assimilate its past. From the 1880s in England, writes historian Jose Harris, there was a distinct decline in a popular sense of continuity with past history. He remarks upon what he calls the emergence of a new race or nation with an unhistorical mentality through forcible mass migration to the cities and where, even in the villages, folk memory was dying.[58] What was true of the late nineteenth century is even more applicable today as the stimulating noise of the present has all but drowned out our collective memory.

Shamballa and Modern Warfare

The destructive consequences arising from the intensifying energy of Shamballa has been most keenly felt in the realm of modern warfare. Of course, the history of the past, as the Tibetan observes, is largely one of aggression, national pride, racial hatreds, materialism, and selfishness.[59] Even so, it has been only within the past two centuries that warfare has gone beyond the battlefield to disrupt whole societies and, in the case of the World Wars, to break up entire civilizations. British military historian, John Keegan, wrote that while the Industrial Revolution generated enormous wealth, energy, and population increase, it also created armies, "the largest and potentially most destructive instruments of war the world had ever seen."[60]

Basically, militarism was a direct outgrowth of industrialization. Keegan writes: "The technology that built the railways also furnished the weapons with which the soldiers of the new mass armies would inflict mass casualties on each other. The development of such weapons was not deliberate, at least not at the outset; later it may have been."[61] It is ironic that whereas the century from 1815 to 1914 was largely viewed as a period of unprecedented peace (particularly when compared to former times) no prior century had ever witnessed such efforts among the major powers to prepare for war. In fact, between 1815 and 1939 there were thirty-one significant wars throughout the world.[62] Since the Second World War, there have been innumerable conflicts on the international stage.

From the perspective of those on the inner planes, according to the Ageless Wisdom, the destruction of impediments to the free flow of spiritual energy brought about by the touch of Shamballa energy raised to the surface conflicts of opposing forces, which then became sealed on the physical plane.[63] Late nineteenth-century Europe was a hotbed of racial, national, class, ethnic, and gender conflicts, which culminated in the disasters of the twentieth century. Paul Thompson, writing about the England of the Edwardian era, observed that the period from 1909 to 1914 was a time of "social and political crisis of exceptional severity: a crisis which might finally be settled through civil violence rather than through parliamentary politics."[64]

These tensions and internal conflicts, characteristic of most of Europe, spilled over into the First World War. While people in the World

Wars (1914-1945) were the unhappy victims of spiritual circumstance, from the angle of our historic past, humanity was the engineer of its own fate.[65]

Estimates of the number of people who died in the World Wars vary, but averaged together they totaled many millions. Death, through the destructive processes of war is esoterically understood to be under the directive and cyclical intervention of the Planetary Logos, working through the council chamber at Shamballa.

The wholesale destruction of forms in the World Wars produced phenomenal changes upon the astral body of the planet, which had the effect of shattering the large accumulation of world glamour, much to the benefit of humanity.[66] Furthermore, the World Wars, particularly the Second World War, provided unparalleled destruction by fire, as seen by the massive bombing of London, Dresden, Tokyo, and other places. This onslaught of fire, generated by Shamballa, touched not only the physical plane but reconfigured the atomic structure of matter which, so it appears, had a regenerative effect on the first kingdom in nature, the mineral kingdom. The most dramatic example of this, of course, was the release of atomic weapons over Japan. One might note that, according to an ancient prophesy, Atlantis would be destroyed by water, which it was, while the Aryan race would be terminated by fire.[67]

Humanity's victory over the forces of darkness in 1945 opened the door to a new phase of evolutionary history, as seen by the elder brothers of the planet. In the final months of battle, the United States used its secret weapon, the atom bomb, on Japan which brought the war to a quick and decisive end. The fission of the atom brought about an unprecedented release of energy on the planet. Whereas the dropping of the bomb is usually debated in terms of ethics and its military advisability, the implications of this act are much greater.

The explosion of the bomb, from the esoteric perspective, led to a pouring-in of the energy of the third aspect of the first ray, which split the thoughtform of materialism on the mental plane as well as created great destruction on the physical plane.[68] The Tibetan observes that the dropping of the bomb "will have future potent, and at present unsuspected results."[69] He offers an enticing but obscure prediction that atomic energy, harnessed to human need, will induce increased amounts of radioactivity that will provide the path to prosperity and riches.[70]

An important offshoot of war is mass migration. The dispersal and uprooting of people across national boundaries and to other parts of the world began in the nineteenth century as a response to the quickening pace of Shamballa, and has accelerated in the present century. One source estimates that between 1850 and 1880 about three million people emigrated from England and Scotland to North America, Australia, and New Zealand.[71] This, of course, was only the tip of the iceberg. The drift of people to the colonies from Great Britain, the movement of families and even entire communities from Europe to America, and the forced evacuation and repatriation of millions of people due to war and social upheaval indicate a breaking down on a world-wide scale of physical boundaries and the institution of a process of blending and amalgamation such as the world has never seen before.[72] The Tibetan notes that the influence of the planet Uranus is also responsible for the steady movement of peoples from East to West, from Asia to Europe in earlier times, and from Europe to the western hemisphere in more modern times.[73]

Great Leaders as Implementors of Shamballa Energy

Since the year 1400, there has been constant appearances of lesser avatars who have responded to minor crises, to national dilemmas, and religious necessity, according to the esoteric doctrine. These men and women had the effect of changing the current of men's thoughts for the good. Essentially, there are four kinds of avatar. Racial avatars are great personages whose appearance is evoked by the genius and destiny of a race. Such an avatar was Abraham Lincoln who spearheaded the efforts to preserve the Union and emancipate the slaves. Another was Giuseppe Mazzini, who provided a spiritual vision of nationalism and tried to unite Italy in accordance with that vision.

The second group of avatars are the teaching avatars who have left their imprint on some field of human living. Martin Luther, Christopher Columbus, Florence Nightingale, William Shakespeare (Francis Bacon), and Leonardo da Vinci would fit into this category.

The third and fourth groups of avatars have a much greater impact on human affairs and their appearance is much less frequent. The ray avatars come forth when a ray is entering into manifestation and embody the quality and force of that particular ray. Thus, with the emerging of the sixth ray at the start of the Piscean age, the presence of a powerful sixth-ray avatar began to be felt. The same would have been true for earlier planetary cycles.

Finally, the transmitting avatars come into the world as manifestations of divinity who appear at great cyclic moments of revelation. Prime examples include the Buddha and the Christ, who have cast their imprint across whole epochs of human history and, essentially, are world redeemers.[74]

First-Ray Leaders

Not surprisingly, the Shamballa force often works through the lives of military leaders. The names of such first-ray military men are obvious: Napoleon, Alexander the Great, George Washington, Mussolini, Hitler, Field Marshal Montgomery, General George Patton, and Marshal Zhukov. The Duke of Wellington, a first-ray personality, told his sister shortly after the famous Battle of Waterloo that during the battle "the finger of God was on me all day—nothing else could have saved me."[75] In a classic insight as to how a synthetic first-ray mind thinks, Wellington recounted to his friend Stanhope:

"There is a curious thing that one feels sometimes. When you are considering a subject, suddenly a whole train of reasoning comes before you like a flash of light. You see it all...yet it takes you perhaps two hours to put on paper all that has occurred to your mind in an instant. Every part of the subject, the bearings of all its parts upon each other, and all the consequences are there before you."[76]

Whereas Wellington is remembered in the annals of history as a great military strategist, as was his antagonist Napoleon, Hitler possessed the will but not the responsibility of a great first-ray leader. Whereas Hitler had total control over military decision-making, he was often curiously irrational in executing military plans and would wildly blame others for the failures of his own policies. Near the end of the war, he ranted that if the war were lost, it would be because the German people had not been worthy of him, but it was he who had not been worthy of the German people and his progressive physical decline was an outward sign of his inner collapse.[77]

In addition to military leaders, the Shamballa force is sometimes used by strong first-ray personalities for the good of humanity. Florence Nightingale, the founder of modern nursing, was an initiate responding to the Shamballa force. Not only did she courageously administer to the sick and wounded during the Crimean War, she also set down the rules and procedures for the nursing profession and championed the cause of more humane treatment for the common soldier. Alexander II, the Czar of Russia, was no doubt an initiate of high standing. In fact his life paralleled that of Abraham Lincoln in several important ways. The Czar was a contemporary of Lincoln, he freed the serfs from virtual slavery a year before Lincoln issued his Emancipation Proclamation, and he, like Lincoln, died as the result of assassination. The day before Alexander II was killed, he presented a declaration for the institution of limited representative government.[78]

Powerful individuals who incarnate as representatives of Shamballa have stood behind the great declarations and pronouncements of history such as the Magna Charta, the Declaration of Independence, and the Atlantic Charter.[79] Names include such as Thomas Jefferson, Benjamin Franklin, and Franklin D. Roosevelt. The Tibetan observes that over the past two thousand years there have been four symbolic happenings which characterize the theme of liberation, as opposed to liberty, which is an important aspect of Shamballa. The first was the life of Christ himself which, as revealed in the gospels, was devoted to service, sacrifice, and liberation.

The second great symbolic happening was the signing of the Magna Charta, of which historian Doris Mary Stenton writes: "No single state document has had more influence on the course of history and its influence is even now not spent. It is the forerunner of the great constructive statutes of the thirteenth century, the first detailed review of necessary reforms. It points the way to the new age, to a kingship controlled not by fear of revolt but by acceptance of the restraint of law."[80]

The third historic act of liberation was the freeing of the slaves, first with the abolition of the slave trade by Britain in 1807, followed by the emancipation of the slaves and the serfs by Lincoln and Alexander II, respectively in America and Russia during the 1860s. It is interesting to note that the three nations on which D.K. and the Hierarchy pinned their hopes to guide humanity in the future were the ones who sounded this important note of liberation.

Finally, the birth of the United Nations stands as a symbolic act of human liberation. Although the U.N. is a half-century old, it has become a fixture for peace, human rights, and global unity in the world today. The Tibetan claims that this has been due in no small part to the efforts of the Hierarchy who overshadowed the creation of the U.N. in San Francisco in 1945 and who continue to channel the impersonal energies of the Christ into the General Assembly as they did from its inception.[81] Robert Muller, for many years the assistant Secretary-General of the United Nations, has this to say: "Things are beginning progressively to fall into a pattern which we had not seen before, because it couldn't be seen, and which foreshadows the world predicted two thousand years ago by someone who had the most luminous insights into the mysteries of life on this planet and in the universe, namely, Christ."[82]

The Fusing Power of Shamballa in National Affairs

It is often through the efforts of strong first-ray leaders that the synthesizing power of Shamballa is utilized, however imperfectly. The impetus towards federation and fusion has also been helped by the inflow of seventh-ray energy, which began to be felt in the late seventeenth century. The fusing power of the seventh ray, which blends spirit and matter, has served as a correcting force to the separative and sectarian tendencies of the sixth ray. Both these rays are active in the department of politics and are charged with the task of producing synthesis.[83]

The Tibetan has made reference to certain great and outstanding personalities who were peculiarly sensitive to the will-to-power and the will-to-change, and who altered the character of their national life and emphasized wider human values. He referred to the men who initiated the French Revolution in the name of divinely inspired ideals; Napoleon, who spread these ideals across Europe; Mussolini, the regenerator of his people; Hitler, who gave a distressed nation hope and employment; Lenin, the idealist, who masterminded the Russian Revolution; also Stalin and Franco, who brought order out of chaos. All these men were expressions of Shamballa force even though they had little or no understanding of the potency or source of this energy.[84] It should be stressed that the energy of Shamballa, as with all spiritual energies, is impersonal and neutral. Because Shamballa flows along first-ray lines, it may be accessible to certain charismatic first-ray types whose will is highly polarized. The motive, whether for good or for evil, behind the use of this energy rests with the personality of the individuals themselves.

A dominant theme in modern history, particularly in the nineteenth century, has been self-determination for ethnic groups seeking to become nation-states. The Tibetan specifically mentions the movements for Italian and German unification that occurred during the mid-nineteenth century. Confederation and unity in Italy was brought about largely through the efforts of three men: Giuseppe Mazzini, who used second- and sixth-ray energy in developing the ideals of nationhood, expressed through his militantly nationalistic organization Young Italy, which laid the basis for Italian unification; Count Camillo Cavour, a pragmatic third-ray type, who shrewdly utilized diplomacy to create a centralized state; and Giuseppe Garibaldi, who, as a first-ray leader, brought about the unity of northern and southern Italy through military conquest.

Of these three men, Mazzini is particularly noteworthy since he had strong esoteric interests, having been a member of the Carbonari, an occult society, and who significantly influenced H.P.B. in the development of some of her ideas. One source suggests that one of the great adepts was probably Mazzini.[85] Whereas Mazzini, Cavour, and Garibaldi made significant contributions to the work of bringing about Italian unity, they operated differently and appear to have had little time for one another. Commenting on Garibaldi in 1867, Mazzini writes: "He looks at the matter more from a materialistic than from a moral point of view, thinking more of the body of Italy than of its real soul."[86]

Perceptions aside, Garibaldi was an active Freemason and adhered to its principles. The Italian Grand Orient was founded in 1859, and in 1864 the Congress of Italian Freemasonry elected Garibaldi as its Grand Master. Attractive to members of the expanding middle class, Freemasonry became an important mechanism for the spread of liberal and republican ideas and for pulling together the various movements, ranging from Mazzini's Young Italy to Garibaldi's redshirts, in the cause of national unity.[87]

Germany, on the other hand, was largely the creation of Otto von Bismarck, a strong first-ray type with a genius for strategy and diplomacy. Bismarck holds a place in esoteric history as a black avatar, "coming forth correspondingly from the realm of cosmic evil, and responsible for the focus of materialism upon the planet today."[88] In a famous speech delivered in October 1862, Bismarck observed that "the great questions of the day will not be settled by revolutions and majority votes...but by blood and iron."[89] His various political and diplomatic maneuverings were all designed to hold back the tide of constitutionalism and to maintain the power of Prussia. A reading of German history in light of the Ageless Wisdom may well show that the decline of this great nation into barbarism began with Bismarck. Curiously, the modern German state, born out of two successful wars with Austria and France, rejected the liberal and democratic trends of Western Europe and embraced the oligarchic rule of a small group of Prussian aristocrats, of which Bismarck was one.

Clearly, we see in the nationalistic movements of the nineteenth century the emergence of the battle between good and evil, which culminated in the Second World War. The vision of nationalism held by the Italian patriot, Mazzini, was characteristically different from that of Bismarck. Mazzini believed that nationalism would encompass the ideals of the French Revolution, namely the brotherhood of man, whereas Bismarck held that nationalism should support traditional hierarchies and the interests of the nation-state. It was the fate of Europe that Bismarck's vision of nationalism would win out over Mazzini's. This provided the environment for the two World Wars in the twentieth century, which nearly destroyed civilization in the West.

In *Destiny of the Nations*, the Tibetan mentions an interesting experiment involving Mustafa Kemal, known as Ataturk, the Turkish dictator who came to power in the 1920s and modernized Turkey after the collapse of the Ottoman Empire in the First World War. Ataturk broke with the Ottoman and Muslim traditions of the past and set about a policy of forced westernization. Ataturk also introduced parliamentary democracy, although political control remained in his hands.[90] "The testimony of future historical records," the Tibetan wrote, "will indicate how wisely, sanely, and disinterestedly he used this type of force [Shamballa] to attain first ray objectives."[91] Thus history in the light of Shamballa can be read in terms of great destruction and cruelty, as in the case of war and forced unification, or in the light of great synthetic ideas which guide humanity further along the path of evolution.

Hitler, Nazism, and the Perversion of Shamballa Energy

It is common to think about Nazism and the era of the Third Reich in Germany as an aberration when the world temporarily plunged into a nightmare of evil. The consequences of Nazi rule speak for themselves but what is less understood is the nature of this evil from an occult perspective. The question, "What is evil?" begs many answers. Throughout his books, the Tibetan gives us several responses to this question. On a very practical level, evil is the result of wrong motive, the tendency to selfishness and separativeness, and the dominance of glamour, illusion, and maya within an individual or a society. As he remarked to one of his disciples, evil is an illusion, "for it is the use that is made of motive and opportunity by personality separativeness and selfishness which constitutes evil."[92]

There is a deeper dimension to evil, however. The Tibetan refers to evil as "the residue of that which earlier was." By this he means that a thing or condition becomes evil once it outlives its purpose and becomes a hindrance to further progress. Hitler's plan to enslave the masses of Eastern Europe, and what he termed "non-Aryan peoples," was a throwback to ancient practices and, if successful, would constitute a major reversal in the evolutionary development of not only the Europeans, but humanity as a whole.

Beyond the aggregate of evil desires, wicked intentions, reactionary tendencies, and selfish purposes, there exists cosmic evil, which flows into the planet from regions beyond the solar system and requires the combined efforts of the planetary Hierarchy and Shamballa to protect humanity from this awesome power of destructiveness. At times, due to the unusually depressed and negative state of humanity, the shield protecting the planet is compromised, thus provoking a severe crisis. In an address delivered in May of 1944, the Tibetan observed that whereas the present conflict resulted from human conditions, it had existed for ages between the Great White Lodge of Masters and the

Lodge of Black Adepts. This struggle, which was fought out during Atlantean times, had returned and, he insisted, it must now be brought to a finish.[93]

The extent of the evils perpetrated by Hitler and the Nazis could not have been so extensive or catastrophic had it not been rooted in the misuse of Shamballic energy, rendered active through association with the Black Lodge on the inner planes. Two factors contributed to this development. In the first place, there was a proliferation of occult thought in the early decades of the twentieth century from a variety of sources, including the Order of the New Templars, the Hermetic Order of the Golden Dawn, the Rosicrucians, the Anthroposophists, and the Theosophists, which became part of the intellectual climate of the times. Secondly, the unprecedented destruction and suffering, brought about by the First World War, left Europe in a state of disarray and hopelessness. In no other country was this more true than in Germany, arguably the strongest nation and military power in the world in 1914, who within four years was defeated militarily, psychologically, and emotionally. To add insult to injury, Germany was forced by the victorious allies to accept full responsibility for the war and to pay the victors staggering reparations.

Within this milieu Hitler emerged. He was born in a small village in Austria in 1889 and, from all accounts, was an undistinguished student in school. After his mother died, he went to live in Vienna where he survived as a struggling artist, living from hand to mouth. It was during this time that Hitler became exposed to the virulent anti-semitism and racial ideas that would later be the cornerstone of his ideology. In 1913, when the war broke out, he went to Munich and joined the German army. After the war he, like many of his comrades, returned to a defeated Germany, angry, bewildered, and looking for revenge. In January 1918, an adventurer who took the name, Baron von Sebottendorf, formed a small group called the Thule Gesselschaft, dedicated to the blending of right-wing politics, extreme nationalism, Teutonic paganism, and occultism. Through his involvement with the Thule Society, Hitler met two individuals who would be his mentors in black magic, Deitrich Eckart and Karl Haushofer. There is some question as to when and how Hitler received his instruction in the black arts but, according to Joscelyn Godwin, he had ample opportunity to learn Thulean mythology in 1924 while imprisoned for leading an abortive uprising against the Bavarian State in 1923.[94] Haushofer, and most likely Hitler, were members of an even more secret society, the Vril Society, which was concerned with researching Atlantean civilization, the origins of the Aryan race, and the secrets of Shamballa, among other things.[95]

Hitler's dramatic rise to power and his military achievements indicate that he was in possession of unusual and extraordinary powers. Throughout his many speeches and writings, Hitler constantly doted on the theme of will and will-power. Germany, he believed, would achieve her destiny through marshaling the collective will of the German people. His obsessive projection of the will (the Tibetan observes that Hitler was enslaved by evil through obsession) underscored his uncanny success. Against all odds he was able to acquire political power and then, in opposition to the advice of his generals, marched his troops into the Rhineland, into Austria and, thanks to British and French appeasement, into Czechoslovakia. Even after the start of the Second World War, Hitler was able to gain the advantage through bold and decisive initiatives. While Hitler clearly demonstrated the power of self-directed will and active intelligence (his mental powers were developed to a high degree), he was virtually devoid of all capacity for love and compassion. Thus, the results of his actions proved to be brutal and destructive. Without the balancing energy of love, the will to conquer and dominate eventually turns in on itself, as it did in the case of Nazi Germany.

It is also apparent that Hitler mastered the occult use of sound. The intonation of certain words or sounds for bringing forth certain desired effects is a closely guarded occult secret and can only be shared with trusted disciples and initiates. Insofar as black magic is the negative reverse aspect of white magic, it stands to reason that Hitler was privy to these secrets and used them to further his diabolical designs. On the other hand, Winston Churchill exemplified the right use of speech, which he used to inspire and mobilize the British nation in its gallant defense against the German air force during the Battle of Britain. To a lesser extent, Franklin Roosevelt, in his speeches and "fireside chats," inspired confidence in the American people.

It was widely believed that Hitler had a mesmerizing effect on the masses who heard his speeches at meetings, Nazi Party rallies, and by means of radio. It was also true that music, chanting, and the spoken word were constantly and deliberately directed at the German people in both public and informal settings. The perversion of sound, writes the Tibetan, builds around the soul a beguiling and deceptive energy that imprisons the senses and is a source of glamour.[96] This is what Hitler effectively did with respect to the folk soul of Germany. Not only that, but Hitler fed upon the psychic energy of his audience and used this energy to stimulate his mental faculties. It was not unusual for Hitler to depart from a three-hour speech refreshed and alert. Interestingly enough, after the German army suffered its first major defeat at the Battle of Stalingrad in Russia at the end of 1942, Hitler ceased to appear in public and give speeches (he made only four public speeches from then up to the end of the war), the lack of which seemed to undermine his power.[97] Moreover, his intuitive insights gave way to doubt and deficient judgment, leading to catastrophic decisions that hastened Germany's ultimate defeat.

Much could be said about the occult interests of individual Nazi leaders and the movement as a whole (an occult bureau was part of the state apparatus up to the end of the war), as well as some of the crazy ideological theories that were seriously entertained by members of the Nazi elite. Within the upper echelons of the movement was a small group of black magicians who appeared to function as a black masonic lodge. It was through this group of seven, who personified in themselves specific aspects of the material forces such as fear, cruelty, aggression, and so on, that the Black Lodge directed its potent forces towards Germany. The Tibetan identified these seven black masons as Hitler, Heinrich Himmler (head of the feared SS), Joachim von Ribbentrop (the German foreign secretary), Joseph Goebbels (the propaganda minister), Hermann Goering (the air force chief), Rudolf Hess (head of the Party Chancery), and Julius Streicher (the fanatical anti-Jewish journalist).[98] The Shamballa force can only be used in group formation. That is why, according to D.K., Hitler, in reversing the reaction to Shamballa in the direction of evil, had to gather around him a group of like-minded personalities. Essentially, Hitler and the black masons expressed the invocative arc of Shamballa, which leads to the intensification of the material aspect.[99]

World Ideologies

In recent times, the Shamballa force has touched humankind by providing the impetus behind great bodies of thought in the modern world. Owing to the vastly increased power of the human mind to respond to ideas within the last two centuries, collective bodies of thought, characterized by the major world ideologies, have captured our imagination.[100] One English clergyman wrote in the mid-nineteenth century that "the mind of the masses is awakening from the slumber of the ages and they are beginning to occupy a more prominent and conspicuous position in the social and political affairs of the modern world."[101] The prevalence of ideologies, which has been replacing orthodox religion as the controlling factor over our minds, is an important unit of measurement in determining the shift in consciousness of humanity from the astral to the mental plane.

Of the major ideologies, democracy is the oldest. Its origins go back to the ancient Athenians but, in the context of modern European history, the idea that all men should be subject to the law, known as constitutionalism, gained strength only as recently as the seventeenth century. The English Civil War created a diverse political climate and led to the emergence of radical groups, such as the Levelers, who believed that each man was a free and independent citizen who had the right to vote and participate in public life. The belief in representative government, the idea of progress, and the expansion of political freedom was fostered by the eighteenth-century philosophers and underscored the democratic revolutions in America and France, as well as liberalism, which has become a dominant political ideology of the last two centuries. From a spiritual perspective, democracy constitutes a response to universality, which is divine love in action: hence it represents love-wisdom in the political sphere.[102]

The Tibetan writes that true democracy does not exist in the world today, since people living in so-called democratic countries are as much at the mercy of politicians, large corporations, and financial interests as people living under dictatorships.[103] The danger of modern democracy is that it depends upon the whims of the majority of people at any time, which can easily be manipulated by those in power. Moreover, democracy is the most complete expression of individualism and often works against group cohesion and community well being.

In classical terms, democracy, if it was not to be perverted into oligarchy, needed to be tempered by a hierarchy of just and selfless leaders as well as an electorate of wise and informed minds. D.K. adds that, at some future date when political life is dominated by enlightened people, when people are told the truth and can judge freely, and when the democratic process is extended to all spheres of society, then we shall see a much better world.[104]

Communism is primarily a third-ray ideology and, as a system of social organization, can be traced to the most ancient of human societies but, as an ideology, it began in the nineteenth century through the writings of Karl Marx. A man of great intellect with a first-ray personality and a fourth-ray mind, Marx sought to explain economic life in terms of class conflict and thus turn society on its head by championing the cause of the poor and oppressed. It was a powerful message and communism became the first modern ideology to mobilize the masses to action. On the eve of the First World War, many thought that socialism would sweep across Europe. It did, as we know, become rooted in Russia, and later China. Moreover, communism has influenced social thought even in those countries which saw it as an anathema. The Tibetan writes that communism as a system is of human origin and, despite its distortions, it is divine in its essential nature and essence.[105]

One must carefully distinguish between communism as a political and economic ideology and communism as a spiritual expression of group life. The former, as has been clearly seen, leads inevitably to social engineering, the extension of social rights at the expense of political and human rights and, ultimately, in the words of Leszek Kolakowski, becomes "merely a repertoire of slogans serving to organize various interests..."[106] On the other hand, as a spiritual alternative to capitalism, which in the words of Marx eventually turns everything into a commodity, communism can be a blueprint for community building through the emphasis on group sharing and cohesion at whatever level.

The most recent of the major ideologies, and the most obscure, is fascism. Unlike democracy and communism, which embody clear principles and theories, fascism is generally a mishmash of ideas incorporating extreme forms of nationalism, authoritarianism, militarism, and the will to conquer. Hitler saw the state as being subordinate to the nation, which he endowed with racial, mythical, and ethnic overtones. In essence, fascism is synonymous with opportunism, which can be adjusted to the whim of the leader or dictator. For Hitler, the Nazi state could be at once socialist or capitalist depending upon the audience or the needs of the moment. While in theory it is often communal, in practice fascism is highly individualistic and discriminatory towards certain groups. The ability of fascism to captivate the idealism of the young and to destroy old political and social forms is reflected in its first-ray nature. From a broader perspective, fascism was the bastard son of the old European order which was mortally wounded in the First World War.

Public Opinion and Awakening Consciousness

Population growth and the emergence of public opinion in the inter-war years gave rise to what the Spanish philosopher Jose Ortega y Gasset called "the revolt of the masses." Ortega would have agreed with the Tibetan's comments about mass psychology "with its unreasoning quality and its blind activity, and massed reaction to solar plexus impressions," however, in this the Tibetan saw the vague intellectual reactions by the mass of humanity as a groping towards mental plane activity.[107] While the Tibetan was aware of the dangers created by the impact that powerful minds have over the masses, he nevertheless knew that a telepathic interplay was emerging which would signify an important leap in consciousness. The Tibetan writes:

"Everywhere and in every country men are being taught in their earliest years that they are not only individuals, not only members of a state, empire or nation, and not only people with an individual future, but that they are intended to be exponents of certain great group ideologies—Democratic, Totalitarian, or Communistic. These ideologies are, in the last analysis, materializing dreams or visions. For these, modern youth is taught that he must work and strive and, if necessary, fight. It is therefore surely apparent that behind all the surface turmoil and chaos so devastatingly present today in the consciousness of humanity, and behind all the fear and apprehension, the hate and separativeness, human beings are beginning to blend in themselves three states of consciousness—that of the individual, of the citizen, and of the idealist. The power to achieve this, and to be all these states simultaneously, is now reaching down into those levels of human life which we call 'submerged classes.'"[108]

Whereas the second half of the twentieth century has witnessed a virtual elimination of fascism, a decline in the appeal of communism, and a rejuvenation of democracy, it has also seen the increased potency of Shamballa. The full impact of the Shamballa force was felt in 1975, which was a benchmark in the transition from old to new ways of thinking, the emergence of new technologies, and the coming into manifestation of new souls who, it is believed, will help to usher in the externalization of esoteric truth in the twenty-first century. The nature of the changes resulting from the "direct hit" from Shamballa at the turn of the century will also be made more clear in the portentous years ahead.

Chapter 5 —
Masters, Sages, and Adepts: Their Influence on Human Affairs

Most religions acknowledge the existence of great beings, whether they are called gods, heroes, angels, saints, avatars, mahatmas, rishis, masters, or arhats, who stand between humanity and the divine and often intercede on humanity's behalf. Throughout antiquity, legends, lore, myths, and sagas spoke of supermen who could accomplish astonishing feats beyond the realm of human capability. The lineage of the Ageless Wisdom refers to these great beings as the planetary Hierarchy, constituting the elder brothers of humanity, who are those souls whose consciousness has transcended the fourth human kingdom and now includes the fifth, or spiritual kingdom. Though not bound by the world of form, certain of the Masters of the Wisdom are those who have chosen to remain on the planet to help guide their fellow people.[1] In relation to humanity, the Hierarchy works through precipitation, by which an idea or archetype is projected from the higher planes of consciousness into human consciousness through the agency of some initiate, disciple, or group of disciples. The organization of the Hierarchy, in its various departments, stands as an inner spiritual government, or model system, towards which humanity, first unconsciously, then consciously, aspires to emulate. In relation to the human kingdom, the Hierarchy functions in a number of ways:[2]

- They stand as a wall between humanity and excessive evil
- They work ceaselessly to awaken consciousness in all forms of life
- They direct world affairs as far as humanity will permit
- They direct and control the unfolding cultural cycles and the resulting forms of civilizations

- They receive and transmit forces and energies from Shamballa
- They help bring to closure cycles, ideologies, organizations, and civilizations
- They prepare people for initiation

The rooting of the Hierarchy on the planet was, as with all things, an evolutionary process. This event occurred at the moment humanity was touched with the spark of consciousness and required rudimentary guidance.

Contacts With the Hierarchy

Efforts to prove the existence of the Hierarchy by means of physical evidence is fruitless since such proofs must of necessity involve a media of limitation, which is both too narrow and too material. By analogy, it would be much like trying to view the workings of an atom with the naked eye. On the inner planes, there is a correspondence between ordinary human consciousness, as expressed through the personality vehicles of concrete mind, emotion, and physical form, and monadic consciousness, as conveyed through the spiritual triad of atma, buddhi, and manas. It is at this higher level where the Hierarchy is to be found. Of course, an adept, higher initiate, or Master of the Wisdom (the terms have specific meaning but can be used in a general sense) can manipulate and function with energy on the lower three planes and, so, appear to possess physical form. However, the physical form is an illusion. What one perceives as a physical body is merely a projection of a master's energy body, which is then materialized by a person's consciousness into form. In essence, so it is said, a master is a lighted being.

There is considerable evidence that points to the active participation in human affairs by members of the Hierarchy. One such master, who is referred to in many memoirs, letters, and monographs of the late eighteenth century as the Comte de St. Germain, is said to have been an incarnation of the Master Rakoczi. He appeared in courts all over Europe, hobnobbed with some of the greatest figures of the age, was accomplished in all the known arts and sciences, and yet was considered to be a mysterious figure. His activities are recorded in one source where it is observed that:

"Comte de St. Germain disappeared from the stage of French mysticism as suddenly and as inexplicably as he had appeared. Nothing is known with positive certainty after that disappearance. It is claimed by transcendentalists that he retired into the secret order which had sent him into the world for a particular and peculiar purpose. Having accomplished this mission, he vanished."[3]

Another mysterious figure seems to have made a propitious appearance during the debate over the signing of the Declaration of Independence. On the eve of the American Revolution, delegates from the various colonies gathered together at the old State House in Philadelphia on July 4, 1776. They weighed the pros and cons of proclaiming the liberty of the American colonies, knowing that if the enterprise failed they would all be hung for treason. As the discussion reached a critical stage, suddenly a man seated in the balcony leaped to his feet and gave a strong, eloquent, and impassioned speech on the virtues of liberty and the impelling need to sign the Declaration, as it was in accordance with divine will and America's destiny. As soon as this unknown speaker fell exhausted into his seat, the delegates rushed to sign the Declaration of Independence. In the meantime, the speaker, later referred to as "the Professor," vanished without notice.[4] The timing and circumstances surrounding this important event point to intervention by the Hierarchy, although one can only speculate on this matter.

Alice Bailey records the experience of meeting her master for the first time on June 30, 1895. She was fifteen years old at the time and was alone at home when in came a tall man dressed in European clothes with a turban on his head. His visit was brief. He told her that there was some work that the Hierarchy had planned for her in the future and that, depending on how she handled herself and the decisions she made, she "would travel all over the world and visit many countries, 'doing your Master's work all the time.'" These words proved to be prophetic.[5]

H.P.B. had a similar experience while visiting the Great Exhibition in London in 1851. Accompanying one of the Indian delegations was one of the masters who directed her to meet him in Hyde Park.[6] In her own account of the matter, published two years before her death, H.P.B. notes that her master informed her that he required her cooperation for a piece of work that he was about to undertake and, to prepare herself for this task, she would have to spend three years in Tibet. Shortly thereafter, H.P.B. departed for India.[7]

One finds in *The Initiate*, a trilogy of books by Cyril Scott, the story of a man under the pseudonym Justin Moreward Haig who lived like an ordinary person in London prior to the First World War, but whose abilities and insights clearly indicate that he was a master or some great adept. Of this man, whose identity he was directed not to reveal, Scott remarks:

"I have before me the absorbing task of writing my impressions concerning a man who has reached a degree of human evolution so greatly in advance of his fellow-creatures that one might regard him almost as a living refutation of the old catch-phrase: 'Nobody is perfect in the whole world.'"[8]

There is much circumstantial evidence of unusual brief appearances by unassuming people that is suggestive of a visitation by a "brother on the inner planes." A recent newspaper account of a story related how an Austrian Jewish couple, in an attempt to flee their country just prior to the Second World War, were stopped at the border and were denied permission to continue on to Italy. At that moment, so the story goes, a mysterious man made his appearance and presented them with two tickets for Zurich, instructing the couple to take the next train to Switzerland where they would find refuge. This all turned out to be true.[9] Stories of this nature are legion.

Origins of the Hierarchy on Earth

The early history of the Hierarchy's involvement in planetary affairs mirrors that of Shamballa. We are told that the White Brotherhood made its headquarters at Shamballa on the etheric plane, where its activities were directed and plans developed for the momentous task of assisting and elevating fledgling humanity. These activities persisted for a long period of time until the first subrace of the Atlantean root race, the age of the Rmoahals, seventeen million years ago, when it was decided to have a dense physical plane headquarters and an organization. The incarnating group of adepts and chohans formed the original Shamballa fraternity at the Temple of Ibez.

These adepts were faced with a difficult problem of dealing with humanity, whose polarization was very unstable, due to their having an overactive emotional body and very little mentality. The Tibetan writes that in those times, adepts, working under instruction from Shamballa, used certain physical-plane methods to stimulate the brains of selected people, employing the laws of energy to activate their centers. These methods no doubt involved regulating the flow of energy through the etheric centers, or chakra points, which would not have seemed terribly out of place given that people during the third root race could see into the etheric. The objective of all this work was to bring about a realization of the kingdom of God within the individual.[10]

A major change in the relationship of the Hierarchy to humanity occurred sometime during the fourth root race of the Atlantean period, when the door by which animal men passed into the human kingdom became closed. This momentous event, so we are told, was occasioned by certain members of the Hierarchy being called to work elsewhere in the solar system which, by necessity, opened the door for a number of highly evolved souls to take their place in the ashrams of the masters. The pressure of these rearrangements forced a decision to separate the human and animal kingdoms.[11]

At the same time, members of the human family who were willing to undergo the intense rigors of discipleship training were allowed into the fifth kingdom of the Hierarchy.[12] It was at this point that the duality between spirit and matter began to appear in human consciousness. We must remember that people in earlier root races lived in a trance-like state, conscious of forms and desires, with only a fleeting awareness of vague higher impulses. The demarcation between the visible world of form and the subtle realms of spirit led to the first faint signs of discrimination among humans. With this came flickerings of moral sensibilities which resulted, over time, in the ability to distinguish between advantageous and disadvantageous stimuli. The Hierarchy was able to take advantage of these efforts at rudimentary thinking so as to train people to make judgments and to have an understanding of cause and effect relationships.[13] On the other hand, these groping efforts at thought, combined with a much more powerful astral nature, left people open to suggestibility from many quarters. This provided an avenue for the entrance of planetary evil and resulted in the "great war" between the white brotherhood and the forces of darkness, which led to the destruction of Atlantis.

The Structure of the Planetary Hierarchy

As noted earlier, most religious traditions recognize and account for the existence of unseen but identifiable entities that act as intermediaries between heaven and earth. Medieval art is full of paintings depicting the Christ surrounded by a host of adoring saints and angels. This impression of the Hierarchy is tinged with a strong flavor of devotion and idealism. Among the ancient Greeks, Socrates declared that there are orders of life which dwell along the shores of the air as people dwell along the shores of the sea. The indigenous peoples of the earth have been known to commune freely with unseen spirits, which are invoked through ritual and ceremonial practices.

In the West there emerged, during the Middle Ages, the idea of a "great chain of being" which, derived from Platonic thought, provided a connecting link from the smallest, most inanimate object to God, the all-powerful creator. Alexander Pope, in his *Essay on Man*, writes, "Vast chain of being! which from God began; natures ethereal, human, angel, man, beast, bird, fish, insect, what no eye can see, no glass can reach; from infinite to thee; from thee to nothing."[14] Within this cosmic superstructure, there are devic and angelic hierarchies which, along with humanity, function within the grand scheme of evolution in accordance with the divine plan. Historian Christopher Hill, writing of seventeenth-century Britain, observes that men and women of that time lived in a world of magic, inhabited by God and the Devil, in which witches, fairies, and angels intervened on a daily basis.[15]

The Tibetan eloquently defines the Hierarchy as "a great salvaging corps of dedicated, liberated units of life, working in group formation with all forms and lives in all kingdoms and with all souls particularly."[16] The key concept in this passage is "liberated units of life" insofar as the masters, as a group, are disciples who have, in consciousness, transcended the threefold world of physical, emotional, and concrete mental forms and, therefore, live without personality attachments in the realm of lighted substance. In the process of undergoing evolution from the fourth kingdom of humanity to the fifth kingdom of souls, the disciple (defined as one who works consciously with energies and forces for the good of humanity and the divine plan) begins to transmute the atomic matter in his body to a more etherialized substance. The completion of this transmutation allows a master, if his service so directs, to move in and out of the form world at will. Stories abound of persons and situations that seem to appear and disappear without cause or notice. In times of crisis, particularly, the veil separating the empirical and unseen worlds momentarily dissolves, resulting in an event often termed magical or mysterious.

Each kingdom in nature is a hierarchy within a hierarchy defined by levels of consciousness and etherialized matter. Mystics who claimed to have penetrated into the kingdom of souls have told us little about the constitutional structure of this kingdom. Occultists have been more explicit. The Tibetan, in his book, *Initiation Human and Solar,* provides a diagram of the relationship between solar and planetary hierarchies, adapted in Table 6.

From a literal standpoint, this diagram appears like the flowchart of any large business corporation with departments, department heads, and a clear chain of command. From another perspective, it exemplifies a flow of energy that is governed by number. Insofar as the Ageless Wisdom is defined and organized by numerical sequences, we can detect reoccurring and corresponding patterns of the numbers, which link the cosmos from the macrocosm to the microcosm into a beautiful, logical, and ordered whole.[17]

All levels of form and consciousness are consistently organized by means of the archetypal numbers: one, three, and seven. The number one represents unity, as exemplified by the Logos, solar and planetary. The three represents the tripartite godhead consisting of will, love-wisdom, and active intelligence. The seven, comprising the divine trinity and the quaternary of form, as demonstrated by the seven rays, rounds out the structure of both the planetary and solar hierarchies. Within this structure lies one of the clues to the structure of Masonry.

The Office of the Manu: The Will Aspect

Within the planetary Hierarchy, the first department, representing the will aspect, is guided by that great being, the Manu. Students of esotericism generally agree that the Vaivasvata Manu has been the driving force behind the fifth root race and it has been he and his successors who have guided the affairs of humanity since the root race began over sixty thousand years ago. The Tibetan notes that the Manu dwells in the Himalayas at Shigatse, where he presides in etheric form over an ashram of advanced initiates and disciples.

Table 6. Solar and Planetary Hierarchies

The Solar Logos

Solar Trinity or Logoi

I	Father	Will
II	Son	Love-Wisdom
III	Holy Spirit	Active Intelligence

The Seven Rays

Three Rays of Aspect • Four Rays of Attribute

I. Will or Power	II. Love-Wisdom	III. Active Intelligence
		4. Harmony or Beauty
		5. Concrete Knowledge
		6. Devotion/Idealism
		7. Ceremonial Magic

The Planetary Hierarchy

Sanat Kumara, the Lord of the World
The Three Kumaras (Buddhas of Activity)

Reflections of the three major and four minor rays

The Three Department Heads

I. Will Aspect	II. Love-Wisdom Aspect	III. Intelligence Aspect
A. The Manu	B. The Bodhisattva (Christ, the World Teacher)	C. The Mahachohan (Lord of Civilization)
Master Jupiter	A European Master	The Venetian Master
Master M.	Master K. H.	4. Master Serapis
		5. Master Hilarion
	Master D. K.	6. Master Jesus
		7. Master R.

Four grades of initiates
Various grades of disciples
People on the Probationary Path
Average humanity of all degrees

In directing the affairs of the present root race as it has evolved in India, Europe, and America, the Manu is concerned largely with government and planetary politics. While not directly intervening in world affairs, he influences the founding, stabilizing, and dissolving of racial types and forms. Clearly, there is much overlapping. Whereas, for example, the fifth root race continues in the West, a remnant of the fourth root race continues in Asia, particularly among the Chinese and Japanese peoples and their neighbors. At the same time the fifth root race, under the guidance of the Manu, is in the process of dissolving while the Manu is simultaneously involved in helping to prepare for the sixth root race.[18]

The Department of Love-Wisdom: The Christ

The second department of the Hierarchy is under the direction of the World Teacher, known as the Christ or Lord Maitreya, who has presided over the spiritual destinies of people since about 600 BCE. By whatever name he is called in the many world religions, the work of the Christ has been to develop an understanding of man's inner godlike nature and his link with the guides and teachers on the inner planes, including the Logos himself.[19] Concerned primarily with the formation and directing of great spiritual ideas, as contained in the dominant world religions, his efforts have been directed towards propagating esoteric truths, which are often veiled teachings found in the world's sacred religious writings. To this end, he appeared in Palestine two millennia ago.

While seeking to uphold the teachings of Judaism, the Christ saw the need to release it from the grip of ethnic exclusivity and spread it across the world. It is interesting to note, and this is a point that Houston Smith made in one of his lectures, that both Hinduism and Judaism were tribal religions which, consequently, were inward-looking and maintained an exclusive hold over the mysteries and practices of these traditions. However, the teachings contained in these religions were too important to remain the property of any one group. Therefore, it was necessary for the Buddha and the Christ, respectively, to appear and essentially, with some modifications and shifts in emphasis, provide a context for these teachings to spread across the world. This was effectively accomplished through the rise of Buddhism and Christianity.[20] The dynamic radiatory influence of the Christ, characteristic of the second ray, was also behind the spread of Islam in the sixth century CE.

The Lord of Civilization: The Mahachohan

The third department of the planetary Hierarchy is under the direction of the Mahachohan. We are told that of the three department heads, he has held his position the longest, over a period of several root races, and ascended to this office when the Hierarchy was founded on the planet during Lemurian times. The present Mahachohan assumed office in the Atlantean period and is the sum total of the intelligence aspect.[21] We are further told that the Master R., during the course of this century, is now taking over this office, releasing the Mahachohan for greater work. Similar to the Manu, who oversees the evolution of root races, the Mahachohan is concerned with the rise, perpetuation, and disintegration of civilizations. It was under his department, for example, that the plans were laid for the rise of Western Civilization, including institutional development, intellectual life, cultural flourishings, scientific and technological change, progress in communications, money and business affairs, and educational development.

The Nature of Ashramic Work

Under each of these three departments the masters and their various ashrams are said to work. According to the Tibetan, there are sixty-three masters (7*9) who are concerned with the evolution of the human family. Of this number, forty-nine work exoterically, meaning that they are actively involved in human affairs, and fourteen work esoterically and are concerned with subjective matters.[22] Those masters who work exoterically have vast responsibilities for political, social, or national development. The Master Morya (M.), along with his many disciples, seeks to guide the political destinies of mankind and is connected with many organizations of an esoteric nature. The Master Koot Hoomi (K.H.), reported to be the next world teacher, works along second-ray lines and is concerned with energizing and vitalizing great philosophies and philanthropic organizations. The spread of democracy as a means for expanding human rights and bringing greater numbers of people into the political sphere is, no doubt, part of this work. Other masters have more specific responsibilities. The Master Jesus works to guide the evolution of the Christian churches, and, indirectly, the course of Islam. The Master Rakoczi (R.) has a particular interest in ritual, and therefore overshadows the work of Freemasonry and the ritualized activities of various religious groups. There are, as well, Master Hilarion who stimulates the subjective development of scientific enterprise; a master who resides in Great Britain and is responsible for labor movements on a global basis; and a Master P., who encourages the evolution of mental sciences, including psychology.[23]

It is important to see the masters not so much as individuals (which technically they are not), but rather as lineages of consciousness. One of the conditions for achieving the fifth initiation (that of a master) is the expansion of awareness over many lifetimes. To be totally conscious of the past, covering a multitude of lives, is to stand in consciousness beyond time and space, and thus comprehend a greater portion of the divine plan, which encapsulates human destiny. Some of these lineages are given to us. The Master R. is said to have lived as the philosopher, Roger Bacon, in the thirteenth century, in which he promoted the study of optics and mathematics, as well as taking an interest in the magical properties of precious gems. He, moreover, fostered the study of Islamic texts with the hope that Moslem thought and culture might become more integrated into Christianity.[24] Next, he incarnated as Francis Bacon in sixteenth-century England. Bacon's enormous contribution to scientific thought, literature, and political life is well documented. Less so are his veiled occult writings. Whether the works of Shakespeare were actually written by Bacon is a matter of endless debate. As Jean Overton Fuller remarks, the point is not that one or the other is the true bard but that they both stand together as the greatest minds of the age.[25] Later, as the Comte de St. Germain, the Master R. worked to promote Jacobian and Masonic ideas.[26]

The Master Jesus appears and reappears throughout Biblical history. Students of esotericism generally believe that he first emerged as Joshua, the Son of Nun, then as Jeshua during the time of Ezra in the sixth century BCE, then as the prophet Joshua, prior to being a vehicle for the use of Christ consciousness. In both a literal and metaphorical sense, Jesus claimed to represent the lineage of the Jewish prophets and to fulfill the law of Israel. Later, as Apollonius of Tyana, he took the fifth initiation and became a Master of the Wisdom.[27]

As with all things, the ashrams of the masters, also known as the Trans-Himalayan Lodge, have their counterparts in human affairs. It is through Freemasonry that the work of externalizing the ashram of the masters (or in Masonic terminology, the Grand Lodge on High) is most clearly effected. Using the symbolism of the craft trades, the focus of various lodges through ritual and esoteric practices is to ground the work of the Hierarchy so as to create a link between the subjective inner lodge and its objective manifestation on the physical plane. The process of building the inner temple is a group process, but it is also a transformative process of spiritual growth, or as one source puts it, "In Freemasonry we are taught that the first preparation for initiation is in our hearts."[28] Over time, much of the impetus that kept alive the inner life of Freemasonry has abated so that the repetition of the forms has replaced the subjective experience of deeper mysteries. This is why recent efforts to rejuvenate and re-spiritualize Masonry through the lodges of Ancient Universal Mysteries is of such importance. The keynote of this work, in keeping with the aims of the Hierarchy, is to train disciples to be conscious, working servants of humanity.

The Hierarchy as Custodians of the Plan

To the Hierarchy is given the task of being the custodians of the divine plan. The Plan, which has been called "the blueprint of the divine purpose," can be interpreted as the perfected goal of cosmic, planetary, and human evolution that is brought by the Hierarchy to humanity, bit by bit, in the form of ideas, which in time become ideals to be desired and fought for.[29] This work, so we are led to believe, occupies much of the master's time, particularly in its relation to the human kingdom. The process of externalizing the Plan, which is the goal of human history, falls into a number of stages. Bringing the Plan into form first originates in what esoteric sources refer to as the Council Chamber of Shamballa where it is registered by the senior members of the Hierarchy who work to formulate the purpose of the Plan in terms of possibility, its immediate need, appropriateness to the moment, the availability of disciples to do the work, and the energies to implement a portion of the Plan. The process then enters the phase of programming wherein it is taken up by a particular ashram and is reduced to the stages of human impression and direction, assuming that all hindrances in bringing about mental contact can be overcome. The Plan is then patterned in the minds of disciples, who are involved in its implementation, and among receptive minds within the body of humanity, including the intelligentsia. Both of these groups, consciously and unconsciously, work to bring the pattern to mass-consciousness. Finally, the idea contained in the pattern of the Plan is precipitated into the minds of ordinary people.[30]

Efforts by Individual Adepts and Masters to Teach Humanity

The extensive, difficult, and often futile process of stepping down energy requires long-term vision on the part of the Hierarchy. For many centuries, since Atlantean times, the Hierarchy directed its efforts to educating and training individual disciples in mystery schools or small religious communities to carry on the work through unobtrusive activities, far removed from the affairs of ordinary life. On the other hand, the work of the masters and their disciples often had a profound social impact. According to one source, the masters guided vast migrations of people into India and the plains of Turkestan, into China and across the land bridge into North America, and into Egypt and Mesopotamia. This took place roughly between 8000 and 5500 BCE.[31]

Between 5500 and 3000 BCE, the masters began to establish hidden sanctuaries where they could pass along their teachings to a small group of disciples and students. It was at this time, during the Neolithic period in Europe and prior to the rise of the first Mesopotamean civilization, the Sumerian civilization, that men began to dominate one another through warfare and the desire to possess greater amounts of territory. There was also a rise in ethnic consciousness and commercial activity, as evidenced by the invention of writing and the use of money. While the masters continued to play an unseen role, they did, in some cases, hold positions of significant power and influence. Great heroes of the ancient Near East such as Menes in Egypt, Sargon the Great of Akkad, and Brihadratha in India, were both kings and priests and had a direct association with the masters, or were masters themselves. Add to this list Hammurabi, Ikshvaku, and Moses, all notable law-givers of their people. The Manu, who inaugurated the civilization of India, was, of course, a Master of the Wisdom himself.[32]

The period falling between the decline of the Greek city-states in the fourth century BCE and the flowering of Roman civilization in the first few centuries of the Christian era saw the rise of many mystery schools and great teachers who were, if not adepts themselves, disciples of high rank. It was during this Hellenistic age that centers for esoteric teaching emerged. One such center was the city of Alexandria in Egypt, which was founded in about 330 BCE by Alexander the Great. The city housed one of the most important libraries in the ancient world, containing a wealth of rare and original documents dealing with esoteric lore. The expansion and beautification of Alexandria was taken on by the Ptolemaic monarchs of Egypt, the first and foremost of whom was Ptolemy Soter. He had been a general in the armies of Alexander and was a man possessed of many gifts. Whereas he is said to have remained on good terms with the state religion of Egypt, Ptolemy Soter was probably an initiate in one of the Egyptian mystery schools. However, the extent of his esoteric knowledge and connections remains unclear.[33]

Hermes and Hermetic Thought

There can be little doubt as to the esoteric nature of the Hermetic literature which, as some have suggested, appeared during the first two centuries of the Christian era. According to Manly P. Hall, using the writer of mysticism, Thomas Taylor, as his source, there may have been two persons by the name of Hermes: the first living in antediluvian times and the second living shortly after the beginning of the Christian era. Hall draws upon another source, one of the fathers of the Western Church, Albertus Magnus, who claims that Hermes was buried in the Valley of Hebron, where his tomb was raided by the armies of Alexander the Great.[34]

Whenever Hermes lived and whatever he did cannot obscure the fact that he was one of the pillars of western occultism whose influence has been timeless. H.P.B. refers to "a wondrous Being called the Initiator" who descended from a high region during the third root race and who, one supposes, played a vital role in the mental awakening of humanity. From this Initiator, whom H.P.B. says must remain nameless, there has emerged in subsequent ages the great sages and hierophants, of whom Hermes was one.[35]

Within the scope of mythology, Hermes holds a place as the god of stones. According to the Greeks, when Hermes killed Argos, he was tried by the gods and was acquitted, in the process of which stones were tossed at his feet. Thus, he was enveloped in a heap of stones and was transformed into the spirit of the stones.[36] Occultly understood, this myth points to the possibility that Hermes released the secrets of the mineral kingdom.

The Cult of Orpheus

Orpheus was another of the great sages who followed in this tradition. According to one source, Orpheus appears to have lived in Thrace during the post-Homeric period—probably the seventh or eighth century BCE—and was a reformer within the cult of Dionysius. Orpheus sought to bring a more ascetic and speculative dimension to this cult that was other-worldly on one hand but was also rigorously intellectual. He probably influenced the religious thinking of Pythagoras. These teachings, conveyed in literary canon in the form of hymns, became the focal point of a cult which spread across Greece and southern Italy during the centuries preceding the birth of Christ. There is some question as to whether the Orphic religion dates from the time of Orpheus, or developed later, during the sixth century.[37] From Orphism emerged a cosmology derived from the Ageless Wisdom, which included among its initiates Plutarch and, some claim, Saul of Tarsus.[38]

The Teachings of Pythagoras

Pythagoras lived during the "golden age" of Greece during the fifth century BCE. In his *Life of Pythagoras*, Iamblichus, an early proponent of Neoplatonism, writes that Pythagoras studied with Egyptian priests for a number of years before going to Babylon where he was initiated by Zoroaster. He stayed there for seven years and learned the wisdom of the Magi.[39] He also studied with the famous Greek philosophers of his day, Pherekydes, Anaximander, and Thales.[40] Pythagoras's brand of esotericism emphasized sacred geometry and number theory, which sought to give numerical proofs and insights to the science of the soul. Specifically, Pythagoras developed a system of pure mathematics, which means that numbers are entities in themselves. This is supported by several facts: 1) numbers are independent of the observer and have a life of their own, 2) they have precise identities and have a universal meaning, 3) they have no history or location and exist in a world where there is no motion or change, and finally, 4) numbers are visible only in the mind and do not have a tangible reality.[41] Seemingly, there is a correspondence between the reality of the soul and the existence of numbers.

Within the lineage of the Ageless Wisdom, there are references to the Master K.H. as the reincarnation of Pythagoras. Legend holds that Pythagoras descended from the lineage of men with "primitive miraculous powers" who came from the Hyperboreans during an earlier root race. Hermotimus of Klazomenai is one of these great beings who is thought to be one of Pythagoras's earlier incarnations.[42]

Plato and Neoplatonism

The mark of a master lies not only in the purity and magnitude of his life, together with the quality of his teaching, but also in the impact that his teaching has over subsequent centuries. If Pythagoras was the greatest scholar of the pre-Christian world, a close second would be Plato. Plato, an avatar of love according to the Tibetan, was a great synthesizer who had a vision of the whole and sought to put forward ideas that would express this vision.[43] Among other things, Plato developed the idea that visible and intangible forms are transitory copies of divine archetypes, which is a reference to the constitution of man. Plato's *Republic* is a veiled description of government as practiced by the planetary Hierarchy and was intended to be a model for the conduct of political affairs of humanity.

After his death, Plato's ideas were perpetuated by a number of adepts, including Plotinus, Porphyry, and Iamblichus, the founder of the Syrian branch of Neoplatonism—all of whom lived in the second century CE. Neoplatonism derived from the ideas of Plato and coalesced into certain esoteric schools, which saw the world as manifestations of ideals expressed through love, truth, and wisdom.[44] Neoplatonism provided one of the pillars that underscored the foundation of the Ageless Wisdom as it has evolved over the past two thousand years.

The Esoteric Context of Christianity

If teaching, as revealed through the thoughts of Plato, Aristotle, and Socrates, has been one of the means for lifting the consciousness of humanity, the other way has been through the evocation of mass desire and the reorientation of humanity towards a fuller life expression. Whereas the former is a more mental approach and is given to the select few, the latter appeals more to the emotions and is disseminated to the masses. This task of transmission and sacrifice is reserved for a great avatar such as the Buddha or the Christ.[45]

The work of the Christ did not occur in a vacuum, but was supported by esotericists in the mystery schools. Esoteric students generally believe that the presence of the masters and their disciples has been pervasive throughout human history, dating from the ancient world to modern times. In particular, H.P.B. observes that Christian and Hebrew scholars understand little of the enormous impact that esotericists, with their knowledge of the Cabala and other mysteries, have had in disseminating occult wisdom. She writes:

"How much less is definitely known of the Oriental, or universal Kabala! Its adepts are few, but these heirs elect of the sages who first discovered 'the starry truths which shone on the great Shemaia of the Chaldean lore' have solved the 'absolute' and are now resting from their grand labor...Travelers have met these adepts on the shores of the sacred Ganges, brushed against them in the silent ruins of Thebes, and in the mysterious deserted chambers of Luxor. Within the walls upon whose blue and golden vaults the weird signs attract attention, but whose secret meaning is never penetrated by the idle gazers, they have been seen but seldom recognized. Historical memoirs have recorded their presence in the brilliantly illuminated salons of the European aristocracy. They have been encountered again on the arid and desolate plains of the Great Sahara, as in the caves of Elephanta. They may be found everywhere, but make themselves known only to those who have devoted their lives to unselfish study, and are not likely to turn back."[46]

These adepts, initiates, and disciples traveled individually or settled into small communities where the mysteries were guarded or given out to receptive seekers. Some state that the Master Jesus was trained and educated among the Essenes, an idiosyncratic sect, who followed rigorous ethical principles and lived according to ascetic principles.[47] Rudolf Steiner notes that the Essenes were an exclusive sect who existed in Palestine at the time of Christ and numbered about four thousand. Their goal was to train aspirants through severe discipline to experience the life of the soul and to overcome the machinations of their lower nature.[48]

Closely akin to the Essenes were the Therapeutae, who were considered to be an offshoot of pre-Christian Hellenistic Judaism. They resided in Egypt and in the vicinity of the Dead Sea.[49] The primary source for our understanding of the Therapeutae comes from the philosopher Philo Judaeus, who portrayed them as a community of men and women who lived simple non-ascetic lives in pursuit of health and wisdom. Little is known of their initiatory rites and ceremonies except that they congregated together every seven weeks for a solemn festival. Music was an important part of their rituals. Quite possibly, the story of the deliverance of Israel from bondage in Egypt to freedom played a part in their rites and their mythology.[50] In the words of Steiner, the Essene and Therapeutae communities provided a natural transition from the mystery schools to Christianity.[51]

Insofar as the Essenes and the Therapeutae provide a bridge from the mysteries to Christ, the Gnostics reversed the process and offered a mystical environment for the development of Christianity. Gnostic sects arose during the first century CE among unorthodox Jews, Greek philosophers, and Persian mystics. Godwin writes that the Gnostics held that the world was a place of sorrow and corruption mistakenly brought into existence by a low-grade demiurge (lesser god) within the celestial hierarchy. Christ was viewed as a being of extreme historical importance insofar as he taught about the true God, who existed beyond the realm of appearances. As the true son of God, Christ was sent to lead humanity home to their eternal source, which was both an external fact and an immanent reality.[52]

According to Steiner, the Gnostics were saturated with the mysteries of the Ageless Wisdom and sought to understand the life of Christ from that perspective. It was the Gnostics who differentiated between the personality of Jesus and his divinity, which was Christ in Jesus.[53] Whereas the spark of Christ's divinity existed within the nature of man himself, it was human destiny to, in the words of the gospels, "perform the same works as I do myself...and even greater works."[54] As Steiner says, "A mystic of this kind does not seek a perfect God; he seeks to experience the divine life. He seeks to be made Divine himself, not to gain an external relation to the Godhead."[55] Through the tradition of Gnosticism, perpetuated by disciples on the inner path, the voice of Christian mysticism was kept alive through the centuries of oppressive domination by the Christian Church.

Hierarchy in the Modern World

While, as we have seen, the masters have been an active force in human affairs throughout human history, the plans and approaches taken by the Hierarchy have been adjusted to compensate for changes in human consciousness. Modern history, esoterically speaking, could be said to have begun around 1400 CE, when the Hierarchy was confronted with the problem of extreme separateness and intense distinctiveness of thought within human civilizations which, if left unchecked, could have dire consequences. The Middle Ages with its emphasis on faith, parochialism, and extremes of passion was, in the words of H.P.B., "a period of intellectual darkness, which degraded the nations of the Occident, and lowered the European of those days almost to the level of a Papuan savage."[56]

After watching this trend for another century, esoteric sources tell us that the elder brothers of the race called a conclave of all departments to articulate plans. Their object was to determine what steps could be taken to bring about synthesis and integration in the realm of thought, which would reflect the purpose of the divine life. Three tasks confronted the masters and their disciples: first, to review the divine plan and refresh their minds as to the vision; second, to note the energies available for a major new initiative; and third, to form chelas and initiates into groups which could be used for work in the centuries ahead.[57]

Hierarchical Experiments in Group Formation

Since the Hierarchy can in no way infringe on human free will, the approach by the masters to human affairs can best be seen in terms of experiments aimed at expanding men's consciousness. Unlike humanity, the Hierarchy always sees the long view of history and their plans are carefully laid so as to take account of conditions, expectations, and requirements of future root races, rounds, and schemes. In terms of the divine plan, human evolution advances through developing, first, self-consciousness, then group-consciousness, and finally, God-consciousness. Many of the experiments over the past five centuries have involved group work, which will be the focal point of human endeavor in the Aquarian age.

The first such experiment involved the creation of groups that have provided the inner dynamic for the great social, political, religious, and artistic movements of modern history. Groups usually formed around a dominant figure, able to intuit ideas from those on the inner planes, who inspired the work of others. This form of group was common among artists and those engaged in the political field. Often there developed among contemporary thinkers a form of telepathy which, for the most part, was unconscious and allowed for the cross-fertilization of ideas. We would expect to find this occurring, for example, between mathematician/scientists Gottfried von Leibniz and Sir Isaac Newton, both of whom worked on inventing differential calculus in the 1660s and 1670s. The same could be said for Charles Lyell and Charles Darwin with respect to the theory of evolution, or Michael Faraday and James Clerk Maxwell with regards to electromagnetism.

Suffice it to say that no great thinker or creative artist works in isolation. He or she is tuned most always to a flow of ideas that is impressed upon a subjective group of thinkers within a given field. Like a pebble tossed into a still pond, thought waves are constantly broadcast out through the ethers until they reach the boundaries of their ring-pass-not. Needless to say, those who are in tune with these thought patterns are easily influenced by them.

Cultural Groups

Cultural groups helped define the Renaissance and included many of the great artists who, under the influence of the fourth ray, dominated the various schools in Italy, such as those in Venice and Florence, and collectively transformed western art. The vision of these artists was backward-looking to the civilizations of Greece and Rome in the Age of Aries. The theme of much of this art, which depended on a very small number of painters, was heroic individualism, symbolizing the emergence of man from the collective unconscious into a distinctive personality.

While men such as Piero della Francesca, Sandro Botticelli, Hieronymus Bosch, Albrecht Durer, Titian, Giovanni Bellini, and the

Venetian painter Giorgione were, it could be argued, among those who responded in some ways to hierarchical impression, three Renaissance artists stand out as initiates or disciples of sufficient quality to serve as conscious interpreters of spiritual ideas. These men were Michelangelo, Raphael, and Leonardo da Vinci. Of this trinity, Michelangelo expressed the will aspect as seen in the power of his paintings and sculpture: witness the mural on the ceiling of the Sistine Chapel, which Kenneth Clark maintains "passionately asserts the unity of man's body, mind, and spirit."[58] Raphael, representing love-wisdom, produced art of great beauty and sensuality. Leonardo, through his myriad of talents and interests, stood for the qualities of active intelligence, possessed great curiosity, and was referred to by Clark as "that great hero of the intellect."[59]

Beginning in the nineteenth century, there were several schools of artists who appear to have been guided from the inner planes. Most notably, the Pre-Raphaelites and Impressionists, who brought attention to the subjective life by revealing a life behind the form, stood in opposition to the forces of materialism which seemed to dominate all fields of human endeavor. Paul Gauguin, an avant-garde artist of the late nineteenth century and a representative of the symbolist school of painting, appears to have been directly influenced by Theosophical ideas.[60]

These schools helped to pave the way for cubism and the revolution in twentieth century art. Wassily Kandinsky (1866-1944), Piet Mondrian (1872-1944), and Paul Klee (1879-1940) were at the forefront of this movement and were students of esoteric ideas. Occult symbolism was pervasive in their paintings. Kandinsky's theories of art drew heavily upon ideas contained in *The Secret Doctrine*. In a letter written by Mondrian, he stated, "It is in my work that I am something, but compared to the Great Initiates, I am nothing." Klee was interested in the "mysterious forces that speak on a different level of human consciousness..."[61]

Among the writers, the Tibetan specifically mentions the Elizabethan poets: Christopher Marlowe, Sir Philip Sydney, Edmund Spenser and, of course, Shakespeare. John Bunyan lived a century later and there is a clear indication that he was receptive to ideas on the inner planes. According to one writer, "Bunyan had the esoteric sense. He recognized that words and symbols were but the outer seeming, containing a hidden meaning."[62] Not to be forgotten are the Neoplatonists, for example, Marsilio Ficino, John Dee, and Pico della Mirandola who, like the above poets, sweetened literature with classical and esoteric references.

Later, inspired groups of musicians underscored the revival of music in Germany during the eighteenth century, numbering among them Bach (J.S., J.C.), Handel, Haydn, Telemann, Mozart, and Beethoven. Mozart (a Mason), Beethoven, and Bach were three artists who possessed extraordinary mental clarity and not only introduced new forms of musical syntax, but served as vehicles for the downflow of divinely impressed ideas. The musical climate for centuries to come, inspired by these three great composers, owed much to the subjective impulse stemming from the Hierarchy.[63] Musician Keith Bailey writes:

"During the 'Romantic' era that followed Beethoven in the nineteenth century, the concrete expression of subtone five appeared to dominate the thoughts of thinkers of the day. It is perhaps for this reason that the Romantic Era was regarded as a failure by the Hierarchy, but the failure was on the part of the general public, for it was they who failed to respond to the essential mystical and subjective impressions, expressed by the artists of the day, continuing the work commenced by Mozart, and to a greater extent by Beethoven."[64]

Religious Groups

Numerous religious groups also emerged in the sixteenth century in response to the need to purify, diversify, and strengthen spiritual life. This was the driving force behind the Protestant Reformation. Martin Luther, of course, was a conscious disciple, and it was his challenge to Catholic authority, with the posting of his ninety-five theses in 1517, which generated widespread religious, political, and social upheaval and schism. Professor A.G. Dickens writes that Luther was indebted to humanism, which connected him to the important synthesizers of his day—men like Erasmus, John Colet, and Sir Thomas More.[65] Humanism, says D.K., with its apparent materialism, has a deeply spiritual program and purpose.[66]

Among those groups spearheading the challenge to the old religious order were the Catholic mystics, the Lutherans, Calvinists, and later the Pilgrim Fathers and the ones whom the Tibetan calls "those sour and earnest men," the Huguenot and Moravian martyrs. The fragmentation of religious groups and their claims to possessing absolute truth substantially heated the religious climate of Europe to a dangerous level. Religious wars devastated first Germany and then France in the sixteenth century, and did not abate until the latter part of the seventeenth century. There was a positive side to this heightened sectarianism, however. Protestant religious groups, seeking to bring about reforms in ritual, dogma, and practice, acted under second- and sixth-ray influence in leading people to the point of revolt and away from acquiescence to authority, as characterized by the Catholic Church. Whereas many of these sects tried to impose new authorities, they did, inadvertently, enable men to start thinking for themselves, by allowing them to interpret and discuss the Bible.[67]

From the late eighteenth century to the twentieth century, there were succeeding waves of reformers, inspired often by religious convictions, whose mission in life was to expose and eliminate social wrongs. Prominent reformers, many of them Quakers, in the transitional period of social and industrial revolution, marking the late eighteenth and early nineteenth centuries, included such persons as Elizabeth Fry, John Howard, Jonas Hanway, Patrick Colquhoun, Henry Fielding, and Jeremy Bentham. They worked to alleviate the plight of the poor, improve prison conditions, establish foundling hospitals for children, rectify the brutal treatment of the mentally ill, and humanize the law.

Towards the end of the nineteenth century, a new generation of reformers included Josephine Butler, who led the crusade against the sexual abuse of women; Jane Addams who opened Hull House in Chicago for abandoned children; William Booth, founder of the Salvation Army, who initiated many projects to help the poor; Roger Baldwin, founder of the American Civil Liberties Union; Helen Keller, who overcame severe physical disabilities and provided an inspiration for others; Dorothy Day, the founder of the Catholic Worker movement; and the two founders of Alcoholics Anonymous, William G. Wilson and Robert H. Smith. Although these and other reformers represented different backgrounds and outlooks on life, there is no doubt that their efforts contributed to the good of humanity and were in line with hierarchical intent.

Political Groups

New political ideas also helped to reshape society along group lines. European society, conditioned by feudalism, had been from the medieval period divided into three estates: the first estate consisting of the clergy, the second estate comprising the aristocracy, and the masses (or everyone else) incorporating the third estate. In this bottom-heavy structure of society, only the civil and ecclesiastical elites were considered significant. In describing the class structure of seventeenth-century France, historian Pierre Goubert writes:

"There was in the kingdom of France a traditional distinction between those who prayed, those who fought and those who toiled. For a long time...the Third Estate had been held to comprise officials, tradesmen and bourgeois, while at the bottom were the most contemptible of all, the rude mechanicals, who worked with their hands: artisans, some tens of thousands of urban workers and the vast mass of peasantry."[68]

During the seventeenth century, when religious and social conflict swept across Europe, new political ideas, emerging along first-ray lines, began to appear. Groups, such as the Levellers and the Diggers, two of the many political and religious sects that made up the firmament of the English Revolution, brought forth the concepts of liberty, equality, and the rights of citizens. In particular, the Levellers wanted religious toleration and an extension of the electoral franchise. The Diggers are a more interesting group insofar as they posited a concise second-ray vision of the proper role of civil society and were inspired by alchemical ideas. Their leader, Gerrard Winstanley, wrote his views on creation in a tract, published in 1649:

"...in the beginning universal love appeared to be the father of all things (though self-love in our experience rules in man first); and as he made mankind to be the lord of the earth, so he made the earth to be a common treasury of livelihood to whole mankind without respect of persons; and for all other creatures likewise that were to proceed from the earth."[69]

The ideas put forth by the Diggers were far too radical for their time and remain a vision for the future. Those of religious tolerance and liberty, expressed by the Levellers, were later transported to the American colonies.

Manly Palmer Hall writes that Francis Bacon was behind the colonization of America, which was brought about along spiritual lines. Bacon, identified by the Tibetan as the Master Rakoczi,[70] was the head of a secret society which included many of the great minds of the seventeenth century. This group, under Bacon's influence, devised a scheme for blending and fusing a new people into a new nation which would bring together many national, religious, and social groups. The German Pietists, alchemists, Cabalists, mystics, Freemasons, and Rosicrucians were among the groups of settlers who populated the colonies and gave America its vision.[71] A century later, the Master Rakoczi, this time as the Comte de St. Germain, was a frequent visitor to the courts of Europe while simultaneously overshadowing the work of many secret societies. The work of these societies gave subjective impetus to the French Revolution.

A number of political reformers in the seventeenth and eighteenth centuries sought to reform the corrupt and decaying institutional structures of the ancient regime. Government ministers, such as Malesherbes, Turgot, and Colbert in France, advocated reform, along with political philosophers such as John Locke, Baron de Montesquieu, Denis Diderot, Jean Jacques Rousseau, Thomas Paine, Thomas Jefferson, Benjamin Franklin, and Voltaire. Paine, in particular, is of interest. He was an activist, political thinker, and spiritual initiate and, more than any other person, he created a favorable climate of opinion for the American Revolution through the publication of his famous treatise, *Common Sense*.

Speaking of Paine, R. Bryant-Jefferies writes: "He also was considered the first to use the term "United States of America" and his vision was for this country to defend freedom. He saw what the price of subjugation was for other countries seeking independence. He was nationalistic in that he believed each country should defend its own freedom, but he saw colonialism as an abomination."[72]

Political change was brought about by a number of persons who inspired movements that were in keeping with the goals of the Hierarchy. The most obvious representative of this group was Giuseppe Mazzini, founder of the Young Italy movement, who set the vision for Italian unification. He once wrote that "Every nation is Humanity's worker; it labours for Humanity, in order to attain a common end for the good of all."[73] Two other political leaders whose group efforts had significant results were James Keir Hardie, the founder of the British Labour Party and a supporter of the franchise for women, and Chief Joseph of the Nez Perce Indian tribe, who demonstrated courage, leadership qualities, and humanitarian concerns that have become legendary.

Scientific Groups

The scientific discoveries of the seventeenth century, which ushered in a whole new paradigm of thought, were the work of groups in academies and societies. The best known of these societies, which sprang up all over Europe, were the Royal Society in England and the Academie des Sciences in France. These groups of scientists established networks of communication for discussing new ideas, provided the cost and means for experimentation, and created a number of publications. Many of the problems presented to the Royal Society in its earliest years were practical issues, such as finding a satisfactory way of measuring longitude.[74]

Francis Bacon's introduction of the inductive method and René Descartes' deductive method, which provided the methodological framework for the Scientific Revolution, generated intense and pervasive inquiries into the nature of matter and empirical thought along third- and seventh-ray lines. This gave rise to a widespread curiosity as to how nature and the material world functioned, leading to discoveries by men like John Kay (flying shuttle), James Hargreaves (spinning jenny), and James Watt (steam engine), all of which contributed to the Industrial Revolution in Britain. By the same token, emerging groups of thinkers, known as philosophes, brought greater clarity to intellectual life by questioning old superstitions and giving vague concepts a systematic meaning. Denis Diderot's *Encyclopedia* was a case in point. With the manifestation of the fifth ray in 1775, the pace of scientific and technological change and discovery began to quicken.

Scientific inquiry blossomed in the nineteenth century, and it is with these groups that the best case for a telepathic interaction can be made. The most significant field of investigation was medical science. One person, whose remarkable achievement led to the emergence of a whole new field of medicine, was Samuel Hahnemann, the founder of homeopathy. His success in treating many serious illnesses with homeopathic preparations influenced others to follow suit. The contribution of homeopathy in dealing with the cholera epidemic in Britain in the 1830s led to the founding of the London Homeopathic Hospital in 1844.[75] Hahnemann's work encouraged efforts by Louis Pasteur, Robert Koch, and others in creating theories about germs. Their work further influenced Joseph Lister, who developed the "antiseptic principle."

From the work of Hahnemann there arose another remarkable person, Dr. Edward Bach, whose mission was to bridge the gap between the then existing schools of healing—allopathic, homeopathic, and naturopathic—and future schools of healing that would recognize the importance of the soul. Bach, who attended the London Homeopathic Hospital, later developed a set of flower remedies that worked on the subtle planes to modify emotional and personality imbalances. It is said that throughout his life "Bach had followed the inner promptings and intuitions with absolute faith, for he recognized these as higher sources of knowledge.[76]

Other scientific efforts that most certainly received attention from members of the Hierarchy were in the field of electricity and radioactivity. Included here would be the work of James Clerk Maxwell, Michael Faraday, Nikola Tesla, Thomas Edison, Pierre and Marie Curie, and Walter Russell. The revolution in physics brought about by Einstein and Max Planck had a telepathic radiatory effect leading to extensive research in quantum mechanics, relativity, and superspace research.

Not to be forgotten are Luther Burbank and other naturalists whose work unlocked some of the mysteries of the vegetable kingdom and promoted within human consciousness environmental and ecological concerns. Burbank, like many disciples, underwent a profound spiritual crisis as a young man, which cut him adrift from the doctrines of orthodox religion and, so it is said, awakened in him "a conscious cosmic power...leaving the deepest and most abiding impression on his young life."[77] Through his work with the forces of nature, Burbank developed his religion of humanity, which became the guidepost of his life and an inspiration for many others.

Educational Groups

Another important outgrowth of the Renaissance was, in the Tibetan's words, a desire for educating the masses of people "so that they can become strictly and consciously human."[78] One of the most noteworthy initiates to address the question of education was Jean Jacques Rousseau, the eighteenth-century French philosopher. Rousseau, one of the early proponents of the so-called "Romantic" movement, denounced the traditional view that children should be beaten into submission and taught only so much as to make them obedient and moral. He believed that children possessed consciousness as well as sensibilities and a potential for growth. His ideas appealed to an emerging band of thinkers and moral activists who were concerned with eliminating suffering and improving the condition of humanity.

Groups devoted to improving the lot of the child through proper education blossomed towards the end of the nineteenth century. One of the leading lights of educational reform was Maria Montessori, who was born in 1870. Montessori, through her work with children from the slums, fostered the idea that youngsters could be the masters of their own nature through development of the will. Her aim was to create a prepared environment by which the child, free from undue adult intervention, could learn to develop his own potential. These ideas have gained great popularity as evidenced by the growing number of Montessori Schools today.[79]

More recently, the thinking of Rudolf Steiner and Robert Muller, two obvious initiates, has sought to place the best of child development theory within a spiritual context. The growing number of Waldorf Schools, with their emphasis on cultivating imagination, spiritual knowledge, holistic approaches, and epistemological synthesis, provides a rough format as to how mass education in the future may evolve.

Needless to say, the last four decades of the twentieth century have witnessed many useful experiments and programs in education. Whereas the limitations of bureaucratic education, found in most public schools, is evident even to the most casual observer, some promising models based on spiritual insight are looming on the horizon.

Psychological Groups

One of the most significant developments in the nineteenth century was the emergence of psychology. This occurrence had its roots in music and the arts, which brought to the surface hitherto hidden emotions and subconscious thoughts and associations. Musician and occultist Cyril Scott has written; "It is this searching power in Beethoven's work which prompted us to write that he was the forerunner of psycho-analysis—he was in one sense a psychoanalyst, and this is why, as his music became more widely diffused and the Victorian age progressed, its women gradually became less hysterical and less subject to fainting and tearfulness."[80] Other composers, according to Scott, conditioned the psychological and social life of the nineteenth century. Chopin brought to consciousness a new sensitivity which led to emancipation for women; Schumann's music spread light into the neglected world of children; whereas Wagner's music drama gave rise to the important spiritual principle of unity in diversity.[81] Musical artists, such as Franck, Grieg, Tschaikowsky, Delius, Debussy, Ravel, and Scriabin, had, in the words of Scott, close associations with the deva kingdom and the world of the nature spirits.[82]

Psychology is of pervasive interest in the world today. Psychoanalysis and other perspectives of the inner life, which sought to place psychology on a sound scientific footing, were greatly influenced by the prevailing spirit of positivism in the nineteenth century and focused exclusively on empirical evidence. However, there were a number of counter-movements at this time. Spiritualism gave rise to research in psychic phenomena, which provided a useful climate for the books of H.P.B. and the development of the Theosophical Society. Mesmerism, and its offsprings phrenology, palmistry, physiognomy, and graphology, have been denounced repeatedly as pseudo-sciences, but the efforts of these practitioners have helped others to better understand human traits and character.

Groups devoted to psychical research have been pervasive since the late nineteenth century. William James was the first of the modern psychologists to take religion seriously. The author of a short biographical sketch of James writes: "William James presented his religious ideals: that the cause of all sickness and human misery is man's sense of separateness from God, and that God still is evolving with His growing universe, and that humanity can help by building a better world..."[83]

Carl Jung extended the study of psychology into previously uncharted territory. His interests included many fields of esotericism, such as alchemy, mythology, and astrology. Roberto Assagioli, an acknowledged disciple of the Master D.K., pioneered the field of pyschosynthesis, which is providing the basis for an understanding of the spiritual dimension of psychology.

Business Groups

The final sphere of group work directed towards enhancing the condition of humanity and furthering the cause of evolution has been that of financiers and the business community. The Tibetan has said of these groups that they control all that can be converted into energy and constitute a dictatorship over all modes of intercourse, commerce, and exchange.[84] Financiers are charged with the control of the world's money and thus utilize third- and seventh-ray energy. Curiously, money has evolved from ancient times, first as coins—the mineral kingdom affecting the physical plane; then as paper bills—the vegetable kingdom impacting the astral plane; and presently, as electronic transfer mechanisms—the animal kingdom corresponding to the mental plane. Since financiers work powerfully, and usually unconsciously, with the laws of manifestation, their responsibility is great, particularly where the welfare of humanity is concerned.

Groups of businessman began to emerge with the commercial revolution of the seventeenth and eighteenth centuries. Whereas most of these men were driven by the desire for huge fortunes, they inadvertently paved the way for economic development, better living standards, and expansionism. Adam Smith, a professor of philosophy, put forward a justification for free-market capitalism in his influential book, *The Wealth of Nations*. In this book, Smith argued that economic life was guided by an invisible hand, which produced an unrecognized harmony in the relations between producers and consumers. Within the framework of the twentieth century, the theories of John Maynard Keynes have served to modify and humanize the economic system that Smith advocated over a century before. More recently, the writings of E.F. Schumacher have questioned the effectiveness and moral integrity of large systems, unregulated growth, and a belief in unlimited resources. The ideas of Smith, Keynes, and Schumacher have had tremendous power and influence.

Capitalism has had a checkered career, to say the least, and in its most negative aspects is the prime contributor to the secular religion of materialism in the modern world. In spite of all the greed and corruption that is often associated with business enterprise, individuals such as Andrew Carneige, John D. Rockefeller, and Henry Ford have, through their philanthropical works, demonstrated the right use of money. Today, visionaries in the business world are taking the lead in developing new models of leadership, group interaction, and organizational dynamics which, with the coming of the seventh ray, will have an important impact on our future.

Formation of the New Group of World Servers

These experiments in group endeavor have brought people from a condition of isolation and parochialism to a point in time where collective interaction has become the norm. Now that people have reached the stage where they are able to transcend nation and race, the Hierarchy, according to the Tibetan, "is faced with another situation which requires careful handling."[85] The goal for humanity in the present century has been to gather up and weld together the various threads of influencing energy and patterns of thought that have been produced by groups since the year 1500.[86] This synthesizing work, representing the best of the past, requires intense efforts by groups of committed disciples who have undergone systematic occult training.

At one of their quarterly meetings, in 1900, so it is written, the Hierarchy outlined plans to expand human consciousness so as to enlarge the horizon of human thought.[87] To bring about this change, it was determined to establish a subjective link between senior disciples, aspirants, and workers in the world to foster global cooperation. The formation of the League of Nations was one immediate consequence of this plan.[88] As the story goes, the idea originated in the fourth-ray ashram of the Master Serapis and was taken up by certain disciples working in the sixth-ray ashram of the Master Jesus. The impact of the sixth ray on this idea was to give it aspirational appeal. The idea was then modified and impressed upon the consciousness of Colonel House, a close confidante of President Woodrow Wilson, and himself an advanced disciple. President Wilson, a sixth-ray aspirant, then became the single-minded proponent of the idea.

Another initiative of the Hierarchy was the formation of the Red Cross, which was established in 1864 by the Geneva Convention and was signed by every world power. The idea behind the Red Cross was, in its formulation and intent, clearly of a second-ray nature insofar as it sought to alleviate human suffering and render compassion. In time each nation instituted its own branch of the Red Cross, making it a truly international organization.

When the Hierarchy met in 1925 to review the proposals they had set down twenty-five years before, the masters decided to put their personal groups in touch with each other, thus giving form to the New Group of World Servers. These seven groups of workers, organized along political, religious, and educational lines, were to act as a liaison between the inner Hierarchy and the thinkers of the world, thus serving as a bridge for the downflow of creative and inspired thought. Animated by a desire to serve and swept by a current of spiritual stimulation, these groups were to be a new and timely experiment in furthering the cause of the Plan.[89]

With the coming of the World War, the Hierarchy hastened its efforts to help mankind. The success of the Hierarchy in establishing what the Tibetan calls "great approaches" to humanity, due to the intense desire of world disciples based on meditation and service, enabled the masters to exercise a greater influence on human affairs. The Tibetan observed that in 1936 "a definite step forward was made as the result of the work done in the last fifty years" so that a point of stabilization was achieved by which plans could be laid to further assist humanity.[90] A year later at Wesak, the Council of the Hierarchy discussed the method of deepening the hold of new ideas on members of the New Group of World Servers and the consequent awakening of the intelligentsia in all countries to the principles of brotherhood and the recognition of the Hierarchy. The Hierarchy was also anxious to use the tremendous energies at its disposal to achieve equilibrium in the world, to stimulate the New Group of World Servers to an understanding of the present emergency, to define the Plan more clearly and radiate it more effectively out into the world of humanity, and to keep the forces that had been set in motion since 1914 within definite limits.[91]

Following the World War, the Hierarchy kept up its efforts to guide humanity through radiating light and love on to the world. We are told that spiritual forces overshadowed the San Francisco conference where the United Nations was created in 1945. The following year, a new alignment was undertaken with humanity which, it was said, would proceed for several hundred years.[92] These steps appear to point to a closer cooperation between humanity and the Hierarchy in the years ahead, through the medium of the New Group of World Servers.

Much could be written about the work of the New Group of World Servers in the world today. The ever-increasing emphasis on group work and organization, thanks to the waxing seventh-ray influence, is now facilitating the development of such groups. In 1942, during the height of the war, the Tibetan wrote that groups of world servers are appearing everywhere all over the world. He commented that where there were three members of the New Group of World Servers found in any exoteric group, then it was linked by a "thread of golden light" to the wider group of world servers. Whereas the grouping of world servers is very tenuous on the physical plane, the links are stronger on the astral and mental planes, where the love of humanity and purpose, as directed by the divine plan, are worked out.[93]

Efforts By Disciples to Assist the Hierarchy

Initiatives by certain disciples did much to promote the cause of peace and brotherhood during the troubled period of the world wars. The efforts taken by Nicholas Roerich to promote a banner of peace to protect institutions harboring the world's cultural treasures was one example. Roerich proposed that a banner, containing three spheres within a circle, be placed over museums and cultural centers so as to protect them from attack and pillage. A movement to adopt the Roerich Peace Pact and Banner of Peace was inaugurated in 1929 at an international congress in Bruges, Belgium. From there the idea spread. Leaders of many nations signed the Pact, including Franklin D. Roosevelt, who said "this treaty possesses a spiritual significance far deeper than the text of the instrument itself."[94]

Another example was the work of the disciple and spiritual healer Wellesley Tudor Pole who initiated the silent minute. According to Sir George Trevelyan, the idea was first presented to Tudor Pole by a fellow officer while serving with the British forces in Palestine during the First World War. The friend, foreseeing his own death and the future Second World War, told him that "when the time comes, remember us. We shall be an unseen but mighty army...Lend us a moment each day and through your Silence give us the opportunity..."[95] When the war did come to Britain in 1940, Tudor Pole went to the King and presented his idea for a silent minute. This moment of silence would be announced each evening by the striking of Big Ben and would be broadcast over the BBC. The King was delighted by the idea and it was quickly taken up. After the war, Air Chief Marshal Sir Hugh Dowding referred to the silent minute by noting that "if it had not been for this intervention, the battle would have been joined in conditions which humanly speaking would have rendered victory impossible."[96]

The work undertaken by Dion Fortune, founder of the Society of the Inner Light, also involved the spiritual defense of Great Britain during the war. It is said that in the years of crisis, 1939 to 1941, when Britain faced Germany as the sole defender of freedom, she, through her groups, "helped to maintain the strength and resilience of the group mind of the nation" by focusing on relevant symbols.[97] Fortune also corresponded weekly with her students during these years and her letters reveal much. In February, 1940 she wrote:

"Still the war is being confined on the inner planes, and the amazing rise in the morale of the nation indicates the way in which the fight is going. A blitzkrieg today would have a different effect on us to what it would have had last autumn. With every week that passes, the spiritual tide is rising, and an energy and confidence is showing itself to which this country has been a stranger many a long day."[98]

The Tibetan also employed his group of disciples on behalf of the Forces of Light during the World War. At one point he told them that they were confronted with the difficult task of standing firm on the physical plane against all that was hateful and destructive and doing what was needed to be done to overcome the prevailing sense of powerlessness, while preserving an inner attitude of complete harmlessness and loving understanding. Given that the practice of total harmlessness is difficult in the best of times, one can only surmise the difficulty that confronted these disciples at a point in history when the psychic atmosphere of the planet was swept by fear, anger, hatred, and suffering. To partake of world suffering, yet stand unmoved by it, was another condition which the Tibetan placed on his group. He wrote: "Those who refuse to share in the world karma and pain will find their entire progress inevitably slowed down, for they will have to put themselves outside the great tide of spiritual force now sweeping in regenerating streams throughout the world of men."[99]

The Impact of Hierarchical Initiation

Every forty-nine years the opportunity comes for the masters to undergo initiation. This is not only a hierarchical event but one that brings about creative changes on earth. The most recent initiation occurred in 1952. While its impact on the planet remains unclear, much of the preparatory work for the New Age was no doubt initiated, which included stimulating the work of the United Nations; creating an international spirit; hastening the process of decolonization; and eroding the illusion of racial, national, and ethnic separation. The Tibetan predicted that a number of spiritually oriented leaders and executives would appear around 1955, and that these leaders would use seventh-ray energy to work towards group fusion and international understanding.[100] Included among this group, one supposes, were Martin Luther King, John F. Kennedy, Pope John XXIII, and Dag Hammarskjold, who brought about new ways of thinking and a redirection of humanity towards the good.

Going backwards in time, the previous hierarchical initiation took place in 1903. Those preparing for initiation were confronted with the rising tide of world evil brought about by materialism and unprecedented separateness. Faced with this situation, the Hierarchy had to decide what they should do to aid humanity, in which situation and at what time, so as to force humanity to recognize what was happening to them and to make choices based on free will. What they decided to do was to stand aside and allow the forces of sectarian nationalism, racism, and militarism to force a crystallization of existing cleavages. This led inevitably to the World War.[101]

Subsequent regressions of time reveal that initiations within the Hierarchy occur in the beginning and at the middle of each century. What consequence such initiations have on the course of human events is unclear except that the three prior initiations in 1854, 1805, and 1756 involved the outbreak of significant wars—the Crimean War, the Battle of Trafalgar, and the Seven Years War, respectively—all involving the British and the French. During the 1707 period of initiation within the Hierarchy, the United Kingdom of Great Britain was formed out of England and Scotland. Clearly, this was an event of some significance. We might deduce from the few hints given to us by the Tibetan that periods of importance within the realm of the Hierarchy have a corresponding effect of breaking down barriers, forcing a synthesis, or impacting an important turn in human affairs. It was in 1609 during one of these initiations, for example, that the Netherlands gained its independence from Spain. The Netherlands went on to become a Mecca for religious and political dissidents seeking freedom and toleration for centuries to come.

Predictions of Contemporary Events

In *A Treatise on Cosmic Fire*, the Tibetan makes a number of predictions for the second half of the twentieth century which, given the advance of time, we can now see in hindsight. He says that a very interesting time will begin in 1966 in which there will be a special effort by the white lodge to advance the ends of evolution along a particular line of force.[102] The social revolution of the 1960s, with its emphasis on individualism, creativity, experimentation, and compassion, could well have been the result of this hierarchical effort. The Tibetan also observed that there will be a reaction against crime, Sovietism, and extreme radicalism in the years ahead, which has certainly happened.[103] He further noted that there would be a re-spiritualization of the Catholic churches and an ecumenical outreach to the Episcopal and Greek churches around 1980, which was also initiated.[104]

Writing in 1934, the Tibetan prophesied that in the coming three generations (ending around 2030) a group of people will enter incarnation who will be equipped to lead humanity out of its present impasse. The impasse that he was referring to was the problem of sex, which has been problematic for most of the twentieth century. Since sex emotion, according to the Tibetan, is connected to crime,[105] that too could also abate.

An analysis of the above statement in no way implies that the issue of sex or crime will be solved by any one group of people. Rather, it suggests that initiates or disciples from some hierarchical ashram will come into manifestation with the sole purpose of teaching humanity, by whatever means, methods of right approach. Opportunities are then created for gaining deeper insight (and thereby expanding conscious) which allows people to view the matter differently, within a larger context, and then take steps to deal effectively with the problem. We are told that the period up to 2025 is a window of opportunity whereby humanity, in cooperation with the Hierarchy, is charged with bringing about an uplift in the collective consciousness of the planet. Whereas humanity is presently in one of its depressive cycles, seeing trouble at every turn and problems as irresolvable, members of the Hierarchy stand as eternal optimists since they know that all the ills which afflict people (individually and collectively) are transitory (hence illusory). It is just a matter of time.

Chapter 6 —
The Evolution of Human
Consciousness

Of the three planetary centers, including Shamballa and the Hierarchy, humanity is the newest and also the least developed. We know that the progress of humanity has been a slow and painful evolutionary process beginning, as the Tibetan observes, on the moon chain during the fifth race of the third round; then individualizing in the third root race of the fourth round (Lemurian times); next gaining the opportunity for higher evolution made possible by the opening of the door to initiation in the Atlantean period; and, presently, nearing a portentous time when the greater part of the fifth root race stands close to the probationary path with the coming of the new age.[1]

We are told that humanity has experienced three periods of manifestation when incarnating egos (human souls, not the human species) have taken form. The first time these egos individualized was during the moon chain (referred to as Old Atlantis). The second time was on Lemuria and, most recently, human egos incarnated on earth in the Atlantean period of the fourth root race, until the final stages of that civilization. There is some ambiguity in the statements made by the Tibetan as to the evolutionary stage of this last group. At one point he says that they are "of a low order as far as the lowest of our present humanity is concerned, but somewhat higher than the egos which individualized upon ancient Lemuria."[2] He then states that "many of the disciples today came into this earth evolution from the moon chain where already much had been unfolded."[3] He further remarks, "the egos which individualised upon the moon chain and which came in steadily, as the planetary conditions fitted them, until the final stages of the Atlantean period, constitute the bulk of our modern humanity."[4] H.P.B. writes that moon worship occurred throughout the ancient world, including the Egyptians, to whom the lunar symbol of the cat was sacred, and the Chaldeans, who worshipped the moon under various names.[5] It is not known whether these moon worshippers were descended from the moon chain and were unconsciously responding to an inner recognition. However, it is an intriguing thought.

Elsewhere, the Tibetan observes that those who now comprise the inner group around the Lord of the World were recruited from the ranks of those who were initiates on the moon chain, including the Mahachohan, whereas the best and brightest of humanity are rapidly increasing in number and are moving into the minor offices beneath the central esoteric group.[6] D.K. makes an interesting point that the Christ was the first of earth humanity to individuate whereas the Buddha was the last of the moon chain egos to enter human evolution. The rapid development of both these great beings has no parallel amongst the rest of humanity, but it does give us a hint as to the relativity of the evolutionary process.[7]

It would stand to reason, therefore, that groups of souls who incarnated on the moon chain would be older in terms of evolutionary development than younger souls who came along later during the second period of manifestation, in Lemuria, and the final phase of incarnation, before the door into the human kingdom closed in Atlantis. It should be noted that the moon chain was considered to be a failure and was aborted before its time. Those who incarnated on this chain reached a certain stage of development but were forced to make adjustments after transferring to the earth chain, the polar opposite of the moon chain.[8]

What percentage of people individuated during each of these three streams is difficult to say, however the Tibetan does indicate that the majority of egos entering from the moon chain constituted the active intelligence aspect of divinity, whereas those incarnating during Lemurian and Atlantean times embodied, in greater percentages, the love-wisdom aspect and the will aspect respectively.[9] Accordingly, by this reckoning, most people on earth today incarnated during the moon chain or in the Lemurian period.

A Definition of Humanity

What is meant by the term *humanity*? The Tibetan defines this term as "that evolution through which the Son aspect is to express itself most perfectly in this cosmic incarnation." This purely esoteric definition points to the condition of humanity as a synthesizing point between higher and lower principles, or aspects of nature. Herein lies the essential importance of the person as a vehicle for the life of God, as a spark of individualized consciousness emanating from the Logos himself, and as a composite of the three lower kingdoms (mineral, plant, and animal) in nature. The outward form of this esoteric dimension is the trinity with the polar opposites of father-spirit and mother-matter, synthesized by the son or man. In Hinduism, man is the Vishnu aspect in the process of development through the intelligence of Brahma, impelled by the will of Mahadeva.[10] Although man was edited out of the Christian trinity, his rightful place is that of the son, embodying the Christ aspect.

Taking a more functional and historical perspective, it is clear that the idea of mankind or humanity is rooted in the great religious teachings, reaching back into earlier root races. Historian W. Warren Wagar edited a useful book entitled, *History and the Idea of Mankind*, which traces the origin of this important concept through five traditional societies and in the modern world. It is useful to see how the concept of humanity sprang from several of these religious traditions.

In Indian thought the idea of mankind constitutes the sum total of four mutually complimentary components of society. These included the priestly class (Brahmans), the warrior class (Ksatriyas), the merchant and producer class (Vaisyas), and the servant class (Sudras). Although division into these four categories implies a functional sociological perspective, it appears evident that such classes emerged from the Hindu notion of diversity within unity.[11] Within Hinduism, static social categories, which crystallized into castes, were overshadowed by the greater sweep of evolution, directed by the great lords of karma, which determined that humans would live a multitude of lives in many different conditions.

The Hindu concept of mankind is juxtaposed by the Jewish notion which places man within the universal order as part of the cosmic unity. One of the key concepts flowing from this ethical universalism is the principle that there should be one law for all people living within a given society. Whereas cosmic universalism speaks to God's relationship to the world, in reality there is no universalism in the history of humanity. Thus humankind does not exist as a historical reality, but as an idea waiting to be realized. Without the evolving vision of human universalism, people have no future, only a past. Herein one finds the role and purpose of the Jews as God's chosen people. The Jews are not favored above and apart from their fellow humanity, but are chosen as a vehicle so as to instruct and broadcast to the peoples of the earth God's plan and mission. Generally speaking, the selection of the Jews as the chosen people is only a temporary arrangement because the goal of history is to choose all people and all nations. It is through carrying out this destiny that the unity of the human race is affirmed.[12]

The unity of mankind is also pronounced within Christianity. Whereas the source of this religion derives from the teachings of the Master Jesus, it evolved as a borrower religion, drawing upon many diverse ethical, religious, and philosophic traditions. The most prominent synthesizer within the Christian community was Paul of Tarsus, who was exposed to Hellenistic thought, including stoicism, as well as the teachings emanating from the various mystery schools. While preaching to the Athenians, Paul affirmed that, from a single stock, God had created the human race so that people could occupy the whole earth and find a way of seeking and realizing him.[13] Paul's epistles affirmed without exception the unity of mankind under God for all of history.[14] Within four centuries following the death of Jesus, the idea of the Christian Church as an outward expression of the living Christ came to be accepted. This provided the basis for the concept of a Christian world state, which flowered during the Middle Ages. What Christ taught, and the Church ignored, was that he, as a being within the heart of every person and with counterparts in the many world religions, was an intermediary agent, guiding humanity to its ultimate evolutionary destiny, which in Biblical terms was unity with the father.

Universality is also a core concept within Islam. The idea of the unity of the human race is underscored in the Koran by the acceptance of the Biblical notion of Adam as the father of all men. At the core of his teachings, the prophet Mohammed called for the concept of one human race united under the umbrella of one religious community, guided by a holy book, stressing submission to an all-powerful deity. The need for unity sought expression in two key components of this religion. The first is service to God through service to humanity. The second is militant messianism, which resulted in the rapid expansion of Islam from 622 CE, the date of Mohammed's flight from Mecca to Medina, to the middle of the ninth century.[15] Whereas Judaism sought to foster universality through the intellect (understanding the meaning of God's plan and human history) and Christianity tried to unite humanity through experiencing the love of God, Islam advanced a vision of a unified humanity through their submission to the power or will of God.

Humanity as an Evolving Concept

In the words of one source, "historians tend to believe that man's consciousness, his psychic faculties, have always been as much as they are now."[16] However, this is not the case. From the esoteric perspective of consciousness, people are ever evolving towards greater self-understanding, group awareness, and service. As units of consciousness, people achieve periodic insights and vague hints of a deeper reality through the incessant trials and tribulations of daily living. Over a period of many lifetimes, people slowly and painfully fight their way through the pitfalls of maya, the fogs of glamour, and the deceptions of illusion until they begin to sense the first flickerings of soul light. It is at this point that one starts to tread the path.

The evolution of consciousness is by no means an individual matter insofar as it is conditioned, structured, and generated by group considerations. Each root race is predominately a body of consciousness which long outlives its physical plane dominance. Throughout his books, the Tibetan observes that the great majority of people in the world today are essentially Atlantean in consciousness and are therefore influenced by the thoughtforms and diseases of that civilization.[17] There are also remnants of Lemurian consciousness among cultures in the present global environment.

Lemurian Consciousness

It has been the goal of the third root race (historically speaking, the first human root race) to gain mastery over the physical plane. The shift from animal consciousness to that, which the Tibetan called "savage man," involved a corresponding change from an emphasis on satisfying purely physical appetites to a response to environmental impacts, which were not intelligently understood.[18] Mastery over the physical plane in simple terms means survival. Humanity, rooted in material form, was compelled to learn the laws of nature and to live by them.

This ability to read the code of nature might well be a residual trait, possessed by the ancient Lemurians. H.P.B. refers to the race of giants or "one-eyed" Cyclopes, who were perhaps the precursors of the present-day aborigines. They appear in the fables of the ancient Greeks and, by some accounts, existed in fact during the last three subraces of Lemuria. The important point about these Cyclopes-like Lemurians is that they were able to see into the etheric through the third eye, and thus visualize the world of subtle vibrations.[19] Of course, lacking a corresponding intelligence, they were unable to employ the intellect to make sense of this inner world, which left them as little more than automatons to their own instincts. Knowing the secrets of the plant and animal kingdoms, they unwittingly indulged in a form of magic. By the same token, the Lemurians saw the lower kingdoms as sources of power and objects of worship and veneration.

Esotericism, of course, teaches that all forms are energy that possess the quality of life. Hence it is reasonable to assume that Lemurians, who were able to see into the etheric, were sensitive to the living currents of energy that flow through all forms. It was not until the beginning of the fourth root race, so we are told, that the two front eyes were fully developed and people gained the perspective of physical sight.[20]

Traces of Lemurian consciousness can still be found today, primarily among the aboriginal peoples of the world (the term meaning the first or earliest of its type). Many of these people, who survive today in small bands or tribes in mostly tropical regions, are listed by organizations, such as Cultural Survival, to be among those societies most in danger of becoming extinct. The Mikea of Madagascar and the Nharo Bushmen of Botswana are two of many examples.[21] Regardless of their geographic setting, the aboriginal peoples share an instinctual understanding of a hidden code which regulates the complex patterns and interrelationships of the lower kingdoms. With reference to her quasi-fictional account of a walkabout with the Aborigines of Australia, Marlo Morgan writes:

"[According to the Aborigines] The purpose of the plant kingdom is to feed animals and humans, to hold the soil together, to enhance beauty, to make air and balance the atmosphere. The primary purpose of the animal kingdom is not to feed man, but it agrees to that when necessary. It is to balance the atmosphere, be a companion and teacher by example and occasionally help with work. So each morning the tribe sends out a thought or message to the animals and plants in front of us … It is up to the plants and animals to make their own arrangements about who will be chosen."[22]

This closeness to nature, and the patterns of relationships occupying the lower three kingdoms, accounts for the birth of man's first religious impulse, which took the form of animism, or the belief that all natural phenomena are inanimate and possess an innate soul. One form of animism, the worship of the life force in animals, has been a strong cultural force, as witnessed by the cave paintings of animals recorded on cave walls by Neolithic peoples. The wisdom of animals was central to the philosophy and religion of Native Americans. Rocks and plants were also seen as spiritualized forms, which accounts for the polytheism found among many native peoples.

Indigenous cultures also place great emphasis on the importance of initiation to highlight important transformations in the life of an individual or a group. Puberty, marking the passage from childhood to adulthood, is always celebrated by extensive rituals, tests, and trials of initiation. The whole idea of initiation is central to the Ageless Wisdom, indicating, as it does, major leaps in consciousness. Seemingly, the inner landscape of initiation involves the recognition in brain consciousness of various spheres and states of divine awareness, which then has a life-reordering impact on thought and behavior.[23] It is this recognition, conscious or otherwise, which has made initiation, in one form or another, a cultural universal. It is only modern materialistic society that has maintained a disregard for the importance of ritual and initiation, resulting, of course, in dire social consequences.

A final characteristic of indigenous societies, which is no doubt a residue of Lemurian consciousness, is the faculty of seeing all life as a web of relationships. This is an aspect of etheric vision, which was active during the Lemurian root race. Indigenous people divide their everyday world into paired sets: man-woman, parent-child, husband-wife, brother-sister, and so on. These dyadic relationships are intended to form stability and balance through partnerships and the social creation of one's alter-ego. The achievement of psychological health through relationships is yet another fundamental principle that was practiced, even if it was not fully understood, over the span of several root races. It is worthwhile noting that the secret to achieving harmony through conflict, according to esoteric teaching, is when "two merge with one."[24] Thus only in duality is there real unity.

Atlantean Consciousness

Whereas the Lemurian root race sought to gain dominance over the physical plane, the Atlantean root race has attempted to do the same with respect to the astral plane. The transfer of consciousness from one plane to the next involves a finer degree of sensitivity. Hence, we can assume that the more highly evolved Lemurians and the "old souls" from the moon chain were the first to manifest the rudimentary faculty of discrimination, which is at the root of emotional life. The primitive stage of this type of consciousness is colored almost entirely by a desire for objects, material comfort, and the craving for pleasure over pain. In time, these base desires transmute themselves into an emotional response to elements in the environment that is paralleled by an intensified "wish-life," which is the first hint of imagination. Among the more emotionally evolved, there is a sense of refinement, sensibility, and creativity. At the highest reaches of the astral plane, one finds the mystic, who with intense aspiration and an awareness of duality, longs for union with God and is characterized by intense devotion.

Throughout the Atlantean root race, people continued to possess the power of clairvoyance. The faculty of clairvoyance enables one to see upon the subtle planes as clearly and easily as we do today upon the physical plane. Disciples who have clairvoyant abilities are far removed from the bulk of Atlanteans insofar as they possess detachment and the maturity of mind to use this faculty in a creative manner. Generally speaking, the Atlanteans were trance mediums, which opened them up to the lower psychic world of glamour and the control of outside entities. This could well explain how the dark forces were able to gain a hold on the astral plane during Atlantean times, which resulted in the "great war" between the forces of light and darkness.

Moreover, insofar as the Atlantean civilization was governed for a long time by the seventh ray of order and ceremonial magic, particularly during the first half of its existence, this contributed to the rise of spiritualism as the religion of the people on Atlantis.[25] Spiritualism is a form of instinctual telepathy, radiating from the solar plexus center, and is characterized by the kind of rapport that a mother would have with her child.[26] We are reminded that spirituality in Atlantean times was very different in quality from that of today. Then there was a vague longing for the hereafter, a desire for beauty, and for emotional completion, without any thought as to how such might be achieved. The Hierarchy, it is said, encouraged these aspirations. Under the guidance of initiates and adepts at that time, the instinctual urge for something better was nurtured and this led eventually to the great temples and beautiful cities, of which the Chaldean and Babylonian civilizations contained the degenerated remnants.[27]

We are told that many of the modern processes of civilization, including science, were known to the priest-kings in Atlantean times, but to the masses, who were not privy to this knowledge, these wonders seem to have been derived from some awesome magic.[28] We must assume that this knowledge was of a general nature without the technical modifications that have been added in recent centuries. The resurgence of spiritualism in the nineteenth century was the revisiting of this ancient Atlantean consciousness into human affairs.[29] Seeing that this phenomenon (spiritually debased though it may have been) could be used to shift people's attention to the subtle and invisible realms, H.P.B. drew upon spiritualism as a basis for promoting Theosophy and experiments in higher psychism.

Lower psychism and exaggerated emotionalism have cast long shadows across human history and are so pervasive as to be almost self-evident. Wars, representing eruptions of energy on the astral plane, have been a continuous feature of human existence throughout man's recorded history. Sociologist Pitirim Sorokin has calculated that from 600 BCE up to 1925 CE there have been in the history of nations approximately 1,623 important disturbances including small and large civil wars.[30]

Much disease is also emotional in origin. Influenza, which the Tibetan specifically indicates is the result of fear, worry, and irritation,[31] produced at least thirty epidemics and panepidemics in Europe (and later throughout the world) from the fourteenth century to the present, according to *The Cambridge World History of Human Disease*. Tuberculosis, which we are told ravished the Atlantean civilization and involves a misuse of second-ray energy,[32] became epidemic throughout much of

Europe and the rest of the world between the eighteenth and twentieth centuries, which coincided with the rise of urban and industrial development. This illness originates in the loss of breath, and in the words of the Tibetan, "he who lives only for material goods, who sacrifices all virtue in order to gain that which cannot last, will die in life, will find breath failing him..."[33] The bubonic plague, which visited Europe on a cyclical basis throughout the Middle Ages up to the early eighteenth century, can be linked to low-grade emotional energy and often followed periods of war and strife. Add to this the pervasive belief in witchcraft and the existence of various demonic entities (all of which were astral entities) which dominated the consciousness of the masses throughout the Middle Ages and the early modern period of western history.

The functional impact of religion (particularly the great world religions such as Islam and Christianity) has been to raise humanity from the lower levels to the higher levels of the astral plane. This refers, of course, to the emphasis which these religions have placed on sin and redemption, images of heaven and hell (both astral constructs of reality), and a fear-inspired morality (fear being the most pervasive emotion and the line of least resistance for most of humanity down through the ages). The examples of highest attainment for Christian believers were the mystic and the saint, which were also models of men and women who had purified their astral natures. Religion, as expressed through the churches, has been a conditioner of Atlantean consciousness that has persisted for hundreds of thousands of years after the fact.

Given the overwhelming astralism that dominated the Atlantean civilization and has had a residual effect on subsequent civilizations, it follows that the center of consciousness for the Atlanteans was in the solar plexus. Students of esoteric knowledge are familiar with the centers, or chakras. These centers are located in the etheric body along an etheric spine. Along the spinal column, energy passes between the centers. Vital energy is stored at the base of the spine and unites the three divine energies (will, love-wisdom, and active intelligence) with the energy of substance, the aggregate of atomic lives out of which all forms are built. At a critical point in evolution, these combined energies pass up the central channel in the spinal column and all the centers are brought into full expression. This process can be very dangerous if it is prematurely forced.[34]

The centers themselves are composed of concentric interblending centers of energy which rotate at varying speeds depending upon their place within the hierarchy of the body. At the center of each chakra is a point of latent fire. Evolution, whether of an individual or a race, is marked by the extent to which the higher centers are open or are becoming sensitive to subtle spiritual impulses.[35]

The seven chakras, in order of descent, include the crown center (top of the head), the ajna center (in the forehead, the area of the third eye), the throat center, the heart center, the solar plexus center, the sacral center (the area of the reproductive organs), and the base of the spine. Whereas these chakras are identifiable within the etheric body of a person, they have a correspondence to other forms. Nations and root races have a spiritual constitution and an array of developed or undeveloped chakra centers.

Table 7. The Chakras and the Root Races[36]

Root Race	Chakra	Expression
Seventh	Head	Will
Sixth	Ajna	Intuition, integration
Fifth	Throat	Creative power, mental development
Fourth	Solar plexus	Psychic sensitivity and mysticism
Third	Sacral center	Physical appearance and generation
Second	Heart or vital center	Coordination of life forces
First	Base of the Spine	The will to be, to exist

From this chart, it is clear that each root race is, in a very real sense, a chakra center within the body of humanity. Whereas the shift from the Lemurian root race to the Atlantean root race was accompanied by the emergence of astral sensitivity, the change from the Atlantean to the Aryan root race gave rise to a sensitivity to ideas and a responsiveness to thought currents. This has been a major step in the evolution of humanity as it represents a transference of energy from those centers figuratively below the diaphragm to those above the diaphragm. In the coming root races, the intuition and will shall be more completely developed. Students of esotericism generally believe that in accordance with the divine plan, it is the goal of humanity to be fully conscious on the mental plane by the end of the round.

Stages of Extraction from the Realm of Glamour

The flooding of emotional perceptions on the astral plane, beginning in Atlantean times, created a problem that has plagued humanity ever since, namely glamour. Though astral in origin, glamour can be seen as representing the bulk of deceptions, illusions, misunderstandings, misinterpretations, and exaggerations which prevent one from seeing clearly.[37]

The process of extracting oneself from glamour follows several stages. The first stage, where the consciousness of the bulk of humanity can be found today, is an acceptance of the world of appearances as an end in itself. The glamours associated with life on the physical plane prompt an almost automatic response to familiar instincts, including the drives for sex, food, and warmth. For many, there is a desire to seek physical or psychological comfort at all costs. For others, the desire for material possessions is stimulated by a wish to incorporate beauty and comfort into physical-plane life.[38]

Pitirim Sorokin, in his useful book, *The Crisis of Our Age*, defines western history in terms of three cultural systems: ideational culture, idealistic culture, and sensate culture. The relevance of Sorokin's book to the topic of glamour is that it provides a scale by which consciousness can be measured historically. Once the focal point of consciousness can be identified, then the various glamours associated with that sphere of consciousness can be detected.

Idealistic culture, according to Sorokin, emphasizes supersensory and superrational ideals, such as those which characterized the Middle Ages. Accordingly, many of the sixth-ray glamours pertaining to devotion are to be found within this culture. Ideational culture, which is an attempt to synthesize diverse cultural threads, was peculiar to Europe in the fourteenth and fifteenth centuries and to Greek culture in the fifth and fourth centuries BCE. At these intervals, there is an accompanying artistic and intellectual flowering, which interjects into the culture a new concept of truth and beauty. Finally, sensate culture, with its focus on the material world, has gathered momentum throughout Europe since the sixteenth century.[39] The rise of sensate culture could be said to coincide with the return to dominance of an Atlantean-based consciousness which, over the last two centuries, has brought about glamours surrounding the desire for material comfort, security of person and possessions, and the rights of the individual.

The second stage of extraction occurs when people become aware of the fact that they and all of humanity are victims of great forces over which they have no control. It is at this point that we become conscious of a duality in our nature. Even though our focus is still primarily on the physical plane, we are also cognizant of inner forces, energies, and worlds of being, opening us to other spheres of reality.[40] Just as medieval man awoke from the materialism of the Roman Empire during the "Dark Ages" and entered an otherworldly ideational phase of cultural development, so we, on a mass scale, may be undergoing a similar transition, as witnessed by the widespread emphasis in many parts of the world on purification, social responsibility, subjective meaning, and the pursuit of virtue in daily life. Underlying all cultural cycles is the slow, ponderous sweep of evolution. So, if we are moving into a new cultural era, as Sorokin believed we would, then it will be on a higher turn of the spiral. This, of course, fits conveniently with Vico's historical typology of cultural development (discussed in Chapter 3).

The third phase of extraction, of which the Tibetan speaks, is the stage of the so-called Arjuna experience, derived from the events surrounding the disciple Arjuna in the *Bhagavad Gita*. Arjuna is forced to enter into battle against his kinsmen, companions, and friends (representing his lower nature), all of whom have now become his enemies. Urged on by Krishna (the voice of his soul), Arjuna is directed to enter into the battle without thought of its outcome.

The phase of extraction is reached when the conflict between the pairs of opposites (higher and lower nature) intensifies and a resolution is made to seek illumination and to transcend the transitory images, glamours, and illusions, which hitherto have dominated one's consciousness.[41] It is at this point that one begins to overcome astral inversion, which is mistaking the unreal for the real. Needless to say, only a relatively small group within the body of humanity have achieved this point of consciousness, but the numbers are increasing, especially now during this present period of transition.

Thinking in terms of Sorokin's model, periods of creative cultural development, such as was noted in reference to fifth-century Greece and the Renaissance, can be seen as bursts of idealistic activity by which a small group of enlightened people generate a synthesis of thought, so as to create a vortex of energy which opens the door to new ideas from the Hierarchy. Hence, as was noted in the last chapter, the period around 1400 BCE was a major turning point in the West, as seen by those on the inner planes.

Aryan Consciousness

"The fifth root race," observes D.K., "marks a point where higher and lower manas approximate, and where the concrete mind, meeting its highest development of this round, gives place to the intuition from above."[42] It may seem curious that the mental development of humanity is so retarded, given that, by Hodson's estimation, the Aryan race is about a million years old,[43] or minus a few hundred thousand years, by some measurements.

The slow pace of mental evolution within humanity is the result of a process of unfoldment whereby a master gives a hint to a disciple whose training has led to a certain degree of mental clarity, which is then radiated into the environment through service.[44] Since disciples capable of such training in this early phase of racial development were few and far between, it stands to reason that conscious and coherent patterns of thought were virtually non-existent well into the period where history began to be recorded, except for among a handful of gifted individuals.

Ideas are generated on the mental plane through the process of building thoughtforms. In the course of astral living, humans have spewed forth into the environment masses of emotionally laden thoughts (referred to by the Tibetan as kama-manasic matter), "which surround practically every unit of the human family, producing a condition of murkiness and fog within, and around, each aura."[45] Through purification of the emotional life, coupled with an ability to concentrate, we begin to dissipate the murky clouds of emotional energy and half-formed thoughtform fragments, thus clearing the ethers, which allows for the downflow of ideas.[46] This, of course, takes time. Even as late as the early to mid-twentieth century, when the Tibetan's books were written, he estimated that eighty-five percent of the human race is surrounded by a "thick swirling fog of half-formed, semi-vitalized forms."[47]

The evolutionary development of thought, as seen historically, is not just an individual matter, but occurs within an ever-expanding field of consciousness. Biologist Rupert Sheldrake in his book, *A New Science of Life*, has put forward a theory that the physical and behavioral traits of an organism progress within the framework of self-organizing fields, which he refers to as morphogenetic fields. These fields cut across time and space and contain the quality of memory that is accumulative through time. The constancy and repetition of forms, consisting of oscillating and rapidly moving systems that display patterns of vibration and rhythm, create an aggregate of structures which eventually provide the template for a more evolved form. Sheldrake calls this process morphic resonance.[48]

What is true of forms is also true of consciousness. Hence, the slow evolutionary development of thought has created and, in turn, has been affected by a mental field, which Teilhard de Chardin referred to as the noosphere. The spread and development of this field of consciousness has increasingly imposed upon the mass of fragmented and "semi-vitalized thought-forms" a coherent pattern of thought, which is beginning to unite humanity through the synchronicity of ideas and embryonic telepathic activity. de Chardin writes:

"It may well be that in its individual capacities and penetrations our brain has reached its organic limits. But the movement does not stop there. From west to east, evolution is henceforth occupied elsewhere, in a richer and more complex domain, constructing, with all minds joined together, *mind*. Beyond all nations and races, the inevitable taking-as-a-whole of mankind has already begun.[49]

An Anthroposophical View of History and the Evolution of Human Consciousness

In a series of lectures delivered in the spring of 1921, Rudolf Steiner discussed the evolution of Western Civilization with respect to three distinctive periods. Whereas Steiner borrows much from the classical Theosophy of H.P.B., his focus is not the integration of eastern and western esotericism, but an analysis of the mystical and occult currents of thought which have underscored conditions and events in the Occident. Steiner's lectures are primarily declarative statements or expository remarks without any attempt to offer documentation for his provocative assertions. We must therefore consider his ideas in this light.

Reflecting on the evolution of human consciousness in the West, Steiner first identified the development of what he called the sentient soul, lasting from 2907 to 747 BCE.[50] This period coincided with what Steiner termed the third post-Atlantean age, or the Egypto-Chaldean epoch. People at this time, he claims, saw the spiritual in all facets of the outer world.[51] Stewart Easton writes that it was not possible for men at this time to engage in intellectual thinking, nor did they have explanations for the workings of earthly phenomena.[52] This suggests that people were still predominately instinctual in nature, lacking the capacity for reasoning in terms of cause and effect.

With the exception of the Egyptians, the leaders of other empires at this time did not establish any great or long-lasting civilizations. Following a period of innovation and creativity, the Sumerians, who rivaled the Egyptians in many ways, ceased to exist as a separate people and their priests do not seem to have inherited any significant body of esoteric knowledge.[53] Lacking significant mental development, the priests and kings of these earlier civilizations and empires tended to be rigidly traditional, as opposed to expansive and dynamic. Only towards the end of this epoch, notes Easton, during the period of the Hebrew prophets did men begin to approach self-consciousness and "prepare the way for the incorporation of the 'I' within the other three bodies, which became possible for the majority of mankind only in the following epoch."[54]

The development of the intellectual or rational soul began in the eighth pre-Christian century in southern Europe and Asia Minor. More particularly, this period coincided with the rise of the Greeks to cultural predominance, at a point when Sorokin identifies the emergence of an ideational culture.[55] With the dawn of the rational soul age, men began to speculate about the natural world and to ask questions. This germ of intellectual curiosity was the trademark of the Greeks who elevated the techniques of speculation to an art form while laying down the general principles of philosophy, mathematics, and science. Much of this speculation concerned an attempt to deduce fundamental elements from abstract principles or virtues. For example, in response to the question "how is happiness acquired?" Aristotle reasoned that happiness was not sent by some divine power, but was achieved through moral goodness and by some kind of intellectual training or study.[56]

According to Steiner, the epoch of the intellectual soul lasted until the fifteenth century, which included the medieval phase of European history. Students of medieval intellectual history have found important similarities between the thought patterns of the Greeks and the schoolmen of the Middle Ages who, of course, borrowed heavily from Greek ideas. The chief difference between the thinking of these two societies was that whereas the Greeks sought to understand the structure or components of things, medieval man attempted to reduce an idea to its universal principle. Professor Huizinga writes of the late Middle Ages:

"Every notion concerning the world or life had its fixed place in a vast hierarchic system of ideas, in which it is linked with ideas of a higher and more general order, on which it depends like a vassal on his lord. The proper business of the medieval mind is discrimination, displaying severally all concepts as if they were many substantial things."[57]

The third epoch in Steiner's historical view of man's intellectual development, which he referred to as the consciousness soul, dates from 1413 to 3513 CE. Why Steiner should have selected 1413 as a commencement date for the start of this new epoch is, at first glance, perplexing since, apart from the death of England's Henry IV, it marks little that is of major historical interest. The date is, however, of numerological value since it points to the completion of the 2,100-year cycle (actually 2,160 years) of the intellectual soul.

All histories, esoteric and exoteric, refer to the fifteenth century as an important period of transition. We know that the Hierarchy developed new initiatives for approaching humanity around this time. For Steiner, what made this period important was the invention of the printing press and the dissemination of the written word, which dates from the 1470s. According to Steiner, something of a psycho-spiritual element resounds through speech, and when spoken words ceased to be the content of human learning, the culture begins to be assimilated in abstract forms, through writing and the printed word.[58]

Whereas the Egyptians and the Chaldeans were the prototypical expression of the sentient soul, and the Greeks (and to a lesser extent the Romans) were the guiding influence behind the expression of the intellectual soul, the Anglo-Saxon people were seen as the representatives for the consciousness soul. Steiner does not talk about a Teutonic subrace, as does Hodson, nor does he say that the Anglo-Saxons were the flowering of Teutonic consciousness. Rather he maintains that the bud of what he calls patriarchal consciousness, which he sees as the essence of the intellectual soul, existed in Greece up to about 1000 BCE, and then was transferred to the inner soul of the Anglo-Saxon peoples, where it was nurtured for centuries.

Steiner maintains that patriarchal consciousness first appeared in the soul condition of Scotland and then spread throughout Britain. The gradual accumulation of this energy exploded on to the physical plane in about the 1770s, giving rise to a new kind of social structure that had far-reaching consequences.[59] At the heart of patriarchal consciousness is a pattern that is defined by the qualities of matter. Hence technology, materialism, and the tendency towards modernism is ultimately an outgrowth of patriarchy. Steiner says that England distanced itself from this patriarchal consciousness between the 1830s and the 1860s, but still had to reckon with the culture of technology, which she had helped to establish.[60] As to this last point, there is much ambiguity.

Whereas individualism, with its emphasis on solving practical problems, as reflected in patriarchal consciousness, has been a dominant feature of the Anglo-Saxons, Steiner argues that the Latin peoples have been characterized by abstract thought and, what he calls, the shadow-like intellect. As evidence, Steiner points to the Roman juridical tradition, which he holds was corroded by abstraction, as was the French Revolution, which he clearly did not like. The end result of these tendencies towards abstraction, notes Steiner, is constant experimentation without a goal. "The shadowy intellect is incapable," he says, "of truly intervening in the actual conditions. Everything basically remains undone and incomplete; it all remains as legacy of ancient Romanism."[61]

Anthroposophy, as noted in Chapter 3, also teaches that, subjectively speaking, European civilization is fed by four mystery streams. Each of these streams linked Europe to earlier subraces and root races. The eastern mystery stream, which is referred to as the Grail stream, flowed from the subraces of India, Persia, Chaldea, and Greece, and represented the spirit self. In this context the spirit self stands for the astral body, which is purified through the blood of the chalice. It is, therefore, the wisdom of these earlier subraces that, using Steiner's mystical language, effectively etherialized the blood of Europe, epitomized by the medieval image of cosmic Christianity.[62] From this mystery stream arose the Slavic racial consciousness, which has come to dominate most of Eastern Europe, including Russia.

The western mystery stream was seen as the repository of the Hibernian or Celtic mysteries. This stream of consciousness was rooted in Atlantis and passed into the Celtic regions of Europe by nomadic tribes during the first post-Atlantean culture. According to the Anthroposophists, the Hibernian mysteries are revealed in the stone circles and megalithic structures of the British Isles, of which Stonehenge is the most famous. The Celtic mysteries focused on time: daybreak, midday, twilight, and the seasons of the year.[63] Research has demonstrated that megalithic sites possess an elaborate geometry and number patterns that are infused with esoteric wisdom. John Michell writes:

"It was this world of the unconscious mind that the former magicians traveled, finding there the knowledge and power by which they were able to predict and influence events in the mundane world. This dream country was also marked out with a pattern of lines and centers, representing both the form in which visions occur and the figure which expresses the most sublime of all cosmic schemes, the cabalistic Tree of Life. So instructed were they in the geography of the unseen world, and so confident were the ordinary people in the wisdom and inspiration of their prophets and philosophers, that a scheme of barely imaginable piety and splendour was initiated, by which the whole world was shaped according to its archetypal ideal."[64]

Through the Germanic peoples flowed the northern stream of mysteries. The Germanic tribes were divided into two groups. The East Goths (Lombards) occupied Greece for a long time and then moved around the Adriatic Sea to Northern Italy. The West Goths (Franks) traveled by way of France and Spain, where they formed the basis for the Merovingian and the Carolingian kingdoms. These tribes and others (Visigoths, Ostrogoths, and Anglo-Saxons) brought with them new ideas of law, religion, and social life, which stressed the communal values of the folk. When the Vikings invaded Europe in the ninth century CE, they implanted the Nordic myths, particularly those surrounding Odin, who was, so it is said, the Bodhisattva of that time. Through sacrifice and heroic deeds, these myths prepared the Germanic and Anglo-Saxon peoples for the consciousness soul.[65] Acting as the avenue of ego impulse, the northern stream of mysteries gave rise to the expression of individuality, which Steiner associates with patriarchal consciousness. This ego, with its emphasis on sensate values, has been an important facet of the Teutonic peoples, representing the fifth subrace.

Finally, there is the southern stream, which the Anthroposophists maintain represents spirit-man. This stream, originated in Lemurian times and then passed through Egypt and Rome before entering Europe. Accordingly, this stream brought with it the consciousness of legalism, which formed the basis for Roman law. Following upon the Grail stream of the East, which culminated in Europe in the thirteenth century, the southern stream sparked the emergence of Rosicrucianism. During the sixteenth and seventeenth centuries, at a time of continuous religious strife, the Rosicrucians appeared in Europe. The argument is put forward that the Rosicrucians were charged with taking up the inner battle against the rise of materialism and power politics, which dominated the Church and the nations at that time, representing "the dark shadow of the Lemurian mystery of man." The southern stream, so we are told, is interwoven with the esotericism of the Jewish people.[66]

Consciousness and Racial Groups

Whether or not we care to accept all that Steiner gives us, his analysis goes far towards filling in the general outline of consciousness development that is presented by the Tibetan. Hodson offers a somewhat different typology which, for the most part, could be considered to be complimentary to that of Steiner. "The Theosophical view of single-sexed human evolution," writes Hodson, "is that it consists of a duality of consciousness and form, and that it has continued on earth for some 18 million years."[67] This duality of consciousness and form implies a relationship between the presentation of a dominant idea and the reaction of humanity to that idea. Hence, a root race is a divinely inspired idea that is developed through the seven subracial periods. According to this view, the entire root race flows from the department of the reigning Bodhisattva, who is an adept of highest standing and is in training to be a Buddha. For the fifth root race, this great adept has been the Manu.

Subsequently, each subrace, as noted in a previous chapter, has been guided by the consciousness of a great teacher. For the Indo-Aryan subrace in India, the teacher was Vyasa, one of the seven sages associated with the Vaivasvata Manu, who taught that the man in the sun was the lord and giver of life. Next came the Arab and Egyptian subrace, guided by Hermes, who imparted the idea that the true light dwells in the heart of every man. In the Persian, or third subrace, the great teacher, Zarathustra, brought to earth the wisdom of sacred fire. This fire purifies all that is unclean within man and purges out evil. There then followed Orpheus, the world teacher of the fourth subrace, which Hodson calls the Celtic or Greek subrace, who brought to consciousness the mysteries of sound. He taught that all phenomena in its various subtones resonate in one divine harmony. Associated with the creative word was also the message of beauty and joy. In our present subrace, the Teutonic or Anglo-Saxon, the great teacher has been the Christ, who has taught the meaning of love in its highest form.[68]

What appears evident from both the writings of Hodson and Steiner is that each subrace, or post-Atlantean civilization, embodies the accumulated teaching, consciousness, and wisdom of the previous subraces and, by implication, earlier root races. Hence the Teutonic subrace, which has been dominant in northern Europe and North America, is a synthesis of the collective streams of the past along with a new impulse, representing the evolution of the individualized ego.

What the Tibetan tells us is that these subracial teachings are steps in the broader evolution of the human mind, which will reach its full development at the end of this root race. He observes that the point of identification of self for modern people in this contemporary stage of evolution (the fifth subrace) is not in the true self, or soul, but in the parts of our lower nature, whether this is expressed through the physical body, or through the astral body, as reflected in the statement "I want" or "I desire" something, or through the mental vehicle, where we regard ourself as the author of thought.

It is this identification that results in the theological differences and the doctrinal and sectarian diversities everywhere to be found and in this fifth root race, and particularly in this fifth subrace, this identification reaches its apotheosis. It is the era of the personal self, not of the spiritual self.[69]

Karma and the Evolution of Consciousness

Karma is an abstruse and complex phenomenon, the full effects of which can be only partially realized. By the same token, it is a rather simple concept. Essentially, karma, as mentioned before, is the expression of the law of cause and effect, or scientifically stated, "for every action there is an equal and opposite reaction." The complexity of karma concerns the magnitude of its activity, which affects the solar system as much as it does the subhuman kingdoms, and is connected to every thought and action. Within the sphere of human history, there are many interlocking spheres of karma, which include world karma, racial karma, national karma, group karma, and individual karma.

Karma, as it acts out in the world, unites together the twin ideas of freedom and responsibility. Freedom is the evolutionary tendency and destiny of all forms and involves the overcoming of limitation. The many obstacles, difficulties, and tests, which are the lot of any life, serve, over the course of many lifetimes, to strengthen the will, purify the heart, and expand the intellect, so as to eventually lead one to the path of higher initiation and, hence, to greater freedom. Responsibility is the mechanism by which freedom is achieved, and can be summed up in the attempt to create right human relationships. In opposition to the unbridled licentiousness of Lemurian times, we are told, there arose the first tendencies towards marriage and family formation, which constituted initial efforts in group formation and humanity's beginning lesson in responsibility.[70] Freedom through responsibility is the essential ingredient of relationships and group work, which is the basis of human existence.

Historically speaking, karma is intertwined with the process of human evolution. For the bulk of infant humanity, whose consciousness is below the threshold of self-awareness, karma is a group matter. Here we see the importance of families and kinship groups, which are to be found in every culture and comprise the basic unit of social stability. Families rooted on the same piece of earth for generations, even centuries, created provincial networks of support and cohesion. While attending to the basic need of the individual, clans and family groupings have also been a focal point of separativeness and extreme parochialism. The mass of peasantry, which has been the dominant social group, at least in Europe, from ancient to modern times, lived within the context of small exclusive family arrangements. If the family afforded its members protection, it also provided a forum for conflict. Historian, Peter Laslett, writes: "In the traditional patriarchal society of Europe, where practically everyone lived out his whole life within the family, often within one family only, tension…must have been incessant and unrelieved, incapable of release except in crisis."[71]

For the mass of humanity, therefore, karmic relationships have been family relationships. Insofar as we are told that it is the soul of the person who chooses when, where, and with whom to incarnate, it stands to reason that family units would incarnate together as a group over many lifetimes so as to gradually develop patterns of goodwill leading to a rudimentary understanding of right human relations. It is for this reason that virtually everyone, regardless of their degree of consciousness or rank in life, goes through a family group experience. Level of development, past karmic obligations, and other factors will determine one's situation in life, range of associations, and avenues for service.[72]

As consciousness evolves and the person begins to see himself as having an identity apart from the mass-consciousness of the group, then karma becomes more personal and definite. At this stage, one begins to work off the effects of actions wrought, in some cases, over many lifetimes.[73] In the recorded history of humanity, there have been times when conditions have been ripe for a significant change of consciousness on a wide scale. Such a time occurred during the period of the Renaissance and subsequent centuries, in which the sphere of public life began to expand at the same time that the realm of private space began to be defined. This could be seen in the emergence of various clubs, societies, and organizations; the visible practice of personal piety in religious matters; the creation of private space in homes; the spread of literacy; and the expansion of one's horizons through travel and mobility.[74]

As individuals evolve towards greater personality integration, their lives take on greater karmic responsibilities. The Reformation and the Counter Reformation of the sixteenth and seventeenth centuries created a climate where self-discipline and adherence to duty became paramount obligations in a person's life. This new emphasis on personal responsibility stood in marked contrast to the relatively licentious and boorish life of the medieval peasant in an earlier age, who was primarily concerned with security and survival. The inner-directed man, fearful of losing self-control and aware of temptations in the world, emerged as a social ideal during the nineteenth century, at a time when the middle classes were coming to dominate society. Dutiful, self-reliant, sensitive, and charitable, yet ambitious, exclusive, and materialistic, the social virtues of the Victorian age reflected the ideals of the separated personality, which has had both positive and negative karmic consequences.

Through pain and suffering, wrought by two world wars and a flood of other disasters in the twentieth century, humanity has worked off much evil karma and, in the words of the Tibetan, "karma based on causes later to be initiated will not generate such dire effects as that of the past."[75] He writes: "When karmic retribution becomes acute and terrible, as it is in today's appalling world experience, it indicates that humanity has reached a point where consequences can be meted out on a large scale and with justice. Very little suffering is attached to karma where there is ignorance, leading to irresponsibility and complete lack of thought and there is attached to affairs but little true sense of guilt. There may be unhappy conditions and distressing circumstances, but the inability to respond to such conditions with commensurate pain is lacking; there is little mental reaction to the processes of karmic retribution."[76]

National Karma

It is said that since the Aryan root race has developed its mental faculties so quickly in such a short period of time that karma on a large scale, which is often horrific in nature, can express itself through world conditions.[77] Various circumstances—such as wars, acts of terrorism, and natural disasters, which are visited on large groups of people— can be seen as the overshadowing of national, racial, or world karma on individual lives.

Through observing the history of nations, clear patterns of cause and effect can be detected, which suggest a network of karmic events. In one sense, national karma is closely associated with great men or leaders who guide the destiny of a people. The political savvy of Queen Elizabeth I, the foolishness of Charles I, the stability and detachment of Queen Victoria, the reform-mindedness of David Lloyd George, and the heroic vision of Winston Churchill all generated national karma and determined the course of British history. In another sense, if Abraham Lincoln had been somewhat less than politically astute and without vision, what sort of karma would have befallen the United States as a result of the Civil War? Also, what kind of karmic responsibilities did Lenin impose on the Russian people? To national leaders and public figures, therefore, are given unique responsibilities because they are entrusted with the karmic destinies of a race or nation.

The process of identifying karmic connections can only be speculative at best since the task of relating cause to effect is complicated by the myriads of unseen variables and correlating events. This is particularly true when we attempt to identify karmic connections on a national or racial scale. Hodson devotes some attention to a discussion of the karma of individual nations and, while some adjustments have been made to his analysis, his comments are worth considering.[78]

Belgium—Hodson asks the question, why did Belgium suffer so heavily in the two world wars? He links the cause of this suffering to the atrocities committed by their colonial administration in the Belgian Congo, which amounted to barbarous treatment, even partial genocide, against the native population.

France—The humiliation of the French by capitulating, with very little opposition, to the German army in 1940 stands in contrast to the pride of French kings and rulers who treated their native populations with cavalier indifference and who waged endless wars of aggression against other nations from the time of Louis XIV to Napoleon.

Spain—The defeat of the Spanish armada by the English in the sixteenth century began a long and painful decline of this once great nation, culminating in the Spanish Civil War in the 1930s and the rise of fascism. However, no other nation was more responsible for the slaughter and enslavement of the Indian populations in the period of colonization, nor in the fanatical slaughter of non-Catholic peoples, through the use of the Inquisition, during a time of political unification in the fifteenth century.

Switzerland—Unlike other European nations, the Swiss have been spared the ravages of war and destruction. Apart from being a neutral state, Switzerland has a long history of democracy, harmonious ethnic pluralism, as well as being the home of many international organizations devoted to peace and the service of humanity, such as the International Red Cross.

Italy—The misfortunes that Italy has suffered in the twentieth century, primarily under Mussolini, who sought to create a new Roman Empire, may be traced back to the aggressive policies of the old Roman Empire, which conquered and enslaved many diverse peoples.

Germany—The crimes perpetuated by Hitler and the Nazis against the Jews and other groups stand as one of the greatest atrocities of all time. The Nazi experience was the culmination of nearly a century of aggressive actions by the Germans under the leadership of Bismarck and others. The destruction of Germany during the Second World War, and her humiliation by means of the Versailles Peace Treaty at the end of the First World War, were karmic paybacks for German imperialistic designs.

Japan—Modern Japanese history up through the Second World War parallels that of Germany in terms of its reliance on industrialism, militarism, and authoritarianism. The brutality accompanying the Japanese invasion of China and Southeast Asia in the 1930s and during the war led, karmically, to her own destruction through massive bombing, culminating in the dropping of the atom bombs on Hiroshima and Nagasaki.

Great Britain—Every nation has positive and negative karmic elements. Britain initiated and perpetuated the trans-Atlantic slave trade for commercial benefit, which predated the wage slavery and suffering that was the lot of most people living in the British Isles during the Industrial Revolution of the nineteenth century. On the other hand, the evolutionary development of fundamental political rights and the willingness of the British government to stand on principle, as in the case of protecting the neutrality of Belgium in the First World War, perhaps, according to the law of karma, saved Britain from disaster and invasion in the Second World War.

United States—As a young nation, the United States is relatively free from the ancient karma shared by peoples and nations in Europe, Asia, and Africa. An inherent generosity and natural bounty has blessed the United States with much wealth, prestige, and comfort, however karmic debts have accrued which are now coming to fruition. One such area is race relations. Another is the epidemic of drug use, which appears to be a karmic reaction to the neo-colonialism of American corporations, which helps to keep many nations in Asia, Africa, and Latin America poor, and the addictive nature of America's mass-consumer society, which saps the will of its citizens.

Russia—More than most countries, Russia has a long history of suffering, which mirrors its own brutal attacks on Jews, Poles, and other subject people. Unlike the nations of Western Europe, much of the population of Russia consisted for centuries of ignorant serfs, whose stature has only risen during the Soviet experience of the twentieth century. The rise of the Russian people to a point where they can participate freely in political and economic life may signal a change in their karmic fortunes. Through absorbing the brunt of the Nazi attack during the Second World War, the Russians paid off much ancient karma.

Racial and Global Karma

The fortunes or misfortunes of one's country aside, aggregates of individuals are also subject to the karma of their racial group. Certain temperamental tendencies are contained in the racial makeup of the physical body and are part of the constitutional structure of that body for an entire life. This is not so much a dense physical phenomenon as a matter of subjective activity. Each racial group resonates to a particular color, sound, and vibratory rate. Hence, an Oriental body will have one set of qualifications, whereas a western body will have another set of qualifications. One is not better than the other; they are merely different. The question of race is more than skin deep and involves other planes of consciousness as well as a whole set of subtle conditions which we, often unwittingly, respond to positively or negatively. An unseen effect of the recent trend towards intermarriage and the mixing of racial groups, for instance, is to force one vibration to the same key as another, which can lead to difficulties both socially and physically.[79]

As with all matters spiritual, the solution to circumstances involving racial karma involves an alteration of consciousness rather than changes in physical-plane circumstances. This is why the Hierarchy constantly puts emphasis on highlighting the positive with respect to dealing with and understanding national or racial groups. "Each nation," writes an unknown contributor to A.A.B.'s *Letters on Occult Meditation*, "has its virtues and each has its defects; it will therefore be the work of the superintending Teacher to apportion meditations that will intensify the virtues and remedy the defects."[80]

All this points to the great opportunity that will be placed at the feet of humanity in the centuries to come. Insofar as the race is becoming receptive to ideas, and increasing numbers are gaining mastery on the mental plane, people will be able, given a proper orientation, to transcend their own karmic responsibilities and work to eliminate group karma at various levels. Global problems involving environmental concerns, racial and ethnic cleavages, world hunger, exploitative capitalism, totalitarianism, and political corruption are essentially the products of age-old thought patterns, which have gained a hold and crystallized in the minds of people.

By understanding the nature of the subtle world—the laws of manifestation and of spiritual evolution, the consciousness structure of root races and their branches, the inner government of the planet, and the cyclical ebb and flow of energy from the seven rays and cosmic sources—humanity can disintegrate the barriers of karmic limitation that inhibit the race from experiencing the inner light of greater soul purpose.

Reincarnation

In principle, the esoteric doctrine of reincarnation has attracted serious attention from men and women in the West, representing many diverse backgrounds. For many people, such as the student I referred to in the introduction to this book, the plausibility of living many lives is an outgrowth of some personal experience. For others, reincarnation provides a compelling answer to one of life's great questions, "what happens to us after death?" Thinkers and writers throughout history have alluded to the reality of reincarnation. Shakespeare, for example, wrote in his sonnet, number 59:

> *If there be nothing new, but that which is*
> *Hath been before, how are our brains beguil'd,*
> *Which, labouring for invention, bear amiss*
> *The second burden of a former child!*

There is strong evidence that the early Christian Church accepted the doctrine of reincarnation, which can be supported by the scriptures. In the book of Matthew, Jesus says: "'Elijah is to come to see that everything is once more as it should be; however, I tell you that Elijah has come already and they did not recognize him but treated him as they pleased; and the Son of Man will suffer similarly at their hands.' The disciples understood then that he had been speaking of John the Baptist."[81]

The Christian Gnostics were all reincarnationists, and references to reincarnation can be found in the writings of Tertullian, the Greek theologian Origen, St. Gregory of Nazianzus, St. Augustine of Hippo, and Synesius, Bishop of Ptolemais, among others.[82] Tolerance for reincarnation ended with the Fifth Ecumenical Council and opposition to this doctrine was later ratified by other church councils.

Recently, there has been a flurry of interest in historical reincarnation, as evidenced by a number of books on the subject. Barbara Lane's book, *Echoes From the Battlefield*, contains testimonies of people living today who remember participating in the American Civil War during a past life. In a similar vein, Rabbi Yonassan Gershom has collected a number of case studies of persons who recall their demise in the Holocaust. A former British journalist, Vicki Mackenzie, has chronicled the lives of Tibetan Buddhist adepts who have chosen to reincarnate in the West to help give impetus to the transformation of consciousness that is taking place during these propitious times.[83]

In essence, reincarnation is nothing more than the cyclic process of manifestation and pralaya that operates through schemes, chains, globes, rounds, and root races. Moreover, it is the logical consequence of a recognition of the Self as a soul, as distinct from a personality. This points to the illusion of death since the essential Self, as opposed to the more obvious impermanent self, does not die. The personality is only the housing unit which defines a life for a brief period within time and space, before it disintegrates. Whereas reincarnation is largely seen in personal terms, in relation to one's previous and/or future incarnations, it is primarily a group phenomenon, affecting the nature and evolutionary development of communities, nations, and civilizations.

Beyond the experience or wisdom that can be garnered from any particular life, or string of lives, supposition about previous existences is of little consequence. An analogy might be made to a random day in one's own life. By itself, what happened on the twenty-second of August fifteen years ago is unimportant, however the sequence of days that comprise a single life has made one what one is. The correspondence holds true in both cases.

A Case Study: Great Britain and Ancient Rome

Because history gives us a wide canvas on which to view the rise and fall of nations, empires, and civilizations, we can see possible connections between the collective existences of a set of people living at different points in time. However, such an exercise is far from being precise. People live, die, and are born again in a variety of circumstances, so the understanding of history in the light of reincarnation is far more speculative than scientific. Having said that, there are some intriguing correlations.

One obvious example is the enthusiasm of the Renaissance Italians who not only sought to emulate the achievements of classical antiquity, but identified themselves almost completely with the ancients. Burckhardt has written that the power of the Renaissance that achieved mastery over the western world was derived from the influence of Greek and Roman culture coupled with the genius of the Italian people.[84] The fact that the passion of the Italians for classical culture did not display itself before the fourteenth century suggests that a whole generation of artists, scholars, builders, and others who possessed an intimate knowledge of the Greek and Roman world came into manifestation as a group.

At other times in history, there have been bursts of nostalgia, creative emulation, and a similarity of activity, which is indicative of reincarnation. The fanatics who championed the cause of Christianity during the time of the Crusades in the eleventh and twelfth centuries might well have been the same souls who championed the cause of the Catholic Church during the Counter Reformation in sixteenth-century Europe.

Likewise, the men of finance and commerce who made Amsterdam the center of bourgeois capitalism during the seventeenth century bear a close resemblance to the Florentines of the fifteenth century. German Field Marshal, Helmuth von Moltke, the architect of the modern German army and a believer in reincarnation, thought that there was a similarity between the politically motivated popes in the ninth century and the chiefs of the German General Staff in his own time.[85] Hitler, like many of the Nazi leaders, believed in reincarnation and identified himself with the black magicians on Atlantis and the German warriors of the ninth century.

Certain nations possess such close similarities in consciousness and evolution so as to invite suspicions of reincarnation on a mass scale. Such a correlation appears to exist between Great Britain and ancient Rome. As a point of departure, one needs to look at the ray structure of each society. The Tibetan observes that the British race in modern times consists of largely reincarnated Romans, based on his knowledge of their ray configurations.[86]

Dr. R. F. Newbold, professor of Classics at the University of Adelaide in Australia, presents a compelling argument that ancient Rome possessed the qualities of a first-ray soul and a seventh-ray personality.[87] Britain possesses a ray-one personality which, in terms of nations, is indicative of strong leadership capabilities, the ability to govern effectively, an impetus towards creating an empire, and detachment in dealing with other nations and peoples. Through its second-ray soul, the first-ray personality of Britain would have a nurturing quality in guiding other peoples towards independence and self-reliance; the seventh-ray personality of Rome would tend towards greater ritual, formalism, and an emphasis on law and order.

There is also a rough correlation between events in British and Roman history that seem noteworthy.

Rome	Britain
Defeat of Etruscans by Romans	Norman conquest of the Anglo-Saxons
Twelve Tables of Roman Law	Issue of the Great Charter
Creation of republican constitution	Creation of Parliament
Punic Wars against Carthage	Hundred Years War against France
Cultural development (synthesis of Greek ideas)	The Elizabethan renaissance
Civil War leading to the end of the Republic	English Civil War leading temporarily to the end of the monarchy
Age of Augustus, golden age of the arts	Augustian age, golden age of the arts
Pax Romana (27 BCE-180 CE)	Pax Britannica (1815-1914)
Construction of roads, temples, and public buildings	Industrial Revolution
Emergence and expansion of the Roman Empire	Global expansion of the British Empire
Wars against the German invaders	World Wars against Germany
Dismemberment of the western Empire	Decolonization

The similarity of these events speaks for themselves. In essence, British history, to some extent, is modeled on a stream of consciousness that was developed by the Romans. Owen Barfield presents an interesting theory that is based on an unpublished manuscript, *Treatise on Logic*, by the poet Samuel Taylor Coleridge. According to Coleridge, the essence of self-consciousness is unity, which has a subjective essence as well as an external nature. He refers to these as active unity and productive unity. From unity is derived the universal law of polarity, which is an esoteric truth as well as a characteristic of all phenomena. In seeking to understand the transition from the dialectic to the organic, Coleridge constructed a diagram of two perpendicular lines, representing the four directions. The north-south axis is recognized as the physical properties of attraction and repulsion, governed by the magnetic force of gravitation. The east-west axis represents the relationship between dilatation and contraction, established through the flow of electricity.[88]

If we apply this model to European history, there are some

interesting correlations. Between the Teutonic peoples of the North (Britain) and the Latin peoples of the South (Romans), there is a magnetic attractive force that draws the one to the other. This could explain similarities in history and culture and also reasons why the souls of the ancient Romans might seek to continue their evolution within a northern, hence English, environment. As to the west-east axis, the tendency for Western Europe to expand beyond its borders and for Eastern Europe to sustain a more provincial focus is clearly seen in history. The reason why this relationship is described as electric is due to the strong current of energy, information, and emotion that has, over time, flowed across Europe from west to east.

Britain, of course, was an outpost in the Roman Empire but, after the fifth century CE, it was overswamped by waves of Anglo-Saxon invaders. Geoffrey of Monmouth, a twelfth-century historian of Britain and one of the proponents of the Arthurian legends, puts forth the theory that Britain had Trojan origins. According to the legend, Brutus, the grandson of Aeneas of Troy, was banished from his country and arrived in the land of Albion with his faithful followers. After his death, the island was divided among his three sons, which resulted in the creation of England, Scotland, and Wales. There is little corroborating evidence to support this story, although it was popularly believed throughout the Middle Ages.[89] More to the point is the fact that following the conquest of England by William the Conqueror, a two-tiered society was created with the largely latinized Normans holding positions of rank and power, while the defeated descendants of the Anglo-Saxons and the Vikings made up the mass of the common folk. Roman consciousness, insofar as it appeared in England, was found only among the upper crust.

Rudolf Steiner argues that the English folk spirit descended in England somewhere around the middle of the seventeenth century.[90] This probably means that as a nation, England was developing self-consciousness. This self-consciousness, if it existed, was hardly a unified phenomenon, particularly in the seventeenth century, and was constantly modified by class divisions. Among the elites, there is solid evidence to support the notion that these patricians, as they called themselves, saw themselves as heirs to the legacy of Rome. Claims to divine right by the Stuart kings owed much to the legacy of the Roman emperors. Whereas the English kings in the seventeenth century sought to rule like Roman emperors, the Hanovarian kings of the eighteenth century desired to live like them. So did the class of noblemen who comprised the patrician class. Secure in their classical-style country homes with gardens, busts of Roman heroes, and temples, they ran the affairs of state in much the same relaxed manner as the aristocratic senatorial Romans. Moreover, Italy attracted the English landed classes like a magnet and it became routine for sons of peers and gentlemen to visit the Roman world as part of their grand tour. In the Augustan age of eighteenth-century England, many noblemen, like Lord Chesterfield, expressed a spiritual identity of their own times with that of Rome.[91] In almost every sphere of life, an English gentleman could make comparisons with his counterparts in Rome.

The strength of Roman consciousness in England and, incidentally, the implication that many Englishmen were reincarnated Romans, comes from the importance of Latin and classical references in English literature and education. Between 1500 and 1650, about 10,000 words were introduced into English, the majority of which were derived from Latin.[92] Education at the best public schools, such as Eton and the two ancient universities of Oxford and Cambridge, was profoundly classical until after the First World War. The mirror of consciousness that a classical education provided was more than a longing for the past. It was an expression of a deep-seated memory and an affinity for what is the line of least resistance. By the nineteenth century, the emphasis had shifted somewhat from an identification with the Romans to that of the Athenians.[93] Here too, reincarnation, as evidenced by historical memory, would appear to play a role.

A final point of similarity concerns the way that both the British and the Romans have ruled subject peoples. "Rome," it is said, "discovered that 'liberation' was the best policy." Many of the Greek city-states had treaties with Rome which gave them great internal autonomy but bound them to give assistance in the case of war. Other conquered territories simply fell within the Roman sphere of influence and were unilaterally free to govern themselves.[94] Rome built roads, temples, aqueducts, columns, and other structures in the outreaches of the empire, which reflected its grandeur. The provinces also contained a two-tiered society. The Romans provided the governors, judges, and military leaders, but did not interfere in the daily life of the inhabitants. According to one source, "the Romans made no attempt to impose uniformity; in some provinces a magistrate, a quaestor, was responsible for the collection of direct taxes, but probably only by overseeing local officials."[95]

Britain governed her colonies in a similar fashion. Unlike the French and the Germans, the British created a colonial society of the ruling elites (themselves) apart from the subject peoples, who were left to their own devices or served their masters in a subordinate role. Like the Romans, the British sought to create a home away from home, which included buildings and other public works that reflected the styles of Victorian architecture. Colonial peoples adopted British customs and laws. Many of those who were better educated and came from the upper echelons of the indigenous society went to England to be educated. Indeed, many colonials sought to transform themselves into Englishmen, in much the same way that conquered people within the Roman Empire desired to become civilized Romans. Whereas the Roman Empire rested on the backs of slaves, the British Empire was supported by masses of colonial servants and laborers. Insofar as the British people are subjectively linked to India (the jewel of the British Empire) through past incarnations and associations, the relationship between these two countries was, quite literally, a family affair.[96]

The retreat of modern Britain from its classical past signals not only an important change in the course of its history but new collective patterns of reincarnating souls. As Britain (like many other countries) breaks down its wall of isolation and becomes an integrated part of a united Europe, it will, no doubt, open itself to a more diverse array of incarnating men and women. This is an important step towards becoming a planetary society of one humanity.

Section Three—
Spirals and Cycles

The wise man knows that a conditionless, changeless period of manifestation is an utter impossibility for man in his present state, he knows that history repeats itself in ever recurring periods through an eternity of time as day follows night; he knows that the democracy of one age will make way for the monarchy of the next, as surely as he knows that the tides will throw up the waters of an ocean on its shores and then fling them back in perfect time and rhythm.

—Teachings of the Temple

The reality of Soul History cannot be demonstrated by its traces, but by the character of its Present Moment. There is a spiritual life that cannot be accounted for in terms of causes transmitted from the past. This life is that of the Collective Soul of Humanity. This soul is present here and now, though still more than embryonic in its development. It lives by a creative action that constantly overcomes the disruptive action of the material world. We do not see its source, but we feel its working. It is a natural working, but not a mechanical or even a vital one.

—J.G. Bennett, *The Dramatic Universe, IV, History*

Chapter 7—
The Seven Rays and The Psychological Dimension of History

A point of constant philosophical debate is whether people possess free will or are conditioned by factors beyond their control. Whereas most political, sociological, economic, and psychological schools lean towards one or the other of these positions, the Ageless Wisdom posits that we are the product of both. In all his writings, the Tibetan clearly states that we possess free will that cannot be infringed upon by the elder brothers of the race. At the same time, people are limited and governed by forces and energies over which they have little knowledge, let alone control. An animal tethered by a rope of varying lengths is symbolic of the human condition. Circumscribed within the planes of consciousness is our own sphere of awareness, which is referred to as the ring-pass-not by esoteric students. Thus while we live, move, and have our being, operating under the illusion that we possess complete freedom of choice, we are, at the same time, being conditioned by a myriad of energies that define our ring-pass-not. Noting the extra planetary and interplanetary energies affecting the planet at the time of the Hierarchical council held at Wesak in 1937, the Tibetan enumerated the following:

- The cumulative forces of the Piscean age that serve as the line of least resistance for the unenlightened masses
- The incoming Aquarian energies that have a wide and general effect upon the ethers surrounding the earth, upon all the kingdoms in nature, and upon thinking humanity
- The cosmic forces pouring into the planet from Betelgeuse and Sirius that stimulate the heart and head centers respectively of world disciples

- Venusian forces of great potency that override the previously dominant Martian forces
- The forces of the planetary entity itself that are behind much of the physical and cataclysmic activity of the present times
- The energy of the united Hierarchy of the planet in their great approaches to the physical plane wherein they seek to stimulate the higher centers of humanity
- The emerging energies of the New Group of World Servers, serving as a bridge between humanity and the Hierarchy
- The powerful vibratory influence of important men and women who, subjectively or objectively, direct human affairs and are regarded by the Hierarchy as "doors into human life"
- Certain evil or dark forces who work ceaselessly to enslave people and hold back human evolution.[1]

The Nature of Motion

All forms, whether one thinks in terms of an atom, a human being, or a solar system, are governed by rotary motion. What is meant by rotary motion is movement around a central axis. Hence, all forms from the angle of etheric vision have a similar shape but are differentiated by the velocity of rotation. Low grades of matter rotate at a slower speed than do more refined grades of matter. This is equally true among a common species of form and between forms of a different nature.[2] Humanity today, comprising billions of individual aggregates, collectively spins at a faster rate than did its Lemurian or Atlantean counterparts. As consciousness evolves, from an esoteric standpoint, a vortex is created, which has the effect of opening the higher chakra centers. As we become more mentally polarized and continue to refine our emotional nature, the throat, heart, and head centers above the diaphragm are stimulated and eventually open, allowing for the transmission of higher energies.

When activity begins to transpire on the plane of mind, then the phenomenon of time comes into play. This second aspect of motion is cyclic in nature insofar as it lends itself to periodicity, which is the appearance and disappearance of all forms whether great or small. The esoteric causes of cyclic motion are beyond the scope of our discussion, or even comprehension. Suffice it to say that, esoterically speaking, it can be linked to the will aspect of divinity and to the impulses originating in Sirius.[3] Cyclic motion explains why individual lives, nations, civilizations, subraces, and root races come into manifestation at a given point, undergo a phase of growth or development, reach an optimal stage of development, begin a process of decline, and then go out of existence.

Throughout history, civilizations, nations, people, and events have been governed by an intricate and endless web of cycles. Unraveling these various cycles is a study in itself and one, though much needed, which would easily be a lifetime's preoccupation. There are many kinds of cycles, astrological cycles being perhaps the most obvious. Other cycles are more subtle. H.P.B. refers to the work of a Dr. E. Zasse, who noted that from the year 1700 there was a cycle of destructive energy in Europe that resulted in a war every fifty years. Dr. Zasse believed that this mysterious law had astronomical implications and was linked to the periodicity of solar sun spots.[4]

Rotary and cyclic motion is impacted by a third stream of movement which travels in a spiral pattern. Spiral-cyclic motion occurs when the locus of a point moving around a fixed center (rotary motion) travels in cyclical orbits while expanding or decreasing in scope. Put another way, the attractive force of rotating matter becomes dominated by a higher vibration and, through its spiraling movement, it sweeps those forms systemically nearer to a stronger and higher point of energy.[5] The driving force behind spiral-cyclic movement is the impulse to forward movement, which means that no two events ever take place in precisely the same spot. The old adage that "history repeats itself" is a statement of cyclical motion. However, in reality, events may go in and out of season but they never replicate the same situations or circumstances. Hence, all persons, places, and things become modified and altered in the course of time.

Spiral-cyclic force manifests itself in seven ways but emanates from three cosmic sources. The Tibetan explains this process as follows: "From these three cosmic planes (embracing the sacred personality of the Logoi, solar and planetary) come the united energies of the three constellations which control and energise our solar system: The Great Bear, the Pleiades and Sirius; these work through the medium of the seven rays and these in turn express themselves through the twelve constellations which form the great zodiacal wheel. The Lords or ruling

Powers of these twelve sources of light and life 'step down' the potency of these three major energies so that our Solar Logos can absorb them; they 'tune out' those aspects of these three Potencies which are not suited to our systemic life at this point in the evolutionary process, just as the Hierarchy upon our little planet tunes out or steps down the energies from Shamballa. In a mysterious manner, these three major energies express themselves through the seven rays, just as all triplicities subdivide into septenates and yet preserve their identity."[6]

The seven types of spiral-cyclic energy, or the seven rays, are vibrating streams of energy. Technically speaking, the seven rays, as intelligent entities through which the divine plan manifests, function ultimately as sound and color. Each ray note vibrates at a certain frequency and has its own shade and quality of intelligent life. Consequently, as the rays radiate through the seven planes of manifestation, they saturate the life forms on each plane in descending order. History is shaped by the interplay of ray notes and light qualities on the three lower planes—mental, astral, and etheric/physical. As these rays are governed by the law of cycles, they play upon the consciousness of humanity according to rhythmic patterns. Thus, the whole of human history can be understood as a melody of ray and subray interactions.

The Length and Impact of Ray Cycles

Not all ray cycles are the same length. Neither are they arbitrary. According to Stephen Pugh, who has made a study of esoteric number theory, Pythagoras developed a cosmic world view centered upon the dyad, or the number ten.[7] Each number, according to Pugh, has a philosophical reference. The number one, for example, is based on universal unity; the number two is characterized by the cipher five and relates to consciousness; three, (9 or 3*3) is represented by the ternary and stands for the trinity, which is the primary geometric form; four, defined by the cipher twenty-five (25), synthesizes duality and perfected form; five, or cipher thirty-five (35), connotes the combination of perfect mind and thinking (e.g. conscious) man; six, symbolized by cipher fifteen (15) links one-pointed focus that embodies form; and, seven (7 or 3+4) signifies the infusion of spirit into matter.

Placed in a cosmic setting, the interplay of these numbers provides an orderly arrangement of inflowing and outflowing ray energies, as seen in the following table.

Table 8. Multiple Time Periods for Each Ray

Short Cycles	Racial Cycle	Planetary Ray Cycle
Ray 1 (10)	10, 100 years	100, 1000 years
Ray 2 (5)	5, 50 years	500, 5,000 years
Ray 3 (9)	9, 90 years	900, 9,000 years
Ray 4 (25)	2.5, 25 years	250, 2,500 years
Ray 5 (35)	3.5, 35 years	350, 3,500 years
Ray 6 (15)	1.5, 15 years	150, 1,500 years
Ray 7 (7)	7, 70 years	700, 7,000 years

In discussing the manner by which time is conditioned by the seven rays, it is important to make a clear distinction between the cyclic movement of the rays, which delineate regular and repetitive units of time, and the spiral movement of the rays, which determine the period when a particular ray is in or out of manifestation. Connecting ray cycles to historical events often falls short of precision in that individuals and groups of men and women make history in response to cyclic influences. Human free will may retard or accelerate the unfoldment of an idea, the invention of a device, the start of a war or its conclusion, or a host of other events. However, rarely, if ever, is history made independent of the determining energies impacting the planet, of which the rays exert a major influence. What may seem to the casual observer as coincidence is, in fact, the synchronization of cyclical impulses.

Cycles Based on the Ray Cipher One

With reference to the cyclic movement of the rays, the decad multiples of a ray cipher enable us to divide time into units and give it meaning. For example, a year, a decade, a century, and a millennium are all expressions of first-ray cycles and reflect the ebb and flow of will energy. According to Pythagorean doctrine, the number one and its multiples are the source of every emanation. Understandably, we give the greatest importance to first-ray cycles. Each year is marked by a variety of annual events. The history of nations is most often written in reference to decades and centuries. A hundred-year cycle appears to be of major significance. Research based on tree rings has shown that warm and cold and wet and dry weather patterns occur in one-hundred-year cycles.[8] Often the history of civilizations is understood in terms of millennia. In a history of the last thousand years, Felipe Fernandez writes: "Decades and centuries are like the clock cases inside which the pendulum of history swings. Strictly speaking, a new millennium begins every day and every moment of every day; yet the approach of the year 2000 makes the present a peculiarly—indeed, an uniquely—good time for taking stock of our last thousand years of history, asking where they have led us and wondering where we go from here."[9]

Cycles Based on the Ray Cipher Five

The second ray, characterized by the cipher five, or half-ten, is also clearly identifiable. We know that the Soviet Union measured its economy in terms of five-year plans; some figures suggest that cycles of inflation, such as those that affected the American economy in rhythmic fashion since World War II, have a five-year duration. Moreover, data collected by the Essex Corporation in 1992 and compiled by the Bureau of Labor Statistics indicate that for the fifty-one-year period between 1940 and 1991, the rate of inflation was close to five percent; 4.54% to be exact.

Historically, a fifty-year period represents a unit of time in which trends and developments often spin their course. The revolutions of the early nineteenth century; the period of European imperialist expansion, beginning around 1870; and the Cold War era all occurred in roughly a fifty-year period. We also find evidence of social movements and counter-movements (which exemplify the second-ray emphasis on duality) occurring roughly within half-century time frames. The Reformation of the sixteenth century, beginning in 1517, was answered by the Counter Reformation, which grew out of the three Councils of Trent, dating from 1545 to 1563. Similarly, the succession of Czar Alexander II to the Russian throne in 1855 was counter-balanced by the ending of absolutism, accompanied by revolts and mutinies, which led to the reforms of the "October Manifesto" in 1905.

Dr. Raymond Wheeler believed that a great transformation of history occurred with the termination of a five-hundred-year cycle. If we take the year 575 BCE as the start of one five-hundred-year cycle, we know this to be an extraordinary period when Greek philosophy was at its height, when Confucius lived in China, when Sidhartha (the Buddha) was alive, and when Zoroaster, Lao-tse, and the Jewish prophets were making an impact on their respective societies. Five hundred years later, shortly after the death of Christ, the Roman Empire reached its geographic limit and began to decline. By the next five-hundred-year cycle, Europe had plunged into the so-called Dark Ages when warfare, plague, and lawlessness reached their height. On the other hand, it was also a time of cultural innovation in the Byzantine world and the start of the Carolingian Empire, with the coronation of Charlemagne. The eleventh century marked the return to stability, the emergence of feudalism, and the rise to supremacy of the Christian Church. Next came the Reformation, humanism, and the growth of centralized bureaucratic states in the sixteenth century.[10] Needless to say, we are presently entering into another five-hundred-year transition period, which is also marked by the end of a two-thousand-year sixth-ray cycle and the start of a seventh-ray cycle.

In developing his periodic table of civilizations, theorist Alvin Barta calculated that the normal duration of each civilization was 2,000 years, which could be divided into roughly five-hundred-year episodes that defined the major benchmarks for these civilizations.[11] Oswald Spengler also appears to have used calculations based on five-hundred-year cycles in charting his study of civilizations.

Cycles Based on the Ray Cipher Nine

We see in the third-ray cycle, based on the cipher nine, a period of manifestation followed by a short interval of pralaya. Nine-year intervals, in their various multiples, often have a profound impact on personal lives as well as those of nations and groups of nations. When Queen Victoria of Britain succeeded to the throne in 1837, she was eighteen years old (or two nine-year cycles). Eighteen years after Queen Victoria was married (1840), her eldest daughter was also married. When Victoria died in 1901, she was eighty-one years old and thereby had completed nine nine-year cycles. Both the French Revolution (1788-1815) and the period of World War (1914-1945) lasted twenty-seven years and thereby constituted three nine-year cycles. In numerology, nine is the number of completion and from an esoteric perspective, nine is the number of initiation, meaning also that it is a cycle of completion.

A nine-year cycle when divided by three into a three-year cycle, or multiplied by three into a nine-year cycle reveals an important and interesting pattern which, it is said, relates to the work of the New Group of World Servers. Essentially, it can be broken down into three waves: the first cycle—crisis/consolidation—creates a precipitating conflict, breakdown, or danger; the second cycle—tension/expansion—reveals heightened anxiety, increased stimulation, and the intensification of emotional, mental, and psychic energy; finally, the third cycle—consciousness impact—leads to a breakthrough into mass-consciousness of some critical idea or avenue of service.

Table 9. Time Cycles Based on the Numbers Three and Nine

	3-year cycle	9-year cycle	27-year cycle
1933-34	crisis/consolidation	crisis/consolidation	crisis/ consolidation
1934-35	tension/expansion		
1935-36	impact on consciousness		
1936-37	crisis/consolidation	tension/expansion	
1937-38	tension/expansion		
1938-39	impact on consciousness		
1939-40	crisis/consolidation	impact on consciousness	
1940-41	tension/expansion		
1941-42	impact on consciousness		
1942-43	crisis/consolidation	crisis/consolidation	tension/expansion
1943-44	tension/expansion		
1944-45	impact on consciousness		
1945-46	crisis/consolidation	tension/expansion	
1946-47	tension/expansion		
1947-48	impact on consciousness		
1948-49	crisis/consolidation	impact on consciousness	
1949-50	tension/expansion		
1950-51	impact on consciousness		
1951-52	crisis/consolidation	crisis/consolidation	impact on consciousness
1952-53	tension/expansion		
1953-54	impact on consciousness		
1954-55	crisis/consolidation	tension/expansion	
1955-56	tension/expansion		
1956-57	impact on consciousness		
1957-58	crisis/consolidation	impact on consciousness	
1958-59	tension/expansion		
1959-60	impact on consciousness		

Much can be read into these cycles. If we look at the twenty-seven-year cycles, it is evident that the period from the coming to power of the Nazis in 1933 and the advent of the Great Depression constituted a period of global crisis, which lasted through the Second World War.

Beginning in 1945, we see a time of tension, resulting from the uncertainties of the post-war world, but also a period of expansion as independent states begin to emerge (India, Israel), and other states are transformed by revolution (China). Throughout the 1950s, we observe a period of stability in which the post-war order started to take form. The year 1987 marked the close of the next twenty-seven-year cycle, and highlighted the beginning of the end for the Soviet Union and the communist governments of Eastern Europe.

Cycles Based on the Ray Ciphers Twenty-Five, Thirty-Five, and Fifteen

Ciphers twenty-five, thirty-five, and fifteen relating to rays four, five, and six are also important divisions of time. A twenty-five year cycle marks the convenient break of a century into four parts. If each century constitutes a particular theme, or set of themes, then the fourth-ray cipher represents the fourfold division of that theme. Suppose we take the theme of warfare in the twentieth century, which is the topic of Gabriel Kolko's book, *Century of War*. We see that the first quarter century was dominated by the First World War, the next quarter by the Second World War, the third quarter by the Cold War, and the fourth decade by the rise of terrorism and nationalist conflict. Also of significance are cycles of two hundred and fifty years (the Industrial Revolution has been more or less of that duration) and a 2,500-year interval, marking the duration of a major astrological cycle, the most recent being the Piscean age.

A period of thirty-five years is the approximate length of a generation. One frequently finds the concept of generations in literature. There are many references in the Old Testament to generations, well over a hundred in fact, and another forty-odd references in the New Testament. In fact, Jesus interpreted historical time in terms of generations. The Spanish philosopher, Julian Marias, noted that the intellectual life of nineteenth-century Europe, which has had a profound influence on history up to the present, was initiated by a small group of men of the same generation, such as Auguste Comte, John Stuart Mill, Charles Darwin, Søren Kierkegaard, Karl Marx, Herbert Spenser, and Johann Fichte. "Looking back," says Marias, "one might have been able to predict in advance to which human 'types' the generations theme would appeal, and therefore, the period in history during which scientific consideration of the theme would begin."[12]

If we look at the other end of the century, we find that virtually all the leaders who guided the fortunes of humanity during the critical period of the world wars were born during the same generation. Numbered among this group would be Churchill (1874), Stalin (1879), Kemal Ataturk (1881), Franklin Roosevelt (1882), Eamon deValera (1882), Benito Mussolini (1883), Harry S. Truman (1884), George Patton (1885), Chiang Kai-Shek (1887), Bernard (Monty) Montgomery (1887), Adolf Hitler (1889), Charles DeGaulle (1890), Dwight Eisenhower (1890), Erwin Rommel (1891), Francisco Franco (1892), Hermann Goering (1893), and Nikita Khruschev (1894), among many others. There is a connection between the fifth ray and concrete mental and scientific work which may account, in part, for the grouping of creative minds and great leaders into particular generations. Also, Theosophy and the Ageless Wisdom teach that souls incarnate at a certain point in time and space so as to learn from the environment and perform a general field of service.

The cipher 15, which in the Pythagorean system related to the sixth ray, also has a broader significance. The Spanish philosopher, Jose Ortega y Gasset, believed that a generation lasted for about thirty years, divided into two fifteen-year cycles. A generation spends its first fifteen years coming of age and challenging the generation that is in power. Over the next fifteen years, it assumes power for itself and then is superseded by another generation in the following fifteen-year period.[13] According to American historian, Arthur Schlesinger, Jr., Ortega's fifteen-year oscillations roughly correspond to Henry Adams's twelve-year cycles. Of course, life expectancy was shorter in the early nineteenth century when Adams lived.[14]

The Romans calculated their "Great Year" cycle to be 1,460 years, rounded off to 1,500 years. This number was obtained by multiplying the days in a year (365) times the four seasons.[15] Major events in a nation's history may occur in regular cycles. One finds, for instance, that the fifteenth year of each century has been significant in French history, as evidenced by the following:

1415 -   King Henry V defeats the French at Agincourt
1515 -   King Louis XII dies and is succeeded by Francis I
1615 -   King Louis XIII marries Anna of Austria. The States General is

dismissed after promising reforms; it will not be called again until the eve of the French Revolution

1715 - Louis XIV dies and is succeeded by his grandson, Louis XV, under the regency of the Duc d' Orleans

1815 - The Duke of Wellington defeats Napoleon at the Battle of Waterloo

1915 - First World War

If we extend these dates another fifteen years, there are some further interesting correlations:

1430 - Joan of Arc is captured by the Burgundians following the siege of Orleans

1530 - Francis I marries Eleanor of Portugal

1630 - Chief minister, Cardinal Richelieu, uncovers a conspiracy of Maria d' Medici, the Queen Mother and regent to Louis XIII, to usurp power

1830 - Revolution in France

1930 - Signing of the London Naval Treaty to limit the production of warships

While these events may, in some cases, lack a direct correlation, there is some suggestion of a cyclical effect. The defeat of Napoleon and the restoration of the Bourbons in 1815 led directly to the Revolution of 1830; which led to another revolution almost fifteen years later (1848); which led to war between France and Austria in 1859; which resulted in an attempted coup d'état nearly thirty years later. It thus becomes evident that patterns of cause and effect, far from being obscure or random processes, conform, as do all things, to the rhythmic law of cycles.

Cycles Based on the Ray Cipher Seven

Finally, we come to the cycles of the seventh ray. At its basic level, each life consists of a cycle of seven years, which corresponds to a developmental stage as well as a period of consciousness unfoldment. In any life, the first seven years marks a close connection with the realm of imagination; the next seven years of childhood marks coordination of the emotional and physical vehicles; and at adolescence there is a point of crisis when the physical, astral, and mental vehicles come into alignment. With the entering of adulthood at the age of twenty-one, one experiences the birth of the soul or ego. From ages twenty-eight to thirty-five, we enter into maturity and assert a degree of moral responsibility. It is at this point that the personality is being contacted by the soul. From thirty-five to forty-two, there is a crisis of values with a transition into a new phase of mental and moral striving when the soul begins to make some claim on the personality. Between the ages of forty-two and forty-nine is also a time of transition when karmic debts have to be paid and the pathway of service is to be defined. After the age of forty-nine, up to age fifty-six, there is a culminating point when the efforts sowed in the past come to fruition. Between the age of fifty-six and sixty-three, the soul decides whether the life will end or continue.

Nations also go through development stages. If we look at American history on the basis of a seventy-year cycle, for example, we see that from 1787, when the Constitution was drawn up and adopted, to the eve of the Civil War in 1857, the United States underwent an important developmental phase of constructing its physical vehicle through westward expansion and internal improvements, along with intense nationalism and regionalism, corresponding to personality growth. The Civil War, of course, was a major crisis in American history. After the war, the country became increasingly united both psychologically and physically. The frontier closed in the 1890s and industrialization expanded rapidly.

From the 1890s to the 1920s, there was also massive immigration, mostly from Central and Eastern Europe. This seventy-year period ended with the Wall Street crash (1929) followed by the Great Depression. In more recent times, particularly after World War II, America has come of age. The country emerged as the dominant world power following the Second World War. Civil Rights and other mass movements have led to a high degree of social assimilation. It might be said that the seventy-year period from the 1930s could be characterized as a time of personality integration in which the physical, emotional, and mental components of the society have come together. Now, as the United States prepares to enter the next millennium, the country is in another crisis, which though unclear, is universally recognized.

The Spiral-Cyclic Impact of the Seven Rays

Overshadowing the cyclical ebb and flow of the rays is a more dominant pattern of spiral-cyclic ray harmonics. These ray spiral-cycles usually have a long duration and signal the beginning and end of great historical epochs. The inflowing and outflowing of the rays gives us, in the words of the Tibetan, "a dramatic picture of the progress of those souls who are carried in and out of manifestation by the appearance or disappearance of a ray."[16]

The quality of civilization, the types of forms that appear in the kingdoms of nature, and the constant stages of human awareness of those persons carried into form life in a particular era result from the constant interplay of the rays.[17] Our present solar system, the second of three solar systems, is governed by the second ray, which can be seen in its expansiveness and the gravitational tension that holds the planetary systems in a rhythmic orbit. It is for this reason that it can accurately be said that the second ray is never out of manifestation.

There are a series of five rays that govern humanity as a whole, which are analogous to each individual human being. In his volume on *Glamour*, the Tibetan gives the ray structure of humanity in its present form, as follows:

Soul ray	Ray 2	Expression of love and wisdom
Personality ray	Ray 3	Development of intelligence for transmutation into love-wisdom
Mental ray	Ray 5	Scientific achievement
Astral ray	Ray 6	Idealistic development
Physical ray	Ray 7	Organization, business sense

It is useful to note that the soul ray governs humanity for its entire life period and, along the same line, is the ray that governs the solar system. The third and fifth rays (personality and mind) are mental in nature and underscore the importance of cognition and abstract thought in humanity's evolution through the Aryan root race. The sixth ray (astral) highlights a pronounced emotional quality and the dualistic phenomenon of idealism that has been the hallmark of the Piscean age.

Moreover, the seventh ray is indicative of the spread of commercial enterprise and organizational development on the physical plane over the past two thousand years.

In the Aquarian age, which is beginning to take shape, the alignment of personality based rays will be somewhat different.

Personality ray	Ray 5	Concrete and scientific focus
Mental ray	Ray 4	The creative effect
Astral ray	Ray 6	Holding to ideals
Physical ray	Ray 7	Organization (incoming ray)

This revised chart is interesting insofar as the orientation of the personality of humanity will continue to be towards mental development, although more strongly through an analysis of concrete forms. The fifth-ray tendency towards critical analysis and methodological approach will be tempered by a more artistic and creative perspective, which will be seen more clearly when the fourth ray comes into manifestation around 2025. The ray structure of humanity's astral and physical natures remains what it was previously, however, the emphasis should shift more to the qualities of the seventh ray due to the reinforcing seventh-ray planetary cycle, which is now emerging into predominance.[18]

Each root race is said to be governed by a particular ray, which denotes the qualities or attributes to be gained from that root-race experience.

Table 10. The Rays and the Races[19]

Soul Ray	Full Expression	Major Influence
1—Will	7th root race Perfection of the Plan	1st & 7th subraces
2—Love-Wisdom	6th root race	2nd & 6th subraces
3—Active Intelligence	5th root race Aryan race Perfected Intellect	3rd & 5th subraces
4—Harmony	4th root race Atlantean race Perfected Emotion	4th & 6th subraces

5—Knowledge	3rd root race	5th & 3rd subraces
	Lemurian race	
	Perfected physical	
6—Idealism/Devotion	2nd root race	6th & 2nd subraces
7—Ceremonial Magic	1st root race	7th & 1st subraces

We see from this table that the goal of the present fifth root race is to develop the perfected intellect, which is indicated by the spiral-cyclic influence of the third ray. Given, according to Hodson, that the egos for the Aryan race were selected a million years ago and the Semite nucleus for this race was formed about a hundred thousand years ago, the third-ray impact over this present root race has been lengthy and will continue for some time into the future.[20] Curiously, the third and fifth subraces of the Aryan root race (the Persian-Mesopotamian-Chaldean race and western people) have, by this reckoning, been the major influences in bringing about the intellectual development of humanity.

Seen from another angle, the second and third rays correspond to the soul and personality of humanity at this point in time. The western and eastern hemispheres of our planet are governed by a different set of rays. The Occident has a second-ray soul and a fourth-ray personality whereas the Orient has a fourth-ray soul and a third-ray personality. In practical terms, this has meant that in the West there is a psychic tension between the second-ray soul characteristics of desire for balance and stability, restraint of passion, kindness, and a spiritual-religious world view, and the fluctuating emotionalism, selfishness, personal expressiveness, depression, and rebelliousness, which are manifestations of the fourth-ray personality. In the East, the fourth-ray soul encourages aesthetic elegance, beauty, refinement, and synthesis while the fourth-ray personality tends towards manipulation, crude commercialism, over-activity, and vague abstraction.

It is useful to contemplate the correlation of the relationship between the two hemispheres of the planet with the two hemispheres of the brain. Both say something about the duality of consciousness.

Table 11. The Seven Rays and Some of Their Qualities

Ray 1   Will and Power   courage, strength, fearlessness,
                                pride, synthesis

Ray 2   Love-Wisdom   faithfulness, magnetic love,
                                sensitivity, fusing power

Ray 3   Active Intelligence   abstract thought, strategizing,
                                action, manipulation of energy

Ray 4   Harmony from Conflict   love of beauty, mediation,
                                mathematical exactitude,
                                creative aspiration

Ray 5   Concrete Knowledge   technical expertise, scientific
                                thought, logic, power to define,
                                accuracy and precision, idea of
                                cause and results

Ray 6   Devotion, Idealism   single-mindedness, humility, self-
                                sacrificing, emotionalism,
                                fanaticism, idealism

Ray 7   Ceremonial Order   planning and organization, power
                                to build, management of detail,
                                sense of rhythm and timing,
                                ritualism

The dominant ray of the past two millennia has been, of course, the sixth ray of devotion and idealism. Generally speaking, rays two and six govern the astral body and the emotional life of the planet. There is no clear date as to when the sixth ray came into manifestation, but the Tibetan notes that it was before the dawn of Christianity. The Tibetan is reticent about giving exact dates for the commencement and termination of the sixth-ray cycle. If we can assume that the length of time the sixth ray has been in manifestation is about 2,160 years (the dates given by the astrologer Dane Rudhyar), it is most likely that the impact of this ray began to be felt around 125 to 100 BCE. Unlike the second ray, which is characterized by regular cycles, the sixth ray increased in potency over a long period of time, reaching its apex in 1625, and since then has been quickly declining. We will still feel the afterglow of this ray for some time to come.

Replacing the sixth ray as the dominant ray for the next two thousand years is the seventh ray. This ray came into manifestation in

1675 and has been gaining strength ever since. Assuming that this ray cycle will be the same as the previous one, it will remain in manifestation until 3775. The great planetary disruptions of the last hundred years are attributable directly to the crossover from the outgoing sixth ray to the incoming seventh ray. As in all transition periods, there is a pronounced change in vibratory energy when a ray enters into manifestation or departs. Given that we are dealing with two rays of a lengthy duration, the force of change and disruption is that much greater. The transition phase, which began in 1875, will conclude in or around 2025. With the seventh ray, there is a tremendous amount of organizing power, the effects of which have already started to be realized.

Table 12. Comparison of Sixth and Seventh Ray Attributes[21]

Characteristics of Ray 6	*Characteristics of Ray 7*
1. fostered the vision	will materialize the vision
2. produced the mystic	will develop the magician
3. created nationalism and sectarianism	will lead to fusion and synthesis
4. groups focused on personality concerns	groups working in concert with the plan
5. created a sense of duality	will foster personality integration
6. created modern electricity for material needs	will see electrical energy in all forms
7. developed theories of the lower three worlds	will convert these theories into facts
8. taught the meaning of personal sacrifice	will inaugurate the age of divine service
9. promoted the spirit of individualism	will foster the rhythm of group work
10. recognized the historical Christ and the religion of narrow idealism	will recognize the cosmic Christ and the scientific religion of light
11. produced great idealistic religions	will foster religious synthesis
12. fostered separative instincts	will recognize wider issues

Table 13. Major Ray Cycles[22]

	Entry	Peak	Completion
Ray 1	2100 CE	——	——
Ray 2	1575 CE	1825	2075 (present cycle)
Ray 3	1425 CE	1875	4425
Ray 4	2025 CE	——	——
Ray 5	1775 CE	——	2000 (estimated)
Ray 6	100 BCE	1625	2062
Ray 7	1675 CE	3425	3775

Of all the rays, the third-ray cycles are the longest. This ray came into objective manifestation in 1425, reached the end of its outgoing cycle in 1875, and has gradually begun to wane. When such a transition occurs, according to the Tibetan, the effect is always of a crystallizing nature, which produces a rigidity of form.[23] However, within this cycle, there are rhythms of pulsation when the energies are periodically strong and weak. Third-ray cycles last for approximately 3,000 years, which means this ray will survive the duration of the Aquarian age.[24] Whereas the combination of rays two and six have stimulated the astral plane and the emotional nature of humanity, rays three and seven, acting together, govern the physical body and the physical life of the planet, which has had the effect, and will continue to have the effect, of conditioning individuals to their environment.[25] The third ray will finally go out of manifestation in about 4425.

Of the remaining rays, only the fifth ray is in manifestation. It appeared in 1775 and is in the process of coming into full power. There is some question as to when the fifth-ray cycle will end. Whereas reference is made to the increasing potency of this ray, suggesting that it will be in manifestation for some time, the Tibetan also clearly states that this ray will be withdrawn soon "thus breaking its normal cycle, because it is deemed that the needed special impulse has been adequate and that the impetus given to the human 'spirit of discovery' has served its purpose."[26] This would mean that the fifth ray will pass out of manifestation shortly after the end of the twentieth century.

The first ray is not in manifestation and, because of its powerful potency, has only appeared during periods of great planetary crisis to compensate for some grave human prevarication under the law of karma. Esoteric students believe that such a time occurred briefly during the Second World War when the fate of humanity was imperiled. The energy of Shamballa has been impacting humanity since the early nineteenth century and, no doubt, will continue to be an influential factor in the years ahead. Two thousand years from today, the full impact of the first ray will be felt on the physical plane.[27]

The fourth ray, on the other hand, is scheduled to come slowly into physical plane manifestation around 2025. This ray, as an aspect of the fourth kingdom in nature, has had a major influence on human development. Moreover, as the personality ray of the Occident and the soul ray of the Orient, the fourth ray has underscored the many wars and conflicts that have engaged men and nations for much of their recorded history. With the coming of this ray into manifestation early in the twenty-first century, more of the harmony and beauty aspects will be seen. Rays one, four, and five govern people's mental development and will continue to be a major factor, it is thought, in lifting humanity from a point of polarization on the astral plane to that of the mental plane.

The Impact of Spiral-Cyclic Rays on Modern History

History at any given point in time is conditioned by the proportion of ray types in manifestation. Little has been said about spiral-cyclic ray patterns in the earlier subraces and root races of this round, and they remain unclear. Our attention will focus more on the past two thousand years of western history. It has been during this period, of course, that humanity has made its greatest progress.

The Sixth-Ray Cycle

Over the past 2,160-year cycle of the Piscean age, the most dominant expression of the governing sixth ray has been Christianity in the West, and Buddhism in the East. One of the major reasons why Christianity rose from being a persecuted cult to the prevailing religion of Europe was that it expressed sixth-ray characteristics. Michael Robbins, in his book, *Tapestry of the Gods*, observes that the dominant positive functions of the sixth ray are uncompromising one-pointedness, single-mindedness without deviation, and an overwhelming desire to follow a motivating vision.[28] Through faith and dedication to a beloved ideal, sixth-ray types have a charismatic and transforming effect on others. In the words of Kenneth Clark, men of the tenth century not only recognized Christ's sacrifice in physical terms, they were able to sublimate it into ritual and powerful symbols. This inspired great art, which ultimately contributed to humanizing a crude and ignorant populace.[29]

Along with the sixth ray, Christianity is ruled by the planet Mars, which has governed the third decanate of the Piscean era for the past 600 years. This explains the emphasis the Christian Church has placed on the blood of Christ and the conflict between life and death. The Tibetan writes: "It is a religion of devotion, fanaticism, of high courage, of idealism, of the spiritual emphasis upon the individual and his worth and problem, of conflict and of death. All those characteristics are familiar to us in the presentation of Christian theology. It is however pre-eminently a religion which has waged cruel and oft illogical war upon sex and its implications; it has emphasized a militant celibacy (militant where women and their rights and natures are concerned); it has regarded the sex relation as one of the primary evils of the world and has laid the emphasis upon the inviolable nature of the marriage bond when endorsed by the Church."[30]

Hence, during the Middle Ages, from the eleventh century to the fifteenth century when the Catholic Church in the West reached its zenith of power, the majority of individuals alive at that time had a dominant sixth-ray orientation. This, of course, was seen in the fanaticism, emotionalism, oscillation, and one-pointed devotion that characterized all aspects of European society. Professor Huizinga observed that "the men of that time always oscillate between the fear of hell and the most naive joy, between cruelty and tenderness, between harsh asceticism and insane attachments to the delights of this world, between hatred and goodness, always running to extremes."[31] Just as valor, courage, and boldness became the hallmark of a knight, these qualities produced an opposite virtue—chivalry—which emphasized courtesy, gentleness, and devotion. Likewise, every event and every action, whether heroic or courtly, were embodied in expressive and solemn forms and thus raised to the dignity of a ritual.[32]

To say that most people incarnated along sixth-ray lines during the Middle Ages is not to say that other ray types were out of season. History does not fall into convenient categories, so events, movements, and ideas that may be seen to coalesce at a particular point in time are present in one form or another in all periods. For example, the same energy that drove many explorers to discover the new world in the late fifteenth and sixteenth centuries also drove Marco Polo to China in the late thirteenth century; the same energy that influenced the Nazi regime to exterminate the Jews in the twentieth century fostered periodic outbreaks against the Jews throughout the Middle Ages; the same energy that led Tycho Brahe to discover a new star in the Milky Way in 1572 led Einstein to put forth his special theory of relativity in 1905; and so on.

The problem of making sense of any historical moment is further complicated by the fact that the rays impact human affairs on the astral and mental planes prior to physical manifestation. Whereas airplanes were not successfully built until the early years of the twentieth century, they existed in the minds of men like Leonardo da Vinci in the sixteenth century. Since there are no absolutes in history, the unraveling of the past must focus on dominant events, which often appear exoterically to be vague and amorphous, yet from the inner planes, where the science of the rays is known, have purpose, clarity, and precision.

The Third-Ray Cycle

Historical transitions, occasioned through the inflow or withdrawal of a ray energy, are usually far more subtle and gradual than would so seem to the casual observer. When the third ray came into manifestation in 1425, it brought into planetary life—through waves of incarnating souls—a gradual tendency towards expansion, discovery, and activity that was hitherto unknown in European history. The historian R. H. Tawney writes that economic power, which through trade had been situated in Italy for centuries, "was leaking through a thousand creeks and inlets into western Europe" during the fifteenth century due to the discovery of new lands and trade routes.[33] Whereas Europe of the Middle Ages had been, to use the words of Tawney, "a closed circle," the economic structure of Europe first began to change from within before the dike burst and the new dynamic energies of capitalism brought about interaction with the wider world.

The push to find new trade routes to the Orient began with the Portuguese who, in the late fifteenth century, were successful in completing a voyage around the Cape of Good Hope to India, where they established commercial enclaves. Whereas the Portuguese sailed to the Orient by way of the East, the Spanish sailed to the Orient by way of the West in the pursuit of Christian souls (a sixth-ray objective) and gold (a third-ray objective). The brutal plantation system that was established by the Spanish conquistadors, like Cortez, was a throwback to feudalism, indicating that although their objectives may have been along third-ray lines, their methods of ordering society were sixth ray.

The influx of wealth from the New World and the quickening of commercial growth were curiously less sensational because it had been long prepared for. Heralded by an economic revolution not less profound than that of three centuries later, the new world of the sixteenth century took its character from the outburst of economic energy in which it had been born. Throughout the city-states of Italy in the fifteenth and early sixteenth centuries, there was an aura of busyness, materialism, and opportunism, all characteristics of the third ray. Great banking and commercial families, like the Medici family, fit the image of the manipulative, mentally agile, third-ray type, who engaged in politics, business, and civic affairs, as well as being patrons of the arts. In comparison with nineteenth-century Britain, Italy saw a swift increase in wealth and an impressive expansion in trade; a concentration of financial power on a scale unknown before; the rise, amid fierce social convulsions, of new classes and the depression of older classes; the triumph of a new culture; and a system of ideas amid struggles not less bitter.[34]

Another manifestation of third-ray energy at this time was the urge towards intellectual enquiry and the expansion of consciousness. The third ray lends itself to the capacity for abstract thinking, the ability for rigorous analysis and reasoning, mental agility, faculty with languages, and skillful communication.[35] This new spirit of enquiry underscored the Renaissance. The desire to imitate, translate, and honor the classics was strongly colored by the third ray. Dr. Newbold believes that ancient Greece possessed a third-ray soul which, of course, would resonate with the incoming third ray. He also states that the Greeks of antiquity had a fourth-ray personality, which would be in line with the fourth-ray personality of Italy, the place where the Renaissance began. The fact that Italy is ruled by the sixth ray indicates a response to that still-dominant energy. It appears that ancient Rome was also strongly affected by the sixth ray.[36]

Reverence for classical antiquity gave rise to humanism. The humanists of the Renaissance period were, in the words of Burckhardt, interested in "discerning and bringing to light the full, whole nature of man."[37] It is problematic whether humanism would have come about at all were it not for the influx of the third ray. The theoretical, analytical, and abstract capacities of this ray fostered individualism and an interest in human nature, resulting in a more worldly turn of mind. The fact that humanity, as the third planetary center, is governed by the third ray of active intelligence underscores the connection between the third ray and humanism.

Dating from the sixteenth century, intellectual intercourse expanded beyond the clergy and the small body of literate burghers, nobles, and others to include a wider range of classes, who by then were receiving a grammar-school level of education.[38] Likewise, a seminal peasant consciousness was starting to take root whereby the mass of ordinary folk were beginning to become more active in the affairs of their villages and to challenge authority.[39] It is worth noting that the capacity for rigorous analysis, abstract thought, and skill with languages all flow from the third ray. We might also observe that vernacular languages began to appear in written form around the beginning of the fifteenth century, just prior to the advent of the manifestation of the third ray.

The Second-Ray Cycle

The next major ray modification to the dominant sixth-ray character of western society occurred with the inflow of the second ray, dating from 1575. Tolerance, empathy, and compassion are characteristics of the second ray and these traits can be detected in the political affairs of the period. Beginning in the late sixteenth century, when Europe was being ravaged by religious wars, a sixth-ray phenomenon, there developed an alternative to the fierce bigotry that dominated the minds of both Protestant and Catholic rulers. The so-called politiques, such as Henry IV in France and Queen Elizabeth I in England, sought to unite men and women of different faiths within a strong and powerful nation-state. Consequently, they were willing to tolerate minority religions so long as they did not undermine or challenge the established religion.

From these lukewarm beginnings, the spirit of toleration began to take root. It could be seen most clearly in the Netherlands which, in gaining its independence from Spain, admitted and even welcomed religious refugees from all over Europe, including Jews. This led to intellectual freedom and a burst of creative and entrepreneurial energy, which catapulted the Dutch nation into the position of being a major power. Tolerance also marked the Restoration settlement in England, which allowed people to hold diverse religious views within a limited sphere. In 1689, Parliament passed a Declaration of Rights, which greatly limited the power of the king to act in an arbitrary manner. This declaration was closely followed by a toleration act that expanded the rights of non-Church-of-England Protestants.

Diversity within unity, which is part of the attractive nature of the second ray, can be found also in the movement towards constitutionalism. Essentially, constitutionalism involves the limitation of government by law. While we tend to take this for granted today, it was a new idea in seventeenth-century Europe and one that was hotly resisted. The English fought a civil war over whether the king or the common law would be the highest authority. Outside of the Netherlands, Britain, and a few other places, constitutionalism would remain an ideal rather than a reality for over a century. Democracy, an embryonic concept at this time, derived its impetus from an acceptance of the rule of law. Diversity within unity is also the conceptual framework for multiculturalism, which has become a dominant ideal in American society. Multiculturalism is an offshoot of the second-ray soul of the United States

Since it is the nature of the second ray to centralize and magnetize, this energy also had the opposite effect of stimulating the movement towards divine-right monarchy and political centralization, which reached its peak in the seventeenth century. In the words of historian Sir George Clark: "Thus the state and the nation each grew in strength and consciousness, or rather each was made stronger and more aware of itself by its own action and that of the other. A great part of the activity of statesmen was directed to bringing recalcitrant elements under control: we have seen it in their dealings with churches, armies, universities, feudal jurisdictions, and foreign infringements of their sovereignty. We have seen in their economic policy how the community came more thoroughly under control as it became more truly a community, and this was so not only in economic affairs but in every activity."[40]

A further reflection of the second ray can be found in a renewed sensitivity and love of beauty. This aspect of the second ray gave birth to Baroque art, which reached its highest form of expression in architecture and music. Baroque provided a sense of grandeur and ornamentation, what Kenneth Clark referred to as "visual exuberance."[41] Baroque was not only pleasing to the senses, it was also expansive. Whereas classicism, with its third-ray qualities of logic and order, was attractive to the mind, Baroque, with its displays of richness, ornateness, and grandeur, was satisfying to the emotions.

Insofar as the second and sixth rays are governed by the department of religion within the Hierarchy, it is not strange that the seventeenth century was dominated by religious wars and fanaticism. The Thirty Years War, 1618 to 1648, in the words of one historian, "demonstrated the dangers of religious passion, and of amateur armies led by soldiers of fortune."[42] At the same time, there was also a spiritual awakening which, as stated by the Tibetan to one of his disciples, "laid emphasis upon a wider, general education and upon a revolt from the imposition of clerical authority."[43]

One could cite numerous examples of challenges to the power of the clergy. In England, many religious sects and political movements emerged, each with their own agendas. There were, for example, Presbyterians, Anabaptists, Seekers, Ranters, Quakers, and Fifth Monarchy Men. Christopher Hill, in his book, *The World Turned Upside Down*, states "that men and women, faced with an unprecedented freedom of choice, passed from sect to sect, trying all things and finding them all wanting."[44]

Throughout Europe, education, as measured by advances in literacy, advanced significantly from the sixteenth to the eighteenth centuries. This was a direct result of the coming into manifestation of numerous third- and second-ray types. Whereas the third ray facilitated the spread of the printed word, the second ray encouraged new lines of pedagogy, which often took the form of preaching. Tawney notes that the spirit of Reformation, which swept through England, Germany, and Switzerland, brought with it, among other things, the encouragement of learning and the diffusion of education.[45] One of the most important occurrences in the modern world, according to historian Philippe Aries, has been the development of a written culture in the West, "which redrew the boundary between the inner life and the life in the community."[46]

The Seventh-Ray Cycle

P. A. Sorokin states that, beginning with the sixteenth century, a new principle became dominant and with it a new form of culture that was sensory, empirical, and secular.[47] The trend towards secularism, initiated by the third ray, took a more decisive turn with the influx of seventh-ray energy through seventh-ray souls who came into incarnation after 1675. The shift in perspective from the Aristotelian cosmology of the Middle Ages to the rational Newtonian world view of the eighteenth century was shaped and colored by the incoming seventh ray. We can see how an interest in practical science and the motivation to investigate all aspects of the physical world relate to the seventh-ray emphasis on form-building, managing detail, and the need to fit observations within an orderly model.

A dominant feature of the seventh ray is the concern for law and order. Lawlessness, sanctioned or otherwise, was not only commonplace in medieval and early modern Europe, but largely went unchecked due to sporadic and ineffective means of law enforcement. By the eighteenth century, however, men were becoming obsessed with the problem of maintaining law and order. The expansion of the criminal law and the elevation of its authority made it possible for men of property in eighteenth-century England to govern without a police force or a large army. During the tumultuous years of the early nineteenth century, police forces began to make their appearance. So did prisons. Gradually, as the seventh ray has waxed more strongly, the apparatus of the criminal justice system has become more extensive and intrusive. By the same token, invasions of privacy have become a concern in recent times due in part to more elaborate technology (a fifth-ray development) but more especially to the powerful impulse of the seventh ray to create order.

The Tibetan notes that around the beginning of the eighteenth century an effort was made, with hierarchical backing, to hasten the entry of souls awaiting incarnation into life on the physical plane. The so-called demographic revolution generated unprecedented increases in population, first in Europe, and later (today) among the peoples of Africa, Asia, and Latin America.

Demographers are in relative agreement that the cause of this dramatic population growth was due to lower mortality rather than to changes in fertility.[48] However, given that birth rates had been uniformly high during the preceding centuries, the key factor was fewer deaths as shown by the fact that more infants were surviving childhood. It seems that the causal factor behind this development was a new consciousness aimed at improving and perpetuating the physical vehicle. Historian Pierre Goubert writes that, dating from the later seventeenth century, kings and their counselors thought that it was a good thing for people to multiply. More people, so the reasoning went, meant more work, more taxes, and thus more money.[49] Since the seventh ray is concerned primarily with the spiritualization of the form life, it follows that the care, well being, and health of children, and the robustness of the population as a whole, would postdate the late seventeenth century, when this ray became active on the physical plane.

There is research to suggest a correlation between certain accretionary events, such as meteorite activity, fireballs, and shooting stars, and the sharp rise in population at the end of the eighteenth century. "The growth of world population…[is] no doubt an important factor affecting the accretionary time series…"[50] What prompted this correlation, assuming that it is a genuine correlation, remains unclear. However, one would suspect the activity of Shamballa, which we have seen was becoming more potent at this time. What impact the seventh ray may have had on this development is hard to say.

The Fifth-Ray Cycle

As more and more rays come into manifestation, there is a natural tendency for a society to become increasingly complex and diverse. Since the end of the eighteenth century, when the fifth ray came into manifestation (1775), it has become more difficult to understand events by distinguishing particular lines of ray energy. The fifth ray, along with the seventh ray, generated a united impulse to divide, clarify, and enlighten the physical and social world and, thereby, initiated the civilization of modern times and a new cultural era that was characteristic of the Victorian age. Together, the fifth ray, in concert with second-, third-, and seventh-ray energies, prompted the major social movements that awakened human consciousness in the nineteenth century to greater freedom. Likewise, the reaction against church dogma, the accelerated developments of science, and the sexual and proletarian revolutions were the results of "the impulsive hastenings into incarnation of souls whose time had not truly come but whose conditioning influence was needed if certain difficulties (from the perspective of the Hierarchy) were to be averted."[51]

Challenges to the social order, beginning in the late eighteenth century with social disturbances in America, Holland, Belgium, Ireland, Switzerland, Austria, Poland and, of course, France, dominated Europe until the middle of the nineteenth century and were a consequence of "the impulsive hastenings," about which the Tibetan speaks. On the other hand, liberalism, with its emphasis on equality, political freedom, tolerance, and rights of the individual was a positive manifestation of population pressure, improvements in education, urbanization, and increased responsiveness to human need. Liberalism was accompanied by a sensitivity for the plight of others which, on a mass scale, was unprecedented. Kenneth Clark, in his talks on *Civilisation*, states his belief that the greatest civilizing achievement of the nineteenth century was humanitarianism. "We are so much accustomed to the humanitarian outlook," he says, "that we forget how little it counted in the earlier ages of civilisation."[52] This observation echoed a comment made by the Tibetan that the work carried forward over the preceding five centuries had definitely been successful, which has caused a vital spiritual awakening in every land.[53]

One sphere where the fifth ray has been singularly and decisively felt concerns the rapid growth of technology. David Landes has observed that it took ten thousand years to move from the agriculturally based society of the Neolithic age to the Industrial Revolution of the eighteenth century. Increased specialization, division of labor, and rapid intellectual progress, products of the fifth ray, coupled with greater numbers of people, have enabled humanity in less than two hundred years to leap from the machine age to atomic power, automation, and nanoscience. The point is, in the words of Landes, "that man can now order technological and scientific advance as one orders a commodity."[54] The fifth ray, with its characteristics of detached objectivity, the mastery of factual detail, and acute discrimination, has set the tone for research methodology and scientific unfoldment.

The Fourth-Ray Cycle

Looking ahead, the fourth ray is scheduled to come slowly into physical-plane manifestation around 2025. This ray, as an aspect of the fourth kingdom in nature, has had a major influence on human development. Moreover, as the personality ray of the Occident and the soul ray of the Orient, the fourth ray has underscored the many wars and conflicts that have engaged people and nations for much of their recorded history. The Tibetan writes that the fourth ray of harmony through conflict has been conditioning national development since 1850, which has underscored the myriad of human conflicts this century. By the same token, this ray has helped generate the desire for liberation among colonial peoples and others suffering from oppression.[55]

Today, the influence of this ray is being felt on the mental and astral planes, which is stimulating the work of mediation and conflict-resolution among individuals, groups, and nations. The principle of harmony, says the Tibetan, will bring about the New World Order: "the new civilization and culture is the trend and the voice of public opinion and the opportunity offered to people everywhere to bring about social security and right human relations."[56]

As the fourth ray waxes stronger in future generations, more emphasis will be placed upon creating beauty through the arts and other spheres of life. Rays one, four, and five govern people's mental development, so with the increased intensity of Shamballa energy, coupled with a population that has more dominant fifth- and fourth-ray characteristics, the shift of humanity's polarized focus from the astral to the mental plane should continue apace.

Historical Impact of Waning Ray Cycles

Each ray cycle undergoes a creative and constructive period when its energies are waxing, followed by a waning phase when the energies crystallize into rigid patterns and thoughtforms. Three of the rays, currently in manifestation, are now in their downward cycle. The dynamic quality of Christianity, which conquered Europe during the Middle Ages and demanded blind faith, was forced on the defensive after the seventeenth century with the waning of the sixth ray and withered in the emerging light of toleration and skepticism. Attacks on the Catholic Church were the most evident just prior to the French Revolution, with the widespread belief in Deism in England, Encyclopaedism in France, and Rationalism in Germany, along with the rise of numerous secret and occult societies, such as the Illuminati and the Freemasons. Assaults on the institution of the Church itself led to the suppression of the Jesuits in 1773 and religious toleration in some Catholic countries.[57]

When in 1825 the potency of the second ray began to decline, religion as a social, political, and intellectual force effectively began a process of withdrawal from public life.[58] Religious historian Owen Chadwick bluntly states that "the churches were less central to the activities of the state in 1901 than in 1837."[59] A similar point could be made with respect to the age-old alliance between religion and education. Whereas up to the early decades of the nineteenth century it was not considered respectable to be a teacher unless one was also a clergyman, after 1870 this link rapidly disappeared.[60] In spite of the illusions of some today that religion can be resurrected through politics into public life, orthodox religion, insofar as it is practiced in the West, remains a local and private matter and is losing its control over the minds of people.

The third ray completed its outgoing cycle in 1875 and occultly began to wane.[61] This means that crystallization began to take place on the inner planes which "causes mental conditions of a set and static nature."[62] Given the length of the third-ray cycle, however, it will probably be some time before the rigidity of third-ray energy will be fully seen on the physical plane.

Nevertheless, there are some interesting parallels. Modern social, political, and economic thought has been sustained by bodies of ideas that emerged during the Enlightenment, or arose from great thinkers in the nineteenth century. Adam Smith, Göethe, Rousseau, Marx, John Stuart Mill, Auguste Comte, Herbert Spenser, Freud, William James, Thorstein Veblen, and Max Weber, to name a few, have cast long shadows over twentieth-century thought. The active, creative, reasoning, eclectic, analytical, deductive, and intellectual mind, characteristic of the third ray, epitomized these great thinkers. The most innovative ideas of the twentieth century have been spawned by scientists expressing fifth-ray mental characteristics. Qualities of the fifth-ray mind include preciseness, convergent thought processes, literalness, detachment, empirical-mindedness, concreteness, fact-ascertaining-mindedness, and an orientation to technical processes.[63]

The waning of the third ray has probably also affected business and economic patterns. Free-market capitalism, which up to the turn of the twentieth century remained largely decentralized within myriads of small industries, began to disappear through competition or absorption into large business conglomerates. The pace of monopoly capitalism or, as some would call it, industrial totalitarianism, characterized by mergers between industrial giants, has accelerated over the past hundred years, and it has, particularly within the past fifty years, achieved global dominance. At the same time, business and financial organizations have become more bureaucratic, specialized, inflexible, impersonal, and technocratic. Whereas the entrepreneurial aspects of business are largely ray-three qualities, the administrative and organizational processes of business resonate more with the seventh ray. Within the global business environment, therefore, both the third ray and the seventh ray are active.

Curiously enough, there has been an explosion in the quality and quantity of communications and transportation systems over the past 125 years, which are governed by the higher expression of the third ray. There is a clue here as to the complexity of historical ray analysis insofar as events and developments, such as the growth of telecommunications, are impacted by a constellation of ray patterns, not to mention other energies that are pouring into the planet. Civilizations are made up of interdependent systems so that energies flowing from cosmic, systemic, and planetary sources intermingle and impact one another. Radio, television, airplanes, cars, cybernetic systems, and so forth are, on one level, manifestations of technological and scientific power, wrought by the waxing fifth ray and to some extent by the seventh ray. By the same token, the third ray, which has a very long cycle of manifestation, remains a potent force and will continue to be so, to a lesser extent, throughout the Aquarian age.

Subrays

The system of ray cycles is made more complex by the activity of lesser rays, known as subrays. Little is known as to how often the subrays are repeated within a major ray cycle, but the Tibetan suggests that it may be as many as seven times. He further observes that each subray has a life span of 150 to 200 years. Insofar as these rays are technically subrays of the dominant ray, in this case the sixth ray, their impact on human affairs essentially has been in the realm of religion.[64] Whereas each of the major religions arises under the influence of a particular ray, it likewise follows that religions would be colored or strengthened by the prevailing subray. For example, while Christianity and Islam resulted from sixth-ray influence, Christianity was conditioned by the sixth subray while Islam arose during a second-subray cycle.

From the vantage point of our own era, we are experiencing the energies of the seventh subray, which has been active since 1860. According to the Tibetan, the first outcome of this seventh subray influence was the Ecumenical council at Rome with its declaration of Papal Infallibility. The Tractarian Movement in England also owes its impetus to this subray. With its emphasis on ritualism and sacerdotalism, the seventh subray has encouraged a tightening of priestly authority in matters of dogma and practice, as well as literal interpretations of scripture, which has encouraged the periodic rise of religious fundamentalism. On the other hand, modern spiritualism was due to seventh-subray influence.[65]

Under the sixth subray, which was active during the eighteenth century, many enthusiastic movements, or religious revivals, such as those which occurred under John Wesley and George Whitfield in England, emerged to challenge the philosophic emphasis on reason. Elsewhere, as the result of the sixth subray, there emerged the Molinos and Quietists in Spain and Central Europe, along with the followers of St. Martin in France.[66] Zealous efforts to spread Christianity to Asia and other parts of the world figure as a thread in the fabric of seventeenth- and eighteenth-century church history. The evangelistic nature of Christianity and other religions relates back to the sixth ray.

Going back further, it has been suggested that the occult revival of the Renaissance period that gave rise to the resurgence of Hermetic philosophy, alchemy, Rosicrucianism, Neoplatonism, and other such movements, occurred during the fifth subray period, whereas the epoch of the Flagellants, and other fanatical enthusiasts who practiced self-torture and mutilation, was inspired by the fourth subray. The revival of interest in astrology around the thirteenth century (when St. Albertus Magnus and St. Thomas Aquinas integrated it into Christian thought) and the rise of the Gnostics may have coincided within the third- and second-subray cycles, respectively.[67]

Rays and the Nations

As students of esotericism are well aware, the Tibetan devotes much attention in his books to a discussion of the rays with respect to the nations. This is entirely understandable. We are informed that one of the great problems for the Hierarchy today is the strength of nationalism and the allegiance offered by most people in the world to their nation, ethnic group, race, or religion. Throughout the Piscean age, nations have been governed by the law of cleavages; in the age to come the law of loving understanding will be felt and this will eventually lead to the development of a world-wide international spirit.[68] Concerning the problems that will need to be resolved over the next two centuries, the Tibetan puts the matter of territorial possessions, or national self-interest, at the top of the list.[69] Through a knowledge of the rays, humanity can more clearly see the matrix of interdependent relationships that binds nations together, as well as points of friction that need to be overcome.

Table 14. Nations, Rays and Mottos[70]

Nation	Personality Ray	Soul Ray	National Motto (Esoteric)
India	Fourth Ray	First Ray	I hide the Light
China	Third Ray	First Ray	I indicate the way
Germany	First Ray	Fourth Ray	I preserve
France	Third Ray	Fifth Ray	I release the Light
Great Britain	First Ray	Second Ray	I serve
Italy	Fourth Ray	Sixth Ray	I carve the Paths
U.S.A.	Sixth Ray	Second Ray	I light the way
Russia	Sixth Ray	Seventh Ray	I link two ways
Austria	Fifth Ray	Fourth Ray	I serve the lighted way
Spain	Seventh Ray	Sixth Ray	I disperse the Cloud
Brazil	Second Ray	Fourth Ray	I hide the seed

One could discuss the rays and the nations at great length and, indeed, the history of a nation could be understood in terms of its ray configurations. Clearly, nations that have common rays often share similar destinies, or at least are in some ways connected. Two nations reflective of first-ray personality types are Great Britain and Germany.

Britain has demonstrated a good use of first-ray energy through the creation of its empire, which has blended many diverse peoples into a common polity and cultural system. With Germany, there has been a similar, albeit a more destructive, attempt to create a nation out of many smaller states and then to expand into an empire through the use of military power. In fact, Germany, like Britain, was an aggressive colonizer, but entered the game late in the nineteenth century and was far less successful.

Apart from competitive rivalries, which resulted in their being on opposite sides during the two world wars, Britain and Germany share many common bonds. It is no accident that the royal family in Britain is by lineage German, dating back to George I and the ascendancy of the Hanovarian line in 1714. In both countries there has traditionally been a strict code of discipline and propriety among the upper classes, which filtered down the social scale.

Other rays affecting Germany are ray six, which lends itself to fanaticism and unreasonable devotion to authority; ray four, the soul ray, which intensifies Germany's idealism and artistic genius, particularly with regard to music; ray seven, which emphasizes a love of order; and ray one, the personality ray, which gives this nation great drive and a tendency towards impetuousness.[71]

Britain, on the other hand, is impacted by ray four, which emphasizes its role as a mediator of conflict; ray five, which connects Britain to France and helps to explain why Britain has been an innovator in science; ray three, which accounts for Britain's expansiveness over the globe; ray one, its personality ray, which has given Britain far more importance in the world than its size would indicate; ray two, the soul ray, which connects Britain to the United States and encourages inclusiveness in foreign affairs; and finally, ray seven, which deals with its organizing abilities and the British emphasis on the rule of law.[72] By the same token, Britain is closely associated with India (which was the Jewel of the British Empire) and China (until recently) through its colony of Hong Kong. Both India and China are, at the soul level, first-ray nations.

Spain, Austria, and France, being governed by the seventh, fifth, and third rays, have experienced a close interrelationship since medieval times and have been dominated, as in the case of Spain and Austria, by the Hapsburg monarchs and by the Bourbons with respect to France and Spain. Both Italy and Spain, each with a sixth-ray soul, have been closely associated with the Catholic Church. Of course, Italy is the home of the papacy, whereas Spain has been the most fanatical of all the Catholic nations, being the force behind the Counter Reformation. Austria and Germany, both fourth-ray souls, have produced many of the world's greatest musicians and artists in other fields.

Similarly, the United States, with its second-ray soul and sixth-ray personality, has strong links with many countries, among which include Brazil, Italy, and Russia. Brazil, with its second-ray personality, has a history, like the United States, of being a magnet for many diverse groups of people who have been assimilated into a common culture. Italy, with a fourth-ray personality and a sixth-ray soul, has had a strong cultural impact upon the United States through the many immigrants from that country who were drawn to America from around the turn of the century to the 1920s. Russia, with its sixth-ray personality, shares with the United States a common psychology and a strong religious idealism. However, the inclusive and open second-ray nature of the United States stands in contrast to the seventh-ray soul of Russia, which is predicated on order and ritualism, hence the misunderstandings which led to and perpetuated the Cold War.[73]

Kurt Abraham, in his book *The Seven Rays and Nations*, focuses his attention on the ray structures of the United States and France. The sixth-ray personality nature of the United States is characterized by fanaticism, personal self-expression, noisy self-assertion, exclusiveness, rampant desire, stubbornness in terms of its sense of rightness, sensationalism with respect to sexual matters, glamours concerning money, and compassion for suffering. The French, on the other hand, with a third-ray personality, often come across as competitive, unfriendly, individualistic, and possessive. These differences, Abraham maintains, are at the root of the mistrust and basic misunderstandings between these two nations. However, the second-ray soul qualities of the United States, which emphasize generosity, friendliness, team spirit, and sharing, enable this country to play a leading role in the spiritual integration of humanity. France, with its fifth-ray soul, has an important role to play in bringing illumination to humankind. In the words of Abraham, "when the intellect of the French is turned towards the discovery and the elucidation of things of the spirit, then they will carry revelation to the world."[74] Interestingly, the zodiacal ruler of the United States at the soul level is Aquarius, the opposite of the personality sign of France, which is Leo. The soul sign of France is Pisces, a feminine sign, and the personality ruler of the United States is Gemini, a masculine sign.

Nations can be grouped in terms of their national psychology. Some nations, such as India, France, the United States, Russia, and Brazil, are feminine in their psychology; express great beauty; are fond of pageantry, display, and color; have strong individualistic tendencies; and are inclined to value money, possessions, and the material aspects of life. Masculine countries, on the other hand, including China, Germany, Great Britain, and Italy, are more mental, political, standardizing, group-conscious, occult by nature, aggressive, full of grandeur, emphasize law and order, possess race- and class-consciousness, and are empire-builders.[75]

Writing in the mid-1930s, the Tibetan indicated that certain obstacles were prevalent in the major industrial states, which prevented the realization of a deeper spiritual vision. Russia was governed by the dictatorship of the proletariat, which glorified the workers and drove out some of the best elements; Germany was controlled by a dictatorship of racial superiority that legitimized racism and separatism by isolating those of non-Germanic stock; the United States was under the control of a dictatorship of organized business, which sought to control government and regulate every department of economic life; and lastly, Great Britain was controlled by the dictatorship of empire, albeit a moderate and balancing empire of the middle classes.[76] Yet, in each instance, the perversion of power masked certain ideals which, if realized, could guide each nation to greater service.

From the perspective of the Hierarchy, the configurations formed by groups of nations can exert enormous power in world affairs. The Three Emperors League between Austria-Hungary, Germany, and Russia, established in 1873, created a triangle of crystallizing energy that served as a catalyst for the eruption of World War I in 1914. Both the world wars were fought between two triadic groups of nations. In the First World War it was the Triple Entente (Britain, France, and Russia) opposed by the Triple Alliance (Germany, Austria-Hungary, and the Ottoman Empire). In the Second World War, the allies, represented by Britain, the United States, and Russia, stood for the forces of light against the axis powers, Japan, Germany, and Italy, which were manipulated by the dark forces.

Much could be written about the esoteric significance of the three allied powers during the Second World War through which their leaders, Churchill, Roosevelt, and Stalin, provided focal points by which the Hierarchy could aid the forces of light. Each of these three nations had their part to play. Britain, as a result of its sophisticated political apparatus and penchant for government, was infused with will energy which, among other things, allowed it to absorb the full weight of German attacks in 1940 without capitulating. The United States, with its second-ray soul and propensity for openness and generosity, was given the task of supplying the allies with vital resources. The Soviet Union, (Russia) having a seventh-ray soul and sixth-ray personality, paid off much ancient karma through the sacrifice of up to twenty million of her citizens and the destruction of many of her cities. To say that Britain provided the time, American the materials, and Russia the blood in winning the war would be entirely true.

Planetary Power Centers

If we reflect on the relationship between the planet and the human body, it will be evident that there are many correspondences. Each comprises an interconnected network of systems that provide certain necessary functions. Like the human chakra system, energies flowing from various sources are released into our planetary life through the medium of certain inlets. At this time there are five such inlets for the inflowing spiritual forces, which are:

Inlet	Soul Ray	Personality Ray	Area
London	Ray five	Ray seven	Covers the Commonwealth regions
New York	Ray two	Ray three	Covers the Western Hemisphere
Geneva	Ray one	Ray two	Covers Europe and Russia
Tokyo	Ray six	Ray four	Covers the Far East
Darjeeling	Ray two	Ray five	Covers India and most of Asia [77]

It is said that later two more centers will be added. One, presumably, will be in Africa (Johannesburg), while the other will most likely be situated in the South Pacific in Australia (Sydney).

Of the five planetary inlets listed above, London, New York, and Tokyo are objective centers while Geneva and Darjeeling are subjective centers.[78] Each of the objective centers are major world cities that have been, and are, focal points of great economic and political power. The subjective centers, on the other hand, exert a less obtrusive but an equally potent energy over a wide area. These two centers, Geneva and Darjeeling, the Tibetan maintains, transmit pure spiritual energy with greater ease than do the objective centers. Together, all of them form five centers of "impelling energy."[79]

New York (along with London) is the most active center. With a second-ray soul and a third-ray personality, this city attracts people from all over the world and, in essence, represents a composite of humanity as a whole. More so because New York is the home of the United Nations. It was to New York (drawn by the magnetic quality of the second ray) that the many immigrants came seeking relief from oppression and a better life. Similarly, for many, the United Nations symbolizes the hope of the world, and in its spiritual aspect the UN seeks to bring about world salvage through human liberation. In terms of its third-ray personality, New York is the center of business and finance on a global scale. It is also characterized by speed and a quality of restlessness, both characteristic of the third ray.

The force expressing itself through New York at this time is the sixth ray. Being the personality ray of the United States, New York may be seen as a place of extremes where excesses of wealth and poverty as well as selfishness and generosity exist side by side. It is also a city of many conflicts between ideologies, principles, and competitive industries.

The connection to the sixth ray dates back to more ancient times when North America was part of the continent of Atlantis. Within the United States itself there is another subsystem of inlets, of which New York, in terms of chakras, is the throat center. The other centers include Washington (head center), Los Angeles (heart center), Kansas City (ajna center), and Chicago (solar plexus center). The Tibetan does not give the centers for the other two chakra points, the sacral center and the base of the spine.[80]

Planetary centers, like all forms, have their outward appearance as well as their inner reality. William Blake saw both sides of London. On one hand it was, to him, a wasteland of materialism, suffering, and cries of woe; on the other hand it was the new Jerusalem, the emanation of Albion over all the world. London, with its fifth-ray soul and seventh-ray personality, was the precursor of modernism and industrialism, both of which Blake deplored. Conversely, the capacity for organization, discrimination, detached objectivity, and intellectual power enabled London to be the center of a global empire upon which it is said "the sun never sets." Influenced by the second-ray soul and the first-ray personality of Great Britain, London, since the seventeenth century, was a haven for political and religious refugees from Europe, and during the Second World War it was a small beacon of light through which the forces of light could work.

The Tibetan places great importance on the role of the Commonwealth, from which the Empire evolved, as a significant step in human evolution, covering, as it does, fifty countries and about a quarter of the world's population. Whereas the Commonwealth has all but dissolved exoterically, it continues to have a strong esoteric influence through which the Hierarchy can work. London exists as the heart center of the Commonwealth, the other points of which include Sydney, Johannesburg, Toronto, and Vancouver. We are told that Calcutta, Delhi, Singapore, Jamaica, and Madras are all subjectively linked.[81]

Tokyo, like New York, is situated in a country with a strong sixth-ray influence, which gives it a somewhat fanatical quality. We have seen manifestations of this sixth-ray aspect (Toyko has a sixth-ray soul and a fourth-ray personality) in its lower material form through the will to conquer much of Southeast Asia, during the Second World War, and the drive for business success in the post-war world. Incidentally, this sixth-ray energy has also helped to materially transform other nations of Asia and has contributed to the elevation of Japan as one of the most literate societies in the world. The sixth ray combined with the fourth ray is a difficult relationship, reflecting, on one hand, unrelenting aspiration, effort, and drive within a milieu of conflict, inconstancy, restlessness, and cyclic pessimism. Tokyo forms a potent triangle with London and New York, which can be seen in the impact these centers have on world affairs.

As to the subjective centers, Darjeeling, with a second-ray soul and a fifth-ray personality, is the repository of wisdom, which has been stored in that region for centuries. This storehouse of energy, when properly invoked, could become a vast circular flow of divine light which can help to regenerate the planet. Located near the foothills of Tibet, Darjeeling also holds the first-ray energy of Shamballa, filtered through the Hierarchy, and the wisdom of India, expressed along first- and fourth-ray lines.

Like Darjeeling, Geneva has more spiritual energy than the other three objective centers and combines the fusing and synthesizing aspect of the first ray along with the harmonizing and magnetic power of the second ray. Geneva expresses these indwelling energies in a number of ways. One is the synthesis of cultural traditions—French, German, and Italian—which is characteristic of Switzerland. It was also the birthplace of Calvinism and a center of religious experiment and activity during the Reformation of the sixteenth century. The League of Nations made its home in Geneva, and Geneva has been the primary center for peace negotiations and international diplomacy. Geneva is also the home of many humanitarian organizations, such as the Red Cross. Governed by the sign of Leo, Geneva, more than any other city, has been the focal point of European self-expression in its highest form.

Chapter 8—
Planetary Harmonics:
Esoteric Astrology and
Historical Events

In his book, *A Treatise on White Magic*, the Tibetan observes that there are three groups of solar energies that impact life on this planet. The first are pranic energies that radiate from the physical sun and vitalize physical forms. The second group of energies emanate from what is occultly termed "the heart of the sun." They sweep through the solar system as seven great streams of consciousness and pour into the soul of man. It is from these energies that one finds the seven grades of consciousness that comprise the constitution of man and the seven rays.[1]

Added to these two groups of energies is a third which forms the basis for astrological research. This third group of energies flows from the twelve constellations of our zodiac. As to the reality of these zodiacal energies as they play upon humanity, there can be little doubt. However, the extent to which they govern human behavior in specific ways is problematic. Much depends, for example, upon a person's level of consciousness. An advanced disciple whose life is an expression of soul qualities, more or less, will respond to these energies differently than will a man or woman who is struggling to integrate his or her personality. Zodiacal energies condition every form and every kingdom in nature, acting either as a retrograding or stimulating force.[2]

The salient point in creating a horoscope, from the perspective of esoteric astrology, is not the relationship of a sign to a given month of the year, such as Pisces to March or Gemini to June, but the ability to comprehend the thoughtform of the constellation as it has evolved over the ages. Here again, an understanding of one's place upon the spiritual path is vital for relating astrology to evolutionary development. For the relatively few aspirants and disciples who are consciously treading the spiritual path, their efforts are directed towards breaking free from the wheel of earthly existence by means of embodying and dominating these inflowing energies. As for the bulk of average humanity, they are governed by the illusion of forms and appearances which makes them largely oblivious to the complex cycles of zodiacal energies that affect their lives in ways they can seldom appreciate.[3]

The field of esoteric astrology can be considered to be, basically, an analysis of the seven rays from a different perspective. Here again, everything on the inner planes is interrelational. In differentiating ray cycles (more accurately spiral-cycles) from astrological cycles, it could be said that the former relate to space whereas the latter are elements of time. As was noted in the previous chapter, the rays themselves are, in the context of human history, really manifestations of human egos who incarnate in large numbers over vast periods of time and thus radiate the qualities of one ray or another across the broad landscape of history. Astrological cycles, on the other hand, are planetary modifications of ray energy that have a direct magnetic impact upon the planet and thereby precipitate a specific quality of events at certain periods. Put another way, such cycles create a force field of potentialities by which certain conditions exist that will make it probable that one or more corresponding events will likely occur. Insofar as the rays and planetary influences on earth are essentially one and the same, it follows that astrological cycles are the result of energy that has been filtered through the solar system so as to reach earth in a modified form.

The seven rays enter our solar system through one of the seven stars (Rishis) forming the Great Bear. They are then transmitted through three major constellations, which the Tibetan identifies as Aries, Leo, and Capricorn (as expressions of first-ray energy) and, in turn, are transformed through the sun itself, formed by three aspects—the central spiritual sun, the heart of the sun, and the physical sun. The seven rays are next transfigured by means of the seven sacred planets (Vulcan—a veiled planet, Mercury, Venus, Jupiter, Saturn, Neptune, and Uranus) before being impressed on the four non-sacred planets, of which our Earth is one.[4]

Yet this is only part of the picture. There are many potent energies which play upon our solar system and planet all the time but go unnoticed since they are of a quality that is beyond the sense apparatus of most individuals, who have not achieved triadal and monadic consciousness. Essentially, the solar system is a great filtering agent by which energies are stepped down so that they can be effective and useful in our, relatively speaking, gross plane of existence. The constellations and planetary systems, which comprise this vast network of the solar system, are pointers and modifiers of energy.

The ancients recognized that individual planets possess specific characteristics. Venus, for example, was associated with radiance or beauty, Mars with assertiveness or dynamic action, Jupiter with expansiveness, Saturn with limitation, and Mercury with relationship or communication. Among the more recently discovered outer planets, Neptune is seen by esoteric astrologers to have a misty, vague, mystical quality; Uranus is associated with unpredictability; and Pluto points to death, rebirth, and regeneration. The sun and the moon (a dead planet) have a polar opposite effect. The sun, symbolized by the soul, represents one's higher nature, whereas the moon symbolizes the forces of one's instinctual or lower nature.

Esoteric astrologers concern themselves essentially with three types of energy. First, there is the energy of the constellation in which the sun is situated at the time of birth; second, there is the rising sign, which is positioned on the eastern horizon at the point of birth; finally, there is the moon which governs the form aspect, especially the physical form. The energy of the constellation under which a person (or some other entity) is born relates to an immediate or present problem to be solved and is associated with the personality. It also governs the activity nature of a life. The ascendant, or rising sign, holds the key to the future. It is connected to the soul of a life and when duly consummated produces sattva, or harmony. If a life evolves according to its soul purpose, then the ascendant will gain greater dominance as it unfolds. Finally, the moon, representing the past, encapsulates the limitations and handicaps under which one must work and, if not confronted and overcome, will hinder the evolution of a life. For this reason, the moon is an element of inertia. The birth month, therefore, represents a point of opportunity between the weight of one's historic past, often stretching over many lifetimes (moon), and the subjective pull of one's inner light, leading to the liberation of consciousness.[5]

Each one of the zodiacal constellations also has its particular characteristics, which can be grouped in several different ways. In terms of elements, Aries, Leo, and Sagittarius are fire signs and possess an element of dynamism or combustibility. Taurus, Virgo, and Capricorn are earth signs, which indicate rootedness or groundedness on the physical plane. Gemini, Libra, and Aquarius are air signs and are related to the quality of mind. Finally, Cancer, Scorpio, and Pisces are water signs and are the most sensitive to any environment.

Central to an understanding of esoteric astrology are the three crosses. As with all things esoteric, there are different dimensions to this phenomenon. The mutable cross, comprising the constellations of Gemini, Virgo, Sagittarius, and Pisces, is said to bring about conditions that generate great changes in the life of a planet, a kingdom in nature, or a human being. Referred to also as the common cross, it characterizes the steady development towards personality integration and thus it is the path of ordinary experience. In human terms, this is the lot of the overwhelming majority of men and women today. It can also be said that the mutable cross is the means by which the soul (or ego) gains experience through the lower three worlds of form.[6]

Taurus, Leo, Scorpio, and Aquarius are the signs of the fixed cross and mark the path of discipleship. Whereas the focus of the mutable cross is towards the outer world, the fixed cross is more inwardly focused and is given to constant and unavoidable crises, leading to a transformation of the subjective nature. This cross is primarily that of soul development whereby one becomes increasingly conscious of greater issues beyond those of personal concern. It is through this cross that one treads the path of service.[7]

The last of the three crosses, the cardinal cross, comprises the constellation of Aries, Cancer, Libra, and Capricorn. The key word signifying this path is synthesis and it represents the path of initiation or, should we say, the path of those who are no longer bound by the mists of glamour and illusion that characterize the lower realms of form. At this point, one is responding to the subtle and powerful energies of the monad. The Tibetan refers to this path as "the beginning of the endless Way of Revelation."[8]

Needless to say, the symbolism of the three crosses lends itself to Christian imagery. The mutable cross, or the cross of the hidden Christ, is predominantly the cross of repeated incarnations; the fixed cross is the cross of the Son of God, the incarnating Christ, or the Christ of planetary experience; the cardinal cross, known as the cross of the risen

Christ, represents the Cosmic Christ, the avatar of pure love.

Astrologically speaking, evolution progresses first by mounting the mutable cross, then moving on to the fixed cross, and finally stepping on to the cardinal cross. Each transference from one cross to the next, which is symbolized by the act of initiation, involves a reversal on the wheel of the zodiac from a clockwise rotation (Aries to Pisces), to a counter-clockwise rotation (Pisces to Aries) and, finally, clockwise again. All three crosses are rotating vortices of energy that are differentiated by velocity and the quality of energy. As an entity (at whatever level) repeatedly incarnates on the mutable cross, for example, the rate of its energy body increasingly gains momentum until it reaches a critical point of tension. Then the wheel is reversed, creating an inevitable condition of chaos until a new rhythm is established on the fixed cross. The same process is then repeated, however at a higher turn of the spiral. This holds true for all manifested forms whether one is considering a person, a nation, or a planetary system.

The downflow of energies pouring through our solar system separates itself out, as all things must, into three streams or vibrations, representing the three aspects of divinity. The tripartite passage of these energies follows a clear line of progression. Hence, we can observe that each of the planetary centers, which have a direct impact on human history, receives energies that have already been modified by greater entities. These energies are then passed from Shamballa through the Hierarchy, and finally to humanity.

Table 15. The Threefold Transmission of Energies[9]

Rays	I.	II.	III.
Nature of Spirit	Will, Purpose	Love-Wisdom	Active Intelligence
Cosmic	Great Bear	Sirius	Pleiades
Zodiacal	Leo	Pisces	Capricorn
Systemic	Saturn	Uranus	Mercury
Planetary Centers	Shamballa	Hierarchy	Humanity

We see from the above table that the energy of will and purpose flows through those constellations, zodiacal patterns, and planetary systems that reflect the nature of this energy. The same could be said of the love-wisdom line and the stream of active intelligence. Energy, following the law of economy, finds its line of least resistance. The ray energy of a particular quality is attractive to constellations, systems, and centers that are receptive to its vibratory essence. Our solar system is governed by the energy of love-wisdom, thus it follows that expansiveness and inclusiveness (both second-ray characteristics) would be dominant. Other solar systems, depending on their ray type, would be configured differently.

A more complete relationship between the rays, groups of constellations, and planetary rulers can be found in the following table. As one can see, there is much interrelationship, which further points to the complexity of this whole subject. It is interesting that, in most cases, the ray transmitted by a planet is different from the ray that is transmitted by a constellation. Each ray, filtered through a particular constellation, has both an orthodox and an esoteric planetary rulership. The orthodox rulership corresponds to the outer form, or personality aspect, whereas esoteric rulership speaks to the subjective or soul nature of a constellation.

Table 16. Rays, Constellations, and Planets[10]

Ray	Constellations	Orthodox Planets	Esoteric Planets
1. Will or Power			
	Aries, The Ram	Mars	Mercury
	Leo, The Lion	Sun	Sun
	Capricorn, The Goat	Saturn	Saturn
2. Love-Wisdom			
	Gemini, The Twins	Mercury	Venus
	Virgo, The Virgin	Mercury	Moon
	Pisces, The Fishes	Jupiter	Pluto
3. Active Intelligence			
	Cancer, The Crab	Moon	Neptune
	Libra, The Scales	Venus	Uranus
	Capricorn, The Goat	Saturn	Saturn

4. Harmony through Conflict

Taurus, The Bull	Venus	Vulcan
Scorpio, The Scorpion	Mars	Mars
Sagittarius, The Archer	Jupiter	Earth

5. Concrete Science

Leo, The Lion	Sun	Sun
Sagittarius, The Archer	Jupiter	Earth
Aquarius, The Water-carrier	Uranus	Jupiter

6. Idealism, Devotion

Virgo, The Virgin	Mercury	Moon
Sagittarius, The Archer	Jupiter	Earth
Pisces, The Fishes	Jupiter	Pluto

7. Ceremonial Order

Aries, The Ram	Mars	Mercury
Cancer, The Crab	Moon	Neptune
Capricorn, The Goat	Saturn	Saturn

The Great Cycle

The above discussion places the mechanics of this difficult subject into a wider context. Fortunately, the impact of planetary ray influences on human history seems more straightforward. From the dawn of recorded history, people have looked to the movement of the stars and planetary systems to understand not only the relationship of the earth to the cosmos, but also the matrix by which human affairs could be understood. Not surprisingly, civilizations up to modern times have tended to see history in terms of cycles. Many civilizations defined time in relation to a Great Year, or the completion of a major cycle. A Great Year of history tended to move through various cyclic stages, which could be pictured as a wheel. At the center of the wheel was the point of eternality, or substance, that was unchanging. The turning of the wheel constituted change and experience, or the passing of time through its various historical phases.[11]

The Great Year can be divided in any number of ways. Oswald Spengler saw it as a fourfold progression whereby a culture went through a seasonal cycle of spring, summer, autumn, and winter phases. Karl Marx saw history as moving through four modes of production from slavery to socialism. William Irwin Thompson's vision of four cultural ecologies in the West further implies a quaternary division of the Great Year. William Butler Yeats, in his *Vision*, thought that historical time was conditioned by four faculties, which he referred to as Will, the Mask, the Creative Mind, and Body of Fate. On the other hand, Francis Bacon divided the Great Year into three phases—growth, maturity, and decline—as did the ancient Sumerians who entertained a threefold cycle. Plato split the Great Year into five segments.[12]

Astrologically speaking, the Great Year is defined by planetary movements. Plato, drawing upon Babylonian historical cosmology, interpreted the Great Year as a 36,000-year cycle.[13] This makes numerical sense insofar as a circle is 360 degrees which, divided by the twelve houses in the zodiac, equates to 3,000-year lesser cycles. Plato's calculations, however, were based not on astronomical cycles but on astrological and numerological metaphors which, though logical in one sense, were basically an abstraction.[14]

From a Theosophical standpoint, the Great Year is characterized by the fourth-ray cipher twenty-five (25), which is based on the calculations of Pythagoras. As with all things, Theosophy and the Ageless Wisdom do not deal with absolutes, but envision the universe as a set of correspondences. In this case, there are three Great Years which relate to the cycles of the monad, the soul, and the personality. The succession of the sun through the rounds of the greater zodiac, the first of the three Great Years most recently ended when the sun entered the sign of Pisces two thousand years ago.[15] It should be noted that there appears to be two zodiacs. The greater zodiac, which lasts for approximately 250,000 years, records the passage of the sun around the solar system and is symbolic of the soul as it relates to the life cycle of the monad. The lesser zodiac is an approximate 25,000-year cycle and corresponds to the path of the sun through the twelve constellations as they impact our planet. Insofar as the greater zodiac records the relationship of the soul to the monad, the lesser zodiac reflects the relationship of the personality to the soul.[16]

The last Great Monadic Year (or greater zodiac) began, according to Hodson, during the Atlantean root race and ended just prior to the birth of Christ.[17] Because root races overlap, precise dating of the ancient past is often wildly speculative and problematic. For example, Wachsmuth estimates that what he calls the Prototype I phase, beginning at the end of the Lemurian root race and approaching the start of the first Atlantean root race, occurred at roughly 25,000 BCE.[18] Hodson implies that the configuration of Atlantis, around the time it split into two island continents, happened 200,000 years ago.[19] Daniel Krummenacher, basing his work on admittedly hypothetical calculations, suggests that the fourth root race ended 3.8 million years ago, before the time, according to Hodson, when the Rmoahal subrace emerged and spread over Atlantis. Such glaring discrepancies of time may be something of a sleight of hand since, aside from the wide parameters given for this root race (Hodson defines it as extending from 12 million years ago to 9564 BCE), there is no indication of the precise dates when any event occurred on Atlantis. In addition, periods of pralaya are difficult to calculate. By Hodson's reckoning, the fifth root race, which reaches back into the past a million years, has undergone four Great Years.

As noted earlier, the passing of the sun through the signs of the lesser zodiac is a 25,000-year cycle, and is analogously equivalent to a complete soul cycle. The time period for this most recent 25,000-year cycle dates back to the early days of the third subrace of the fifth race (Persian), prior to the last Ice Age, and before the final deluge of Atlantis. The significance of this cycle, in terms of historical evolution, is determined by the sum total of experiences gained in each of the constellations of the zodiacal wheel. The return of this cycle, which from all accounts began sometime during the Atlantean root race as well as during the early subraces of the Aryan root race, points to a re-emergence of the consciousness found in this earlier period. The surfacing of emotionalism, which is evident in many parts of the world today, reflects the revisitation of Atlantean astralism. "There are millions of such souls in existence," observes the Tibetan, and "they may be regarded as modern Atlanteans."[20]

The passage of the sun through the various signs of the zodiac on a yearly basis is the focal point of conventional astrology. According to the Ageless Wisdom, this projection of a horoscope is an illusion since it places the universe around the central life of the personality. Esoterically speaking, this makes as much sense as putting the earth at the center of the universe, which was the error made by medieval cosmologists. The personality exists only as a vehicle for the light of the soul, and beyond that, as a vehicle for the energies flowing through the monad and modified by the spiritual triad of atma, buddhi, and manas. Seen as a separate entity, the personality is an illusion. This speaks to the distinction between conventional astrology, which relates planetary influences to the individual, and esoteric astrology, which views all phenomenon as the embodiment of modified ray energies. Accordingly, nothing is separate or isolated in the universe. This is the first great principle of the Ageless Wisdom.

The Great Age

The Great Year can be divided into twelve lesser cycles, which relates to the predominance of a particular astrological constellation. Since humanity is still on the wheel of the common cross, the progression of ages is now in a clockwise direction, which accounts for the fact that we are presently moving from the Piscean age to the Aquarian age. According to the Tibetan, when humanity individuated in the Lemurian period some eighteen million years ago, there was an interrelation of extreme potency between three constellations, Leo, Capricorn, and Pisces. To these was added a fourth energy, that of Aquarius.[21] While the intensified vibration of this particular alignment has only occurred a few times in the past, there have been roughly 8,572 ages of Leo, Capricorn, Pisces, and Aquarius since that time. Also, there have been six times since the dawning of the fifth root race when the sun in Aquarius has coincided with a seventh-ray cycle, creating a moment of planetary crisis.[22] These facts reveal that evolution proceeds very slowly, more so in the past when humanity lived in a relative state of unconsciousness. Insofar as each of the twelve ages, marked by one of the astrological signs, represents a particular quality or impulse, humanity is imbued with the collective wisdom of the zodiac through the constant turning of the wheel.

The teaching or significance of each of the signs can be found in any book on astrology, ranging from the simplistic to the profound. One should always be mindful of the fact that each sign represents a certain configuration of energy, which may be fluid (as in the case of water signs), stable (earth signs), interactive (air signs), or dynamic (fire signs). As with all things esoteric, there is never one meaning for a sign since the message corresponds to one's level of evolution. For example, Capricorn (an earth sign) would be characterized by an attachment to form for undeveloped humanity on the mutable cross; for people beginning to tread the path of discipleship on the fixed cross, it would involve relating through form; whereas on the cardinal cross, in reference to a disciple who has gained mastery on the mental plane, it would provide the freedom to transform the form.[23] In each case, the relationship to matter (or the form world) is quite different. The same could be said for each of the other signs. Moreover, no sign is an entity unto itself and must be understood, through various patterns, in relationship to other signs of the zodiac, mostly with the signs belonging to the same cross and the various triangles between signs, as described in *Esoteric Astrology*.

Having said this, it is necessary to outline some of the key qualities for each of the zodiacal signs; these qualities possess a seed and a hint of their wider impact.[24]

- Aries—Initiating, beginnings, will or power expressed through creative processes, thrusting forward
- Taurus—Desire, possessiveness, will or directed purpose, worldliness elevated to the search for illumination
- Gemini—Duality, love-wisdom, fluidity, versatility, control over pairs of opposites
- Cancer—Mass-sensitivity, mass-identification, protectiveness, service for the masses
- Leo—Sensitivity leading to individual awareness, self-consciousness, self-assertion, vitality, authority, the will to rule and illumine
- Virgo—Nurturing form and spirit, critical analysis, industriousness, discrimination, methodicalness
- Libra—Equilibrium, balance of spirit and form life, relationships, companionship, harmony
- Scorpio—Testing, trial, points of crisis, re-orientation, degeneration, regeneration, secrecy
- Sagittarius—Focused direction, one-pointed activity, satisfaction of desire leading to a higher goal
- Capricorn—Extreme characteristics of the best and the worst, ambition, crystallization, struggle to overcome, encasement by structure leading to creation of structure

- Aquarius—Will to serve, individual consciousness transmuted into group consciousness, humanitarianism
- Pisces—Duality, fluidity endowed with instinctual consciousness, mediumism, release of the captive soul, undisciplined life leading to the resurrected life, renunciation, universality

The Piscean Age

The Age of Pisces, which is now drawing to an end, has been dominated by the light of the Christ. The Danish astrologer, Holger Stavnsbjerg, has calculated the horoscope of Christianity in the light of the hypothetical horoscope of Jesus. His research shows that the 150 most important events in Christian history are each related to a significant zodiacal conjunction, square, transit, or opposition.[25] The power of Christianity, and the reason for its ultimate success, has had less to do with the life and teachings of Jesus and more to do with the resurrection. It was through the resurrection that the crucifixion and death of Jesus was turned inside out and elevated into a story of triumph and glory. Christ was no longer a human figure, who walked among men performing healings and miracles, but a cosmic figure who sat at the right hand of God and, through the holy spirit, radiated love into the world. Through the resurrection, Christ was seen as the world savior who could forgive all sin and raise humanity to eternal life.

The power of this message is undeniable but, without the physical presence of Christ, the ability of the newly formed religious entity of Christianity, which nurtured the Christian message, to maintain its impetus would be clearly stymied. The cross was an ancient symbol, which also conveyed the meaning of the crucifixion and resurrection. Another symbol associated with Christianity is the fish. Houston Smith tells us that if we had been living in the region of the Mediterranean during the early centuries of the Christian era, we would have noticed the crude outlines of a fish scrawled on walls and in caves.[26] Whereas there are a number of references to fish in the Bible, most notably the story of the loaves and fishes, the more ancient meaning behind this symbol is astrological. We also know that the Greek letters of the word fish are also the first letters of the words, "Jesus Christ, Son of God, Savior."[27]

Pisces, we are told, is a sign of extremes. The symbol of this constellation, the two fishes swimming in opposite directions connected by a cord, represent personality and soul. Through renunciation or detachment, the soul, which is captive in form, is liberated and is free to return to its father's house—the higher plane of the monad. This journey is brought about by means of sacrifice (which literally means letting go of the lower so one can do something sacred from the plane of the higher self) and the death of any attachment to the form world.[28]

Pisces, therefore, reflects three conditions of being or states of consciousness. The first condition is imprisonment in the realm of form. Here the mass of men are locked into a sea of glamours, illusions, and false perceptions while, at the same time, they eagerly seek to escape these limiting conditions. The desire to escape the harsh realities of life is central to this state of consciousness. Although information about earlier periods is somewhat sketchy, there is massive evidence to suggest that escapism through alcohol and drugs has been the most pronounced over the past two thousand years. Wine and beer were consumed in large quantities for centuries, but it was the emergence of hard liquor that elevated alcoholism (and consequently, escapism) to epidemic proportions. The word alcohol was coined in the sixteenth century, when it is said that immoderate drinking became a fashion.[29] The use of opiates surfaced in the nineteenth century and, of course, drug use has been a major problem, especially during the latter half of the twentieth century. Some newspaper accounts have suggested that the illegal drug trade today rivals the global oil trade in terms of revenues.[30]

Renunciation or detachment is the second sphere of Piscean consciousness. During the Middle Ages, many men and women entered religious orders so as to, in part, segregate or detach themselves from the low quality of life around them. The emergence of private spheres of life as a social reality, outside of the public domain, began with the Reformation. This took many forms, ranging from the affirmation of personal piety to the retreat of families into separate quarters. The rise of the middle classes brought with it a strong commitment to the nuclear family. This distancing of oneself from the masses helped to raise the collective standard of manners and morals. By the nineteenth century, nearly everything had been segregated into separate spheres of life. A further step along these lines can be found in the present era. One of the forces behind the growing trend towards individualism has been the consciousness to detach oneself from mass norms, values, and controls, which has had severe consequences with respect to civic virtue, community awareness, and even public decency. There are other energies and forces, of course, which have encouraged this trend as well.

The final stage of Piscean consciousness is self-sacrifice and death. This is not the heroic death of Aries or the fiery cataclysmic death of Scorpio, but death related to renunciation and idealism. The archetype of this form of death is the martyr, of which there have been many over the past two thousand years of the Piscean age. Since one of the manifestations of Pisces is the sixth ray, there is often a fanatical desire to bring about reforms or to rectify a condition, based on some lofty goal or ideal. The Crusades of the eleventh and twelfth centuries were certainly characterized by self-sacrifice, fanaticism, and death. The Inquisition, the conquest of Mexico and Peru by the Spanish, the religious wars of the sixteenth and seventeenth centuries, the French and Russian Revolutions, and the two world wars all revolved around the theme of sacrifice and death for a greater goal. Throughout the Piscean age, the blind loyalty of soldiers in the face of death has been noteworthy. In a passage from the classic novel about World War I, *All Quiet on the Western Front*, one of the young German soldiers, before going off to war, says, "With our young, awakened eyes we saw that the classical conception of the Fatherland held by our teachers resolved itself here into a renunciation of personality such as one would not ask of the meanest servants."[31]

The Piscean age must likewise be seen in relation to the other signs of the mutable cross. Virgo, the polar opposite of Pisces, is concerned with discrimination and bringing order out of chaos on the physical plane and, esoterically, the purification of the instrument for the inner birth of the Christ principle. In one sense, Virgo relates to our use of space. The environmental effects of Virgo in recent times has been more pronounced due to the inflowing of Shamballa energy from about 1825. It has been the lot of western man over the past several centuries to surround nature with civilization so as to control and regulate space. This can be seen in terms of the growth of towns and cities and, consequently, technology. The creation of an urban environment is not just a matter of demographics and lifestyle, but relates to the development of a planetary consciousness. Cities are to a society, in a very real sense, what the brain is to a living organism. As a society solves its basic problem of survival through abundant food production, it moves into the sphere of industrialization by which energy and raw materials are extracted and converted into finished products for use. From the standpoint of global industrial growth, a society that has reached a high state of development moves to the next stage, which is the centralization of information by which cities and sophisticated centers of technology become nodes of information-gathering and distribution. This creates what William Irwin Thompson calls a dialectic between the center and the periphery.[32]

It is worth bearing in mind that Virgo creates the form which nurtures the light. Thompson sees a natural evolution from what he calls industrial consciousness, based on patterns of consumption, to planetary consciousness, which will center around images of community, ecological connectedness, a sense of right livelihood, and appropriate technology.[33] Thus it is projected that the new age (or the next upward turn of the spiral) will, in a very real sense, be the birthing of a new Christ spirit.

Astrologer Dane Rudhyar believes that the Piscean age should actually be called the Pisces-Virgo age since the Pisces polarity has dominated the first half of this two-thousand-year cycle, while the Virgo polarity and the qualities it characterizes have gained strength over the second half of the cycle. In particular, the Virgo impact has overshadowed the last quarter of the Piscean age, historically speaking, since the sixteenth century. Much that is today thought to be an expression of the Aquarian age is really a protest against the Virgo influence that has fostered a reactive nostalgic return to the mysticism and mass-consciousness of Pisces.[34]

The other two sides of the mutable or common cross, Gemini and Sagittarius, represent, respectively, the interplay of duality and one-pointed direction and fusion. It is through this dialectical tension between duality or conflict and synthesis that one finds the great historical ideas of Eckhart, Hegel, and Marx. Meister Eckhart (1260-1327), who lived as a Dominican monk, developed a theology centered around Christianity and Neoplatonism, which stressed a dialectical duality between the unconscious innocence of the Garden of Eden state and the worldly cognitive consciousness of the fallen state. This duality is synthesized in the transcendental consciousness of soul-enlightened awareness.

At another level, Georg Wilhelm Friedrich Hegel (1770-1831) believed that every idea (thesis) has its opposite concept (antithesis), which combined together create a unity, or synthesis. Karl Marx (1818-1883) applied Hegel's model to the material evolution of history and concluded that economic forces reflect a class struggle between those who own the means of production and those who produce. This conflict, which is not limited to economics but covers every sphere of cultural and social life, is resolved through synthesis and the resurgence of a new form of production. The power of dialectical paradigms peculiar to the Piscean age, therefore, has resulted directly from the tension between Gemini and Sagittarian planetary influences.

The four signs of the mutable cross would seem to have a direct relationship to the four mystery streams, posited by Anthroposophy, which were discussed at length in chapter six. It is difficult to make precise connections between these two patterns beyond what seems to be an obvious correlation. However, if we overlay a map of the mystery streams with that of the zodiacal positions of the mutable cross, placed in their respective houses, there is an interesting pattern.

Table 17. Mystery Streams and the Mutable Cross[35]

Northern Stream
(Nordic Myths)

Western Stream   Eastern Stream
(Hibernian, Druid,   (Slavic, Indian,
Christian)   Persian, Greek)

Southern Stream
(Rosicrucian
Roman Empire,
Egyptian, Lemurian)

Sagittarius
(ninth house)
philosophy
religion
one-pointed direction
fire

Pisces (twelfth house)   Virgo (sixth house)
mysticism   nurturance of life
other-worldliness   analytical
world saviorship   critically conscious
water   earth

Gemini
(third house)
communication
relationship
duality
air

The western mystery stream, which was seen as the repository of Atlantean consciousness and carried by the Celtic peoples who integrated the Hibernian mysteries with Christianity, most clearly embodies the energies flowing through Pisces. The divine world, according to the Celts, was present in the elements of water and light. Water, or a well, was considered to be especially sacred, and a river was an entity to be experienced and worshipped.[36] Pisces, being one of the water signs, has a connection here.

The eastern stream, in contrast, which Steiner and others have likened to the carrier of the Grail legend and mysteries, represents the inflow of the post-Atlantean consciousness of the Indian, Persian, Greek sub and branch races and, logically by association, the Slavic branch races. The Grail, being the form which nurtures the light (spirit) of Christ, has a direct relationship to Virgo, which is characterized in the esoteric keywords for that sign; from the angle of the soul, "I am the mother and the child. I, God, I, matter am."[37]

Through the southern stream, carried by waves of incarnating souls, flow the mysteries of man in his earthly physical form. This stream began in Lemuria and traveled through Egypt, which in mythical terms is the whole body of Osiris, then to Rome, which represented the materialism of empire, and finally was lodged in Rosicrucian rituals and practices. The southern stream is interwoven with the esotericism of the Jewish people and is rooted in the duality of spirit and matter, expressed Biblically through the symbolic figures of Cain and Abel.[38] Thus the twins, who characterize the opposite polarities of human nature, are represented by the sign of Gemini, which is the guiding force behind this dualistic flow of consciousness.

Finally, the mysteries of the Nordic myths are transported through the northern stream of consciousness. Whereas the Celtic stream focuses more on sacred places, the northern stream highlights sacred objects and feats of strength and cunning. According to legend, Odin, the Nordic God, for his third initiation had to leave behind his third eye so he could read the runic script and thus gain power over the mind.[39] The third eye, among other things, represents a point of synthesis. Odin, as the epitome of courage and tenacity, embraces the Sagittarian quality of one-pointed activity. This ego impulse, around which the Nordic myths revolve, bears a close similarity to the Sagittarian archer whose keywords are, from the angle of the soul, "I see the goal. I reach that goal and then I see another."[40]

Transitions

Energy translates itself according to whatever ray patterns or constellations (mutable cross, fixed cross, or cardinal cross) are in season. Thus, during the Age of Aries, which was overshadowed by the energies of Aries, Libra, Cancer, and Capricorn, those mystery streams that ran through the various civilizations and subraces, including Greece, Rome, Persia, China, Babylonia, and the ancient Hebrews, expressed the qualities of the cardinal cross. The same could be said for the fixed cross constellations (Taurus, Scorpio, Leo, Aquarius), which had been the prevailing ones during the earlier Age of Taurus.

Rudhyar writes that, according to the Hindu tradition, the transition between the 2,000-year cycle of two great ages lasts a tenth of the length of the cycle at its close, which he calls the seed period, and the same amount of time at the start of a new cycle, which he refers to as the germinal period.[41] By Rudhyar's reckoning, the first 216 years of the Piscean age (he calculates a great age to be 2,160 years, which may be an approximation of the real figure) would be the germinal phase of that age, and the last 216 years would be the seed phase. If we assume, based upon Rudhyar's calculations, that the Piscean age began at 100 BCE, then the germinal phase would have ended in 160 CE, near the time of the death of the Roman emperor Antoninus Pius, who was best known for building the Antonine Wall in what is now Scotland. Generally speaking, the second century marked the furthest extent of Roman jurisdiction before the troubles of the third century began to compromise Roman power and size.

If we look at the other end of the present age and conclude (for the sake of argument) that the Piscean age will complete its cycle at the beginning of the twenty-first century, then the seed period would date back to 1784. Congress, during that year, ratified the Treaty of Paris, thus ending the American War of Independence, and the Danes abolished serfdom in their territories, among other things. This seed phase coincides with the flooding forth of the direct line of Shamballa energy at the end of the eighteenth century, bringing in its wake the various revolutions of the nineteenth century, along with the impact of the fifth ray, which was a primary factor behind the growth of science and technology. Moreover, it should be pointed out, that the keynotes for humanity in the next planetary cycle—liberty, equality, fraternity—were given form by the democratic revolutions of the late eighteenth century.

Rudhyar's calculation that the Piscean age will end in 2062 means that the seed period would have commenced in 1846. This date seems to have less importance, although it does mark a time of significant transition when the evils of materialism were being exposed and the industrial system was taking hold in many parts of Western Europe. The planet Neptune was discovered in 1846 and American spiritualism also emerged around this time. It was also a period of social unrest, when (two years later) revolution took place in cities all over the continent. The revolutions of 1848 were a major turning point in European history as revolts broke out in Paris, Vienna, Prague, and elsewhere among the German and Italian states of central Europe and among the Slav nationalities in the east. These revolutions, led by middle-class intellectuals, were fought to promote both constitutional freedoms and national ideas. In spite of the victory of counter-revolutionary forces, these brush-fire revolts opened a Pandora's box of national agitation which would dominate European political affairs until the First World War.

The assumption that the seed phase for the coming age is in the latter part of the nineteenth century or in the twentieth century is consistent with the many instances of new beginnings we have seen during this time period. Most important, this period marks the advent of new lifestyles, economic arrangements, and a new political order which replaced those institutional forms that were destroyed in the First World War. In 1920, the League of Nations came into being as did the International Court of Justice at the Hague. The first public radio station opened that same year and there was also a major earthquake in China that claimed 200,000 victims.

In truth, exact dates are less significant than the reality of the transition process. The important point is that there is much overlapping insofar as the forms of the old age cast a long shadow over the new age which, in turn, gives way to that of a future new age. In addition to the germinal and seed transitions, of which Rudhyar speaks, there are longer shadows. Two of the streams, which have had a modifying effect on Western Civilization, namely the patriarchal tradition of Rome and the intellectual tradition of Greek classicism, were woven into the fabric of European culture for much of its existence during the Piscean age.

We can also divide a great age into three parts corresponding to the decanates of an astrological cycle. Each decanate lasts roughly 700 years. With respect to Pisces, the first decanate extended from 100 BCE to 600 CE, when Europe was controlled by the Germanic tribes after the fall of Rome; the second decanate ended around 1300, when the power of the papacy reached its zenith; and the final decanate, which is rapidly coming to a close, will coincide with the end of the Piscean cycle. The Tibetan gives two different sequential planetary rulerships for Pisces, one exoteric and the other esoteric. The exoteric rulerships, given by the astrologer, Sepharial, are Saturn-Jupiter-Mars, which present humanity with the opportunity to work off karma through war and other social conflicts. The esoteric rulerships offered by Alan Leo are Jupiter-Moon-Mars. These planetary modifications have a more obscure impact and relate to discipleship training and the path of initiation.[42]

The Piscean age can further be analyzed by dividing it into twelve sub-periods of about 180 years. The first sub-period (100-99 BCE to 82 CE) coincided with the life and times of Christ and the Roman Emperor, Julius Caesar. While the Roman Empire was nearing its height, the otherworldly influence of the Age of Pisces was beginning to be felt. The second sub-period (82 to 262 CE) saw the rise of Gnosticism and early church organization.

It was at this time that Roman power reached its zenith. From 262 to 442 CE, ideological disputes broke out within the body of Christianity and the Roman Empire fell under attack from corruption within and invasion from without. The emperor Diocletian in 285 CE divided the Empire into eastern and western spheres. During the fourth period (442 to 622 CE), the Germanic races and tribes from the East poured into the Empire and began to set up new kingdoms. The fifth period (622 to 802 CE) saw the rise of a new religion, Islam, and a continued time of turmoil with the invasions of the Normans and Magyars. As the Piscean age entered into its sixth phase (802 to 982 CE), we find the rise of the Holy Roman Empire under Charlemagne, which essentially brought to an end the Roman Empire in the West.

This is also the time of the Viking invasions and the beginning of urban development in northern Europe. The period (982 to 1162) witnessed the political and social stabilization of Europe and the start of the Crusades, which revived commercial interchange between East and West. The Crusades continued during the next period (1162 to 1342 CE). It was also a time of cultural flowering with the rise of the great Gothic cathedrals and an outpouring of literature from Roger Bacon, Thomas Aquinas, Dante, and others.

From this high point of medieval culture, we enter the ninth phase when medieval institutions came under attack from incessant warfare and the revival of classical ideas. This era (ninth house) witnessed the exploration of new territories, the fall of Constantinople to the Turks, and widescale heresies leading to a significant shift in social perceptions. It was also the point at which the third ray came into manifestation. The tenth house (1522 to 1702 CE) saw a renaissance in occult ideas, as well as the arts, which gave way to the classical era, with the rise of absolutism (which coincided with the manifestation of the second ray) and the end of religious warfare. It was also the period designated as the Scientific Revolution. The eleventh house (1702 to 1882) could be characterized as a time of revolution: political revolutions in France, America, and elsewhere; the Industrial Revolution; the demographic revolution; and the agricultural revolution. On the inner planes, the fifth ray joined the seventh ray in manifestation and the full impact of Shamballa began to impact humanity. These ray forces laid the basis for the coming new age. If the eleventh house was the era of revolution, the twelfth house (1882 to 2062) could be seen as the era of breakdown and renewal. By the end of this period, humanity will have entered into the Aquarian age, and the next twelve-house cycle will be well under way.[43]

John P. Sedgwick, Jr. in his book, *Harmonics of History*, maintains that each century comes under the sway of a particular astrological sign which strikes a particular keynote for that hundred-year period. It is first interesting to note that the progression of the signs corresponds to the counter-clockwise direction of the common wheel, indicating a pattern of mundane events. Secondly, it is interesting that the completion of a cycle of the lesser zodiac (2100 years) roughly corresponds to two cyclical turn-of-the-century astrological wheels. Sedgwick gives only the second turn of the wheel, as seen below.

Table 18. Astrological Influences for Each Century[44]

Century	Dates	Sign	Effects
11th	995-1094 CE	Capricorn	Impact of Saturn, thoroughness and power
12th	1094-1193 CE	Sagittarius	Travel (Crusades), revival of learning
13th	1193-1292 CE	Scorpio	Cruelty, death (Inquisition), heresy
14th	1292-1391 CE	Libra	Impact of Venus, age of chivalry (poets: Dante, Petrarch, Boccaccio)
15th	1391-1490 CE	Virgo	Development of craftsmanship (guilds), the cult of the virgin

16th	1490-1589 CE	Leo	Pomp, ceremony, the emergence of state bureaucracies, origins of royal absolutism, the hero in art
17th	1589-1688 CE	Cancer	Concealed roles, the rise of great ministers of state (Richelieu, Colbert, Mazarin, Olivares), age of mirrors and reflections, new ideas impacting mass-consciousness
18th	1688-1787 CE	Gemini	Outpourings of words, debate and the interchange of ideas, satire, wit, repartee
19th	1787-1886	Taurus	Romanticism and realism, love of possessions, materiality, practicality, business
20th	1886-1985	Aries	Impact of Mars, tendency to impulsiveness and abruptness, everything in a hurry, militarism, war, violence, firepower
21st	1985-2084	Pisces	The last fling of the Piscean age. Outpouring of sixth-ray energy: emotionalism, otherworldliness
22nd	2085-2183	Aquarius	Advent of the Age of Aquarius

Thus far from being clear or distinct, a great age cycle is a conglomerate of criss-crossing energy patterns, waves, and cycles supported by certain decipherable themes or energies. This speaks to the truism that past, present, and future occur simultaneously at any given point in time.

Interplanetary Cycles and Conjunctions

Planetary systems cover broad cycles of time but they also form certain alignments that can precipitate particular events. When the cycles of planets intersect and hold the same position in the firmament, albeit briefly, they are said to make a transit or form a conjunction. Because the planets are directly aligned with one another, these transits/ conjunctions greatly increase the potency of energy directed to Earth. Insofar as planets modify energy in different ways, a Pluto-Saturn conjunction will have a different impact than a Uranus-Saturn conjunction or a Jupiter-Neptune conjunction. Rudhyar defines a transit as "the focused manifestation of the unending pressure applied by Nature upon the natal, archetypal structure of our selfhood."[45] Put more directly, transits indicate trends. A conjunction differs from a transit insofar as the conjunction occurs when two or more planets fall within a narrowly defined range of the zodiac. Due to the potency of the directed energy, transits and conjunctions cause disruptions in the flow of energy on the inner planes, which then work themselves out on the physical plane. Therefore, crises, whether personal or national, are often allied to a transit or conjunction of one sort or another.

Of historical interest are the transits of the slow-moving, or outer planets, which take many years to complete their revolutions around the sun. It might generally be said that these outer planets have a greater impact on mass-consciousness and behavior. Of all the slower moving planets, the most distant is Pluto. It is also the most recently known, having been discovered in 1930. Pluto is the esoteric ruler of Pisces and modifies first-ray energy. It is generally considered by astrologers to be the planet of death, destruction, regeneration, and healing, which brings to the surface all the dark elements of a civilization.

The most infrequent of the planetary transits/conjunctions is the Pluto-Neptune cycle, which repeats every 493 years and corresponds roughly to a five-hundred-year cycle. Neptune, the esoteric ruler of Cancer, has a profound effect on mass-consciousness. It is also the ruler of the Piscean age.[46] Thus the combined effect of the transit of these two planets would have a powerful impact on the astral plane of humanity in dredging up the baser aspects of emotionalism. Pluto-

Neptune transits occurred most recently in 1891 through 1892. Prior to this, there were such transits in the years 1398, 905, and 412.

At each of these times there was a major upheaval. In 412 CE, the Visigoths moved into Gaul and shortly thereafter onto the Iberian Peninsula. There were also mob riots in Alexandria and political eruptions in the Middle East. Over the course of the fifth century, various invaders from the Huns to the Vandals rampaged across Europe, culminating with the sack of Rome by the Vandals in 455 CE.

At the next Pluto-Neptune conjunction in 905, the Holy Roman Empire came under attack from the invading Lombards, China's Tang dynasty fell to the Mongol invaders, the Russians attacked Constantinople, and famine swept across Europe. This century was marked by struggles between Muslims and Christians, Greeks and Russians, also Lombards, Bulgarians, Arabs, and Byzantines.

In 1398, when Pluto and Neptune were conjunct again, the Tatar hordes from Russia swarmed into India and slaughtered nearly 100,000 Hindu prisoners. Shortly before, the black plague had spread throughout Europe and there was widespread rebellion and unrest. No other period in the Middle Ages had experienced so much social unrest as the hundred years between 1350 and 1450.

When a Pluto-Neptune conjunction last occurred in 1891-92, great strides were being made in the field of science. Around this time wireless telegraphy was invented (1891), the first combustion engine was patented (1892), cinematography was invented (1894), and Wilhelm Röntgen discovered X-rays (1895). It was also a time of great upheaval. There was a major earthquake in Japan (1891), which killed as many as 10,000 people, and there was labor violence in the United States involving iron and steel workers. Shortly after the turn of the century, Europe was beset with political struggles, social conflict, psychological ennui, and a revolution of dissonance in the arts. The churning up of emotions on the astral plane helped to set the stage for the great war in 1914.

Neptune and Uranus conjunctions occur every 171 years. While Neptune has the tendency to create illusion, Uranus modifies energy in a very unpredictable manner. Uranus also represents freedom and liberation. It was during the most recent Neptune-Uranus conjunction in 1992-93 that the Soviet Union ceased to exist, that Croatia and Slovenia declared independence from Yugoslavia, and that the Persian

Gulf War began. Each of these events represented liberation but also had an element of unpredictability.

When Neptune and Uranus appeared in 1821, there were numerous wars of independence which took place in Greece, Switzerland, Mexico, and Peru. Other states which declared independence from Spain in that year include Costa Rica, El Salvador, Guatemala, and Honduras. Britain abolished the death penalty for over 100 offenses and the antislavery society was established by William Wilberforce in London in 1822. The following year, the Royal Society for the Prevention of Cruelty to Animals was formed. At about the same time, Vesey's Rebellion took place in South Carolina. Even though it failed, the rebellion remains one of the most important slave uprisings in American history.

The year 1650, the time of the previous Neptune-Uranus conjunction, was a time of major transition. England had executed its king in 1649 and was embarking upon a bold and unprecedented experiment in republican government. The Peace of Westphalia brought to an end the Thirty Years War and, for all practical purposes, over a hundred years of religious warfare. In the century to follow, conflicts between European nations would focus more on commercial and territorial matters.

One hundred and seventy one years earlier—1479—there was also a flurry of peace treaties, beginning with the Treaty of Constantinople, which ended a fifteen-year war between Venice and the Ottoman Empire; Ferdinand and Isabella of Spain made peace with Portugal; and a relative peace was brought about by the grand duke of Muscovy, Ivan III, who was able to free Moscow and the surrounding countryside from Tatar domination. Ironically, at about the same time, Isabel of Castile launched the Inquisition against the Jews in Spain, which was later broadened to embrace all heretics, including Muslims. Within a few years, Pope Innocent III issued a papal bull against witchcraft and sorcery that led to open warfare against witches and magicians, especially in Germany. This period was generally a time of millennial expectation when many people felt that history would end and that certain Biblical prophesies would be fulfilled.

The third of the long cycles, involving Uranus and Pluto, usually leads to major upheavals in consciousness. These conjunctions, unlike the other Pluto cycles, appear to be uneven and unpredictable, which is the nature of Uranus.[47]

The 1457 Uranus-Pluto conjunction again occurred during a culturally significant period. In that same year, one of the great painters of the early Florentine renaissance, Donatello, moved to that city at the age of 71 after working for many years in Rome. Several significant works of art appeared that year, such as *Madonna with Saint Francis and Jerome* by Petrus Christus, *The Rout of San Romano* by Paolo Uccello, and *The Duke of Urbino* by Piero della Francesca. One could speculate that the passing of this auspicious transit gave a boost to new creative approaches to the visual arts, which came to fruition a century later.

When the Uranus-Pluto conjunction visited in 1598, France had entered into another civil war. England was also at the height of the Elizabethan renaissance, in which some of the most profound literature in the English language was written. It was at this time that Edmund Spenser wrote *The Faerie Queen* and Sir Philip Sidney was writing his sonnets. Shakespeare's plays began to appear and would continue to be produced into the next century.

The Scottish philosopher, David Hume, was born in 1711, during the next Uranus-Pluto conjunction. This period coincided with the first generation of Enlightenment writers who believed that the universe operated according to natural laws and that all human affairs could be reduced to explanations based on reason. Freemasonry, with the establishment of the Grand Lodge in London in 1717, was also influenced by this transit.

Although unlike the great cultural movements that coincided with the earlier Uranus-Pluto conjunctions, there were a number of events in 1850-51 that signified a change in consciousness. The Great Exhibition opened in London in 1851, which reflected the achievements of the first phase of the Industrial Age. Europe had been shaken by the revolutions of 1848, which hastened the process of liberal constitutionalism and nationalism.

Whereas the impacting events brought on by planetary transits may not always be clear, this could hardly be said about the Uranus-Pluto conjunction in the late 1960s. The so-called youth revolt which rocked college campuses around the world, the civil rights movement, the anti-war movement, the Cultural Revolution in China, the rise of the new left in Europe and America, the interest in spiritual practices and eastern mysticism, and the vast amount of sexual and drug experimentation all were connected in some way to this transit. In Paris a student revolt led to a national strike. Also, the massing of seven planets in Virgo, plus a solar eclipse on September 22, may have underscored some of the tumultuous events of the year 1968.

Saturn Conjunctions

Saturn conjunctions with the outer planets, which occur with Uranus every forty-five years, with Neptune every thirty-six years, and with Pluto every thirty-three years, are too numerous to detail over a broad landscape of history. However, the influence of Saturn is too important to ignore completely. Saturn represents stability, order, and crystallization. It is often said to be the taskmaster of the zodiac and the disciplinarian for those who are treading the path of discipleship. Saturn also signifies the working out of the law of karma. A Saturn-Pluto conjunction, which occurs every thirty-three years, generates cathartic change and the upheaval of internal structures. In a negative sense it may lead to xenophobia or periods of political reaction. Saturn-Neptune conjunctions relate to the ossification of worn-out structures and the crystallization of forms, especially religious forms. This is also true of ideologies. A Saturn-Uranus conjunction, on the other hand, brings with it innovation that challenges convention and creative ideas into concrete manifestation.

Table 19. Saturn Conjunctions From 1400 CE

Saturn-Pluto	Saturn-Neptune	Saturn-Uranus
1402	1413	1419
1447	1449	1452
1492	1485	1485
	1521	1518
1537		
	1557	1551
1582	1593	1584
1627	1629	
		1617
1650		

Saturn-Pluto	Saturn-Neptune	Saturn-Uranus
1683		
	1665	1672
	1701	
1716		1717
1749	1737	
1782	1773	
		1762
1815	1809	1807
1848	1845	1852
1881	1881	1897
1914-15	1917	
1947		1942
	1952	
1982	1989	1988
2015	2025	

What is interesting about these dates is their synchronicity. In the year 1485, there was both a Saturn-Neptune and a Saturn-Uranus conjunction. That same year Henry Tudor defeated the English king, Richard III, and established the Tudor dynasty. This marked a shattering of medieval feudalism in England. Saturn-Pluto and Saturn-Uranus conjunctions occurred in 1716 and 1717 respectively, which coincided with the establishment of the Grand Lodge of Freemasons in London. The Dutch in that year began a long period of financial decline and the finances of the French government, after years of warfare and extravagance, were in a state of crisis.

The year 1881, when there was both a Saturn-Pluto and a Saturn-Uranus transit, was a time of political assassination, with the shooting deaths of both the Russian Czar, Alexander II, and the American president, James A. Garfield. Romania and Serbia also won their independence from Turkey at this time. The year 1914 saw the start of World War I; this was also the occasion for another Saturn-Pluto conjunction. It is worth remembering that this kind of transit brings about a cathartic upheaval, which was certainly the case with the start of the great war. Three years later, a Saturn-Neptune conjunction, which dissolves crystallized structures, heralded the start of the Russian Revolution.

The Saturn-Uranus conjunction of 1942, the turning point of the Second World War; the Saturn-Pluto conjunction of 1947, the year of Indian Independence, the creation of the Central Intelligence Agency, and the start of the Cold War; and the Saturn-Neptune conjunction of 1952, when Britain's king George VI died, Egypt's king Farouk was deposed, Jordan's king Talal was deposed, and General Dwight Eisenhower won the American presidential election, all mark a period of great transition. The three Saturn transits in the 1980s signified the imposition of economic restraints and the trend towards downsizing in many western countries. Looking ahead, the year 2025, when the fourth ray will be coming into manifestation, will also be joined by a Saturn-Neptune conjunction.

The Outer Planets Through the Zodiac

The passage of the outer planets through the zodiac colors each of the twelve houses with their particular characteristics. Given that Uranus, Neptune, and Pluto were discovered in the eighteenth, nineteenth, and twentieth centuries, respectively, their influences are more apparent over the past few centuries than they would have been earlier. However, they can be easily extrapolated into the distant past. It is possible that in the future other planets will be discovered and their qualities determined, which will add another layer to our existing knowledge of planetary influences on history.

We must constantly bear in mind that each planet is not just a physical body in itself but includes levels of energy, which exist in their exoteric, esoteric, and hierarchical manifestations. As a consequence, we do not see the whole picture. Certain planets are veiled planets; for example, it is noted that the moon veils the planet Vulcan (which seems to exist in etheric form and not as a visible physical entity) and that the sun veils Neptune and Uranus. This does not mean that these planets are hidden from sight, rather, in metaphoric and symbolic terms, that the higher consciousness emanating from these planets has temporarily been veiled by the veiling entity, but are increasingly reachable as evolution proceeds. In due time, after the consciousness of humanity has evolved to an appropriate degree, the veils, it is said, will be lifted and these potent energies, radiating a deeper consciousness, will be felt.[48] Of course, this may take millions of years and there is little that can be said with any accuracy of future rounds, globes, or even solar systems.

What all this suggests is that the range of planetary energy is much more potent and significant than we can realize, and we are far from having a full understanding of the extent to which humanity is affected by these energies. We can understand some of the pieces, however. A look at the flow of energy passing from each of the outer planets, through the geocentric model of the universe (also known as the zodiac), to the lower three planes of human existence will reveal a broad causal context for the unfoldment of human affairs in recent times.

Table 20. Pluto, Neptune, Uranus in the Zodical Signs[49]

	Pluto	Neptune	Uranus
Aquarius	1778-1798	1834-1848	1912-1919
Pisces	1798-1823	1848-1862	1919-1927
Aries	1823-1852	1861-1875	1927-1935
Taurus	1852-1884	1874-1888	1935-1942
Gemini	1884-1913	1888-1902	1942-1949
Cancer	1913-1938	1902-1915	1949-1956
Leo	1938-1957	1915-1929	1956-1962
Virgo	1957-1971	1929-1942	1962-1968
Libra	1971-1984	1942-1957	1968-1974
Scorpio	1984-1995	1957-1970	1974-1980
Sagittarius	1995-2010	1970-1984	1980-1986
Capricorn	2010-2025	1984-1998	1986-1992
Aquarius	2025-2040	1998-2012	1992-1998

Clearly, there are many correspondences among these cycles. Pluto, as we may recall, is the sign of death and regeneration and is often the vehicle for the first ray, given its destructive power to blow apart old forms and bring to the surface that which is hidden. Thus the passage of Pluto causes great disruption—emotionally, psychically, and physically. When Pluto moved through Aquarius between 1778 through 1797-98, it stimulated the spread of revolution in Europe and America.

Being the sign of humanitarian ideals and service to the race, ruled by the seventh ray, Aquarius seeks to put great ideals into concrete form. With respect to the advent of the French Revolution, this gave rise to powerful slogans of liberty, equality, and fraternity, which stimulated the popular imagination. Plutonian influence brought to an end the old order of Europe and created a vehicle for new institutions and republican forms of government.

Likewise, when Neptune entered Aquarius during 1834 through 1848, there was revolutionary fervor, but of a different nature. Neptune, ruled by the sixth ray in its lower manifestation and by ray two in its higher state, has a far more mystical and emotional quality than does the more direct and destructive Pluto energy. The revolutionaries of 1848, unlike those of 1789, were driven less by clear ideas and more by vague nationalistic feelings. As historian Lewis Namier writes of the 1848 revolutions: "The mob had come out in revolt, moved by passions and distress rather than by ideas: they had no articulate aims, and no one will ever be able to supply a rational explanation of what it was they fought for, or what made them fight."[50]

Uranus entered Aquarius in 1912, the date of the first Balkan War. This period leading up to the First World War was also a time of widespread idealism, but still yet of a different nature. It is a well known fact that men went to war with great enthusiasm and with the expectation that it would be a decisive conflict of short duration. Uranus, the planet of unpredictability, determined that the reality of the war would stand in sharp contrast to the high expectations that preceded it. This seven-year Uranian cycle covered the duration of World War I and also brought in its wake another unexpected event, the Russian Revolution.

A year after Uranus moved into Aquarius, Pluto entered the sign of Cancer. Here we find that the mass-consciousness of much of the world's population was turned inside out as the result of the war. The elation that swept across Europe at the start of the war plunged into the depths of despair as the death toll rose to unprecedented heights and hardship became a reality. Pluto, through the vehicle of the war, also drastically affected another aspect of life ruled by Cancer: families and domestic circumstances. The Russian Revolution, the elimination of centuries-old monarchies and dynasties, the post-war influenza epidemic, and the rise of Hitler to power—all, to some extent, related to the passage of Pluto through Cancer.

Neptune's journey through Leo, which began in 1915, added another element to this period of history. Leo, the sign of ego development and self-expression, could be seen in the sense of pride and honor, which not only led the nations of Europe into war, but perpetuated the struggle to the point of exhaustion. After the war, the Neptunian aspect contributed to the sense of escapism, which took many forms. The rise of gangsterism in the United States and the emergence of dictatorships in Russia and Italy, along with fascist movements in many other countries, relate directly to the Neptunian and Leo energies. Insofar as Neptune possesses a tendency towards internationalism and world brotherhood, the League of Nations and the various groups that emerged in the inter-war period devoted to bettering the cause of humanity (which the Tibetan identified as the New Group of World Servers) can be traced, in part, to that planetary influence.

When Pluto passes through Leo, some great leader or group of leaders appears at the center of the historical stage. Such was the case in the Roman Empire when Julius Caesar came to power and was later assassinated during a Pluto-Leo cycle. When this cycle next appeared, the Huns, under their infamous leader Attila, were advancing across Europe. Several Pluto-Leo cycles later, at the end of the seventeenth century (1690-1705), the quintessential Leo monarch, Louis XIV, the Sun King, was in his glory years and Peter I (the Great) was beginning to modernize Russia. In its most recent visitation (1938-1957), the passage of Pluto through Leo coincided with the rise of Hitler to power in Germany and the formation of an allied military opposition led by Churchill, Roosevelt, and Stalin. Strong leaders behind Indian independence (Gandhi and Nehru) and the formation of Israel (Ben Gurion) were also prominent at this time.

Uranus entered Leo at the point that Pluto was passing out of this sign. The period of the late 1950s witnessed the growing ego expression of young people and the creation of a definable youth culture. It was also a time when many former African and Asian colonies achieved independence, liberation being a particular aspect of Uranus. Wars of liberation in Algeria and Cuba took place during this period, along with the formation of the European Common Market.

Between the years 1957 and 1995, Neptune, then Uranus, and finally

Pluto have passed through the sign of Scorpio. Ruled as it is by a sixth-ray planet (Mars) and the fourth ray of harmony through conflict, it is not surprising that this period has been characterized by fanaticism and disharmony of all sorts. Astronomical crime rates, urban decay, drug abuse, and widespread political corruption all over the world have been some of the more noteworthy trends of this era. In its lowest form, Scorpio is the sign of selfish desire, degeneration, the urge for death, enslavement, and violence, but Scorpio also impels regeneration and victory over one's materialistic tendencies. It is by no means accidental that the global AIDS epidemic has arisen while Pluto, in particular, has passed through Scorpio. The higher, or regenerative, characteristics of Scorpio include healing, enlightening, sustainability, and revitalization. Though often less obvious, these elements have been present and are slowly working their way into public consciousness.[51]

With the commencement of the twenty-first century, all three outer planets (Pluto a bit later) will be in (or will soon be in) the sign of Aquarius. This is a significant development, given the advent of the Aquarian age and the superseding of the sixth ray by the seventh ray. As in their previous phases, when the passage of these signs through Aquarius brought in their wake revolution and wars of independence, so the new turn of the cycle promises to be a time of great social, political, and economic upheaval, this time on a far more global scale. On the other hand, there might well be an unprecedented outpouring of humanitarian concern and group work, as well as service activities stretching from the local community to the international community. Whereas the Aquarian age, as such, is predicted by some astrologers to begin in the second half of the twenty-first century, it is important to look at this phenomenon not as a date but a phase of transition. When the three outer planets move into Pisces in the immediate future, or soon thereafter, the Piscean age will all but have dissolved into historical memory.[52]

Epilogue

Oliver L. Reiser, professor of philosophy at the University of Pittsburgh, wrote the preface for *Education in the New Age*, which he entitled "Educational Trends in a World Crisis." One of the salient points that he made in this short introduction is that education must meet the needs of the human spirit if we are not to fall prey to "the standardizing forces of Western machine civilization," which are so prevalent at this time. Our problem, he says, is to attain an overall synthesis by integrating trans-temporal and trans-spatial truths about humanity and the universe. This new synthesis, he believes, will go far towards restoring the cultural and spiritual unity of mankind through the integration of eastern and western thought, the unification of knowledge in accordance with eternal verities, and a return to the basic questions underscoring human existence, such as "What is man?" "What kind of universe does man inhabit?" "How did the human species emerge from the matrix of nature to self-consciousness?" and "What is the best kind of society to foster man's progressive self-evolution?"[1]

These questions, which Reiser asks, relate to the necessity to revision history in a new light. According to the Tibetan, written history reflects most of the vices of humanity and few of the virtues. The historical record, he observes, stresses wars and acts of aggression, nationalistic self-interest, racial hatreds, and the spirit of separateness. British history usually starts with William the Conqueror; American history begins with the landing of the Pilgrims and the theft of land from the Native Americans; most heroes in history are warriors; and the history of discovery is largely a tale of land seizure, greed, ambition, cruelty, and pride.[2]

The historical trends over the past half century have seen a reversal of these narrow historiographical perspectives, as witnessed by a revisionist approach to the crimes of the past, a growing interest in the underdogs of history, and a marked sensitivity to human values and the natural environment. These trends were anticipated by the Tibetan who wrote that the history of civilizations and cultures will be revised and brought to life "and the dry-as-dust information, dates, and names will fall into discard."[3] His vision of a unified humanity that is highly assimilated; united in liberty by those concepts of freedom as expressed in the American Bill of Rights, the Atlantic Charter, and Franklin D. Roosevelt's Four Freedoms; and enjoying a common culture,[4] would, however, not be shared by some historians today.

Whether the lofty goals that the Tibetan sees as humanity's destiny are true or desirable is beside the point. Time and human free will ultimately determine the course of human destiny. What matters is the perspective that one takes in reading history. The approach I have adopted in writing this book has been to try and envision history as seen by the spiritual Hierarchy. This effort by necessity has been something of a lost cause due to my, relatively speaking, limited and distorted consciousness. As viewed from the exalted and rarefied spheres of the inner planes, this history, as with all other written histories, is just an illusion fraught with glamour, as all things are which are derived from physical-plane consciousness.

Yet, to attempt the writing of an esoteric history is not a fruitless task in that it forces us to make certain fundamental shifts in consciousness. For one thing, as we have seen, history is largely concerned with periodicity. This is structured, on one hand, by the endless system of cycles, which encompasses rounds, root races, and subraces. This elaborate structure, as we have observed, is a complex map for charting the consciousness of humanity. By the same token, periodicity is determined by the impact and interplay of ray lives, as comprehended through the ebb and flow of souls passing in and out of manifestation, guided by the ray lords; and by means of planetary activity, whereby reflected ray energy is radiated and magnetized into nodes of probabilities around which the collective crises and events of humanity are clustered.

Another fundamental shift in consciousness, reflected in this book, is the view that human history is marked by the interplay of the three planetary centers: Shamballa, Hierarchy, and Humanity. The potent energies of Shamballa correspond to monadic consciousness and represent the driving force of the divine will. In human affairs, it is the carrier of first-ray energy, which serves to destroy old forms and brings diverse cultural trends and streams into synthesis. Essentially,

Shamballa is the evolutionary current of history.

Hierarchy, the second planetary center, comprising the ashrams and departments of the masters, seeks to guide humanity on its evolutionary journey in accordance with the divine plan. Within the lesser sphere of cosmic cycles, each round and root race embodies lessons to be learned and goals to be achieved. As we have seen, the most recent initiatives by the Hierarchy, broadly speaking, have been to raise human consciousness from the level of the emotions to the mental plane and to develop group-consciousness.

The state of human consciousness, and the ways it is modified and changed by occurrences and developments on the physical plane, is largely the story of the planetary center of humanity, as viewed esoterically. Seen from the inner planes, the pain, suffering, and tragedies of human history, which have been recorded in great detail, are of little consequence, especially if they contribute in some small measure to a widening and deepening of consciousness. This is why the Tibetan strongly encouraged humanity to give particular notice to those great moments in history "when man's divinity flamed forth and indicated new ways of thinking."[5]

Finally, the timeliness of this book corresponds to the era in which we now find ourselves. Everyone realizes that we are living in a period of great transition. Evidence that we are at the end of an age is not hard to find. Historian J.H. Plumb writes:

"An epoch that started 10,000 years ago is ending. We are involved in a revolution of society that is complete and as profound as the one that changed man from hunter and food gatherer to settled farmer and craftsman. Ten thousand years ago the Neolithic revolution closed an age that lasted for hundreds of thousands of years. The foundations of society created by that revolution have endured, no matter how sophisticated and elaborate the superstructure of civilization has become; only within the last century have these foundations begun to crumble, as the new scientific and industrial revolutions spread with ever increasing speed throughout the world."[6]

Plumb might also have mentioned a revolution in consciousness. One of the more telltale characteristics of this present period is our almost total alienation from the past which, of course, is one of the primary reasons why our vision of the future is so uncertain and problematic. Times of transition are also times of great opportunity.

Historians of the future may well look back to the period of the twentieth and early twenty-first centuries as a time when humanity made either a great leap forward in consciousness, or missed such an advantageous moment and thereby condemned itself to much needless pain and suffering. If esoteric history has any practical value, it would be to help us make the most of this opportunity.

References and Notes

Introduction

[1] Alice A. Bailey, *Esoteric Healing*, p. 683

[2] Fritjof Capra, *The Tao of Physics*, p. 81

[3] Alice A. Bailey, *Esoteric Healing*, pp. 583-584; and *The Destiny of the Nations*, p. 16

[4] Alice A. Bailey, *Esoteric Healing*, p. 180

[5] Alice A. Bailey, *The Externalisation of the Hierarchy*, p. 337

[6] Alice A. Bailey, *Esoteric Healing*, p. 30

[7] Renee Weber, ed. *Dialogues with Scientists and Sages*, p. 147

[8] Alice A. Bailey, *The Consciousness of the Atom*, p. 57

[9] Alice A. Bailey, *A Treatise on Cosmic Fire*, p. 881

[10] Alice A. Bailey, *The Consciousness of the Atom*, p. 20

[11] Karl R. Popper, *The Poverty of Historicism*, p. 111

[12] Dane Rudhyar, *Occult Preparations for a New Age*, p. 83

[13] Karl R. Popper, *The Poverty of Historicism*, p. 3

[14] Teilhard de Chardin, *The Phenomenon of Man*, p. 243

[15] Alice A. Bailey, *The Soul and Its Mechanism*, pp. 99-103

[16] Alice A. Bailey, *Discipleship in the New Age, Vol. II*, pp. 284

[17] Alice A. Bailey, *The Light of the Soul*, p. 106

[18] Alice A. Bailey, *A Treatise on Cosmic Fire*, pp. 798-799, 76

Chapter 1

[1] Herbert Butterfield, *The Origins of Modern Science*, p. 13

[2] Bill Moyers, *Healing and the Mind*, p. 308

[3] *Ibid.*, p. 233

[4] Herbert Butterfield, *The Origins of Modern Science*, p. 19

[5] Keith Thomas, *Religion and the Decline of Magic*, pp. 660-661

[6] Fritjof Capra, *The Turning Point: Science, Society, and the Rising Culture*, p. 47

[7] Marilyn Ferguson, *The Aquarian Conspiracy*, p. 23

[8] Morris Berman, *The Reenchantment of the World*, p. 10

[9] Houston Smith, *Religions of the World*, Judaism-tape 6

[10] *Ibid.*

[11] *Ibid.*

[12] *Ibid.*

[13] Alice A. Bailey, *The Rays and the Initiations*, pp. 105-106

[14] John McManners, *The Oxford Illustrated History of Christianity*, pp. 140-141

[15] Houston Smith, *The Religions of Man*, p. 362

[16] Carl L. Becker, *The Heavenly City of the Eighteenth Century Philosophers*, p. 95

[17] Stephen J. Gendzier ed., *Denis Diderot's The Encyclopedia Selections*, p. 135

[18] Pieter Geyl, *Debates With Historians*, p. 9

[19] Fritjof Capra, *The Tao of Physics*, p. 70-71. See also Stanislav Grof, *Ancient Wisdom and Modern Science* (Albany, NY: SUNY Press, 1984; Werner Heisenberg, *Physics and Philosophy* (New York: Harper & Row, 1958); Michael Talbot, *Mysticism and the New Physics* (London: Routledge & Kegan Paul, 1981)

[20] John McManners, *The Oxford Illustrated History of Christianity*, pp. 149,151

[21] *Ibid.*, p. 294

[22] H.P. Blavatsky, *Studies in Occultism*, p. 12

[23] Frances Yates, *The Occult Philosophy*, p. 61

[24] Kenneth Clark, *Civilisation*, p. 33

[25] *Ibid.*

[26] Alice A. Bailey, *A Treatise on Cosmic Fire*, pp. 1078-1079

[27] Joscelyn Godwin, *Mystery Religions in the Ancient World*, p. 98

[28] See Manly P. Hall, *The Adepts in the Esoteric Classical Tradition, Vol. I*, (Los Angeles: Philosophical Research Society, 1981) for a more complete discussion of advanced disciples and initiates in the ancient Greek and Roman world.

[29] Michael Howard, *The Occult Conspiracy*, p. 33

[30] *Ibid.*, 33-41; Eliphas Levi, *The History of Magic*, p. 211

[31] Michael Baigent and Richard Leigh, *The Temple and the Lodge*, p. 149

[32] Christopher McIntosh, *Eliphas Levi and the French Occult Revival*, p. 19

[33] Taken from a talk presented by Keith Bailey at the University of the Seven Rays Conference held in San Diego on April 21, 1996

[34]Ronald C. Davison, *Astrology*, p. 13

[35]Manly P. Hall, *Old Testament Wisdom*, p. 31

[36]A discussion of the Secret Doctrine can be found in Magus Incognito, *The Secret Doctrine of the Rosicrucians* (New York: Barnes & Noble, 1993) and in Max Heindel, *The Rosicrucian Cosmo-Conception* (Oceanside, CA: The Rosicrucian Fellowship, 1973)

[37]Joscelyn Godwin, *The Theosophical Enlightenment*, p. xi

[38]Sylvia Cranston, *HPB*; Charles J. Ryan *H.P. Blavatsky and the Theosophical Movement*; A. P. Sinnett, *Incidents in the Life of Madame Blavatsky*

[39]Alice A. Bailey, *The Light of the Soul*, pp. 275-276

[40]Alice A. Bailey, *Esoteric Psychology, Vol. I*, p. 107

[41]*The Mahatma Letters to A.P. Sinnett*, p. 324

[42]*Ibid.*, pp. 191-197

[43]Helen S. Burmeister, *The Seven Rays Made Visible*, p. xiii

[44]Alice A. Bailey, *Initiation Human and Solar*, pp. 223-224

[45]Eric Hobsbawm, *The Age of Extremes*, p. 5

[46]Alice A. Bailey, *The Rays and the Initiations*, p. 255

[47]Corinne McLaughlin, *How to Evaluate Psychic Guidance and Channeling*, p. 9. See also Alice A. Bailey, *Telepathy and the Etheric Vehicle*

[48]*Ibid.*, p. 6

[49]*Ibid.*, p. 7

[50]Alice A. Bailey, *The Reappearance of the Christ*, p. 148

[51]Rudolf Steiner, *Methods of Spiritual Research*, pp. 14-15

[52]Alice A. Bailey, *Esoteric Psychology, Vol. I*, pp. 98-99

[53]E.H. Carr, *What is History?*, p. 9

[54]Alice A. Bailey, *Reappearance of the Christ*, p. 129

[55]Alice A. Bailey, *The Destiny of the Nations*, p. 3

[56]Alice A. Bailey, *Esoteric Psychology, Vol. I*, p. 3

[57]Alice A. Bailey, *Education in the New Age*, p. 85

[58]Alice A. Bailey, *Esoteric Psychology, Vol. II*, p. 255

[59]Alice A. Bailey, *The Externalisation of the Hierarchy*, p. 292

[60]Alice A. Bailey, *Glamour A World Problem*, p. 14

[61]Alice A. Bailey, *From Intellect to Intuition*, pp. 238-239

[62]Willian Irwin Thompson, *The Time Falling Bodies Take to Light*, p. 39

[63]Ken Wilber, *Up From Eden*, p. 7

[64]Bertrand Russell, *The Autobiography of Bertrand Russell, Vol. I*, p. 3

[65]Joseph Campbell, *The Inner Reaches of Outer Space*, p. 35

Chapter 2

[1]Robert Rosenblum, *Cubism and Twentieth-Century Art*, p. 9

[2]Keith Bailey, "Musical Composition and the Rays," *The Journal of Esoteric Psychology*, Vol. III, No. 3, 1987, p. 132

[3]Thomas Harrison, *1910: The Emancipation of Dissonance*, p. 4

[4]Carlos Castaneda, *Tales of Power*, pp. 120-124

[5]Alice A. Bailey, *The Consciousness of the Atom*, p. 59

[6]Alice A. Bailey, *Esoteric Psychology, Vol. I*, pp. 20-21

[7]Alice A. Bailey, *A Treatise on Cosmic Fire*, p. 51

[8]Oscar Wilde, *The Soul of Man Under Socialism*, p. 9

[9]Genesis 1:26.

[10]H.P. Blavatsky, *The Secret Doctrine: Cosmogenesis, Vol. I*, p. 16

[11]Alice A. Bailey, *A Treatise on Cosmic Fire*, p. 602

[12]Joseph Campbell, *The Masks of God: Primitive Mythology*, p. 189

[13]Nicholas Campion, *The Great Year*, pp. 199-200

[14]Joscelyn Godwin ed., *Cosmic Music*, pp. 53-74

[15]Arthur M. Young, *The Reflexive Universe*, pp. 84-88

[16]Shirley Nicholson, *Ancient Wisdom: Modern Insight*, p. 142

[17]Alice A. Bailey, *The Consciousness of the Atom*, p. 62

[18]Alice A. Bailey, *A Treatise on Cosmic Fire*, pp. 94-95, 321-322

[19]Jeremy Rifkin, *Entropy: A New World View*

[20]Arthur Young, *The Reflexive Universe*, pp. 36-42

[21]Dane Rudhyar, *Occult Preparations for a New Age*, p. 90

[22]See E.L. Gardner's pamphlet, *Chains and Rounds*, published by the London Theosophical Society; H. Saraydarian, *Cosmos in Man*, pp. 25-30; C.W. Leadbeater, *A Textbook of Theosophy*, pp. 121-133

[23]Alice A. Bailey, *A Treatise on Cosmic Fire*, pp. 86-87

[24]H. P. Blavatsky, *The Secret Doctrine: Cosmogenesis, Vol. I*, pp. 370-373

[25]*Ibid.*, p. 371

[26]Rudolf Steiner, *Cosmic Memory: Prehistory of Earth and Man*, pp. 172-173

[27]Geoffrey Hodson, *Basic Theosophy: The Living Wisdom*, p. 382

[28]Rudolf Steiner, *Cosmic Memory: Prehistory of Earth and Man*, pp. 158-172

[29]The following discussion is based on a talk by Daniel Krummenacher, entitled "Chains, Rounds, and Geological Evidence," delivered at the University of the Seven Rays Conference, San Diego, CA on April 6, 1997

[30]G. de Purucker, *The Esoteric Tradition, Vol. I*, p. 308; Blavatsky, *The Secret Doctrine, Vol. II*, p. 115

[31]G. de Purucker, *The Esoteric Tradition*, pp. 311-312

[32]*Ibid.*, p. 313

Chapter 3

[1]Race is differentiated on each of the seven planes of consciousness and has a correspondence to the various root races. Consequently, one may have different racial designations. For example, South African Prime Minister, Nelson Mandela, may have a Lemurian physical body but he most surely has an Aryan mental body.

[2]Alice A. Bailey, *Education in the New Age*, p. 90

[3]Geoffrey Hodson, *Basic Theosophy*, pp. 386-387

[4]Brian Swimme and Thomas Berry, *The Universe Story*, p. 123

[5]H. P. Blavatsky, *The Secret Doctrine: Anthropogenesis Vol. II*, pp. 164, 227

[6]Geoffrey Hodson, *Basic Theosophy*, p. 387

[7]Alice A. Bailey, *A Treatise on Cosmic Fire*, fn. p. 122

[8] G. dePurucker, *The Esoteric Tradition, Vol. I*, pp. 310-311

[9]H. P. Blavatsky, *The Secret Doctrine: Anthropogenesis, Vol. II*, p. 138

[10]Geoffrey Hodson, *Basic Theosophy*, p. 388

[11]G. de Purucker, *The Esoteric Tradition, Vol. I*, p. 312

[12]H.P. Blavatsky, *Isis Unveiled: Science, Vol. I*, p. 303

[13]Annie Besant, *Esoteric Christianity*, p. 184

[14]H.P. Blavatsky, *The Secret Doctrine: Anthropogenesis, Vol. II*, pp. 118-119

[15]*Ibid.*, p. 684

[16]*Ibid.*, p. 170

[17]Rudolf Steiner, *The Influence of Spiritual Beings Upon Man*, p. 74

[18]Brian Swimme and Thomas Berry, *The Universe Story*, pp. 273-274

[19]J.G. Bennett, *The Dramatic Universe: History, Vol. IV*, pp. 184-185

[20]C.D. Darlington, *The Evolution of Man and Society*, p. 22

[21]Alice A. Bailey, *A Treatise on Cosmic Fire*, pp. 689-690

[22]Alice A. Bailey, *Esoteric Astrology*, p. 46

[23]H.P. Blavatsky, *The Secret Doctrine: Anthropogenesis, Vol. II*, p. 62

[24]Guenther Wachsmuth, *The Evolution of Mankind*, p. 17

[25]Rudolf Steiner, *Cosmic Memory: Atlantis and Lemuria*, p. 89

[26]Alice A. Bailey, *Esoteric Healing*, pp. 226-229

[27]G. dePurucker, *The Esoteric Tradition, Vol. I*, p. 334

[28]*Ibid.*, pp. 277, 317, 331, 336, 337

[29]H.P. Blavatsky, *The Secret Doctrine: Anthropogenesis, Vol. II*, p. 341

[30]Guenther Wachsmuth, *The Evolution of Mankind*, pp. 18-19

[31]Geoffrey Hodson, *Basic Theosophy*, p. 389

[32]H.P. Blavatsky, *The Secret Doctrine: Anthropogenesis, Vol. II*, pp. 316-319

[33]Ignatius Donnelly, *Atlantis*, pp. 1-21

[34]*Ibid.*, p. 24

[35]Manly P. Hall, *Atlantis: An Interpretation*, pp. 25-43

[36]L. Sprague de Camp, *Lost Continents*, pp. 62-63

[37]Geoffrey Hodson, *Basic Theosophy*, p. 393

[38]H.P. Blavatsky, *The Secret Doctrine: Anthropogenesis, Vol. II*, pp. 371-372

[39]L. Sprague de Camp, *Lost Continents*, pp. 63-64

[40]*Ibid.*, pp. 64-65

[41]*Ibid.*, pp. 106-107

[42]H.P. Blavatsky, *The Secret Doctrine: Anthropogenesis, Vol. II*, pp. 2, 436, 334

[43]Geoffrey Hodson, *Basic Theosophy*, p. 421

[44]*Ibid.*, pp. 383-394

[45]Brian Swimme and Thomas Berry, *The Universe Story*, pp. 272-273

[46]H.P. Blavatsky, *The Secret Doctrine: Anthropogenesis, Vol. II*, pp. 434-435

[47]Pitirim A. Sorokin, *Social Philosophies of an Age of Crisis*, p. 59

[48]Alice A. Bailey, *Education in the New Age*, p. 39

[49]Alice A. Bailey, *The Reappearance of the Christ*, p. 129

[50]Alice A. Bailey, *Education in the New Age*, p. 39

[51]Geoffrey Hodson, *Basic Theosophy*, pp. 426-427

[52]Rudolf Steiner, *The Driving Force of Spiritual Powers in World History*, p. 79

[53]Geoffrey Hodson, *Basic Theosophy*, p. 398

[54]Rudolf Steiner, *The Driving Force of Spiritual Powers in World History*, p. 81

[55]Romila Thapar, *A History of India, Vol. I*, p. 337

[56]Guenther Wachsmuth, *The Evolution of Mankind*, p. 99

[57]Romila Thapar, *A History of India, Vol. I*, p. 28

[58]Alice A. Bailey, *Initiation Human and Solar*, pp. 41-42

[59]Romila Thapar, *A History of India, Vol. I*, p. 28

[60]*Ibid.*, p. 30

[61]Geoffrey Hodson, *Basic Theosophy*, pp. 422-423

[62]*Ibid.*, p. 395

[63]Alice A. Bailey, *The Reappearance of the Christ*, p. 104

[64]Manly P. Hall, *Twelve World Teachers*, p. 23

[65]Arnold Toynbee, *A Study of History*, p. 30

[66]Geoffrey Hodson, *Basic Theosophy*, p. 426

[67]H.P. Blavatsky, *The Secret Doctrine: Anthropogenesis, Vol. II*, p. 6

[68]Manly P. Hall, *Twelve World Teachers*, pp. 69-77

[69]H.P. Blavatsky, *The Secret Doctrine: Anthropogenesis, Vol. II*, p. 356

[70]Manly P. Hall, *Twelve World Teachers*, p. 80

[71]Arnold Toynbee, *A Study of History*, pp. 27-29

[72]Manly P. Hall, *Twelve World Teachers*, pp. 58-60

[73]*Ibid.*, pp. 60-61

[74]*Ibid.*, p. 62

[75]Geoffrey Hodson, *Basic Theosophy*, p. 396

[76]James Trager, *The People's Chronology*, p. 6

[77]Rudolf Steiner, *The Driving Force of Spiritual Powers in World History*, p. 84

[78]A mystery stream may represent the subjective nature of a people but these streams are also the product of incarnating souls who reincarnate from earlier subraces and root races along certain lines. This may seem to be in conflict with the outward evolution of civilizations, as recorded in history. A history of any group of people must take account of these objective and subjective trends.

[79]B.C.J. Lievegoed, *Mystery Streams in Europe and the New Mysteries*

[80]Geoffrey Hodson, *Basic Theosophy*, p. 396

[81]Geoffrey Barraclough, *History in a Changing World*, p. 33

[82]Christopher Dawson, *Understanding Europe*, p. 26

[83]Emmanuel Le Roy Ladurie, *Montaillou*, p. 23

[84]Isaiah Berlin, "The Question of Machiavelli," *New York Review of Books*, 4, November 1971, pp. 20-32

[85]William Irwin Thompson, *The Time Falling Bodies Take to Light*, p. 160

[86]Michael Kammen, *Spheres of Liberty*, pp. 24-25

[87]Alice A. Bailey, *The Externalisation of the Hierarchy*, pp. 167, 271

[88]Alice A. Bailey, *Esoteric Psychology, Vol. I*, pp. 172-174

[89]Alice A. Bailey, *A Treatise on White Magic*, pp. 326-327

[90] Alice A. Bailey, *Esoteric Psychology, Vol. I*, p. 176

[91] Fritjof Capra, *The Tao of Physics*, p. 53

[92] See T.S. Eliot, *Notes Towards the Definition of Culture*

[93] Alice A. Bailey, *A Treatise on White Magic*, p. 242

[94] *Five Years of Theosophy*, pp. 487-489

[95] *Ibid.*, pp. 489-491

[96] Guenther Wachsmuth, *The Evolution of Mankind*, p. 116; B.C.J. Lievegoed, *Mystery Streams in Europe and the New Mysteries*, pp. 15-36

[97] Giambattista Vico, *The New Science of Giambattista Vico*, p. 64

[98] Alice A. Bailey, *The Rays and the Initiations*, p. 646

[99] Giambattista Vico, *The New Science*, p. 106

[100] Johan Huizinga, *The Waning of the Middle Ages*, p. 193

[101] Giambattista Vico, *The New Science*, p. 106

[102] Jacob Burckhardt, *The Civilization of the Renaissance in Italy*, p. 128

[103] Alice A. Bailey, *The Externalisation of the Hierarchy*, p. 49

[104] Giambattista Vico, *The New Science*, p. 106

[105] Bernard Nesfield-Cookson, *William Blake: Prophet of Universal Brotherhood*, p. 233

[106] V.S. Naipaul, "Among the Republicans," *New York Review of* Books, Oct. 25, 1984, p. 17

[107] Eric Hobsbawm, *The Age of Extremes*, p. 1

[108] Alice A. Bailey, *Discipleship in the New Age, Vol. I*, p. 99

Chapter 4

[1] Chogyam Trungpa, *Shamballa: The Sacred Path of the Warrior*, p. 26

[2] Victoria LePage, "A Trafficway of Angels: The Myth of Shamballa," *The Quest*, June 1997, p. 21

[3] Chogyam Trungpa, *Shamballa: The Sacred Path of the Warrior*, pp. 26-27

[4] Ezekiel 38

[5] Manly P. Hall, *Old Testament Wisdom*, pp. 280-281

[6] Joscelyn Godwin, *Arkos: The Polar Myth*, pp. 96-97

[7] Alice A. Bailey, *A Treatise on White Magic*, p. 378

[8] *Ibid.*, 379; Alice A. Bailey, *A Treatise on Cosmic Fire*, fn. p. 211

[9] Alice A. Bailey, *A Treatise on White Magic*, pp. 381-382

[10] Alice A. Bailey, *Discipleship in the New Age, Vol. II*, pp. 292-293

[11] Alice A. Bailey, *Esoteric Healing*, p. 503

[12]Alice A. Bailey, *The Rays and the Initiations*, p. 306

[13]*Ibid.*, pp. 308-309

[14]Alice A. Bailey, *The Destiny of the Nations*, p. 13

[15]*Ibid.*

[16]Alice A. Bailey, *A Treatise on Cosmic Fire*, p. 581

[17]Brian Swimme and Thomas Berry, *The Universe Story*, p. 271

[18]*Ibid.*, p. 272

[19]David Morrison, "Target Earth," *Astronomy*, October 1995, p. 36

[20]H.P. Blavatsky, *The Secret Doctrine: Anthropogenesis*, *Vol. II*, p. 16

[21]Brian Swimme and Thomas Berry, *The Universe Story*, p. 124

[22]Wishar S. Cerve, *Lemuria: The Lost Continent of the Pacific*, p. 105

[23]Alice A. Bailey, *Esoteric Healing*, p. 229

[24]Wishar S. Cerve, *Lemuria: The Lost Continent of the Pacific*, pp. 156-157

[25]Alice A. Bailey, *Esoteric Healing*, pp. 231-232

[26]H.P. Blavatsky, *The Secret Doctrine: Anthropogenesis*, *Vol. II*, p. 141

[27]Brian Swimme and Thomas Berry, *The Universe Story*, p. 273

[28]Alice A. Bailey, *A Treatise on White Magic*, p. 225

[29]Alice A. Bailey, *A Treatise on Cosmic Fire*, p. 467

[30]William Irwin Thompson, *Pacific Shift*, p. 62

[31]*Ibid.*, p. 78

[32]*Ibid.*, p. 79

[33]Alice A. Bailey, *A Treatise on Cosmic Fire*, pp. 391-392

[34]*Ibid.*, pp. 390-391

[35]Alice A. Bailey, *A Treatise on Cosmic Fire*, p. 439

[36]Arnold Toynbee, *A Study of History*, pp. 364-367

[37]Oswald Spengler, *The Decline of the West*, p. 222

[38]*Ibid.*, p. 21

[39]Alice O. Howell, *Jungian Synchronicity in Astrological Signs and Ages*, p. 149

[40]William Irwin Thompson, *The Time Falling Bodies Take to Light*, pp. 159-161

[41]Arnold Toynbee, *A Study of History*, p. 360

[42]William McNeill, *The Rise of the West*, p. 32

[43]*Ibid.*, p. 69

[44]Alice A. Bailey, *The Destiny of the Nations*, pp. 15-16

[45]Michael I. Rostovtzeff, *Social and Economic History of the Roman Empire*, second edition, pp. 532-535

[46]Alice A. Bailey, *Esoteric Healing*, p. 232

[47]Philippe Aries and Georges Duby, eds. *A History of Private Life: From Pagan Rome to Byzantium, Vol. I*, p. 178

[48]A.H.M. Jones, *Constantine and the Conversion of Europe*, p. 14

[49]*Ibid.*, 14-24

[50]Alice A. Bailey, *The Externalisation of the Hierarchy*, pp. 132-133, 536. It is unclear what the Tibetan means by the Great Council of Shamballa. We can be certain, however, that this is not intended to be a literal statement. The limitations of language in describing matters of an esoteric nature hinder the Tibetan throughout his writings. We can only assume that there is some sort of telepathic interplay taking place between great intelligent entities and leave it at that.

[51]Alice A. Bailey, *The Rays and the Initiations*, p. 145

[52]Alice A. Bailey, *The Externalisation of the Hierarchy*, p. 407

[53]Alasdair Clayre, ed. *Nature and Industrialization*, p. 177

[54]David S. Landes, *The Unbound Prometheus*, p. 98

[55]*Ibid.*, p. 1

[56]*Ibid.*, p. 5

[57]J. A. Banks, "The Contagion of Numbers," *The Victorian City: Images and Realities*, ed. by H.J. Dyos and Michael Wolff, p. 105

[58]Jose Harris, *Private Lives, Public Spirit: Britain 1870-1914*, p. 33

[59]Alice A. Bailey, *Education in the New Age*, p. 45

[60]John Keegan, *The Second World War*, p. 12

[61]*Ibid.*, p. 16

[62]Geoffrey Blainey, *The Causes of War*, p. 71

[63]Alice A. Bailey, *The Externalisation of the Hierarchy*, p. 536

[64]Paul Thompson, *The Edwardians*, p. 240

[65]Alice A. Bailey, *The Externalisation of the Hierarchy*, p. 536

[66]Alice A. Bailey, *Esoteric Healing*, pp. 431-432, 503

[67]Alice A. Bailey, *Esoteric Astrology*, pp. 586-587

[68]Alice A. Bailey, *The Rays and the Initiations*, pp. 646-647

[69]Alice A. Bailey, *Discipleship in the New Age, Vol. II*, p. 61

[70]Alice A. Bailey, *A Treatise on Cosmic Fire*, p. 496

[71]Francois Bedarida, *A Social History of England 1851-1875*, p. 15

[72]Alice A. Bailey, *The Externalisation of the Hierarchy*, p. 134

[73]Alice A. Bailey, *Esoteric Astrology*, p. 446

[74]Alice A. Bailey, *The Externalisation of the Hierarchy*, pp. 297-299

[75]John Keegan, *The Mask of Command*, p. 145

[76]*Ibid.*, p. 136

[77]*Ibid.*, p. 310

[78]Johan Quanjer, "The Will—Its Manifestation in Global Politics," *Pathway to Shamballa: Talks and Sharings from the 1988 Specialized Group Conference*, p. 46

[79]Alice A. Bailey, *The Externalisation of the Hierarchy*, p. 408

[80]D.M. Stenton, *English Society in the Early Middle Ages 1066-1307*, pp. 46-47

[81]Alice A. Bailey, *The Reappearance of the Christ*, p. 93

[82]Robert Muller, *New Genesis*, p. 118

[83]Alice A. Bailey, *Esoteric Psychology, Vol. I*, pp. 360, 178

[84]Alice A. Bailey, *The Externalisation of the Hierarchy*, p. 133

[85]K. Paul Johnson, *The Masters Revealed: Madame Blavatsky and the Myth of the great White Lodge*, pp. 38-43

[86]Denis Mack Smith ed., *Garibaldi*, p. 112

[87]Dana Lloyd Thomas, "A Modern Pythagorean," *Gnosis Magazine*, No. 44, Summer 1997, p. 54

[88]Alice A. Bailey, *The Externalisation of the Hierarchy*, p. 298

[89]A.J.P. Taylor, *The Course of German History*, pp. 100-101

[90]J.A.S. Grenville, *A History of the World in the Twentieth Century*, p. 440

[91]Alice A. Bailey, *The Destiny of the Nations*, p. 16

[92]Alice A. Bailey, *Discipleship in the New Age, Vol. I*, p. 241

[93]Alice A. Bailey, *The Externalisation of the Hierarchy*, p. 433

[94]Joscelyn Godwin, *Arktos: The Polar Myth in Science, Symbolism, and Nazi Survival*, p. 52

[95]Michael FitzGerald, *Storm-Troopers of Satan: An Occult History of the Second World War*, pp. 85-87

[96]Alice A. Bailey, *The Rays and the Initiations*, p. 52

[97]Gerald Suster, *Hitler: The Occult Messiah*, p. 193

[98]Alice A. Bailey, *The Externalisation of the Hierarchy*, p. 258

[99]Alice A. Bailey, *The Rays and the Initiations*, pp. 35-36

[100]Alice A. Bailey, *The Externalisation of the Hierarchy*, pp. 408-409

[101]Thomas Hutton, *A Lecture on the Social Improvement of the Working Classes*, p. 3

[102]Alice A. Bailey, *The Destiny of the Nations*, p. 22

[103]Alice A. Bailey, *The Externalisation of the Hierarchy*, p. 52

[104]Alice A. Bailey, *The Reappearance of the Christ*, pp. 164-165

[105]Alice A. Bailey, *The Destiny of the Nations*, p. 22

[106]Leszek Kolakowski, *Main Currents of Marxism, Vol. III*, p. 530

[107]Alice A. Bailey, *Telepathy and the Etheric Vehicle*, p. 24

[108]Alice A. Bailey, *Education in the New Age*, p. 103

Chapter 5

[1]Alice A. Bailey, *Letters on Occult Meditation*, pp. 259, 262

[2]Ian Gordon Brown, "Spiritual Government: The Principles of Hierarchical Control," *The Beacon*, Vol. XXXIX, No. 5, September/ October 1961, pp. 133-134

[3]Manly P. Hall, *The Most Holy Trinosophia of the Comte de St. Germain*, p. XXVIII

[4]Manly P. Hall, *The Secret Destiny of America*, pp. 165-172

[5]Alice A. Bailey, *The Unfinished Autobiography*, pp. 35-36

[6]Sylvia Cranston, *HPB*, p. 45

[7]Sylvia Cranston, *HPB*, pp. 45-47

[8]Cyril Scott, *The Initiate: Some Impressions of a Great Soul*, p. 3

[9]*New York Times*, March 1, 1997

[10]Alice A. Bailey, *A Treatise on White Magic*, p. 380

[11]Alice A. Bailey, *Initiation Human and Solar*, p. 33-34

[12]*Ibid.*, p. 34

[13]*Ibid.*, pp. 34-35

[14]*The British Anthology; or, Poetical Library, Vol. IV*, p. 17

[15]Christopher Hill, *The World Turned Upside Down*, p. 87

[16]Alice A. Bailey, *The Externalisation of the Hierarchy*, p. 526

[17]The various departments of the Hierarchy might best be seen as vortices of ray energy, vibrating at a very high frequency.

[18]Alice A. Bailey, *Initiation Human and Solar*, pp. 41-43

[19]*Ibid.*, pp. 43-44

[20]Houston Smith, *Religions of the World: Judaism*, tape 6

[21]Alice A. Bailey, *Initiation Human and Solar*, pp. 45-46

[22]*Ibid.*, p. 51

[23]*Ibid.*, pp. 53-60

[24]Maurice Keen, *The Pelican History of Medieval Europe*, pp. 155, 191

[25]Jean Overton Fuller, *Sir Francis Bacon*, p. 79

[26]J. M. Roberts, *The Mythology of the Secret Societies*, p. 207

[27]Alice A. Bailey, *Initiation Human and Solar*, pp. 56-57

[28]Thomas D. Worrel, "The Initiatic Symbolism of Freemasonry," *Gnosis Magazine*, No. 44, Summer 1997, p. 19

[29]Alice A. Bailey, *The Externalisation of the Hierarchy*, p. 674; Bailey, *Esoteric Psychology, Vol. II*, p. 224

[30]Alice A. Bailey, *Discipleship in the New Age, Vol. II*, p. 361

[31]John G. Bennett, *The Masters of the Wisdom*, pp. 36-37

[32]*Ibid.*, pp. 38-40

[33]Manly P. Hall, *The Adepts in the Esoteric Classical Tradition, Vol. II: Mystics and Mysteries of Alexandria*, pp. 5-14

[34]*Ibid.*, p. 17

[35]H. P. Blavatsky, *The Secret Doctrine, Vol. I*, p. 207

[36]W. K. C. Guthrie, *The Greeks and Their Gods*, p. 88

[37]*Ibid.*, p. 314

[38]Joscelyn Godwin, *Mystery Religions in the Ancient World*, p. 144

[39]John G. Bennett, *The Masters of the Wisdom*, p. 48

[40]Joscelyn Godwin, *Mystery Religions in the Ancient World*, p. 72

[41]Robert S. Brumbaugh, *The Philosophers of Greece*, pp. 33-34

[42]W. K. C. Guthrie, *The Greeks and Their Gods*, pp. 195-196

[43]Alice A. Bailey, *Esoteric Psychology, Vol. II*, pp. 398-399

[44]Manly P. Hall, *The Adepts: Mystics and Mysteries of Alexandria, Vol. II*, pp. 65-75

[45]Alice A. Bailey, *The Externalisatiojn of the Hierarchy*, pp. 28-29

[46]H.P. Blavatsky, *Isis Unveiled: Science, Vol. I*, p. 17

[47]Joscelyn Godwin, *Mystery Religions in the Ancient World*, p. 12

[48]Rudolf Steiner, *Christianity as a Mystical Fact*, pp. 160-161

[49]Manly P. Hall, *The Adepts:: Mystics and Mysteries of Alexandria, Vol. II*, p. 57

[50]*Ibid.*, pp. 60-61

[51]Rudolph Steiner, *Christianity as a Mystical Fact*, p. 162

[52]Joscelyn Godwin, *Mystery Religions in the Ancient World*, pp. 84-85

[53]Rudolph Steiner, *Christianity as a Mystical Fact*, pp. 170-171

[54]John 14:12

[55]Rudolph Steiner, *Christianity as a Mystical Fact*, p. 172

[56]H.P. Blavatsky, *Isis Unveiled, Vol. II*, p. 253

[57]Alice A. Bailey, *A Treatise on White Magic*, pp. 401-402

[58]Kenneth Clark, *Civilisation*, p. 128

[59]*Ibid.*, p. 135

[60]Sylvia Cranston, *HPB*, pp. 490-491

[61]*Ibid.*, pp. 485, 488, 490

[62]Margaret Taylor, "John Bunyan: A Forerunner," *The Beacon*, Vol. LI, No. 12, November/December 1986, p. 373

[63]Alice A. Bailey, *A Treatise on White Magic*, pp. 408-409

[64]Keith Bailey, "Musical Composition and the Rays," *The Journal of Esoteric Psychology*, Vol. III, No. 3, 1987, pp. 130-131

[65]A.G. Dickens, *The German Nation and Martin Luther*, pp. 49-71

[66]Alice A. Bailey, *Externalisation of the Hierarchy*, p. 49

[67]Alice A. Bailey, *A Treatise on White Magic*, pp. 409-410

[68]Pierre Goubert, *Louis XIV and Twenty Million Frenchmen*, p. 38

[69]Christopher Hill, ed., *Winstanley: The Law of Freedom and Other Writings*, p. 187

[70]Alice A. Bailey, *Initiation Human and Solar*, p. 58

[71]Manly P. Hall, *The Secret Destiny of America*, pp. 129-131

[72]R. Bryant-Jeffreys, "Thomas Paine 1737-1809: A Forerunner," *The Beacon*, Vol. L, No. 10, July/August 1984, p. 311

[73]Carol Brubaker Smith, "Giuseppe Mazzini; A Forerunner," *The Beacon*, Vol. L, No. 5, September/October 1983, p. 150

[74]Herbert Butterfield, *The Origins of Modern Science, 1300-1800*, pp. 105-107

[75]N.G. Wilmut, "Samuel Hahnemann, Physician and Healer: A Forerunner," *The Beacon*, Vol. XLIX, No. 4, July/August 1981, p. 117

[76]D.J. Nichol, "Doctor Edward Bach: A Forerunner," *The Beacon*, Vol. XLVII, No. 9, May/June 1978, pp. 283, 286

[77]Frederick W. Clampett, *Luther Burbank "Our Beloved Infidel,"* p. 67

[78]Alice A. Bailey, *The Externalisation of the Hierarchy*, p. 49

[79]Renee Bennett, "Maria Montessori: A Forerunner," *The Beacon*, Vol. XLVII, No. 10, July/August 1978, pp. 310-313

[80]Cyril Scott, *Music: Its Secret Influence Throughout the Ages*, p. 67

[81]*Ibid.*, pp. 75-97

[82]*Ibid.*, pp. 118-134

[83]Richard A. Wolfe, "William James: A Forerunner," *The Beacon*, Vol. LI, No. 1, January/February 1985, p. 13

[84]Alice A. Bailey, *A Treatise on White Magic*, p. 412

[85]*Ibid.*

[86]*Ibid.*

[87]The language of Hierarchical meetings and conclaves is taken directly from the Tibetan's own words and we can only speculate on the

form of these gatherings. Again, we need to be reminded that what takes place on the inner planes is different in quality and nature to our conventional understanding. How the Hierarchy works remains a mystery that is yet unrevealed.

[88] Alice A. Bailey, *Esoteric Psychology, Vol. I*, pp. 170-173

[89] *Ibid.*, pp. 170-171

[90] Alice A. Bailey, *Esoteric Psychology, Vol. II*, pp. 702-703

[91] *Ibid.*, pp. 717-720

[92] Alice A. Bailey, *The Externalisation of the Hierarchy*, pp. 449-480

[93] *Ibid.*, pp. 196-197

[94] *The Roerich Pact and The Banner of Peace*, p. 3

[95] *The Lamplighter Movement*, March 1978, p. 2

[96] *Ibid.*

[97] Dion Fortune, *The Magical Battle of Britain*, p. ix

[98] *Ibid.*, p. 24

[99] Alice A. Bailey, *Discipleship in the New Age, Vol. I*, pp. 771-772

[100] Alice A. Bailey, *The Rays and the Initiations*, pp. 721-722

[101] *Ibid.*

[102] Alice A. Bailey, *A Treatise on Cosmic Fire*, p. 753

[103] *Ibid.*, p. 755

[104] *Ibid.*, p. 759

[105] *Ibid*, pp. 297-298

Chapter 6

[1] Alice A. Bailey, *Esoteric Psychology, Vol. II*, p. 209; Alice A. Bailey, *A Treatise on White Magic*, p. 391

[2] Alice A. Bailey, *Esoteric Psychology, Vol. II*, p. 210

[3] *Ibid.*

[4] *Ibid.*, pp. 210-211

[5] H. P. Blavatsky, *The Secret Doctrine: Cosmogenesis, Vol. I*, pp. 387-388

[6] Alice A. Bailey, *Initiation Human and Solar*, pp. 29-30, 45

[7] Alice A. Bailey, *Esoteric Psychology, Vol. II*, p. 210

[8] Alice A. Bailey, *A Treatise on Cosmic Fire*, pp. 413-414

[9] Alice A. Bailey, *Esoteric Psychology, Vol. II*, p. 211

[10] Alice A. Bailey, *A Treatise on Cosmic Fire*, pp. 241-242

[11] W. Warren Wagar, ed. *History and the Idea of Mankind*, pp. 8-14

[12] *Ibid.*, pp. 49-58

[13] Acts 17:24-29

[14] W. Warren Wagar, ed. *History and the Idea of Mankind*, pp. 99-103

[15] *Ibid.*, pp. 74-85

[16] Stewart C. Easton, *Man and the World in the Light of Anthroposophy*, p. 20

[17] Alice A. Bailey, *Esoteric Healing*, p. 252; Alice A. Bailey, *The Destiny of the Nations*, p. 44

[18] Alice A. Bailey, *Esoteric Psychology, Vol. II*, p. 336

[19] H.P. Blavatsky, *The Secret Doctrine: Anthropogenesis, II*, p. 769

[20] *Ibid.*

[21] *State of the Peoples: A Global Human Rights Report on Societies in Danger*, Boston: Beacon Press, 1993, pp. 171-172

[22] Marlo Morgan, *Mutant Message: Downunder*, p. 46

[23] Alice A. Bailey, *The Rays and The Initiations*, p. 259

[24] *Ibid.*, p. 518

[25] Alice A. Bailey, *The Destiny of the Nations*, p. 43

[26] Alice A. Bailey, *Telepathy and the Etheric Vehicle*, p. 8

[27] Alice A. Bailey, *The Externalisation of the Hierarchy*, pp. 121-122

[28] *Ibid.*, p. 122

[29] Alice A. Bailey, *The Destiny of the Nations*, pp. 43-44

[30] Pitirim A. Sorokin, *The Reconstruction of Humanity*, p. 11

[31] Alice A. Bailey, *Esoteric Healing*, p. 70

[32] *Ibid.*, pp. 59, 383

[33] *Ibid.*, p. 232

[34] *Ibid.*, pp. 210-211

[35] Alice A. Bailey, *A Treatise on Cosmic Fire*, pp. 362-363

[36] Alice A. Bailey, *Esoteric Psychology, Vol. I*, p. 319

[37] Alice A. Bailey, *Glamour: A World Problem*, p. 94

[38] *Ibid.*, p. 95

[39] Pitirim A. Sorokin, *The Crisis of Our Age*, pp. 19-21

[40] Alice A Bailey, *Glamour: A World Problem*, pp. 96-97

[41] *Ibid.*, pp. 99-100

[42] Alice A Bailey, *A Treatise on Cosmic Fire*, p. 599

[43] Geoffrey Hodson, *Basic Theosophy*, p. 421

[44] Alice A Bailey, *A Treatise on Cosmic Fire*, p. 953

[45] Alice A Bailey, *Discipleship in the New Age, Vol. II*, p. 412

[46] Alice A Bailey, *A Treatise on Cosmic Fire*, pp. 954-955

[47] *Ibid.*, p. 956

[48] Rupert Sheldrake, *A New Science of Life*, pp. 92-98

[49]Teilhard de Chardin, *The Phenomenon of Man*, pp. 277-278

[50]The soul, as it is applied to a national or group culture, is referred to by both Steiner and the Tibetan as the highest ideals which guide the culture of that nation or group. These values and ideals are not static but follow an evolutionary pattern.

[51]Rudolf Steiner, *Materialism and the Task of Anthroposophy*, p. 175

[52]Stewart C. Easton, *Man and World in the Light of Anthroposophy*, p. 35

[53]*Ibid.*, p. 44

[54]*Ibid.*, p. 35

[55]Rudolph Steiner, *Materialism and the Task of Anthroposophy*, p. 175

[56]J.A.K. Thomson, trans. *The Ethics of Aristotle*, p. 80

[57]Johan Huizinga, *The Waning of the Middle Ages*, p. 207

[58]Rudolph Steiner, *Materialism and the Task of Anthroposophy*, p. 194

[59]Why this form of consciousness should first appear in Britain at the time that it allegedly did is not clearly explained. The most obvious reason has to do with the rise of Britain to preeminence during this period, first as a great commercial power and, later, as an industrial power. Also, through primogeniture, Britain was clearly a patriarchal society.

[60]Rudolph Steiner, *Materialism and the Task of Anthroposophy*, pp. 195-200

[61]*Ibid.*, p. 201

[62]B.C.J. Lievegoed, *Mystery Streams in Europe and the New Mysteries*, pp. 15-24

[63]*Ibid.*, pp. 25-35

[64]John Michell, *The New View Over Atlantis*, p. 211

[65]B.C.J. Lievegoed, *Mystery Streams in Europe and the New Mysteries*, pp. 37-47

[66]*Ibid.*, pp. 49-65

[67]Geoffrey Hodson, *Basic Theosophy*, p. 437

[68]Ibid., pp. 437-441

[69]Alice A. Bailey, *The Light of the Soul*, p. 167

[70]Alice A. Bailey, *Esoteric Healing*, pp. 229-230

[71]Peter Laslett, *The World We Have Lost*, p. 5

[72]Alice A. Bailey, *Esoteric Healing*, p. 290

[73]*Ibid.*

[74]Philippe Aries and Georges Duby, gen. eds. *A History of Private Life, Vol. III, Passions of the Renaissance*, edited by Roger Chartier, pp. 16-19

[75] Alice A. Bailey, *Esoteric Healing*, p. 291

[76] *Ibid.*

[77] *Ibid.*

[78] Geoffrey Hodson, *Basic Theosophy*, pp. 196-213

[79] Alice A. Bailey, *Letters on Occult Meditation*, p. 45

[80] *Ibid.*, p. 46

[81] Matthew 17:10-13.

[82] Joseph Head and S.L. Cranston, eds. *Reincarnation: The Phoenix Fire Mystery*, pp. 142-156

[83] Barbara Lane, *Echoes From the Battlefield* (Virginia Beach, VA: ARE Press, 1996); Yonassan Gershon, *Beyond the Ashes: Cases of Reincarnation From the Holocaust* (Virginia Beach, VA: ARE Press, 1992); Vicki Mackenzie, *Reborn in the West* (New York: Marlowe & Company, 1995

[84] Jacob Burckhardt, *The Civilization of the Renaissance in Italy*, pp. 104, 106

[85] Trevor Ravenscroft, *The Spear of Destiny*, pp. 128-130

[86] Alice A. Bailey, *Destiny of the Nations*, p. 59

[87] R.F. Newbold, "The Rays of Ancient Greece and Rome," *The Journal of Esoteric Psychology*, Vol. VII, No. 2, 1992, pp. 24-35

[88] Owen Barfield, *Romanticism Comes of Age*, pp. 144-163

[89] Hugh A. MacDougall, *Racial Myth in English History*, pp. 7-9

[90] Rudolf Steiner, *The Destinies of Individuals and of Nations*, p. 175

[91] R.M. Ogilvie, *Latin and Greek: A History of the Influence of the Classics on English Life from 1600 to 1918*, p. 47

[92] *Ibid.*, p. 20

[93] *Ibid.*, p. 106

[94] Elizabeth Rawson, "The Expansion of Rome," *The Oxford History of the Classical World*, John Boardman, Jasper Griffin, and Oswyn Murray eds., p. 430

[95] *Ibid.*

[96] Alice A. Bailey, *The Destiny of the Nations*, p. 53

Chapter 7

[1] Alice A. Bailey, *Esoteric Psychology, Vol. II*, pp. 719-723

[2] Alice A. Bailey, *A Treatise on Cosmic Fire*, p. 1032

[3] *Ibid.*, p. 1033

[4]*Five Years of Theosophy*, "The Theory of Cycles," p. 491

[5]Alice A. Bailey, *A Treatise on Cosmic Fire*, pp. 1033, 1034

[6]Alice A. Bailey, *Esoteric Astrology*, p. 595

[7]The following information is taken from two talks given by Stephen Pugh at the annual University of the Seven Rays Conference in April, 1992. The two talks were entitled, "The Seven Rays and the Ten Sacred Numerals, Part I," and "Ten Sacred Numbers of the Manifested Universe." See also Stephen Pugh, "The 10 Sacred Numbers of the Manifest Universe," *The Journal of Esoteric Psychology*, Vol. VII, No.1, pp. 20-24

[8]Brad Steiger, *Brad Steiger Predicts the Future*, p. 25

[9]Felipe Fernandez Armesto, *Millennium: A History of the Last Thousand Years*, p. 12

[10]Brad Steiger, *Brad Steiger Predicts the Future*, pp. 35-41

[11]Alvin Barta, *Timetable of Civilizations*, pp. 2-3, periodic table

[12]Julian Marias, *Generations*, pp. 18-19

[13]Jose Ortega y Gassett, *Man and Crisis*, pp. 55-66

[14]Arthur Schlesinger, Jr., *The Cycles of American History*, p. 30

[15]Nicholas Campion, *The Great Year*, p. 519

[16]Alice A. Bailey, *Esoteric Psychology, Vol. I*, p. 3

[17]*Ibid.*, pp. 3-4

[18]Alice A. Bailey, *Glamour: A World Problem*, pp. 156-157

[19]Alice A. Bailey, *Esoteric Psychology, Vol. I*, pp. 316-317

[20]Geoffrey Hodson, *Basic Theosophy*, p. 398

[21]Alice A. Bailey, *Esoteric Psychology, Vol. I*, pp. 359-362

[22]Dane Rudyhar, *Astrological Timing*, pp. 127-136

[23]Alice A. Bailey, *Esoteric Psychology, Vol. I*, pp. 348-349

[24]Alice A. Bailey, *Destiny of the Nations*, p. 136

[25]Alice A. Bailey, *Esoteric Psychology, Vol. I*, pp. 321-322

[26]Alice A. Bailey, *Destiny of the Nations*, p. 143

[27]*Ibid.*, p. 142

[28]Michael Robbins, *Tapestry of the Gods, Vol. I*, p. 329

[29]Kenneth Clark, *Civilisation*, p. 29

[30]Alice A. Bailey, *Esoteric Astrology*, pp. 212-213

[31]Johan Huizinga, *The Waning of the Middle Ages*, p. 25

[32]*Ibid.*, p. 9

[33]R. H. Tawney, *Religion and the Rise of Capitalism*, p. 77

[34]*Ibid.*, p. 79

[35]Michael Robbins, *Tapestry of the Gods, Vol. I*, pp. 36-49

[36]R. F. Newbold, "The Rays of Ancient Greece and Rome," *The Journal of Esoteric Psychology*, Vol. VII, No. 2, 1992, pp. 28-30

[37]Jacob Burckhardt, *The Civilization of the Renaissance in Italy*, p. 184

[38]Johan Huizinga, *Erasmus and the Age of Reformation*, p. 42

[39]Emmaniel LeRoy Ladurie, *Carnival in Romans: A People's Uprising at Romans 1579-1580*, pp. 63-64

[40]Sir George Clark, *Early Modern Europe*, p. 153

[41]Kenneth Clark, *Civilisation*, p. 192

[42]Richard S. Dunn, *The Age of Religious Wars, 1559-1689*, p. 78

[43]Alice A. Bailey, *Discipleship in the New Age, Vol. II*, p. 407

[44]Christopher Hill, *The World Turned Upside Down*, p. 190

[45]R.H. Tawney, *Religion and the Rise of Capitalism*, p. 146

[46]Philippe Aries and Georges Duby, eds., *A History of Private Life, Vol. III, Passions of the Renaissance*, Roger Chartier, ed., p. 111

[47]Pitirim A. Sorokin, *The Crisis of Our Age*, p. 20

[48]D.V. Glass and D.E.C. Eversley, *Population in History*, p. 15

[49]Pierre Goubert, *Louis XIV and Twenty Million Frenchmen*, p. 26

[50]Kaare L. Rasmussen, "Historical Accretionary Events from 700 BC to AD 1850—A 1050-year Periodicity?" *The Quarterly Journal of the Royal Astronomical Society*, Vol. 3, No. 1, 1990

[51]Alice A. Bailey, *Esoteric Psychology Vol. II*, p. 261

[52]Kenneth Clark, *Civilisation*, p. 329

[53]Alice A. Bailey, *Esoteric Psychology, Vol. II*, p. 718

[54]David Landes, *The Unbound Prometheus*, p. 538

[55]Alice A. Bailey, *The Rays and the Initiations*, pp. 620-621

[56]*Ibid.*, p. 622

[57]Max Beloff, *The Age of Absolutism 1660-1815*, pp. 128

[58]Alice A. Bailey, *Esoteric Psychology, Vol. I*, p. 349

[59]Anthony Symondson, ed. *The Victorian Crisis of Faith*, p. 100

[60]*Ibid.*, p. 101

[61]Alice A. Bailey, *Esoteric Psychology, Vol. I*, p. 348

[62]*Ibid.*, p. 349

[63]Michael D. Robbins, *Tapestry of the Gods, Vol. I*, pp. 352, 371

[64]*Ibid.*,pp. 165-167

[65]*Ibid.*, p. 165

[66]*Ibid.*

[67]*Ibid.*, p. 166

[68]Alice A. Bailey, *Destiny of the Nations*, p. 47

[69]*Ibid.*, p. 34

[70]*Ibid.*, p. 50

[71]*Ibid.*, pp. 78-79

[72]*Ibid.*, pp. 83-84

[73]*Ibid.*, p. 56

[74]Kurt Abraham, *The Seven Rays and Nations*, pp. 41-59

[75]Alice A. Bailey, *Destiny of the Nations*, pp. 55-56

[76]Alice A. Bailey, *Esoteric Psychology, Vol. I*, pp. 174-175

[77]Alice A. Bailey, *Destiny of the Nations*, p. 92

[78]Information contained in this section is derived from the presentations at the Arcane School Conference, held May 15-16, 1992

[79]Alice A. Bailey, *Destiny of the Nations*, p. 93

[80]*Ibid.*, p. 103

[81]*Ibid.*, p. 104

Chapter 8

[1]Alice A. Bailey, *A Treatise on White Magic*, p. 433

[2]*Ibid.*, p. 434

[3]*Ibid.*, p. 437

[4]Alice A. Bailey, *Esoteric Astrology*, pp. 609-611

[5]Alice A. Bailey, *A Treatise on White Magic*, pp. 434-436

[6]Alice A. Bailey, *Esoteric Astrology*, pp. 350, 553

[7]*Ibid.*, pp. 350, 554-555

[8]*Ibid.*, p. 555

[9]*Ibid.*, p. 427

[10]*Ibid.*, p. 86

[11]Nicholas Campion, *The Great Year*, p. 20

[12]*Ibid.*, pp. 20, 87, 229, 412

[13]*Ibid.*, pp. 243-245

[14]*Ibid.*, p. 243

[15]Alice A. Bailey, *Esoteric Astrology*, pp. 409-410

[16]*Ibid.*, pp. 112, 410

[17]Geoffrey Hodson, *Basic Theosophy*, pp. 392

[18]Guenther Wachsmuth, *The Evolution of Mankind*, pp. 21, 29

[19]Geoffrey Hodson, *Basic Theosophy*, p. 392

[20]Alice A. Bailey, *Esoteric Psychology II*, p. 205

[21] Alice A. Bailey, *Esoteric Astrology*, p. 537

[22] Alice A. Bailey, *Discipleship in the New Age, Vol. II*, pp. 425-426

[23] Alan Oken, *Soul-Centered Astrology*, p. 230

[24] *Ibid.*, pp. 165-166, 171-172, 177-178, 184, 191, 198, 206, 214, 221, 229-230, 238-239, 248; Alice A. Bailey, *The Labours of Hercules*, pp. 210-214; Derek and Julia Parker, *The Compleat Astrologer*, pp. 106-128; James David and John Raifsnider, *Astrology of the Seven Rays*, pp. 55-69; Frances Sakoian and Louis S. Acker, *The Astrologer's Handbook*, pp. 33-52

[25] Holger Stavnsbjerg, *The Astrology of Initiation and the Horoscopes of Big Cities*, pp. 61-77

[26] Houston Smith, *The Religions of Man*, p. 426

[27] *Ibid.*

[28] Clara A. Weiss, *Astrological Keys to Self-actualization and Self-realization*, p. 95

[29] Reay Tannahill, *Food in History*, p. 243; Fernand Braudel, *The Structures of Everyday Life, Vol. I*, p. 241

[30] *Ithaca Journal*, October 31, 1996

[31] Erich Maria Remarque, *All Quiet on the Western Front*, pp. 25-26

[32] William Irwin Thompson, *Darkness and Scattered Light*, p. 59

[33] *Ibid.*, pp. 75-80

[34] Dane Rudhyar, *Occult Preparations for a New Age*, fn. p. 143

[35] B.C.J. Lievegoed, *Mystery Streams in Europe and the New Mysteries*, p. xii

[36] *Ibid.*, p. 30

[37] Alice A. Bailey, *The Labours of Hercules*, p. 212

[38] B.C.J. Lievegoed, *Mystery Streams in Europe and the New Mysteries*, pp. 52-53

[39] *Ibid.*, p. 42

[40] Alice A. Bailey, *The Labours of Hercules*, p. 213

[41] Dane Rudhyar, *Occult Preparations for a New Age*, p. 127

[42] Alice A. Bailey, *Esoteric Astrology*, p. 132

[43] Dane Rudhyar, *Astrological Timing*, pp. 126-136

[44] John P. Sedgwick, *Harmonics of History*, pp. 29-56

[45] Dane Rudhyar, *The Practice of Astrology*, p. 105

[46] Alice A. Bailey, *Esoteric Astrology*, p. 220

[47] Dane Rudhyar, *Astrological Timing*, pp. 79-82

[48] Kurt Abraham, *The Moon Veils Vulcan and the Sun Veils Neptune*, pp. 31-34, 42-43

[49]Dane Rudhyar, *The Sun Is Also A Star: The Galactic Dimension of Astrology*, pp. 88-115

[50]Lewis Namier, *1848: The Revolution of the Intellectuals*, p. 6

[51]Alan Oken, *Soul-Centered Astrology*, p. 214

[52]Note that the above discussion regarding the passage of the outer planets through the Piscean zodiac is taken from Rudhyar, *The Sun is Also a Star*, pp. 88-115

Epilogue

[1]Alice A. Bailey, *Education in the New Age*, pp. v-xii

[2]*Ibid.*, p. 45

[3]*Ibid.*, p. 85

[4]*Ibid.*, pp. 46-47

[5]*Ibid.*, p. 47

[6]J.H. Plumb, "The Perspective of History," *The Making of an Historian: The collected essays of J. H. Plumb*, Vol. I, 1988, p. 310

Bibliography

Abraham, Kurt, *The Moon Veils Vulcan and the Sun Veils Neptune*. Jacksonville, OR: Lampus Press, 1989

——*The Seven Rays and Nations*. Cape May, NJ: Lampus Press, 1987

Aries, Phillippe and Georges Duby, gen. eds. *A History of Private Life, Vol. III, Passions of the Renaissance*, edited by Roger Chartier. Cambridge, MA: Harvard University Press, 1989

Armesto, Felipe Fernandez, *Millennium: A History of the Last Thousand Years*. New York: Scribner, 1995

Baigent, Michael and Richard Leigh, The *Temple and the Lodge*. New York: Arcade Publishing, 1989

Bailey, Alice A., *A Treatise on Cosmic Fire*. New York: Lucis Publishing, 1962

——*A Treatise on White Magic*. New York: Lucis Publishing, 1951

——*Destiny of the Nations*. New York: Lucis Publishing, 1949

——*Discipleship in the New Age, Vol. I*. New York: Lucis Publishing, 1972

——*Discipleship in the New Age, Vol. II*. New York: Lucis Publishing, 1955

——*Education in the New Age*. New York: Lucis Publishing, 1954

——*Esoteric Astrology*. New York: Lucis Publishing, 1951

——*Esoteric Healing*. New York: Lucis Publishing, 1953

——*Esoteric Psychology, Vol. I*. New York: Lucis Publishing, 1962

——*Esoteric Psychology, Vol. II*. New York: Lucis Publishing, 1970

——*Externalization of the Hierarchy*. New York: Lucis Publishing, 1957

——*From Intellect to Intuition*. New York: Lucis Publishing, 1960

——*Glamour: A World Problem*. New York: Lucis Publishing, 1950

——*Initiation Human and Solar*. New York: Lucis Publishing, 1951

——*Letters on Occult Meditation*. New York: Lucis Publishing, 1950

——*Problems of Humanity*. New York: Lucis Publishing, 1964

——*Telepathy and the Etheric Vehicle*. New York: Lucis Publishing, 1950

——*The Consciousness of the Atom*. New York: Lucis Publishing, 1922

——*The Labours of Hercules*. New York: Lucis Publishing, 1974

——*The Light of the Soul*. New York: Lucis Publishing, 1955

——*The Rays and the Initiations.* New York: Lucis Publishing, 1960

——*The Reappearance of the Christ.* New York: Lucis Publishing, 1948

——*The Soul and Its Mechanism.* New York: Lucis Publishing, 1930

——*The Unfinished Autobiography.* New York: Lucis Publishing, 1951

Bailey, Foster, *The Spirit of Masonry.* New York: Lucis Publishing, 1957

Bailey, Keith, "Musical Composition and the Rays," *The Journal of Esoteric Psychology,* Vol. III, No. 3, 1987

Balyoz, Harold, *Three Remarkable Women.* Flagstaff, AZ: Altai Publishers, 1986

Banks, J.A., "The Contagion of Numbers," *The Victorian City: Images and Realities,* ed. by H.J. Dyos and Michael Wolff. London & Boston: Routledge and Kegan Paul, 1976

Barfield, Owen, *Romanticism Comes of Age.* Middletown, CT: Wesleyan University Press, 1966

Barraclough, Geoffrey, *History in a Changing World.* Norman, OK: University of Oklahoma Press, 1955

Barta, Alvin, *Timetable of Civilizations.* New York: Vantage Press, 1958

Becker, Carl L., *The Heavenly City of the Eighteenth Century Philosophers.* New Haven: Yale University Press, 1970

Bedarida, Francois, *A Social History of England 1851-1875.* London & New York: Methuen, 1979

Beloff, Max, *The Age of Absolutism 1660-1815.* New York: Harper & Row, 1962

Bennett, J.G., *The Dramatic Universe: History, Vol. IV.* Charles Town, WV: Claymont Communications, 1966

Bennett, John G., *The Masters of the Wisdom.* Sante Fe, NM: Bennett Books, 1995

Bennett, Renee, "Maria Montessori: A Forerunner," *The Beacon,* Vol. XLVII, No. 10, July/August, 1978

Berlin, Isaiah, "The Question of Machiavelli," *New York Review of Books,* 4, November 1971

Berman, Morris, *The Reenchantment of the World.* Toronto, New York: Bantam Books, 1984

Besant, Annie, *Esoteric Christianity.* Wheaton, IL: The Theosophical Publishing House, 1953

Blainey, Geoffrey, *The Causes of War.* New York: The Free Press, 1973

Blavatsky, H. P., *Isis Unveiled: Science, Vol. I,* Pasadena, CA: Theosophical University Press, 1976

——*Studies in Occultism*. Pasadena, CA: Theosophical University Press, 1980

——*The Secret Doctrine: Anthropogenesis, Vol. II*. Pasedena, CA: Theosophical University Press, 1970

——*The Secret Doctrine: Cosmogenesis, Vol. I*. Pasadena, CA: Theosophical University Press, 1970

Braudel, Fernand, *A History of Civilizations*. New York: Allen Lane, 1994

——*The Structures of Everyday Life, Vol. I*. New York: Harper & Row, 1979

British Anthology or *Poetical Library, Vol. IV*. London: John Sharpe, 1825

Brumbaugh, Robert S., *The Philosophers of Greece*. Albany, NY: State University of New York Press, 1981

Bryant-Jeffreys, Richard, "Thomas Paine 1737-1809: A Forerunner," *The Beacon*, Vol. L, No. 10, July/August, 1984

Burckhardt, Jacob, *The Civilization of the Renaissance in Italy*. New York: Phaidon Publishers, 1951

Burmeister, Helen S., *The Seven Rays Made Visible*. Marina del Rey, CA: DeVorss & Company, 1986

Butterfield, Herbert, *The Origins of Modern Science, 1300-1800*. New York: The Free Press, 1957

Campbell, Joseph, *Myths to Live By*. Toronto, New York: Bantam Books, 1972

——*The Inner Reaches of Outer Space*. New York: Harper & Row, 1986

——*The Masks of God: Primitive Mythology*. Penguin Books, 1976

Campion, Nicholas, *The Great Year*. Penguin Books, 1994

Capra, Fritjof, *The Tao of Physics*. Fontana/Collins, 1976

——*The Turning Point: Science, Society, and the Rising Culture*. New York: Simon & Schuster, 1982

Carr, E.H., *What is History?* Penguin Books, 1961

Castaneda, Carlos, *Tales of Power*. Penguin Books, 1974

Cerve, Wishar S., *Lemuria: The Lost Continent of the Pacific*. San Jose, CA: Rosicrucian Press, 1931

Clampett, Frederick W., *Luther Burbank "Our Beloved Infidel."* New York: The Macmillan Company, 1926

Clark, Sir George, *Early Modern Europe*. London, Oxford: Oxford University Press, 1966

Clark, Kenneth, *Civilisation*. New York: Harper & Row, 1969

Clayre, Alasdair, ed., *Nature and Industrialization*. Oxford: Oxford University Press, 1977

Cohn, Norman, *The Pursuit of the Millennium*. London: Paladin, 1970

Cranston, Sylvia, *H. P. B.: Helena Blavatsky*. New York: Tarcher/Putnam, 1993

Darlington, C. D., *The Evolution of Man and Society*. New York: Simon & Schuster, 1969

David, James and John Raifsnider, *Astrology of the Seven Rays*. San Diego: Infinity Books, 1977

Dawson, Christopher, *Understanding Europe*. New York: Sheed and Ward, 1952

de Camp, L. Sprague, *Lost Continents*. New York: Dover, 1970

de Chardin, Teilhard, *The Phenomenon of Man*. New York and Evanston: Harper & Row, 1959

de Purucker, G., *The Esoteric Tradition, Vols. I & II*. Pasadena, CA: Theosophical University Press, 1973

Dickens, A.G., *The German Nation and Martin Luther*. Fontana/Collins, 1974

Donnelly, Ignatius, *Atlantis*. San Francisco: Harper & Row, 1971

Dunn, Richard S., *The Age of Religious Wars, 1559-1689*. New York: W.W. Norton & Company, 1970

Easton, Stewart C., *Man and the World in the Light of Anthroposophy*. Hudson, NY: Anthroposophic Press, 1989

Eliot, T.S., *Notes Towards the Definition of Culture*. New York: Harcourt, Brace and Company, 1949

Ferguson, Marilyn, *The Aquarian Conspiracy*. Los Angeles: J.P. Tarcher, Inc., 1980

FitzGerald, Michael, *Storm-Troopers of Satan: An Occult History of the Second World War*. London: Robert Hale, 1990

Five Years of Theosophy. Los Angeles: The Theosophical Company, 1980

Five Years of Theosophy, "The Theory of Cycles." London: Reeves and Turner, 1885

Fortune, Dion, *The Magical Battle of Britain*. Bradford-on-Avon, England: Golden Gate Press, 1993

Fuller, Jean Overton, *Sir Francis Bacon*. Maidstone, England: George Mann, 1994

Gardner, E.L., *Chains and Rounds*. London: The Theosophical Society, 1966

Gay, Peter, *The Party of Humanity*. New York: W.W. Norton & Company, 1971

Gendzier, Stephen J. ed., *Denis Diderot's The Encyclopedia Selections*. New York: Harper Torchbooks, 1967

Gershon, Yonassan, *Beyond the Ashes: Cases of Reincarnation From the Holocaust*. Virginia Beach, VA: ARE Press, 1992

Geyl, Pieter, *Debates With Historians*. Cleveland and New York: Meridian Books, 1964

Glass, D.V. and D.E.C. Eversley, *Population in History*. London: Edward Arnold, 1965

Godwin, Joscelyn, *Arkos: The Polar Myth*. Grand Rapids, MI: Phanes Press, 1993

——*Mystery Religions in the Ancient World*. San Francisco: Harper & Row, 1981

——*The Theosophical Enlightenment*. Albany, NY: State University of New York Press, 1994

Godwin, Joscelyn, ed., *Cosmic Music*. Rochester, VT: Inner Traditions, 1989

Goubert, Pierre, *Louis XIV and Twenty Million Frenchmen*. New York: Vintage Books, 1972

Grenville, J.A.S., *A History of the World in the Twentieth Century*. Cambridge, MA: The Belnap Press of Harvard University Press, 1994

Grof, Stanislav, *Ancient Wisdom and Modern Science*. Albany, NY: SUNY Press, 1984

Guthrie, W.K.C., *The Greeks and Their Gods*. Boston: Beacon Press, 1950

Hall, Manly P., *Atlantis: An Interpretation*. Los Angeles: Philosophical Research Society, 1976

——*Old Testament Wisdom*. Los Angeles: Philosophical Research Society, 1957

——*The Adepts in the Esoteric Classical Tradition, Vol. I*. Los Angeles: Philosophical Research Society, 1981

——*The Adepts in the Esoteric Classical Tradition, Vol. II: Mystics and Mysteries of Alexandria*. Los Angeles, CA: The Philosophical Research Society, 1988

——*The Most Holy Trinosophia of the Comte De St. Germain*. Los Angeles: The Phoenix Press, 1937

——*The Secret Destiny of America*. Los Angeles: Philosophical Research Society, 1972

——*Twelve World Teachers*. Los Angeles: Philosophical Research Society, 1965

Harris, Jose, *Private Lives, Public Spirit: Britain 1870-1914*. Penguin Books, 1993

Harrison, Thomas, *1910: The Emancipation of Dissonance*. Berkeley, Los Angeles, London: University of California Press, 1996

Hay, Douglas, Peter Linebaugh, and E.P. Thompson, *Albion's Fatal Tree*. London: Allen Lane, 1975

Head, Joseph and S.L. Cranston, eds. *Reincarnation: The Phoenix Fire Mystery*. New York: Julian Press/Crown Publishers, 1977

Heindel, Max, *The Rosicrucian Cosmo-Conception*. Oceanside, CA: The Rosicrucian Fellowship, 1973

——*Teachings of an Initiate*. Oceanside, CA: The Rosicrucian Fellowship, 1979

Heisenberg, Werner, *Physics and Philosophy*. New York: Harper & Row, 1958

Hill, Christopher, *The World Turned Upside Down*. Penguin Books, 1975

Hill, Christopher, ed., *Winstanley: The Law of Freedom and Other Writings*. Penguin Books, 1973

Hobsbawm, Eric J., *The Age of Extremes*. New York: Pantheon Books, 1994

Hodson, Geoffrey, *Basic Theosophy: The Living Wisdom*. Adyar, India: The Theosophical Publishing House, 1981

Howard, Michael, *The Occult Conspiracy*. Rochester, VT: Destiny Books, 1989

Howell, Alice O., *Jungian Synchronicity in Astrological Signs and Ages*. Wheaton, IL: Quest Books, 1990

Huizinga, Johan. *The Autumn of the Middle Ages*. Chicago: University of Chicago Press, 1996

——*Erasmus and the Age of Reformation*. New York: Harper & Row, 1957

——*The Waning of the Middle Ages*. Penguin Books, 1972

Hutton, Thomas, *A Lectutre on the Social Improvement of the Working Classes*. 1853

Incognito, Magus, *The Secret Doctrine of the Rosicrucians*. New York: Barnes & Noble, 1993

Ithaca Journal.

Johnson, K. Paul, *The Masters Revealed: Madame Blavatsky and the Myth of the Great White Lodge*. Albany, NY: State University of New York Press, 1994

Jones, A.H.M., *Constantine and the Conversion of Europe*. New York: Collier Books, 1962

Kammen, Michael, *Spheres of Liberty*. Madison: The University of Wisconsin Press, 1986

Keegan, John, *The Mask of Command*. Penguin Books, 1988

Keen, Maurice, *The Pelican History of Medieval Europe*. Penguin Books, 1968

Kolakowski, Leszek, *Main Currents of Marxism, Vol. III*. Oxford, New York: Oxford University Press, 1981

Krummenacher, Daniel, talk entitled "Chains, Rounds, and Geological Evidence," delivered at the University of the Seven Rays Conference, San Diego, CA, April 6, 1997

Ladurie, Emmanuel LeRoy, *Carnival in Romans: A People's Uprising at Romans 1579-1580*. Penguin Books, 1979

——*Montaillou*. New York: Vintage Books, 1979

Landes, David S., *The Unbound Prometheus*. Cambridge: Cambridge University Press, 1969

The Lamplighter Movement, March 1978

Lane, Barbara, *Echoes From the Battlefield*. Virginia Beach, VA: ARE Press, 1996

Laslett, Peter, *The World We Have Lost*. New York: Charles Scribner's Sons, 1965

Leadbeater, C.W., *A Textbook of Theosophy*. Adyar, India: The Theosophical Publishing House, 1962

——*The Hidden Life in Freemasonry*. Kila, MT: Kessinger Publishing Company, n.d.

LePage, Victoria, "A Trafficway of Angels: The Myth of Shamballa," *The Quest*, June 1997

Levi, Eliphas, *The History of Magic*. London: Rider & Company, 1969

Lievegoed, B.C.J., *Mystery Streams in Europe and the New Mysteries*. Spring Valley, NY: The Anthroposophic Press, 1982

MacDougall, Hugh A., *Racial Myth in English History*. Hanover and London: University Press of New England, 1982

The Mahatma Letters to A.P. Sinnett. Pasadena, CA: Theosophical University Press, 1992

Mackenzie, Vicki, *Reborn in the West*. New York: Marlowe & Co., 1995

Marias, Julian, *Generations*. University, AL: The University of Alabama Press, 1967

McLaughlin, Corinne, *How to Evaluate Psychic Guidance and Channeling*. Shutesbury, MA: Sirius Publishing, 1987

McLaughlin, Corinne and Gordon Davidson, *Spiritual Politics*. New York: Ballantine Books, 1994

McManners, John, *The Oxford Illustrated History of Christianity*. London: Guild Publishing, 1990

McNeill, William, *The Rise of the West*. Chicago & London: University of Chicago Press, 1963

Michell, John, *The New View Over Atlantis*. San Francisco: Harper & Row, 1983

Morgan, Marlo, *Mutant Message: Downunder*. Lees Summit, MO: Marlo Morgan, 1991

Morrison, David, "Target Earth," *Astronomy*, October 1995

Moyers, Bill, *Healing and the Mind*. New York: Doubleday, 1993

Mulder, David, *The Alchemy of Revolution*. New York: Peter Lang Publishing Company, 1990

Muller, Robert, *New Genesis*. Garden City, NY: Doubleday & Company, 1962

Naipaul, V.S., "Among the Republicans," *New York Review of Books*, Oct. 25, 1984

Namier, Lewis, *1848: The Revolution of the Intellectuals*. Garden City, NY: Anchor Books, 1964

Nesfield-Cookson, Bernard, *William Blake: Prophet of Universal Brotherhood*. Crucible, 1987

Newbold, R.F. "The Rays of Ancient Greece and Rome," *The Journal of Esoteric Psychology*, Vol. VII, No. 2, 1992

New York Times.

Nichol, D.J., "Doctor Edward Bach: A Forerunner," *The Beacon*, Vol. XLVII, No. 9, May/June 1978

Nicholson, Shirley, *Ancient Wisdom: Modern Insight*. Wheaton, IL: Quest Theosophical Publishing House, 1985

Ogilvie, R.M., *Latin and Greek: A History of the Influence of the Classics on English Life from 600 to 1918*. Archon Books, 1964

Oken, Alan, *Soul-Centered Astrology*. New York: Bantam Books, 1990

Ortega y Gassett, Jose, *Man and Crisis*. New York: W.W. Norton & Company, 1962

——*The Revolt of the Masses*. New York: W.W. Norton & Company, 1960

Parker, Derek and Julia, *The Compleat Astrologer*. New York: McGraw-Hill, 1971

Patrides, C.A., ed., *Sir Walter Raleigh: The History of the World*. Philadelphia: Temple University Press, 1971

Plumb. J. H., "The Perspective of History," *The Making of an Historian*: The collected essays of J H. Plumb, Vol. 1, 1988

Popper, Karl R., *The Poverty of Historicism*. New York: Harper & Row, 1964

Pugh, Stephen, "The 10 Sacred Numbers of the Manifest Universe," *The Journal of Esoteric Psychology*, Vol. VII, No.1, 1991

Quanjer, Johan, "The Will—Its Manifestation in Global Politics," *Pathway to Shamballa: Talks and Sharings from the 1988 Specialized Group Conference*

Ramage, Edwin S., *Atlantis: Fact or Fiction*. Bloomington and London: Indiana University Press, 1978

Rasmussen, Kaare L., "Historical Accretionary Events from 700 BC to AD 1850—a 1050-year Periodicity?" *The Quarterly Journal of the Royal Astronomical Society*, Vol. 3, No. 1, 1990

Ravenscroft, Trevor, *The Spear of Destiny*. New York: Bantam Books, 1973

Rawson, Elizabeth "The Expansion of Rome," *The Oxford History of the Classical World*, John Boardman, Jasper Griggin, and Oswyn Murray, eds. Oxford, New York: Oxford University Press, 1986

Remarque, Erich Maria, *All Quiet on the Western Front*. New York: Fawcett Crest, 1984

Rifkin, Jeremy, *Entropy: A New World View*. Toronto, New York: Bantam Books, 1981

Robbins, Michael, *Tapestry of the Gods, Vol. I* & *II*. Jersey City Heights, NJ: The University of the Seven Rays Publishing House, 1988

Roberts, J. M., *The Mythology of the Secret Societies*. London: Paladin, 1974

Roerich, Nicholas, *The Invincible*. New York: Nicholas Roerich Museum, 1974

The Roerich Pact and The Banner of Peace. New York: Roerich Pact and Banner of Peace Committee, 1947

Rosenblum, Robert, *Cubism and Twentieth-Century Art*. New York: Harry N. Abrams, Inc., 1966

Rostovtzeff, Michael I., *Social and Economic History of the Roman Empire*, second edition, Oxford: Clarendon Press, 1957

Rudhyar, Dane, *Astrological Timing*. New York: Harper & Row, 1969

——*Occult Preparations for a New Age*. Wheaton, IL: The Theosophical Publishing House, 1975

——*The Practice of Astrology*. New York, Baltimore: Penguin Books, 1968

——*The Sun Is Also A Star: The Galactic Dimension of Astrology*. New York: E.P. Dutton & Company, 1975

Russell, Bertrand, *A History of Western Philosophy*. New York: Simon & Schuster, 1945

——*The Autobiography of Bertrand Russell*. New York: Bantam Books, 1968

Ryan, Charles J., *H.P. Blavatsky and the Theosophical Movement*. San Diego, CA: Point Loma Publications, 1975

Sakoian, Frances and Louis S. Acker, *The Astrologer's Handbook*. New York: Harper & Row, 1973

Saraydarian, H., *Cosmos in Man*. Sedona, AZ: Aquarian Educational Group, 1973

Schlesinger, Arthur, Jr., *The Cycles of American History*. Boston: Houghton Mifflin Company, 1986

Scott, Cyril, *Music: Its Secret Influence Throughout the Ages*. Wellingborough, England: Aquarian Press, 1958

——*The Initiate: Some Impressions of a Great Soul*. York Beach, ME: Samuel Weiser, Inc., 1971

Sedgwick, John P., *Harmonics of History*. New York, 1985

Sheldrake, Rupert, *A New Science of Life*. Los Angeles: J.P. Tarcher, 1981

Shepherd, A.P., *Scientist of the Invisible: Rudolf Steiner*. Rochester, VT: Inner Traditions International, 1983

Sinnett, A.P., *Incidents in the Life of Madame Blavatsky*. London: The Theosophical Publishing Company, 1913

Smith, Carol Brubaker, "Giuseppi Mazzini: A Forerunner," The Beacon, Vol. L, No. 5, September/October 1983

Smith, Denis Mack, ed., *Garibaldi*. Great Lives Observed Series. Englewood Cliffs, NJ: Prentice-Hall, 1969

Smith, Houston, *Religions of the World: Judaism*, tape 6, Boulder, CO: Sounds True Audio, 1995

——*The Religions of Man*. New York: Harper Perennial, 1986

Sorokin, Pitirim A., *Social Philosophies of an Age of Crisis*. Boston: Beacon Press, 1951

——*The Crisis of Our Age*. New York: E.P. Dutton, 1941

——*The Reconstruction of Humanity*. Boston: The Beacon Press, 1948

Spengler, Oswald, *The Decline of the West*. New York: Alfred A. Knopf, 1962

State of the Peoples: A Global Human Rights Report on Societies in Danger. Boston: Beacon Press, 1993

Stavnsbjerg, Holger, *The Astrology of Initiation and the Horoscope of Big Cities*. Holger Stavnsbjerg, 1966

Steiner, Rudolf, *Christianity as a Mystical Fact*. Anthroposophical Press, 1972

——*Cosmic Memory: Prehistory of Earth and Man*. Englewood, NJ: Rudolf Steiner Publications, 1959

——*Destinies of Individuals and of Nations*. New York: Anthroposophic Press, 1986

——*Materialism and the Task of Anthroposophy*. Hudson, NY: The Anthroposophic Press, 1987

——*Methods of Spiritual Research*. Blauvelt, NY: Rudolf Steiner Publications, 1971

——*The Driving Force of Spiritual Powers in World History*. Toronto: Steiner Book Center, 1972

——*The Influence of Spiritual Beings Upon Man*. Spring Valley, NY: Anthroposophic Press, 1961

Steiger, Brad, *Brad Steiger Predicts the Future*. West Chester, PA: Whitford Press, 1984

Stenton, D.M., *English Society in the Early Middle Ages: 1066-1307*. Baltimore: Pelican Books, 1962

Stephenson, James, *Prophecy on Trial*. Greenwich, CT: Trans-Himalaya Incorporated, 1983

Suster, Gerald, *Hitler: The Occult Messiah*. New York: St. Martin's Press, 1981

Swimme, Brian and Thomas Berry, *The Universe Story*. San Francisco: Harper San Francisco, 1992

Symondson, Anthony, ed., *The Victorian Crisis of Faith*. London: S.P.C.K., 1974

Talbot, Michael, *Mysticism and the New Physics*. London: Routledge & Kegan Paul, 1981

Tannahill, Reay, *Food in History*. New York: Crown Publishers, 1988

Tawney, R. H., *Religion and the Rise of Capitalism*. Penguin Books, 1961

Taylor, A.J.P., *The Course of German History*. New York: Capricorn Books, 1962

Taylor, Margaret, "John Bunyan: A Forerunner," *The Beacon*, Vol. LI, No. 12, November/December 1986

Thapar, Romila, *A History of India, Vol. I*, Penguin Books, 1966

Thomas, Dana Lloyd, "A Modern Pythagorean," *Gnosis Magazine*, No. 44, Summer 1997

Thomas, Keith, *Religion & the Decline of Magic.* New York: Charles Scribner's Sons, 1971

Thomson, J.A.K., trans., *The Ethics of Aristotle.* Penguin Books, 1976

Thompson, Paul, *The Edwardians.* St. Albans, England: Paladin, 1977

Thompson, William Irwin, *Darkness and Scattered Light.* New York: Anchor Books, 1978

——*Pacific Shift.* San Francisco: Sierra Club Books, 1985

——*The Time Falling Bodies Take to Light.* New York: St. Martin's Press, 1981

Toynbee, Arnold, *A Study of History.* New York & London: Oxford University Press, 1947, Abridge. Vols. I-VI

——*A Study of History.* New York & London: Oxford University Press, 1957, Abridge. Vols. VII-X

——*Civilization on Trial.* New York: Oxford University Press, 1948

——*Change and Habit.* New York and London: Oxford University Press, 1966

Trager, James, *The People's Chronology.* New York: Henry Holt and Company, 1992

Trungpa, Chogyam, *Shamballa: The Sacred Path of the Warrior.* Boston & London: Shamballa, 1985

Vico, Giambattista, *The New Science of Giambattista Vico.* Ithaca and London: Cornell University Press, 1970

Wachsmuth, Guenther, *The Evolution of Mankind.* Anthroposophic Press, 1961

Wagar, W. Warren, *The City of Man.* Boston: Houghton Mifflin Company, 1963

Wagar, W. Warren, ed. *History and the Idea of Mankind.* Albuquerque, NM: University of New Mexico Press, 1971

Waite, Arthur Edward, *The Brotherhood of the Rosy Cross.* New York: Barnes & Noble Books, 1993

Weber, Renee, ed., *Dialogues with Scientists and Sages.* London and New York: Routledge & Kegan Paul, 1986

Weiss, Clara A., *Astrological Keys to Self-actualization and Self-realization.* New York: Samuel Weiser, 1980

Whyte, Jacqueline C., *Cycles of Time.* So. Hamilton, MA: Manifest Press, 1989

Wilber, Ken, *Up From Eden.* Garden City, NY: Anchor Press Doubleday, 1981

Wilde, Oscar, *The Soul of Man Under Socialism*. London: The Porcupine
    Press, n.d.

Wilmut, N.G., "Samuel Hahnemann, Physician and Healer: A
    Forerunner," The Beacon, Vol. XLIX, No. 4, July/August 1981

Wolfe, Richard A., "William James: A Forerunner," *The Beacon*, Vol. LI,
    No. 1, January/February 1985

Worrel, Thomas D., "The Initiatic Symbolism of Freemasonry," *Gnosis
    Magazine*, No. 44, Summer 1997

Yates, Frances, *The Occult Philosophy*. London: ARK Paperbacks, 1983

Yeats, W.B., *A Vision*. New York: Collier Books, 1966

Young, Arthur M. *The Reflexive Universe*. Mill Valley, CA: Robert Briggs
    Associates, 1976

Index